Official Signs & Icons 2

Official Signs & Icons 2 by Ultimate Symbol

Published by Ultimate Symbol Inc. New York

Mies Hora

Library of Congress Control Number: 2005904803
ISBN: 0-9769513-0-4

First Edition paperback published in 1996

Ultimate Symbol™

Published by
Ultimate Symbol Inc.
31 Wilderness Drive
Stony Point, New York 10980 USA
www.ultimatesymbol.com
800.611.4761 Sales & Upgrades
845.942.0004 Fax Orders
845.942.5342 Technical Support
845.942.0003 Business Office

This book is dedicated to my wonderful mother, Helena,
who always believed in me and whose love and
compassion continue to inform my belief in myself,
and to my father, Richard, whose drive, discipline
and immeasurable talents shine brightly on my path.

Acknowledgements

Official Signs & Icons 2 was built upon the solid foundation of the first edition that was published in 1996. It is over the period of more than a decade that I have had the privilege to work with a remarkable group of visual professionals and individuals whose interest, skill, dedication, support and sheer stamina enabled me to evolve this project into a 21st century reference work. I am deeply indebted to every person who has contributed to this effort.

Development
Mies Hora, *Concept / Writing / Design Direction*

Research / Design / Production / Operations
Gillian Ashworth
Kate Bauer
Shaun Charity
Emily Flynn
Frances Hora
Jill Sabrina Joy
Andrew Koval III
Stephen Lestch
Meng-Yen Pan
Keely Stahl
Elizabeth Sweeney
Kristofor Weinrich
Chisa Yagi

Illustration / Design
Jen Alspach
Chris O'Hara
Michael Wong

Special Thanks
Gary Cosimini, Tom Geismar, Steff Geissbuhler, Caryn Leland, Don Meeker, Paul Mijksenaar, Robert Millstein, Tim Murphy, Jose Luis Ortiz, Paul Singer, Douglas Viehland, and Lance Wyman

Production Notes
Official Signs & Icons 2 and all of the images in it were designed and produced in Adobe Illustrator. This book is typeset in Univers. Printed and bound in China through Colorcraft Ltd., Hong Kong

Cover and book design by Mies Hora

The last few decades have seen major changes in communications, transportation and manufacturing as the world has become more of a global nation. Products are mass produced for sale internationally. People travel between continents for brief vacations. Foreign workers seek employment in developed countries. One can find the products of IBM, Sony, and Mercedes-Benz around the world, but what continues to separate us are the thousands of different languages still spoken.

To help relieve this problem, at least at a very basic level of communication, various governmental and industry organizations have attempted to develop standardized systems of symbols and icons that can be understood internationally without regard to language or culture. As the need for these devices has become more urgent, many groups have worked to upgrade the quality of their standards. Today's systems are considerably more sophisticated than those used just twenty years ago. This book represents a first attempt to gather together in one document the most recent official markings, and to present them in a highly accurate, beautifully drawn manner. In undertaking this daunting task, Mies Hora and his colleagues have made a major contribution to the use, study, and understanding of this visual language.

Seeing the systems of symbols all together this way makes it evident that there are still considerable differences between systems, in terms of both concept and design language. It is clear for example, that a non-English speaking visitor must find it very difficult to negotiate highways in the United States compared to those countries using the international standards. While there is still much work to do to improve, test, and coordinate the systems, having a chance to review and compare the marks as provided by this collection is an important next step.

Meanwhile, it is only through the consistent and repetitive use of such standardized marks that we can help the foreign traveler to find her luggage at the airport, locate the light switch on a rental car, negotiate strange roads, and recognize the presence of a dangerous chemical.

Thomas H. Geismar
Principal, Chermayeff & Geismar Inc.

Tom Geismar is one of America's leading designers. As a founding partner in Chermayeff & Geismar Inc., he has developed more than 100 graphic identification programs, including such well-known marks as those for Mobil, Chase Bank, Xerox, and PBS. His work also encompasses all aspects of graphic design, environmental graphics, and the curating and design of major museum exhibitions, such as the permanent galleries at Ellis Island and the Statue of Liberty. He organized and acted as Chairman of the AIGA/DOT Committee that developed the Symbol Signs project - the comprehensive study that resulted in the first truly internationally adopted system of pictogram symbols.

Wayfinding, or spatial orientation, is an essential aspect of everyday life: knowing where one is, knowing the destination, following the best route, recognizing the destination, and finding the way back. Humanity's ability to survive and thrive has always depended to some degree upon a sense of direction, not becoming disoriented or losing one's way. Relying on visual cues in our physical environment to find our way becomes most important when we encounter demanding, unfamiliar environments and circumstances.

Whether navigating the Internet, the Puget Sound, the inputs and outputs of a surround-sound audio visual system, the operation of a new miter saw, the hallways of a large hospital, a forest trail in grizzly country, a Hong Kong street, a trip through a suburban mall, a mountain pass in Afghanistan, or just finding a restroom during a visit to Disney World, wayfinding "devices" often play an integral role in the success or failure of an endeavor. Even the simplest of settings can involve a jumble of information that must be sorted and processed before it becomes meaningful.[1] Coined in 1960 by architect Kevin Lynch in *The Image of the City*, the term "way-finding" was further described by Romedi Passini and Paul Arthur in their books *Wayfinding in Architecture* and *Wayfinding, People, Signs and Architecture*. They articulated wayfinding as a two-stage process during which people must solve a wide variety of problems that involve both "decision making" (formulating an action plan) and "decision executing" (implementing the plan).[2] There is little question that the positive or negative consequences of people navigating unfamiliar and increasingly complex environments – and whether users perceive a wayfinding system as easy to use or not – is directly related to the quality, consistency, thoughtfulness, and placement of wayfinding devices, directional and informational signs, maps, diagrams, street numbers, labels, colors, typography, icons, and symbol sets. The expanding interactivity of global economies makes requisite ever more refined and sophisticated non-verbal communication systems.

***Official Signs & Icons 2* is the second edition of a** work-in-progress dedicated to the comprehensive collection, clear organization, and accurate reproduction of official symbol and sign systems that are being developed by standards institutions worldwide. The deluge of requests resulting from the 1996 publication of *Official Signs & Icons* for more symbols, covering more specializations, speaks of a desire among communicators and wayfinding designers for easier access to professional level research of symbols and reproduction art.

For this new edition, existing volumes were updated and amended to reflect the current state of national and international standards. In one case, the American Red Cross requested the removal of its ubiquitous, but copyright-protected emblem so that it not be confused as a generic symbol for "first aid" or "emergency medical services", requiring the change of the classic Greek cross symbol colors in the SEGD, AIGA and TCRP systems from red to green. *Volume 3* underwent the addition of many new recreational symbols, mapping versions, and accessibility symbols that meet ADA guidelines. The SEGD accessibility symbols are here gathered for the first time in an up-to-date display, with final changes made in collaboration with the originating designers.

***Official Signs & Icons 2* represents a watershed event** for Ultimate Symbol in that instead of simply collecting and presenting the work of others, new symbol systems are being developed in-house to meet the needs so clearly articulated by the industries that use them. A case in point is *Volume 6: Hospitality Symbol Signs System*, which is the result of three years of R&D to develop a much needed system of communications designed specifically for lodging and hotel facilities. *Volume 7: Safety Symbols Labeling* is my response to the lack of a comprehensive, well-organized set of symbols that harmonize current U.S. and international safety standards.

Much has occurred in the nine years since the first edition was published, and I'm finding ways to exert some influence on how quickly needed symbol systems are brought to bear on the challenge of guiding people on their way through the intricate world in which we find ourselves. It is my sincerest hope that this new effort, now published as a full-color hardcover reference book, as a book with electronic art on CD, and available online as single image and volume downloads, will further stimulate the standardization of messages into forms that more people can easily understand and benefit from immediately. *Where there's a will, there's a way.*

Mies Hora
President & Founder, Ultimate Symbol Inc.

May 2005

Anyone attempting to catalog signs, symbols, icons, pictographs, marks, sigils, and emblems today necessarily walks in the footsteps of the late industrial and corporate designer Henry Dreyfuss. Few have done as much to collect and codify the universe of icons and groups of symbols and signs used throughout the world. Yet he would be the first to remind us that such a compilation is never complete. Technology and communications are developing at an ever quickening pace. To understand and utilize advances in technology, new symbols and icons are constantly being created.

The world wide web may be the most important advance in communications to date. Icons are an essential component of negotiating the net, and most object-oriented computer interfaces as well. Symbols have retained their power to inform us from caveplace to cyberspace.

While attempts at a universal language like Esperanto and Franglais have essentially failed, great leaps have been made in the universal visual language of wayfinding. Traffic control, recreation, travel, safety, and electronics, are only some of the areas benefiting from the growing class of communicators dedicated to simplifying guidance systems for people swept along in a sometimes bewildering modern existence.

***Official Signs & Icons* came into being because of a** simple fact. It has become obvious that while the volume of art work being created for the computerized design professional has increased, the quality remains inconsistent. Official signs and symbol sets meticulously created by some of the best designers and organizations in the world have all too often been bastardized when reproduced and/or transformed into digital media. Stripped of their context, heritage, and original purpose, many symbols are thrown into incomplete collections and misidentified. The worst bear only a resemblance to their original forms or serve primarily as "attention-getters".

This comprehensive collection is a response to the need voiced by many of my peers in the design field to make available carefully compiled, classified, and rendered electronic versions of the most common and effective signs and icons. While just a beginning, I hope that this rigorous work, the fruit of a lot of collaborative research, time, and labor, rises to the standard set by Mr. Dreyfuss and picks up his trail where it ended. New ideas, symbol sources, suggestions for improvement, and comments are more than welcome.

Mies Hora
President & Founder, Ultimate Symbol Inc.

About the Author

Mies Hora founded the software content publishing firm Ultimate Symbol Inc. in 1992 and is responsible for directing the design, development, and marketing of the print and electronic versions of its growing library of titles. Mies coauthored a series of best-selling design reference books, Design Elements 1, 2, 3, *and* 4, *which were produced during 1980-85 in collaboration with his father, architect, designer and artist, Richard Hora. Ultimate Symbol digitized the book series and released* Design Elements by Ultimate Symbol *in 1994 as a catalog with CD in Mac/PC formats. Other titles currently include* Nature Icons, WebPage Graphics, Pictorial Symbols, *and* Official Signs & Icons. *The internet has allowed Mies to reach a global design audience with his collections of visual material.*

A graduate of Parsons School of Design, Mies has also been since 1979 the design director and principal of Hora Associates, where his experience includes positioning, corporate identity, advertising, product and interface design, web site design, publications and print media, packaging, photography, architectural signage, store display, and interior design. An Adjunct Professor at the State University of New York (SUNY) since 1996, he has received numerous awards for his work, and has been a longtime member of the American Institute of Graphic Arts, the Society for Environmental Graphic Design, and the International Interactive Communications Society.

Highway Signs I: U.S. (MUTCD)

1

Overview

Traffic control devices are all signs, signals, markings, and devices placed on, over, or adjacent to a street or highway by authority of a public body or official having jurisdiction to regulate, warn, or guide traffic.

Purpose

The purpose of traffic control devices and warrants for their use is to help ensure highway safety by providing for the orderly and predictable movement of all traffic, motorized and non-motorized, throughout the national highway transportation system, and to provide such guidance and warnings as are needed to ensure the safe and informed operation of individual elements of the traffic stream.

History

The American Association of State Highway and Transportation Officials published a manual for rural highways in 1927 and the National Conference on Street and Highway Safety published a manual for urban streets in 1929. But the necessity for unification of the standards applicable to the different classes of road and street systems was obvious. To meet this need, a joint committee of the American Association of State Highway and Transportation Officials (AASHTO) and the National Conference on Street and Highway Safety developed, and published in 1935, the original edition of the *Manual of Uniform Traffic Control Devices* (MUTCD). That committee, though changed from time to time in organization and personnel, has been in continuous existence and has contributed to periodic revisions of the Manual. The committee's name was formally changed to the National Committee (NC) on Uniform Traffic Control Devices. The Federal Highway Administration (FHWA) has administered the MUTCD since the 1971 edition.[1]

Requirements

To be effective, a traffic control device should meet five basic requirements:

1. Fulfill a need.
2. Command attention.
3. Convey a clear, simple meaning.
4. Command respect of road users.
5. Give adequate time for proper response.

Description

Highway signs fall into the following categories: Warning Signs, Guide Signs for Conventional Roads, Guide Signs for Freeways and Expressways, Specific Service Signs, Tourist-Oriented Directional Signs, Recreational and Cultural Interest Area Signs, and Emergency Management Signing.

Other traffic controls include: Pavement and Curb Markings, Object Markers, Delineators, Colored Pavements, Barricades and Channelizing Devices, Islands, Highway Traffic Signals, Temporary Traffic Control, Traffic Controls for School Areas, Highway-Rail Grade Crossings, Bicycle Facilities, and Highway-Light Rail Transit Grade Crossings.

Lettering

Sign lettering is in upper-case letters of the type approved by the Federal Highway Administration, except that destination names may be in lower-case lettering, with initial upper-case. Highway Gothic upper-case and lower-case alphabets (*Standard Alphabets for Highway Signs*; Series B, C, D, E, Em and F) are available from the Federal Highway Administration (HTO-20), Washington, D.C. 20590 or elsewhere commercially.

Electronic Artwork

The highway signs in *Official Signs & Icons 2* are based on the 2003 Edition of the *Manual on Uniform Traffic Control Devices for Streets and Highways.* In preparing the electronic artwork for this collection, it was decided to not substantially improve the signage typography. In the interest of verisimilitude, the letter and word spacing represents that which is set forth in the MUTCD, thereby providing a look and feel close to what one will encounter on the nation's highways.

Technical Note: the EPS files on the accompanying CD and also available online are vinyl-ready for signmakers. They were created in Adobe Illustrator, and saved as color, grouped EPS files. The image vectors have been substantially cleaned up and are consequently of a higher reproduction quality than that available by accessing images from the FHWA manual. Please note that because the manual is constantly being annexed and revised, generally it should be obtained and specifications reviewed for absolute accuracy.

Color Code

The following color code establishes general meanings for nine colors that have been identified as being appropriate for use in conveying traffic control information. To facilitate print reproduction, the nearest PMS (Pantone®) colors have been assigned to the highway signs as shown to the right.

Color	PMS	Meaning
Yellow	124 C	General Warning
Red	1797 C	Stop or Prohibition
Blue	287 C	Motorist Services Guidance
Green	341 C	Indicated Movements Permitted, Direction Guidance
Light Green	382 C	School Caution
Brown	469 C	Recreational and Cultural Interest Guidance
Orange	165 C	Construction and Maintenance Warning
Black	Process Black	Regulation
White	Process White	Regulation

Regulatory Signs

X201A01
Stop
R1-1

X201A02
Yield
R1-2

X201A03
To Oncoming Traffic
R1-2a

X201A04
4 - Way
R1-3

X201A05
All Way
R1-4

X201A06
Speed Limit, 10 M.P.H.
R2-1

SPEED
LIMIT
15

X201A07
Speed Limit, 15 M.P.H.
R2-1

X201A08
Speed Limit, 20 M.P.H.
R2-1

X201A09
Speed Limit, 25 M.P.H.
R2-1

X201A10
Speed Limit, 30 M.P.H.
R2-1

X201A11
Speed Limit, 35 M.P.H.
R2-1

X201A12
Speed Limit, 40 M.P.H.
R2-1

X201A13
Truck Speed Limit, 40 M.P.H
R 2-2

OR

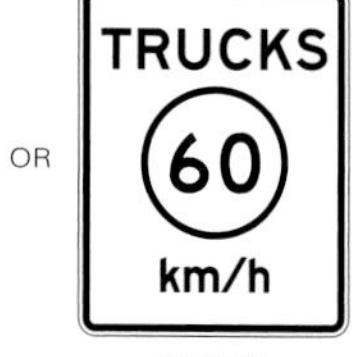

X201A14
Trucks Speed Limit, 60 km/h
R2-2

X201A15
Night Speed Limit
R2-3

OR

X201A16
Night Speed Limit
R2-3

X201A17
Speed Limit, 45 M.P.H.
R2-1

X201A18
Speed Limit, 50 M.P.H.
R2-1

X201A19
Speed Limit, 80 km/h
R2-1

X201A20
Speed Limit, 55 M.P.H.
R2-1

X201A21
Speed Limit, 60 M.P.H.
R2-1

X201A22
Speed Limit, 65 M.P.H.
R2-1

X201A23
Reduced Speed Ahead
R2-5a

X201A24
Speed Zone Ahead
R2-5c

MINIMUM
SPEED
40

X201A25
Minimum Speed
40 M.P.H, R2-4

OR

X201A26
Minimum Speed
60 km/h, R2-4

X201A27
Speed Limit 50 M.P.H.
Min. 30 M.P.H., R2-4a

OR

X201A28
Speed Limit 80 km/h
Min. 30 km/h., R2-4a

X201A29
Fines Higher
R2-6

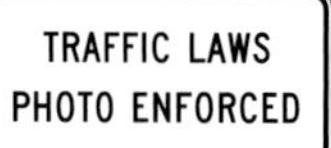

X201A30
Traffic Laws Photo Enforced
R10-18

X201A31
Photo Enforced
R10-19

X201A32
No Right Turn
R3-1

X201A33
No Left Turn
R3-2

X201A34
No Turns
R3-3

X201A35
No U-Turn
R3-4

X201A36
No U-Turn / No Left Turn
R3-18

Note: All symbols and signs are available as fully editable vector image files: see page 238 or www.ultimatesymbol.com

Regulatory Signs continued

X201**B**01
Mandatory Movement
Straight Through Only, R3-5a

X201**B**02
Mandatory Movement (Right)
R3-5

X201**B**03
Mandatory Movement (Left)
R3-5

X201**B**04
Optional Movement (Right)
R3-6

X201**B**05
Optional Movement OK (Left)
R3-6

X201**B**06
Optional Movement (Left)
R3-6

RIGHT LANE MUST TURN RIGHT

X201**B**07
Mandatory Turn (right)
R3-7

X201**B**08
Mandatory Turn (left)
R3-7

X201**B**09
Left Lane (Supplemental)
R3-5b

HOV 2+

X201**B**10
HOV 2+ (Supplemental)
R3-5c

TAXI LANE

X201**B**11
Taxi Lane (Supplemental)
R3-5d

X201**B**12
Center Lane (Supplemental)
R3-5e

RIGHT LANE

X201**B**13
Right Lane (Supplemental)
R3-5f

BUS LANE

X201**B**14
Bus Lane (Supplemental)
R3 -5g

X201**B**15
Advance Intersection Lane
R3-8

ONLY OK

X201**B**16
Advance Intersection Lane
R3-8

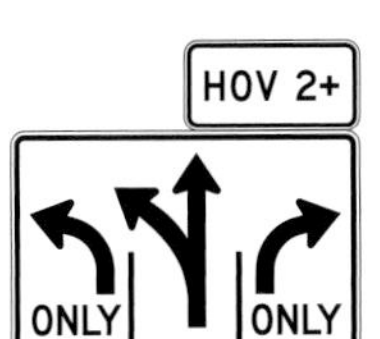

X201**B**17
Advance Intersection Lane
R3-8a

X201**B**18
Advance Intersection Lane
R3-8b

X201**B**19
Two Way Left Turn Only
R3-9b

X201**B**20
Advance Intersection Lane
R3-9d

X201**B**21
Center Lane
R3-9f

X201**B**22
End Reverse Lane
R3-9i

X201**B**23
Bus Lane Ahead
R3-10a

X201**B**24
Preferential Only
R3-10b

X201**B**25
Preferential Only
R3-11a

X201**B**26
Preferential Only
R3-12a

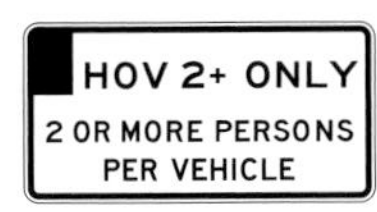

X201**B**27
Preferential Only
R3-13

X201**B**28
Preferential Only
R3-14

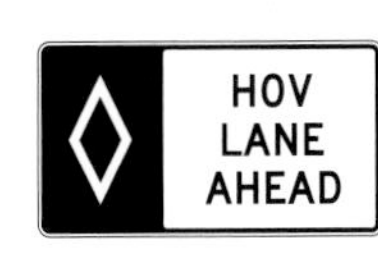

X201**B**29
HOV Lane Ahead
Preferential Only, R3-15

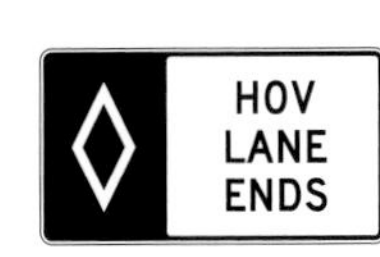

X201**B**30
Hov Lane Ends
Preferential Only, R3-15a

X201**B**31
Restricted Lane Ahead
R3-13

X201**B**32
Restricted Lane Ends
R3-15

X201**B**33
Do Not Pass
R4-1

X201**B**34
Pass with Care
R4-2

X201**B**35
Slower Traffic Keep Right
R4-3

X201**B**36
Truck Route
R14-1

X201**B**37
Trucks Use Right Lane
R4-5

X201**B**38
Truck Lane 500 Feet
R4-6

METRIC
TRUCK LANE 150 METERS

X201**B**39
Truck Lane 150 Meters
R4-6

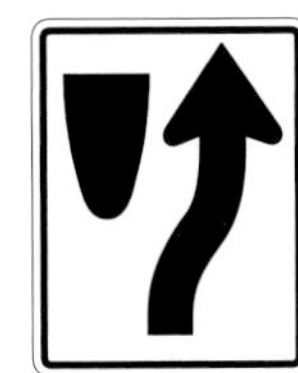
X201**B**40
Keep Right
R4-7

X201**B**41
Keep Left
R4-8

X201**B**42
Keep Right
R4-7a

Regulatory Signs continued

X201C01
Keep Left
R4-7a

X201C02
Keep Right
R4-7b

X201C03
Stay in Lane
R4-9

X201C04
Runaway Vehicles Only
R4-10

X201C05
Do Not Enter
R5-1

X201C06
Wrong Way
R5-1a

X201C07
No Trucks
R5-2

X201C08
No Trucks / Vans (Alternate)
R5-2

X201C09
No Motor Vehicles
R5-3

X201C10
Commercial Vehicles Excluded
R5-4

X201C11
Vehicles With Lugs Prohibited
R5-5

X201C12
No Bicycles
R5-6

NON-MOTORIZED
TRAFFIC
PROHIBITED

X201C13
Non-Motorized Traffic
Prohibited, R5-7

X201C14
Motor-Driven Cycles
Prohibited, R5-8

X201C15
Pedestrians, Bicycles, Motor-Driven Cycles Prohibited, R5-10a

X201C16
Pedestrians and Bicycles
Prohibited, R5-10b

X201C17
Pedestrians Prohibited
R5-10c

X201C18
One Way (Right)
R6-1

X201C19
One Way (Left)
R6-1

ONE
WAY

X201C20
One Way (Right)
R6-2

X201C21
One Way (Left)
R6-2

X201C22
Divided Highway Crossing
R6-3

X201C23
Divided Highway Crossing
R6-3a

X201C24
No Parking Any Time (Right)
R7-1

X201C25
No Parking Any Time (Left)
R7-1

X201C26
No Parking
8:30 AM to 5:30 PM, R7-2

X201C27
No Parking
8:30 AM to 5:30 PM, R7-2a

X201C28
No Parking Except Sundays
and Holidays, R7-3

X201C29
No Standing Any Time
R7-4

X201C30
No Parking Loading Zone
R7-6

X201C31
No Parking Bus Stop
R7-7

NO PARKING
BUS
STOP

X201C32
No Parking Bus Stop
R7-107

X201C33
No Parking Bus stop
R7-107a

X201C34
Reserved Parking
(Handicapped), R7-8

X201C35
Van Accessible (Handicapped)
R7-8a

X201C36
Van Accessible (Handicapped)
R7-8b

X201C37
2 Hour Parking
8:30 AM to 5:30 PM, R7-108

X201C38
No Parking Anytime /
One Hour Parking, R7-200

OR

X201C39
No Parking Anytime /
One Hour Parking, R7-200

X201C40
No Parking, Street Cleaning
(NYC, Unofficial)

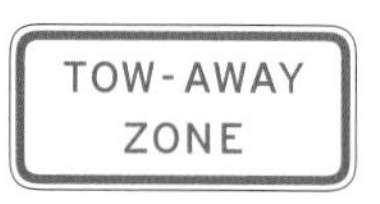

X201C41
Tow-Away Zone
R7-201

X201C42
Tow-Away Zone
R7-201a

Regulatory
Signs
continued

X201**D**01
This Side of Sign
R7-202

X201**D**02
Emergency Snow Route
R7-203

NO
PARKING
ON
PAVEMENT

X201**D**03
No Parking On Pavement
R8-1

NO
PARKING
EXCEPT ON
SHOULDER

X201**D**04
No Parking
Except on Shoulder, R8-2

X201**D**05
No Parking
R8-3

X201**D**06
No Parking
R8-3a

ON
PAVEMENT

X201**D**07
On Pavement (Supplemental)
R8-3c

ON
BRIDGE

X201**D**08
On Bridge (Supplemental)
R8-3d

EMERGENCY
PARKING
ONLY

X201**D**09
Emergency Parking Only
R8-4

NO
STOPPING
ON
PAVEMENT

X201**D**10
No Stopping on Pavement
R8-5

NO
STOPPING
EXCEPT ON
SHOULDER

X201**D**11
No Stopping Except
on Shoulder, R8-6

EMERGENCY
STOPPING
ONLY

X201**D**12
Emergency Stopping Only
R8-7

X201**C**13
Walk on Left Facing Traffic
R9-1

CROSS
ONLY
AT
CROSS
WALKS

X201**D**14
Cross Only at Crosswalks
R9-2

NO
PEDESTRIAN
CROSSING

X201**D**15
No Pedestrian Crossing
R9-3

X201**D**16
No Pedestrian Crossing
R9-3a

X201**D**17
Use Crosswalk
R9-3b

X201**D**18
No Hitchhiking
R9-4

X201**D**19
No Hitchhiking
R9-4a

X201**D**20
Cross on Green Light Only
R10-1

X201**D**21
Cross on Walk Signal Only
R10-2a

X201**D**22
Push Button for Green Light
R10-3

X201**D**23
To Cross Street Push Button
R10-3a

X201**D**24
To Cross Street Push Button
R10-3b

X201**D**25
To Cross Street Push Button
R10-3c

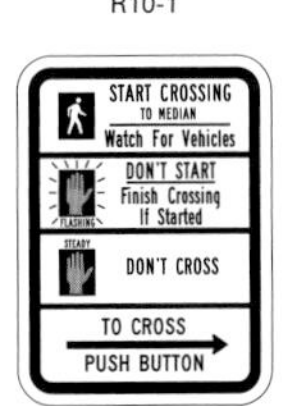

X201**D**26
To Cross Street Push Button
R10-3d

X201**D**27
To Cross Street Push Button
R10-3e

X201**D**28
Push Button for Walk Signal
R10-4

X201**D**29
Push Button Wait for
Walk Signal, R10-4a

X201**D**30
Push Button for Walk Signal
R10-4b

X201**D**31
Yield to Pedestrians Crossing

X201**D**32
Yield Here to Pedestrians
R1-5

X201**D**33
Yield Here to Pedestrians
R1-5a

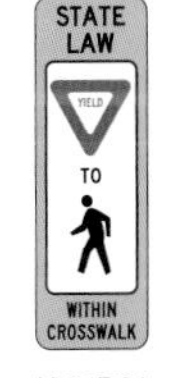

X201**D**34
In-Street Pedestrian Crossing
R1-6

X201**D**35
In-Street Pedestrian Crossing
R1-6a

X201**D**36
Left on Green Arrow Only
R10-5

X201**D**37
Stop Here on Red
R10-6

X201**D**38
Stop Here on Red
R10-6a

X201**D**39
Do Not Block Intersection
R10-7

X201**D**40
Use Lane with Green Arrow
R10-8

X201**D**41
Left Turn Signal
R10-10

X201**D**42
Right Turn Signal
R10-10(R)

Regulatory Signs continued

X201**E**01
No Turn on Red
R10-11

NO TURN ON RED

X201**E**02
No Turn on Red
R10-11a

NO TURN ON RED

X201**E**03
No Turn on Red
R10-11b

LEFT TURN YIELD ON GREEN

X201**E**04
Left Turn Yield on Green
R10-12

EMERGENCY SIGNAL

X201**E**05
Emergency Signal
R10-13

TURNING TRAFFIC MUST YIELD TO PEDESTRIANS

X201**E**06
Turning Traffic Must Yield
R10-15

U-TURN YIELD TO RIGHT TURN

X201**E**07
U-Turn Yield to Right Turn
R10-16

RIGHT ON RED ARROW AFTER STOP

X201**E**08
Right on Red Arrow After Stop
R10-17a

MON-FRI 7-9 AM 4-7 PM

X201**E**09
Mon-Fri 7-9 AM
R10-20a

SUNDAY 7-11 AM

X201**E**10
Sunday 7-11AM
R10-20a

LEFT TURN SIGNAL YIELD ON GREEN

X201**E**11
Left Turn Signal
Yield on Green
R10-21

X201**E**12
Keep Off Median
R11-1

SIDEWALK CLOSED AHEAD CROSS HERE

X201**E**13
Sidewalk Closed Ahead
Cross Here, R9-11

SIDEWALK CLOSED CROSS HERE

X201**E**14
Sidewalk Closed Ahead
Cross Here, R9-11a

SIDEWALK CLOSED

X201**E**15
Sidewalk Closed
R9-9

SIDEWALK CLOSED USE OTHER SIDE

X201**E**16
Sidewalk Closed
Use Other Side, R9-10

ROAD CLOSED

X201**E**17
Road Closed
R11-2

ROAD CLOSED 10 MILES AHEAD LOCAL TRAFFIC ONLY

X201**E**18
Road Closed 10 Miles Ahead
R11-3a

BRIDGE OUT 10 MILES AHEAD LOCAL TRAFFIC ONLY

X201**E**19
Bridge Out 10 Miles Ahead
R11-3b

ROAD CLOSED TO THRU TRAFFIC

X201**E**20
Road Closed to Thru Traffic
R11-4

WEIGHT LIMIT 10 TONS

X201**E**21
Weight Limit 10 Tons
R12-1

METRIC WEIGHT LIMIT 9t

X201**E**22
Weight Limit 9 Tons (Metric)
R12-1/ R12-5

NO TRUCKS OVER 7000 LBS EMPTY WT

X201**E**23
No Trucks Over 7000 lbs
Empty WT, R12-3

OR

METRIC NO TRUCKS OVER 3200 kg EMPTY WT

X201**E**24
No Trucks Over 3200 kg
Empty WT, R12-3 / R12-6

WEIGHT LIMIT 2 TONS PER AXLE 10 TONS GROSS

X201**E**25
Weight Limit 1.8 Tons Per Axle
10 Tons Gross, R12-4

METRIC WEIGHT LIMIT 1.8t PER AXLE 9t GROSS

X201**E**26
Weight Limit 1.8 Tons Per Axle
9 Tons Gross, R12-4 / R12-6

AXLE WEIGHT LIMIT 5 TONS

X201**E**27
Axle Weight Limit 5 Tons
R12-2

METRIC AXLE WEIGHT LIMIT 4.5t

X201**E**28
Axle Weight Limit 4.5 Tons
R12-2 / R12-6

WEIGHT LIMIT 8T 12T 16T

X201**E**29
Weight Limit 8 Tons,
12 Tons, 16 Tons, R12-5

OR

METRIC WEIGHT LIMIT 7.2t 10.8t 14.5t

X201**E**30
Weight Limit 7.2 Tons, 10.8 Tons,
14.5 Tons, R12-5 / R12-6

METRIC

X201**E**31
Metric (Supplemental)
R12-6

ALL TRUCKS COMMERCIAL VEHICLES NEXT RIGHT

X201**E**32
All Trucks Commercial Vehicles
Next Right, Weigh Station
R13-1

X201**E**33
Truck Route
R14-1

X201**E**34
Hazardous Material Route
R14-2

X201**E**35
Hazardous Material Prohibition
R14-3

X201**E**36
National Network Route
R14-4

X201**E**37
National Network Prohibition
R14-5

Warning Signs

X201**F**01 Turn to the Right W1-1

X201**F**02 Turn to the Left W1-1

X201**F**03 Curve to the Right W1-2(R)

X201**F**04 Curve to the Left W1-2(L)

X201**F**05 Reverse Turn W1-3

X201**F**06 Reverse Turn W1-3

X201**F**07 Reverse Curve W1-4

X201**F**08 Reverse Curve W1-4

X201**F**09 Reverse Curve (Two Lanes) W1-4b

X201**F**10 Reverse Curve (Two Lanes) W1-4b

X201**F**11 Reverse Curve (Three Lanes) W1-4c

X201**F**12 Reverse Curve (Three Lanes) W1-4c

X201**F**13 Winding Road W1-5

X201**F**14 One Direction (Right) W1-6

X201**F**15 One Direction (Left) W1-6

X201**F**16 Chevron Alignment (Right) W1-8

X201**F**17 Chevron Alignment (Left) W1-8

X201**F**18 Hairpin Curve W1-11

X201**F**19 Truck Rollover W1-13

X201**F**20 270 - Degree Curve W1-15

X201**F**21 Combination Horizontal Alignment Advisory Speed W1-1a

X201**F**22 Combination Horizontal Alignment Advisory Speed W1-1a

X201**F**23 Combination Horizontal Alignment Advisory Speed W1-2a

X201**F**24 Combination Horizontal Alignment Advisory Speed W1-2a

X201**F**25 Combination Horizontal Alignment Intersection W1-10

X201**F**26 Steep Hill (Caution Trucks) W7-1

X201**F**27 Hill W7-1a

X201**F**28 Hill 8% Grade W7-1b

X201**F**29 Runaway Truck Ramp 1 Mile W 7-4

X201**F**30 Runaway Truck Ramp W 7-4b

X201**F**31 Truck Escape Ramp W7-4c

X201**F**32 Hill Blocks View W7-6

X201**F**33 Sand W7-4d

X201**F**34 Gravel W7-4e

X201**F**35 Paved W 7-4f

X201**F**36 Use Low Gear W7-2

X201**F**37 Trucks Use Lower Gear W7-2b

X201**F**38 9% Grade W7-3

X201**F**39 Next 7 Miles W7-3a

X201**F**40 Next 11 km W7-3a

X201**F**41 9% Grade 7 Miles W7-3b

X201**F**42 9% Grade 11km W7-3b

Warning Signs continued

X201**G**01 Stop Ahead W3-1

X201**G**02 Yield Ahead W3-2

X201**G**03 Stop Ahead W3-1

X201**G**04 Signal Ahead W3-3

X201**G**05 Be Prepared to Stop W3-4

X201**G**06 Speed Reduction W3-5

X201**G**07 Bump W8-1

X201**G**08 Dip W8-2

X201**G**09 Pavement Ends W8-3

X201**G**10 Soft Shoulder W8-4

X201**G**11 Slippery When Wet W8-5

X201**G**12 Loose Gravel W8-7

X201**G**13 Rough Road W8-8

X201**G**14 Low Shoulder W8-9

X201**G**15 Shoulder Drop Off W8-9a

X201**G**16 No Center Stripe W8-12

X201**G**17 Bridge Ices Before Road W8-13

X201**G**18 Speed Hump W17-1

X201**G**19 Road Narrows W5-1

X201**G**20 Narrow Bridge W5-2

X201**G**21 Narrow Bridge W5-2a

X201**G**22 One Lane Bridge W5-3

X201**G**23 Ramp Narrows W5-4

X201**G**24 Divided Highway W6-1

X201**G**25 Divided Highway Ends W6-2

X201**G**26 Steep Hill (Caution Bicyclists) W7-5

X201**G**27 Hill W7-5

X201**G**28 Pavement Ends W8-3a

X201**G**29 Shoulder Drop-Off W8-9a

X201**G**30 Hazardous Condition W8-10

X201**G**31 Slippery When Wet W8-10

X201**G**32 No Passing Zone W14-3

X201**G**33 Speed Zone Ahead W3-5a

X201**G**34 Speed Zone Ahead W3-5a

X201**G**35 Advisory Speed W13-1

X201**G**36 Advisory Speed W13-1

Warning Signs continued

X201H01 Advisory Exit Speed W13-2

X201H02 Advisory Exit Speed W13-2

X201H03 Advisory Ramp Speed W13-3

X201H04 Advisory Ramp Speed W13-3

X201H05 Advisory Curve Speed W13-5

X201H06 Advisory Curve Speed W13-5

X201H07 Low Clearance W12-2

X201H08 Low Clearance W12-2

X201H09 Merge (Right) W4-1

X201H10 Merge (Left) W4-1

X201H11 Lane Ends W4-2

X201H12 Lane Ends W4-2

X201H13 Pavement Width Transition W4-2

X201H14 Pavement Width Transition W4-2

X201H15 Added Lane (left) W4-3

X201H16 Added Lane (right) W4-3

X201H17 Entering Roadway Merge W4-5

X201H18 Entering Roadway Merge W4-5

X201H19 Entering Roadway Added Lane W4-6

X201H20 Entering Roadway Added Lane W4-6

X201H21 Two Way Traffic W6-3

X201H22 Two Way Traffic W 6-4

X201H23 Two Directions (Left and Right) W1-7

X201H24 Cross Road W2-1

X201H25 Side Road - Right (Perpendicular), W2-2

X201H26 Side Road - Left (Perpendicular), W2-2

X201H27 Side Road - Right (Oblique), W2-3

X201H28 Side Road - Left (Oblique), W2-3

X201H29 T-Intersection Ahead W2-4

X201H30 Y-Intersection Ahead W2-5

X201H31 Traffic Circle W16-12p

X201H32 Cross Traffic Does Not Stop W4-4p

X201H33 Oncoming Traffic Has Extended Green, W25-1

X201H34 Oncoming Traffic May Have Extended Green, W25-2

X201H35 Truck Crossing W8-6

X201H36 Bicycle Crossing W11-1

X201H37 Farm Vehicles Crossing W11-5

X201H38 Farm Vehicles Crossing W11-5a

X201H39 Fire Station W11-8

X201H40 Truck Crossing W11-10

X201H41 Golf Cart Crossing W11-11

X201H42 Emergency Signal Ahead W11-12p

Warning
Signs
continued

X201**J**01
Horse-drawn Vehicles
W11-12p

X201**J**02
Pedestrian Crossing
W11A-2

X201**J**03
Pedestrian (Advanced Warning)
W11-2

X201**J**04
Deer Crossing
W11-3

X201**J**05
Cattle Crossing
W11-4

X201**J**06
Snowmobile
W11-6

X201**J**07
Kangaroo Crossing
(Unofficial)

X201**J**08
Equestrian Crossing
W11-7

X201**J**09
Handicapped Crossing
W11-9

X201**J**10
Playground
W15-1

X201**J**11
Share the Road
(Supplemental Plaque)
W16-1

X201**J**12
Distance Ahead 500 Feet
(Supplemental Plaque)
W16-2

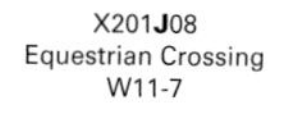

X201**J**13
Distance Ahead 500 Feet
(Supplemental Plaque)
W16-2a

X201**J**14
Distance Ahead 500 Feet
(Supplemental Plaque)
W16-4

X201**J**15
Distance Ahead 2 Miles
(Supplemental Plaque)
W16-3

X201**J**16
Distance Ahead 2 Miles
(Supplemental Plaque)
W16-3a

X201**J**17
Ahead
(Supplemental Plaque)
W16-9p

X201**J**18
Advance Street Name
W16-8

X201**J**19
Advance Street Name
W16-8a

X201**J**20
Photo Enforced
W16-10

X201**J**21
HOV (High Occupancy Vehicle)
Plaque, W16-11

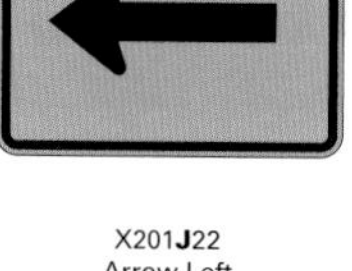

X201**J**22
Arrow Left
(Supplemental Plaque)
W16-5p

X201**J**23
Arrow Left
(Supplemental Plaque)
W16-6p

X201**J**24
Arrow Left
(Supplemental Plaque)
W16-7p

X201**J**25
When Flashing
W16-13p

X201**J**26
Left Lane Ends
W 9-1

X201**J**27
Lane Ends Merge Left
W9-2

X201**J**28
Right Lane Ends
W9-1

X201**J**29
No Outlet
W14-2

X201**J**30
Dead End
W14-1

X201**J**31
Road Construction 500 Feet
W20-1

X201**J**32
Detour 1000 Feet
W20-2

X201**J**33
Road Closed (street)
W20-3

X201**J**34
500 Feet (flagger)
W20-7a

X201**J**35
Flagger
W20-7a

X201**J**36
Blasting Zone Ahead
W22-1

Warning Signs continued

X201**K**01
Blasting Zone 500 Feet
W22-1

X201**K**02
Blasting Zone 1000 Feet
W22-1

X201**K**03
Turn Off 2- Way Radio
W22-2

X201**K**04
End Blasting Zone
W22-3

X201**K**05
Slow Traffic Ahead
W23-1

X201**K**06
Worker
W21-1a

X201**K**07
Men Working / Worker
W21-1

X201**K**08
Road Machinery Ahead
W21-3

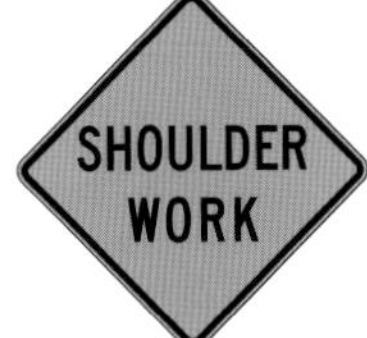

X201**K**09
Shoulder Work
W21-5

X201**K**10
Survey Crew
W21-6

X201**K**11
Utility Work Ahead
W21-7

X201**K**12
Two Arrow
W12-1

X201**K**13
Center Lane Closed Ahead
W9-3a

X201**K**14
Center Lane Closed Ahead
W9-3

X201**K**15
Right Lane Ends
W9-1

X201**K**16
Uneven Lanes
W8-11

X201**K**17
Double Reverse Curve
(1 Lane), W24-1

X201**K**18
Double Reverse Curve
(1 Lane), W24-1

X201**K**19
Double Reverse Curve
(2 Lanes), W24-1a

X201**K**20
Double Reverse Curve
(2 Lanes), W24-1a

X201**K**21
Double Reverse Curve
(3 Lanes), W24-1b

X201**K**22
Double Reverse Curve
(3 Lanes), W24-1b

X201**K**23
Exit Open
E5-2

X201**K**24
Exit Closed
E5-2a

X201**K**25
Exit Only
E5-3

X201**K**26
Detour (Plaque)
M4-8

X201**K**27
End Detour (Plaque)
M4-8a

X201**K**28
End (Plaque)
M4-8b

X201**K**29
Detour (Inside Right Arrow)
M4-10

X201**K**30
Detour (Inside Left Arrow)
M4-10

X201**K**31
Detour (With Right Arrow)
M4-9

X201**K**32
Detour (With Left Arrow)
M4-9

X201**K**33
Pedestrian Detour
(With Left Arrow), M4-9b

X201**K**34
Bike Detour (With Left Arrow)
M4-9c

X201**K**35
Bike/ Pedestrian Detour
(With Left Arrow), M4-9a

Warning Signs continued

X201**L**01
Channelizing Device Drum

X201**L**02
Tubular Marker

X201**L**03
Tubular Marker 2

X201**L**04
Vertical Panel

X201**L**05
Cone

X201**L**06
Cone 2

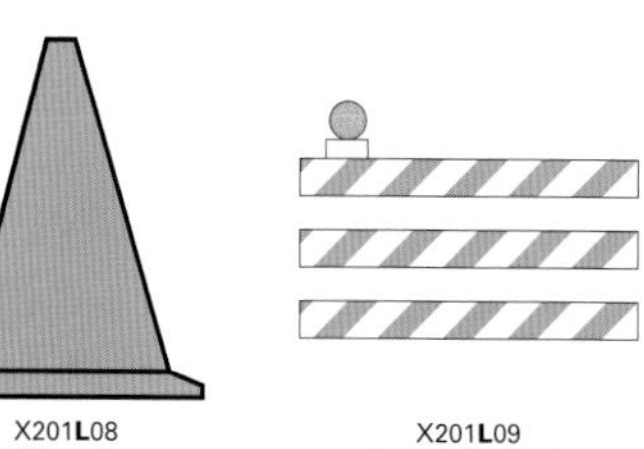
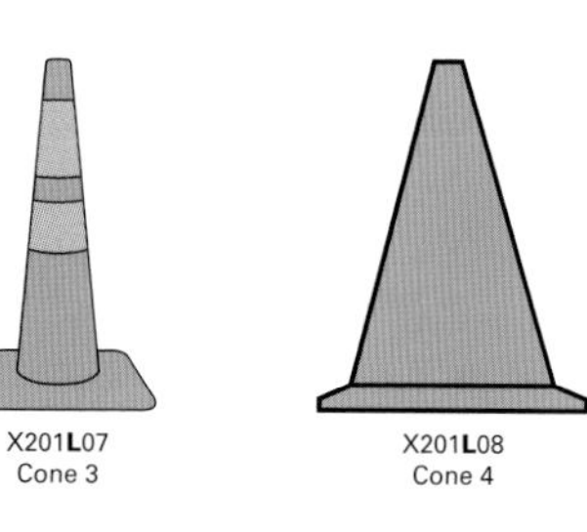
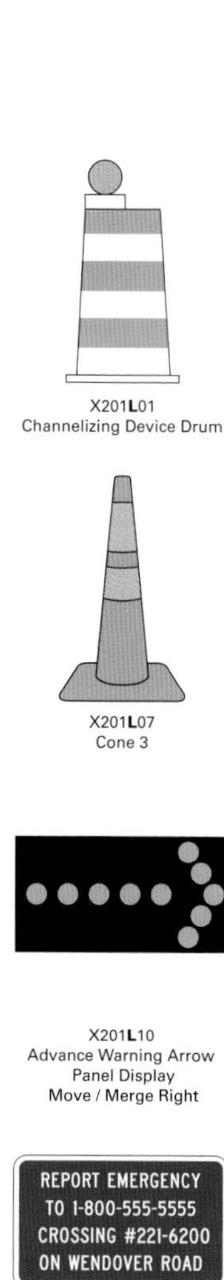

X201**L**07
Cone 3

X201**L**08
Cone 4

X201**L**09
Type **3** Barricade
with Warning Light

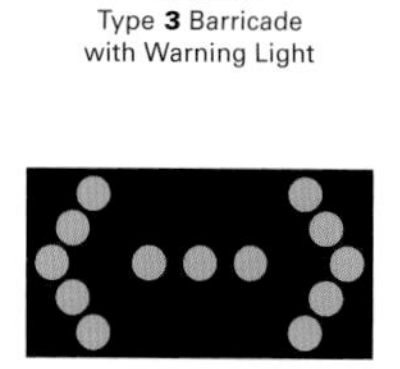
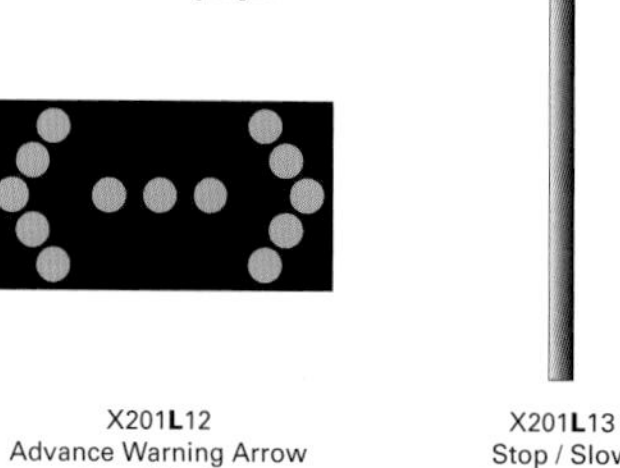

X201**L**10
Advance Warning Arrow
Panel Display
Move / Merge Right

X201**L**11
Advance Warning Arrow
Panel Display
Move / Merge Right

X201**L**12
Advance Warning Arrow
Panel Display
Move / Merge Right or Left

X201**L**13
Stop / Slow
Paddle (Front)

X201**L**14
Stop / Slow
Paddle (Back)

X201**L**15
Portable / Temporary
Mounting

X201**L**16
Report Emergency
I-13a

X201**L**17
Railroad Crossing
W10-1

X201**L**18
Exempt (Plaque)
W10-1a

X201**L**19
Advance Railroad Warning
W10-2

X201**L**20
Advance Railroad Warning
W10-3

X201**L**21
Advance Railroad Warning
W10-4

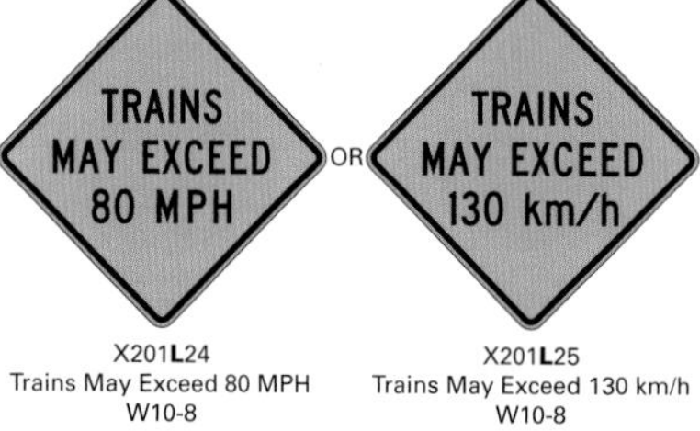

X201**L**22
Light Rail Station
S1-1

X201**L**23
Low Ground Clearance Highway
- Rail Grade Crossing, W10-5

X201**L**24
Trains May Exceed 80 MPH
W10-8

X201**L**25
Trains May Exceed 130 km/h
W10-8

X201**L**26
Storage Space Symbol
W10-11

X201**L**27
Skewed Crossing
W10-12

X201**L**28
Storage Space Between
Tracks and Highway 100 Feet
W10-11a

X201**L**29
Storage Space Between
Tracks and Highway 30 Meters
W10-11a

X201**L**30
Storage Space Between
Tracks and Highway 150 Feet
W10-11b

X201**L**31
Storage Space Between
Tracks and Highway 45 Meters
W10-11b

X201**L**32
No Train Horn
W10-9

X201**L**33
No Signal
W10-10

Warning Signs continued

X201**M**01
No Gates or Lights
W10-13

NEXT
CROSSING

X201**M**02
Next Crossing
W10-14

USE NEXT
CROSSING

X201**M**03
Use Next Crossing
W10-14a

ROUGH
CROSSING

X201**M**04
Rough Crossing
W10-15

RAILROAD CROSSING

X201**M**05
Railroad Crossing
R15-1

3
TRACKS

X201**M**06
3 Tracks
R15-2

X201**M**107
Railroad-Highway
Crossing Sign

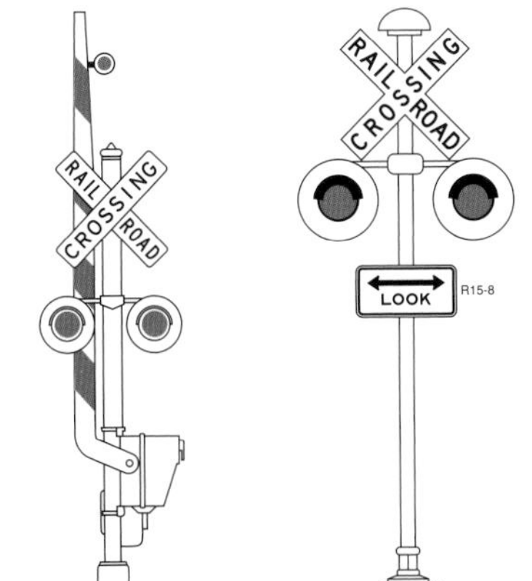

X201**M**08
Automatic Gate / Light Signals
for Railroad Crossing

X201**M**09
Automatic Gate / Light Signals
for Railroad Crossing (Look)

RAILROAD CROSSING

X201**M**10
Automatic Gates / Light Signals
for Railroad Crossing

Regulatory Signs - Railroad

X201**M**11
No Right Turn Across Tracks
Turn Prohibition, R3-1a

NO
LEFT
TURN
ACROSS
TRACKS

X201**M**12
No Right Turn Across Tracks
Turn Prohibition, R3-2a

DO NOT
STOP
ON
TRACKS

X201**M**13
Do Not Stop On Tracks
R8-8

TRACKS
OUT OF
SERVICE

X201**M**14
Tracks Out Of Service
R8-9

STOP
HERE
WHEN
FLASHING

X201**M**15
Stop Here When Flashing
R8-10

X201**M**16
Stop Here On Red
R10-6

NO
TURN
ON
RED

X201**M**17
No Turn On Red
R10-11a

X201**M**18
Exempt
R15-3

X201**M**19
Look
R15-8

X201**M**20
Light Rail Right Lane Only
R15-4a

X201**M**21
Light Rail Left Lane Only
R15-4b

X201**M**22
Light Rail Only Center Lane
R15-4c

X201**M**23
Light Rail Do Not Pass
R15-5

X201**M**24
Do not Pass Stopped Train
R15-5a

X201**M**25
Do Not Drive On Tracks
R15-6

X201**M**26
Do Not Drive On Tracks
R15-6a

X201**M**27
Light Rail Divided Highway
R15-7

X201**M**28
Light Rail Divided Highway
(T-Intersection), R15-7a

Emergency Management Signs

X201**M**29
Hurricane Evacuation Route
EM-1

X201**M**30
Area Closed
EM-2

X201**M**31
Maintain Top Safe Speed
EM-4

X201**M**32
Medical Center
EM-6a

X201**M**33
Registration Center
EM-6d

X201**M**34
Fallout Shelter Directional
Sign, EM7c

School Signs

X201N01
School (Advance Warning)
S1-1

X201N02
School Crossing
S2-1

X201N03
School Bus Stop Ahead
S3-1

X201N04
School
S4-3

X201N05
When Flashing
S4-4

X201N06
School Speed Limit 20 M.P.H.
When Flashing, S5-1

X201N07
Single-Lane Pavement Marking

X201N08
Slow Children at Play

X201N09
Reduced Speed School Zone
Ahead, S4-5

X201N10
Reduced Speed
School Zone Ahead
S4-5a

X201N11
End School Zone
S5-2

X201N12
School Advance Warning
S1-1/ W 16-9p

X201N13
School Yield to Pedestrian
Within Crosswalk
S4-3 / R1-6

X201N14
School Stop for Pedestrian
Within Crosswalk
S4-3 / R1-6a

X201N15
School Crossing Right Arrow
S1-1 / W16-7p

Bicycle Signs

X201N16
Bike Lane
R3-17

X201N17
Ahead (Supplemental Plaque)
R3-17a

X201N18
Ends (Supplemental Plaque)
R3-17b

X201N19
Do Not Pass
R4-1

X201N20
Pass With Care
R4-2

X201N21
Slower Traffic Keep Right
R4-3

X201N22
Begin Right Turn Lane
Yield to Bikes, R4-4

X201N23
Movement Restriction
R4-7

X201N24
Movement Restriction
R4-7

X201N25
Bicycle Wrong Way
R5-1b / R9-3c

X201N26
No Motor Vehicles
R5-3

X201N27
No Bicycles
R5-6

X201N28
No Parking Bike Lane
R7-9

X201N29
No Parking Bike Lane
R7-9a

X201N30
Pedestrians Prohibited
R9-3a

X201N31
Use Pedestrian Signal
R9-5

X201N32
Yield to Pedestrians
R9-6

X201N33
Shared Use Path Restriction
R9-7

X201N34
Push button For Green Light
R10-3

X201N35
To Request Green
Wait on Signal
R10-22

X201N36
Bikeway Narrows
W5-4a

X201N37
Hill
W7-5

X201N38
Bicycle Surface Condition
W8-10 / W8-10p

X201N39
Share The Road
W11-1 / W16-1

Bicycle Signs continued

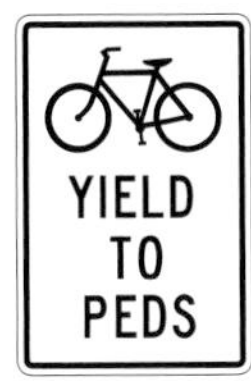

X201**P**01
Bicyclists Yield to Pedestrians
R9-6

X201**P**02
Bicycle Parking Left
D4-3

X201**P**03
Bike Route
D11-1

X201**P**04
Bicycle Route
M1-8

X201**P**05
Interstate Bicycle Route
M1-9

X201**P**06
Begin
(Supplemental Plaque)
M4-11

X201**P**07
End
(Supplemental Plaque)
M4-12

X201**P**08
To
(Supplemental Plaque)
M4-13

X201**P**09
Destination Sign
D1-1

X201**P**10
Supplemental Plaque
to Bicycle Route Sign, D1-1b

X201**P**11
Supplemental Plaque
to Bicycle Route Sign, D1-1b

X201**P**12
Directional Arrow Right
(Supplemental Plaque)
M7-1

X201**P**13
Directional Arrow Left / Right
(Supplemental Plaque)
M7-5

X201**P**14
Directional Arrow Straight Ahead (Supplemental Plaque)
M7-2

X201**P**15
Directional Arrows
(Supplemental Plaque)
M7-3

X201**P**16
Directional Arrow
(Supplemental Plaque)
M7-4

X201**P**17
Directional Arrows
(Supplemental Plaque)
M7-6

X201**P**18
Directional Arrows
(Supplemental Plaque)
M7-7

X201**P**19
Advance Turn Arrow (Left)
M5-1

X201**P**20
Advance Turn Arrow (Right)
M5-1

X201**P**21
Directional Arrow (Bicycle)
M6-1

X201**P**22
Directional Arrow (Bicycle)
M6-1

X201**P**23
Directional Arrow (Bicycle)
M6-3

X201**P**24
Directional Arrows (Bicycle)
M6-4

X201**P**25
Directional Arrows (Bicycle)
M6-5

X201**P**26
Directional Arrows (Bicycle)
M6-5

X201**P**27
Directional Arrows (Bicycle)
M6-7

X201**P**28
Directional Arrows (Bicycle)
M6-7

X201**P**29
Directional Arrow (Bicycle)
M6-2

X201**P**30
Directional Arrow (Bicycle)
M6-2

X201**P**31
Advance Turn Arrow (Bicycle)
M5-2

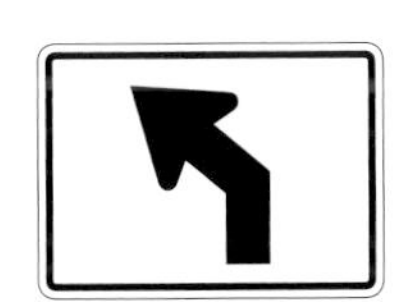
X201**P**32
Advance Turn Arrow (Bicycle)
M5-2

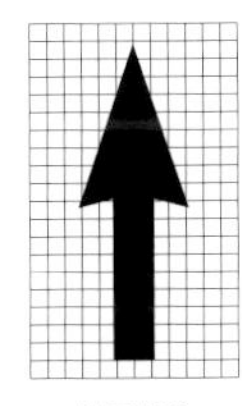
X201**P**33
Directional Arrow
Pavement Marking

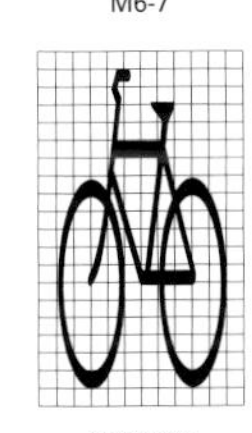
X201**P**34
Bicycle Lane
Pavement Marking

X201**P**35
Bicycle Lane
Pavement Marking

X201**P**36
Directional Arrows (Bicycle)
M6-6

X201**P**37
Directional Arrows (Bicycle)
M6-6

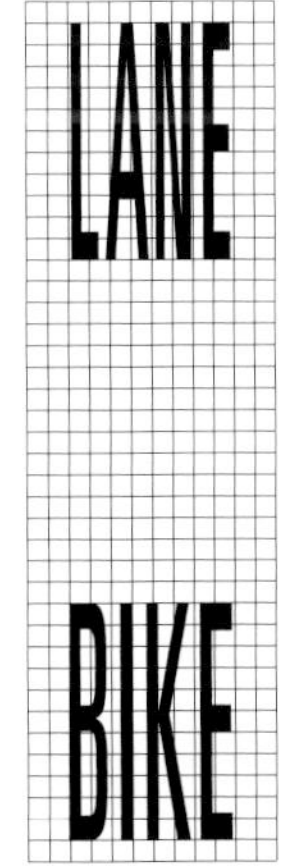

X201**P**38
Bicycle Lane
Pavement Marking

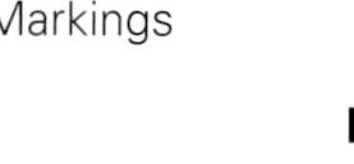

Pavement Markings

X201Q01
Through Lane-Use Arrow
Pavement Marking

X201Q02
Turn Lane-Use Arrow
Pavement Marking

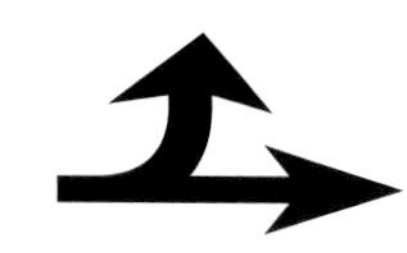

X201Q03
Turn and Through Lane-Use
Arrow, Pavement Marking

X201Q04
Wrong Way Arrow
Pavement Marking

X201Q05
Lane Reduction Arrow
Pavement Marking

X201Q06
Only
Pavement Marking

Guide Signs

X201Q07
Two-way Left-turn Arrow
Lane-Use Control Signal

X201Q08
One-way Left-turn Arrow
Lane-Use Control Signal

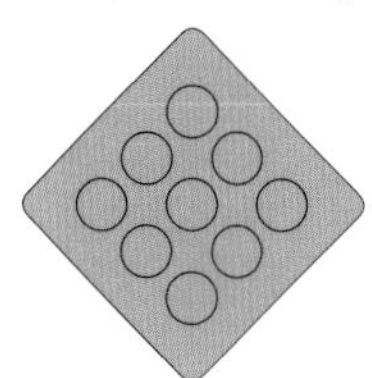

X201Q09
Type 1 Object Marker
OM1-1

X201Q10
Type 1 Object Marker
OM1-2

X201Q11
Type 1 Object Marker
OM1-3

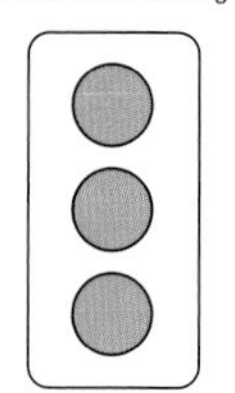

X201Q12
Type 2 Object Marker
OM2-1V

X201Q13
Type 2 Object Marker
OM2-2V

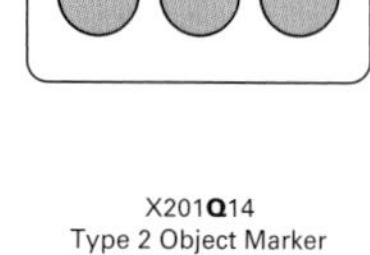

X201Q14
Type 2 Object Marker
OM2-1H

X201Q15
Type 2 Object Marker
OM2-2H

X201Q16
Type 3 Object Marker
OM-3L

X201Q17
Type 3 Object Marker
OM-3C

X201Q18
Type 3 Object Marker
OM-3R

X201Q19
End of Road Marker
OM4-1

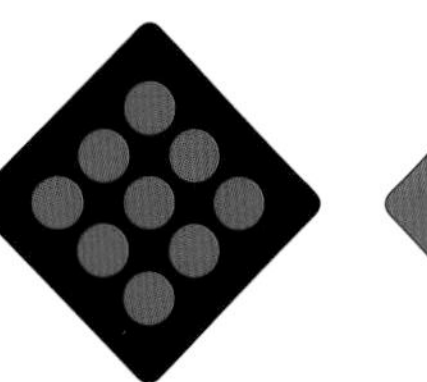

X201Q20
End of Road Marker
OM4-2

X201Q21
End of Road Marker
OM4-3

X201Q22
Interstate Shield
M1-1

X201Q23
Interstate Shield
M1-1

X201Q24
Off-Interstate Business
Loop Marker, M1-3

X201Q25
Off-Interstate Business
Route Sign, M1-2 / M1-3

X201Q26
U.S. Route Sign
M1-4

X201Q27
U.S. Route Marker
(Independent Use), M1-4

X201Q28
U.S. Route Marker
(Guide Sign Use), M1-4

X201Q29
U.S. Route Marker
(Guide Sign Use), M1-4

X201Q30
County Route Marker
M1-5

X201Q31
State Route Marker
M1-6

X201Q32
State Route Sign
M1-5

X201Q33
National Forest Route Sign
M1-7

X201Q34
Eisenhower State System

X201Q35
Eisenhower State System

X201Q36
Junction Auxiliary
M2-1

X201Q37
Junction Auxiliary (Interstate)
M2-1

X201Q38
Combination Junction Sign
M2-2

X201Q39
North, Cardinal Direction
Auxiliary, M3-1

Guide Signs continued

X201**R**01
East
Cardinal Direction Auxiliary
M3-2

X201**R**02
South
Cardinal Direction Auxiliary
M3-3

X201**R**03
West
Cardinal Direction Auxiliary
M3-4

X201**R**04
North (Interstate)
Cardinal Direction Auxiliary
M3-1

X201**R**05
East (Interstate)
Cardinal Direction Auxiliary
M3-2

X201**R**06
South (Interstate)
Cardinal Direction Auxiliary
M3-3

X201**R**07
West (Interstate)
Cardinal Direction Auxiliary
M3-4

X201**R**08
Alternate
Auxiliary
M4-1

X201**R**09
Alt
Auxiliary
M4-1a

X201**R**10
Bypass
Auxiliary
M4-2

X201**R**11
Business Route
Auxiliary
M4-3

X201**R**12
Truck Route
Auxiliary
M4-4

X201**R**13
To
Auxiliary
M4-5

X201**R**14
End
Auxiliary
M4-6

X201**R**15
Temporary
Auxiliary
M4-7

X201**R**16
Temp
Auxiliary, M4-7a

X201**R**17
Rest Area 1 Mile
Auxiliary, D5-1

X201**R**18
Rest Area
Auxiliary, D5-2

X201**R**19
Parking Area 1 Mile
D5-3

X201**R**20
Parking Area
D5-4

X201**R**21
Roadside Table
D5-5

X201**R**22
Picnic Area
D5-5a

X201**R**23
Roadside Park
D5-5b

X201**R**24
Picnic Area
D5-5c

X201**R**25
Scenic Area
D6-1

X201**R**26
Scenic Overlook 2 Miles
D6-2

X201**R**27
Scenic Area
D6-3

X201**R**28
America's Byways
D6-4

X201**R**29
America's Byways
D6-4a

X201**R**30
Recreational and Cultural
Interest Sign, D7-2

X201**R**31
Telephone
D9-1

X201**R**32
Telephone With Arrow
D9-1a

X201**R**33
Telephone 1/4 Mile
D9-1b

X201**R**34
Hospital
D9-2

X201**R**35
Camping
D9-3

X201**R**36
Trailer Camping
D9-3a

Guide Signs continued

X201**S**01
Litter Container
D9-4

X201**S**02
Trash Receptacle
D9-4

X201**S**03
Handicapped
D9-6

X201**S**04
Gas
D9-7

X201**S**05
Food
D9-8

X201**S**06
Lodging
D9-9

X201**S**07
Tourist Information
D9-10

X201**S**08
Diesel Fuel
D9-11

X201**S**09
Alternative Fuel
D9-11a

X201**S**10
Electric Vehicle Charging
D9-11b

X201**S**11
RV Sanitary Station
D9-12

X201**S**12
Emergency Medical Services
D9-13

X201**S**13
Hospital
D9-13a

X201**S**14
Ambulance Station
D9-13c

X201**S**15
Emergency Medical Care
D9-13c

X201**S**16
Propane Gas
D9-15

X201**S**17
Truck Parking
D9-16

X201**S**18
General Information Sign
I-2

X201**S**19
Signals Set for 25 MPH
I1-1

OR

X201**S**20
Signals Set for 40 km/h
I1-1

X201**S**21
General Information Sign
I-3

X201**S**22
Airport
I-5

X201**S**23
Bus Station
I-6

X201**S**24
Train Station
I-7

X201**S**25
Library
I-8

X201**S**26
Recycling Collection Center
I-11

X201**S**27
Police
D9-14

X201**S**28
Weather Info
D12-1

X201**S**29
Car Pool Info Monitor
D12-2

X201**S**30
State Police Monitor
D12-3

X201**S**31
Emergency Dial 911
D12-4

X201**S**32
Travel Info Call 511 (Logo)
D12-4

X201**S**33
Crossover Left
D13-1

X201**S**34
Crossover 1/4 Mile
D13-2

X201**S**35
Reference Location Sign (Mile)
D10-1

OR

X201**S**36
Reference Location Sign (km)
D10-1

X201**S**37
Reference Location Sign
(Intermediate Mile), D10-1a

OR

X201**S**38
Reference Location Sign
(Intermediate km), D10-1a

X201**S**39
Reference Location Sign
(Mile), D10-2

OR

X201**S**40
Reference Location Sign (km)
D10-2

X201**S**41
Reference Location Sign
(Intermediate Mile), D10-2a

OR

X201**S**42
Reference Location Sign
(Intermediate km), D10-2a

Guide Signs continued

X201T01
Reference Location Sign (Mile), D10-3

OR

X201T02
Reference Location Sign (km), D10-3

X201T03
Reference Location Sign (Intermediate Mile), D10-3a

OR

X201T04
Reference Location Sign (Intermediate km), D10-3a

X201T05
Enhanced Reference Location (Mile)

X201T06
Enhanced Reference Location (km)

X201T07
Enhanced Reference Location (Intermediate Mile)

X201T08
Enhanced Reference Location (Intermediate km)

X201T09
Exit Only Panel
E11-1

X201T10
Exit Only Panel
E11-1a

X201T11
Exit Only Panel
E11-1b

X201T12
Exit Only Panel
E11-1c

X201T13
Next Exit 12 Miles

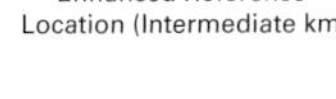

X201T14
Community Interchanges Identification (Example)

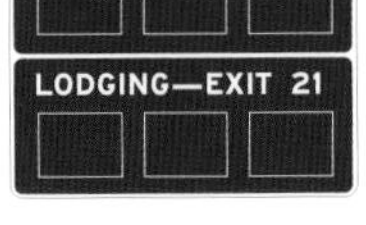

X201T15
Specific Services (Example)

X201T16
General Services (Example)

X201T17
Destination Sign
D1-2

X201T18
Destination Sign
D1-3a

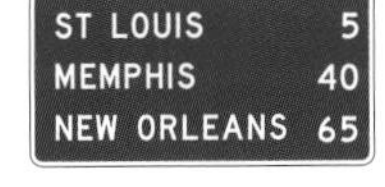

X201T19
Distance Sign
D2-3

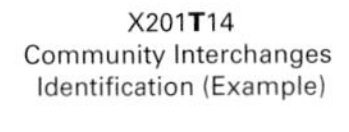

X201T20
Street Name Sign
D-3

X201T21
Diagrammatic Sign (Example)

X201T22
Diagrammatic Sign (Example)

X201T23
Gore Sign

X201T24
Parking Area
D4-1

X201T25
Park & Ride Next Right

X201T26
Park & Ride
D4-2

X201T27
End Construction
G20-2

X201T28
End Road Work
G20-2a

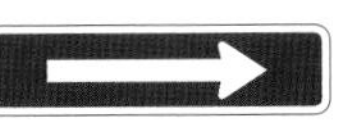
X201T29
Directional Sign (Right)

X201T30
Directional Sign (Left)

X201T31
Weigh Station
D8-3

X201T32
Trail
I-4

X201T33
Rest Area Gore

X201T34
Tourist Information Center (Supplemental)

X201T35
Tourist Oriented Directional (Example), E2-1A

X201T36
General Directional Guide (Example)

X201T37
Roadside Table
D5-5a

X201T38
Parking Directional (Example)

X201T39
No Campfires Prohibition

X201T40
No Smoking Prohibition

Guide Signs

Recreational and Cultural Interest Area Symbol Signs

- General Information

X201**U**01
Automobile
RG-010

X201**U**02
Bear Viewing Area
RG-020

X201**U**03
Dam
RG-030

X201**U**04
Deer Viewing Area
RG-040

X201**U**05
Drinking Water
RG-050

X201**U**06
Environmental Study Area
RG-060

X201**U**07
Falling Rocks
RG-070

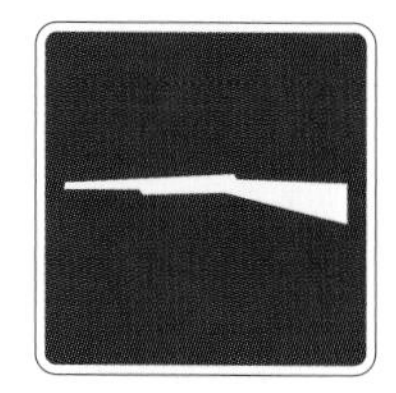
X201**U**08
Firearms
RG-080

X201**U**09
Fish Hatchery
RG-090

X201**U**10
Information
RG-100

X201**U**11
Leashed Pets
RG-110

X201**U**12
Lighthouse
RG-120

X201**U**13
Litter Container
RG-130

X201**U**14
Lookout Tower
RG-140

X201**U**15
Ped Xing
RG-150

X201**U**16
Point of Interest
RG-160

X201**U**17
Ranger Station
RG-170

X201**U**18
Smoking
RG-180

X201**U**19
Truck
RG-190

X201**U**20
Tunnel
RG-200

X201**U**21
Dog
RG-240

X201**U**22
Seaplane
RG-260

- Motorist Services

X201**U**23
Camping (Tent)
RM-010

X201**U**24
Camping (Trailer)
RM-020

X201**U**25
Ferry
RM-030

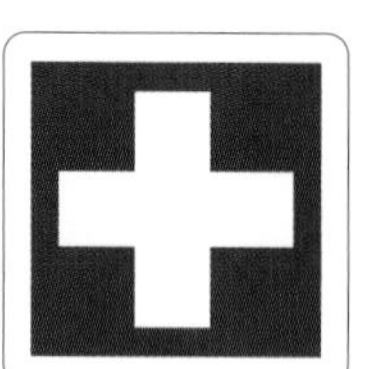
X201**U**26
First Aid
RM-040

X201**U**27
Food
RM-050

X201**U**28
Gas
RM-060

X201**U**29
Grocery Store
RM-070

X201**U**30
Handicapped
RM-080

X201**U**31
Lodging
RM-090

X201**U**32
Mechanic
RM-100

X201**U**33
Post Office
RM-110

X201**U**34
Picnic Area
RM-120

X201**U**35
Picnic Shelter
RM-130

X201**U**36
Rest Room
RM-140

Guide Signs continued

Recreational and Cultural Interest Area Symbol Signs

X201**V**01 Telephone RM-150

X201**V**02 Trailer Sanitary Station RM-160

X201**V**03 Viewing Area RM-170

X201**V**04 Motor Home RM-200

X201**V**05 Group Camping RM-210

X201**V**06 Group Picnicking RM-220

- Accommodation Services

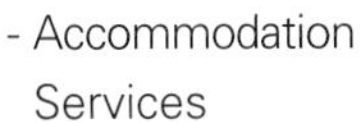

X201**V**07 Airport RA-010

X201**V**08 Bus Stop RA-020

X201**V**09 Campfire RA-030

X201**V**10 Elevator RM-040

X201**V**11 Kennel RA-050

X201**V**12 Laundry RA-060

X201**V**13 Locker RA-070

X201**V**14 Parking RA-080

X201**V**15 Rest Room (Men) RA-090

X201**V**16 Rest Room (Women) RA-100

X201**V**17 Shelter (Sleeping) RA-110

X201**V**18 Shelter (Trail) RA-120

X201**V**19 Showers RA-130

X201**V**20 Family Rest Room RA-150

X201**V**21 Helicopter RA-160

- Land Recreation

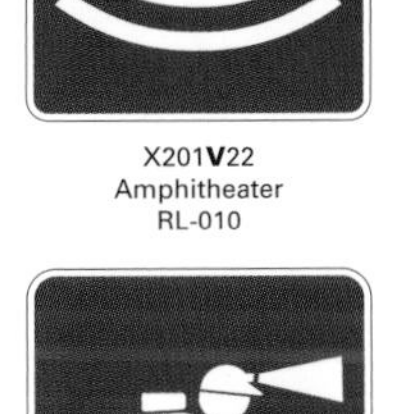
X201**V**22 Amphitheater RL-010

X201**V**23 Climbing RL-020

X201**V**24 Climbing (Rock) RL-030

X201**V**25 Hunting RL-040

X201**V**26 Playground RL-050

X201**V**27 Rock Collecting RL-060

X201**V**28 Spelunking RL-070

X201**V**29 Stable RL-080

X201**V**30 Trail (Bicycle) RL-090

X201**V**31 Trail (Hiking) RL-100

X201**V**32 Trail (Horse) RL-110

X201**V**33 Trail (Interpretive, Auto) RL-120

X201**V**34 Trail (Interpretive, Pedestrian) RL-130

X201**V**35 Trail/ Road (4 WD Vehicle) RL-140

X201**V**36 Trail (Trail Bike) RL-150

X201**V**37 Tramway RL-160

X201**V**38 All-Terrain Vehicle RL-170

X201**V**39 Archer RL-190

Guide Signs continued

Recreational and Cultural Interest Area Symbol Signs

X201**W**01
Hang Glider
RL-210

- Water Recreation

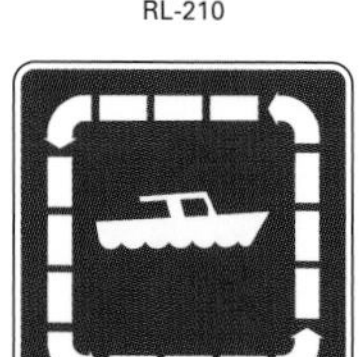

X201**W**02
Boat Tours
RW-010

X201**W**03
Canoeing
RW-020

X201**W**04
Diving
RW-030

X201**W**05
Diving (Scuba)
RW-040

X201**W**06
Fishing
RW-050

X201**W**07
Marine Recreation Area
RW-060

X201**W**08
Motorboating
RW-070

X201**W**09
Ramp (Launch)
RW-080

X201**W**10
Rowboating
RW-090

X201**W**11
Sailboating
RW-100

X201**W**12
Skiing (Water)
RW-110

X201**W**13
Surfing
RW-120

X201**W**14
Swimming
RW-130

X201**W**15
Wading
RW-140

X201**W**16
Fishing Pier
RW-160

X201**W**17
Hand Launch
RW-170

X201**W**18
Kayak
RW-190

X201**W**19
Wind Surf
RW-210

- Winter Recreation

X201**W**20
Skating (Ice)
RW-010

X201**W**21
Ski Jumping
RS-020

X201**W**22
Skiing (Bobbing)
RS-030

X201**W**23
Skiing (Cross Country)
RS-040

X201**W**24
Skiing (Downhill)
RS-050

X201**W**25
Sledding
RS-060

X201**W**26
Snowmobiling
RS-070

X201**W**27
Snowshoeing
RS-080

X201**W**28
Winter Recreation Area
RS-090

X201**W**29
Chairlift
RS-100

Pedestrian Signal Indicators

X201X01
Do Not Walk

X201X02
Walk

X201X03
Don't Walk

X201X04
Walk

X201X05
Don't Walk / Walk

X201X06
Do Not Walk / Walk

General

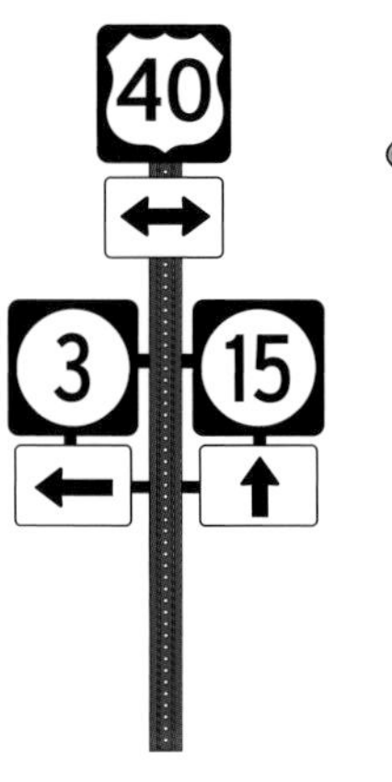

X201X07
Roadside Assembly

X201X08
Warning Sign with
Advisory Speed Plate
Assembly

X201X09
Post

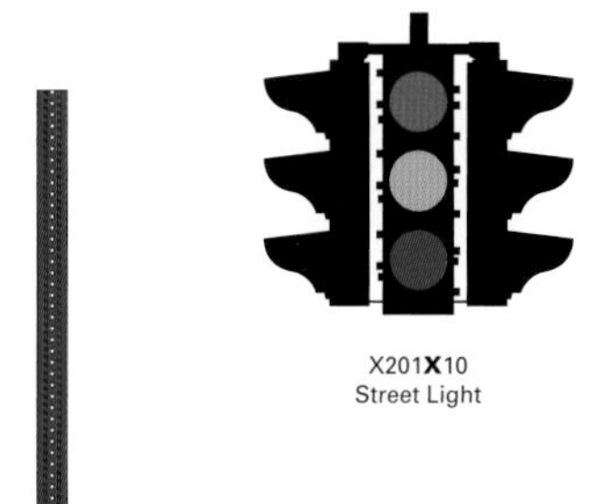

X201X10
Street Light

X01X11
Signal Lenses in Signal Faces
Example

X201X12
Clean Up After
Your Dog
(custom/unofficial)

Blank Standards

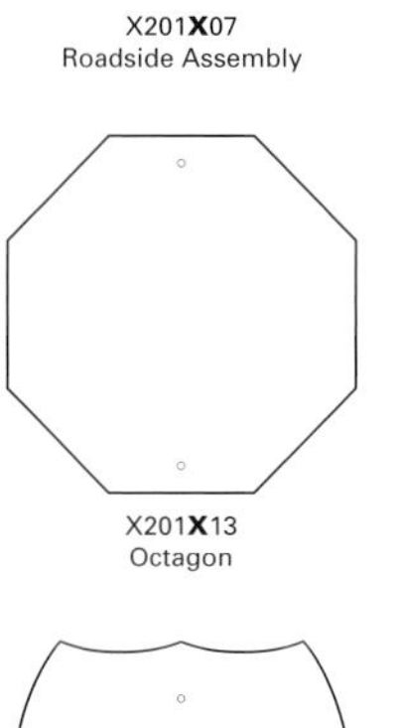

X201X13
Octagon

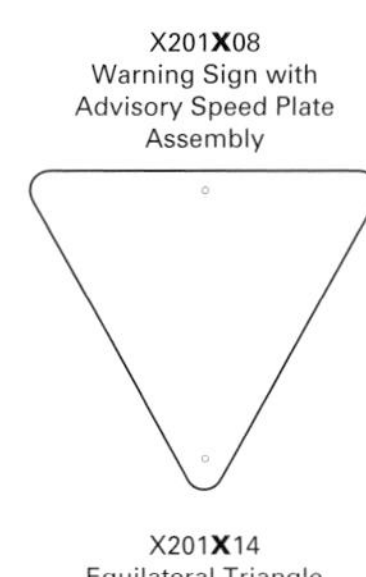

X201X14
Equilateral Triangle

X201X15
Vertical Rectangle

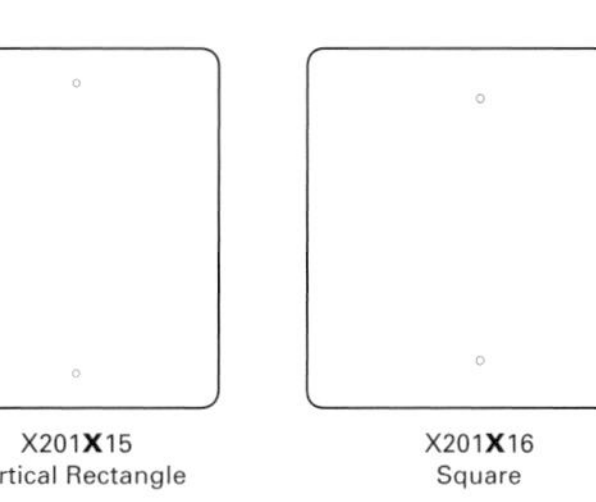

X201X16
Square

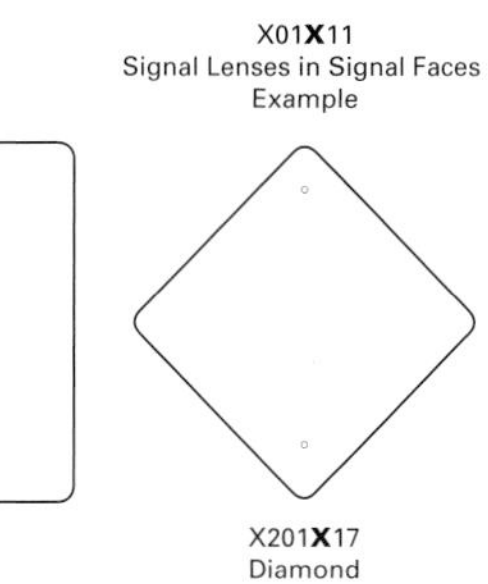

X201X17
Diamond

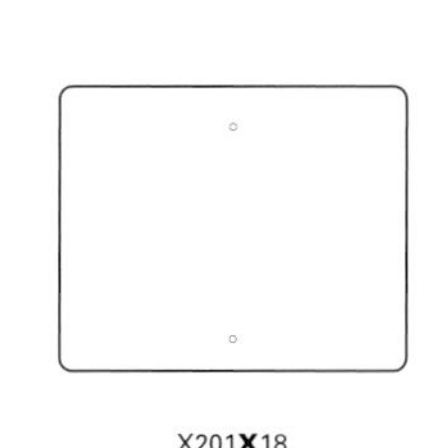

X201X18
Horizontal Rectangle

X201X19
Interstate Shield

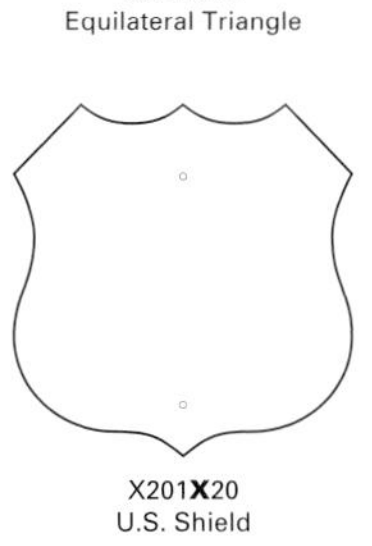

X201X20
U.S. Shield

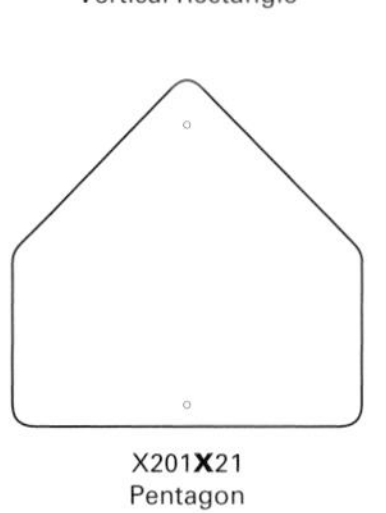

X201X21
Pentagon

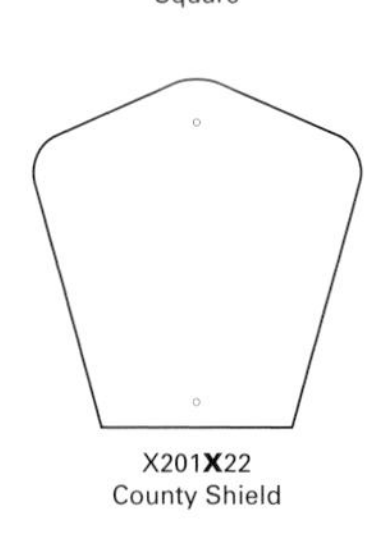

X201X22
County Shield

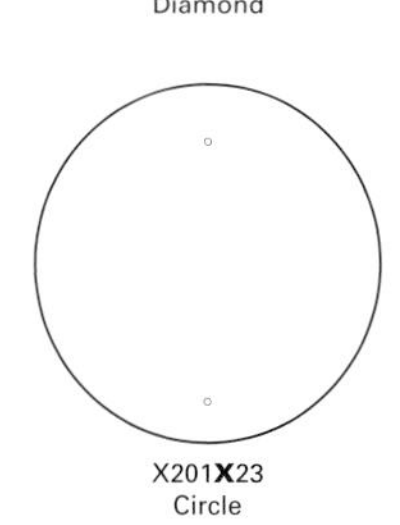

X201X23
Circle

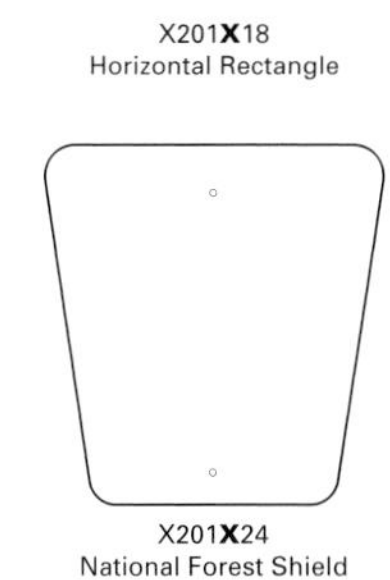

X201X24
National Forest Shield

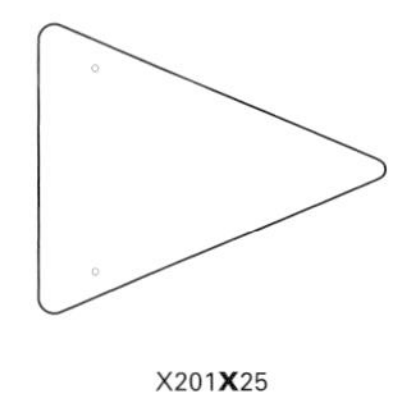

X201X25
Isosceles Triangle

Name	MUTCD	UltSym
A		
Added Lane (Left)	W4-3	X201H15
Added Lane (Right)	W4-3	X201H16
Advance Intersection Lane	R3-8	X201B15
"	R3-8	X201B16
"	R3-8a	X201B17
"	R3-8b	X201B18
"	R3-9d	X201B20
Advance Railroad Warning	W10-2	X201L19
"	W10-3	X201L20
"	W10-4	X201L21
Advance Street Name	W16-8	X201J18
"	W16-8a	X201J19
Advance Turn Arrow (Bicycle)	M5-2	X201P31
"	M5-2	X201P32
Advance Turn Arrow (Left)	M5-1	X201P19
Advance Turn Arrow (Right)	M5-1	X201P20
Advance Warning Arrow Panel Display Move / Merge Right or Left	NA	X201L12
Advance Warning Arrow Panel Display Move / Merge Right	NA	X201L10
"	NA	X201L11
Advisory Curve Speed	W13-5	X201H05
"	W13-5	X201H06
Advisory Exit Speed	W13-2	X201H01
"	W13-2	X201H02
Advisory Ramp Speed	W13-3	X201H03
"	W13-3	X201H04
Advisory Speed	W13-1	X201G35
"	W13-1	X201G36
Ahead (Supplemental Plaque)	W16-9p	X201J17
"	R3-17a	X201N17
Airport	I-5	X201S22
"	RA-010	X201V07
All-Terrain Vehicle	RL-170	X201V38
All Way	R1-4	X201A05
Alt Auxiliary	M4-1a	X201R09
Alternate Auxiliary	M4-1	X201R08
Alternative Fuel	D9-11a	X201S09
Ambulance Station	D9-13c	X201S14
America's Byways	D6-4	X201R28
"	D6-4a	X201R29
Amphitheater	RL-010	X201V22
Area Closed	EM-2	X201M30
Arrow (Supplemental Plaque)	W16-5p	X201J22
"	W16-6p	X201J23
"	W16-7p	X201J24
Automatic Gate / Light Signals for Railroad Crossing	NA	X201M08
Automatic Gate / Light Signals for Railroad Crossing (Look)	NA	X201M09
Automatic Gates / Light Signals for Railroad Crossing	NA	X201M10
Automobile	RG-010	X201U01
B		
Bear Viewing Area	RG-020	X201U02
Begin Right Turn Lane Yield to Bikes	R4-4	X201N22
Begin (Supplemental Plaque)	M4-11	X201P06
Be Prepared to Stop	W3-4	X201G05
Bicycle Crossing	W11-1	X201H36
Bicycle Lane, Pavement Marking	NA	X201P34
"	NA	X201P35
"	NA	X201P38
Bicycle Route	M1-8	X201P04
Bicycle Surface Condition	W8-10, W8-10p	X201N38
Bicycle Wrong Way	R5-1b, R9-3c	X201N25
Bicycle Parking Left	D4-3	X201P02
Bicyclists Yield to Pedestrians	R9-6	X201P05
Bike Detour (With Left Arrow)	M4-9c	X201K34
Bike / Pedestrian Detour (With Left Arrow)	M4-9a	X201K35
Bike Lane	R3-17	X201N16
Bike Route	D11-1	X201P03
Bikeway Narrows	W5-4a	X201N36
Blasting Zone Ahead	W22-1	X201J36
Blasting Zone 500 Feet	W22-1	X201K01
Blasting Zone 1000 Feet	W22-1	X201K02
Boat Tours	RW-010	X201W02
Bridge Ices Before Road	W8-13	X201G17
Bump	W8-1	X201G07
Business Route Auxiliary	M4-3	X201R11
Bus Lane Ahead	R3-10a	X201B23
Bus Lane (Supplemental)	R3-5g	X201B14
Bus Station	I-6	X201S23
Bus Stop	RA-020	X201V08
Bypass Auxiliary	M4-2	X201R10
C		
Campfire	RA-030	X201V09
Camping	D9-3	X201R35
Car Pool Info Monitor	D12-2	X201S29, X201S28
Chairlift	RS-100	X201W29
Climbing	RL-020	X201V23
Climbing (Rock)	RL-030	X201V24
Camping (Trailer)	RM-020	X201U24
Canoeing	RW-020	X201W03
Cattle Crossing	W11-4	X201J05
Center Lane Closed Ahead	W9-3a	X201K13
"	W9-3	X201K14
Center Lane	R3-9f	X201B21
Center Lane (Supplemental)	R3-5e	X201B12
Channelizing Device Drum	NA	X201L01
Circle	NA	X201X23
Clean Up After Your Dog (Custom / Unofficial)	NA	X201X12
Combination Junction Sign	M2-2	X201Q38
Commercial Vehicles Excluded	R5-4	X201C10
Community Interchanges Identification (Example)	NA	X201T14
Cone	NA	X201L05
"	NA	X201L06
"	NA	X201L07
"	NA	X201L08
County Route Marker	M1-5	X201Q31
County Shield	NA	X201X22
Crossover Left	D13-1	X201S33
Crossover 1/4 Mile	D13-2	X201S34
Cross Road	W2-1	X201H24
Cross Traffic Does Not Stop	W4-4p	X201H32

Name	MUTCD	UltSym
D		
Dam	RG-030	X201U03
Dead End	W14-1	X201J30
Deer Crossing	W11-3	X201J04
Deer Viewing Area	RG-040	X201U04
Destination Sign	D1-2	X201T17
"	D1-3a	X201T18
Detour (Inside Arrow)	M4-10	X201K29
"	M4-10	X201K30
Detour 1000 Feet	W20-2	X201J32
Detour (Plaque)	M4-8	X201K26
Detour (With Left Arrow)	M4-9	X201K32
Detour (With Right Arrow)	M4-9	X201K31
Diagrammatic Sign (Example)	NA	X201T21
"	NA	X201T22
Diamond	NA	X201X17
Diesel Fuel	D9-11	X201S08
Dip	W8-2	X201G08
Directional Arrow (Bicycle)	M6-1	X201P21
"	M6-1	X201P22
"	M6-3	X201P23
"	M6-4	X201P24
"	M6-5	X201P25
"	M6-5	X201P26
"	M6-7	X201P27
"	M6-7	X201P28
"	M6-2	X201P29
"	M6-6	X201P36
"	M6-6	X201P37
"	M6-2	X201P30
Directional Arrow Left / Right (Supplemental Plaque)	M7-5	X201P13
Directional Arrow, Pavement Marking	NA	X201P33
Directional Arrow Right (Supplemental Plaque)	M7-1	X201P12
Directional Arrow Straight Ahead (Supplemental Plaque)	M7-2	X201P14
Directional Arrow (Supplemental Plaque)	M7-4	X201P16
Directional Arrows (Supplemental Plaque)	M7-3	X201P15
"	M7-6	X201P17
"	M7-7	X201P18
Directional Sign (Right)	NA	X201T29
Directional Sign (Left)	NA	X201T30
Distance Sign	D2-3	X201T19
Distance Ahead 500 Feet (Supplemental Plaque)	W16-2	X201J12
"	W16-2a	X201J13
"	W16-4	X201J14
Distance Ahead 2 Miles (Supplemental Plaque)	W16-3	X201J15
"	W16-3a	X201J16
Divided Highway	W6-1	X201G24
Divided Highway Crossing	R6-3a	X201C23
"	R6-3	X201C22
Divided Highway Ends	W6-2	X201G25
Diving	RW-030	X201W04
Diving (Scuba)	RW-040	X201W05
Dog	RG-240	X201U21
Do Not Drive On Tracks	R15-6	X201M25
"	R15-6a	X201M26
Do Not Enter	R5-1	X201C05
Do Not Pass	R4-1	X201B33
"	R4-1	X201N19
Do Not Pass Stopped Train	R15-5a	X201M24
Do Not Stop On Tracks	R8-8	X201M13
Do Not Walk	NA	X201X01
Do Not Walk / Walk	NA	X201X06
Don't Walk	NA	X201X03
Don't Walk / Walk	NA	X201X05
Double Reverse Curve (1 Lane)	W24-1	X201K17, X201K18
Double Reverse Curve (2 Lanes)	W24-1a	X201K19, X201K20
Double Reverse Curve (3 Lanes)	W24-1b	X201K21, X201K22
Drinking Water	RG-050	X201U05
E		
East Cardinal Direction Auxiliary	M3-2	X201R01
East (Interstate) Cardinal Direction Auxiliary	M3-2	X201R05
Eisenhower State System	NA	X201Q34
"	NA	X201Q35
Electric Vehicle Charging	D9-11b	X201S10
Elevator	RM-040	X201V10
Emergency Dial 911	D12-4	X201S31
Emergency Medical Care	D9-13c	X201S15
Emergency Medical Services	D9-13	X201S12
Emergency Signal Ahead	W11-12p	X201H42
End Auxiliary	M4-6	X201R14
End Blasting Zone	W22-3	X201K04
End Construction	G20-2	X201T27
End Detour (Plaque)	M4-8a	X201K27
End of Road Marker	OM4-1	X201Q19
"	OM4-2	X201Q20
"	OM4-3	X201Q21
End (Plaque)	M4-8b	X201K28
End Reverse Lane	R3-9i	X201B22
End Road Work	G20-2a	X201T28
End School Zone	S5-2	X201N11
Ends (Supplemental Plaque)	R3-17b	X201N18
Enhanced Reference Location (Intermediate km)	NA	X201T08
Enhanced Reference Location (Intermediate Mile)	NA	X201T07
Enhanced Reference Location (km)	NA	X201T06
Enhanced Reference Location (Mile)	NA	X201T05
Entering Roadway Added Lane	W4-6	X201H19
"	W4-6	X201H20
Entering Roadway Merge	W4-5	X201H17
"	W4-5	X201H18
Environmental Study Area	RG-060	X201U06
Equestrian Crossing	W11-7	X201J08
Equilateral Triangle	NA	X201X14
Exempt	R15-3	X201M18
Exit Closed	E5-2a	X201K24
Exit Only	E5-3	X201K25
Exit Only Panel	E11-1	X201T09
"	E11-1a	X201T10
"	E11-1b	X201T11
"	E11-1c	X201T12
Exit Open	E5-2	X201K23

F-M

Name	MUTCD	UltSym
F		
Falling Rocks	RG-070	X201U07
Fallout Center Directional Sign	EM7c	X201M34
Family Rest Room	RA-150	X201V20
Farm Vehicles Crossing	W11-5	X201H37
"	W11-5a	X201H38
Ferry	RM-030	X201U25
Fines Higher	R2-6	X201A25
Fishing	RW-050	X201W06
Fishing Pier	RW-160	X201W16
Firearms	RG-080	X201U08
Fire Station	W11-8	X201H39
First Aid	RM-040	X201U26
Fish Hatchery	RG-090	X201U09
500 Feet (Flagger)	W20-7a	X201J34
Flagger	W20-7a	X201J35
Food	D9-8	X201S05
"	RM-050	X201U27
4 - Way	R1-3	X201A04
G		
Gas	D9-7	X201S04
"	RM-060	X201U28
General Directional Guide (Example)	NA	X201T36
General Information Sign	I-2	X201S18
"	I-3	X201S21
General Services (Example)	NA	X201T16
Golf Cart Crossing	W11-11	X201H41
Gore Sign	NA	X201T23
Gravel	W7-4e	X201F34
Grocery Store	RM-070	X201U29
Group Camping	RM-210	X201V05
Group Picnicking	RM-220	X201V06
H		
Handicapped	D9-6	X201S03
"	RM-080	X201U30
Handicapped Crossing	W11-9	X201J09
Hand Launch	RW-170	X201W17
Hang Glider	RL-210	X201W01
Hazardous Condition	W8-10	X201G30
Helicopter	RA-160	X201V21
Hill	W7-5	X201G27
"	W7-5	X201N37
Hills Block View	W7-6	X201F32
Horizontal Rectangle	NA	X201X18
Horse-drawn Vehicles	W11-12p	X201J01
Hospital	D9-2	X201R34
"	D9-13a	X201S13
HOV (High Occupancy Vehicle) Plaque	W16-11	X201J21
Hov Lane Ahead Preferential Only	R3-15	X201B29
Hov Lane Ends Preferential Only	R3-15a	X201B30
HOV 2+ (Supplemental)	R3-5c	X201B10
Hunting	RL-040	X201V25
Hurricane Evacuation Route	EM-1	X201M29
I		
Information	RG-100	X201U10
Interstate Bicycle Route	M1-9	X201P05
Interstate Shield	M1-1	X201Q22
"	M1-1	X201Q23
"	NA	X201X19
Isosceles Triangle	NA	X201X25

Name	MUTCD	UltSym
J		
Junction Auxiliary	M2-1	X201Q36
Junction Auxiliary (Interstate)	M2-1	X201Q37
K		
Kangaroo Crossing (Unofficial)	NA	X201J07
Kayak	RW-190	X201W18
Kennel	RA-050	X201V11
Keep Left	R4-8	X201B39
"	R4-7a	X201C01
Keep Right	R4-7	X201B40
"	R4-7a	X201B42
"	R4-7b	X201C02
L		
Lane Ends	W 4-2	X201H11
"	W 4-2	X201H12
Lane Ends Merge Left	W9-2	X201J27
Lane Reduction Arrow, Pavement Marking	NA	X201Q05
Laundry	RA-060	X201V12
Leashed Pets	RG-110	X201U11
Left Lane Ends	W9-1	X201J26
Left Lane (Supplemental)	R3-5b	X201B09
Library	I-8	X201S25
Lighthouse	RG-120	X201U12
Light Rail Divided Highway	R15-7	X201M27
Light Rail Divided Highway (T-Intersection)	R15-7a	X201M28
Light Rail Do Not Pass	R15-5	X201M23
Light Rail Only Center Lane	R15-4c	X201M22
Light Rail Only Left Lane	R15-4b	X201M21
Light Rail Only Right Lane	R15-4a	X201M20
Light Rail Station	S1-1	X201L22
Litter Container	D9-4	X201S01
"	RG-130	X201U13
Locker	RA-070	X201V13
Lodging	D9-9	X201S06
"	RM-090	X201U31
Look	R15-8	X201M19
Lookout Tower	RG-140	X201U14
Loose Gravel	W8-7	X201G12
Low Clearance	W12-2	X201H07
"	W12-2	X201H08
Low Ground Clearance Highway - Rail Grade Crossing	W10-5	X201L23
Low Shoulder	W8-9	X201G14
M		
Maintain Top Safe Speed	EM-4	X201M31
Mandatory Movement (Left)	R3-5	X201B03
Mandatory Movement (Right)	R3-5	X201B04
Mandatory Movement, Straight Through Only	R3-5a	X201B01
Mandatory Turn (Left)	R3-7	X201B08
Mandatory Turn (Right)	R3-7	X201B07
Marine Recreation Area	RW-060	X201W07
Mechanic	RM-100	X201U32
Medical Center	EM-6a	X201M32
Men Working / Worker	W21-1	X201K07
Merge (Right)	W4-1	X201H09
Merge (Left)	W4-1	X201H10
Minimum Speed 40 M.P.H.	R2-4	X201A25
Minimum Speed 60 km/h	R2-4	X201A26
Motorboating	RW-070	X201W08
Motor-Driven Cycles Prohibited	R5-8	X201C14

M-P

R-S

Name	MUTCD	UltSym
R		
Railroad Crossing	R15-1	X201M05
"	W10-1	X201L17
Railroad-Highway Crossing Sign	NA	X201M07
Ramp (Launch)	RW-080	X201W09
Ramp Narrows	W5-4	X201G23
Ranger Station	RG-170	X201U17
Recreational and Cultural Interest Sign	D7-2	X201R30
Recycling Collection Center	I-11	X201S26
Reduced Speed Ahead	R2-5a	X201A23
Reduced Speed School Zone Ahead	S4-5	X201N09
"	S4-5a	X201N10
Reference Location Sign (Intermediate km)	D10-1a	X201S32
"	D10-2a	X201S36
"	D10-3a	X201T04
Reference Location Sign (Intermediate Mile)	D10-1a	X201S31
"	D10-2a	X201S35
"	D10-3a	X201T03
Reference Location Sign (km)	D10-1	X201S30
"	D10-2	X201S34
"	D10-3	X201T02
Reference Location Sign (Mile)	D10-1	X201S29
"	D10-2	X201S33
"	D10-3	X201T01
Registration Center	EM-6d	X201M33
Report Emergency	I-13a	X201L16
Reserved Parking (Handicapped)	R7-8	X201C34
Rest Area Auxiliary	D5-2	X201R18
Rest Area Gore	NA	X201T33
Rest Area 1 Mile Auxiliary	D5-1	X201R17
Restricted Lane Ahead	R3-13	X201B31
Restricted Lane Ends	R3-15	X201B32
Rest Room	RM-140	X201U36
Rest Room (Men)	RA-090	X201V15
Rest Room (Women)	RA-100	X201V16
Right Lane Ends	W9-1	X201J28
"	W9-1	X201K15
Right Lane (Supplemental)	R3-5f	X201B13
Road Closed (Street)	W20-3	X201J33
Road Construction 500 Feet	W20-1	X201J31
Road Machinery Ahead	W21-3	X201K08
Road Narrows	W 5-1	X201G19
Roadside Assembly	NA	X201X07
Roadside Park	D5-5b	X201R23
Roadside Table	D5-5	X201R21
"	D5-5a	X201T37
Rock Collecting	RL-060	X201V27
Rough Crossing	W10-15	X201M04
Rough Road	W8-8	X201G13
Rowboating	RW-090	X201W10
Runaway Vehicles Only	R4-10	X201C04
RV Sanitary Station	D9-12	X201S11
S		
Sailboating	RW-100	X201W11
Sand	W7-4d	X201F33
Scenic Area	D6-1	X201R25
"	D6-3	X201R27
Scenic Overlook 2 Miles	D6-2	X201R26
School	S4-3	X201N04

Name	MUTCD	UltSym
School (Advance Warning)	S1-1	X201N01
"	S1-1, W16-9p	X201N12
School Bus Stop Ahead	S3-1	X201N03
School Crossing	S2-1	X201N02
School Crossing Right Arrow	S1-1, W16-7p	X201N15
School Speed Limit 20 M.P.H. When Flashing	S5-1	X201N06
School Stop for Pedestrian Within Crosswalk	S4-3, R1-6a	X201N14
School Yield to Pedestrian Within Crosswalk	S4-3, R1-6	X201N13
Seaplane	RG-260	X201U22
Shared Use Path Restriction	R9-7	X201N33
Share The Road	W11-1 / W16-1	X201N39
Share The Road (Supplemental Plaque)	W16-1	X201J11
Shelter (Sleeping)	RA-110	X201V17
Shelter (Trail)	RA-120	X201V18
Shoulder Drop Off	W8-9a	X201G15
"	W8-9a	X201G29
Shoulder Work	W21-5	X201K09
Showers	RA-130	X201V19
Side Road - Left (Oblique)	W2-3	X201H28
Side Road - Right (Oblique)	W2-3	X201H27
Side Road - Left (Perpendicular)	W2-2	X201H26
Side Road - Right (Perpendicular)	W2-2	X201H25
Signal Ahead	W3-3	X201G04
Signal Lenses in Signal Faces Example	NA	X201X11
Signals Set for 40 km/h	I1-1	X201S20
Signals Set for 25 MPH	I1-1	X201S19
Single-Lane Pavement Marking	NA	X201N07
Skating (Ice)	RW-010	X201W20
Skewed Crossing	W10-12	X201L27
Skiing (Bobbing)	RS-030	X201W22
Skiing (Cross Country)	RS-040	X201W23
Skiing (Downhill)	RS-050	X201W24
Skiing (Water)	RW-110	X201W12
Ski Jumping	RS-020	X201W21
Sledding	RS-060	X201W25
Slippery When Wet	W8-5	X201G11
"	W8-10	X201G31
Slow Children at Play	NA	X201N08
Slow Traffic Ahead	W23-1	X201K05
Slower Traffic Keep Right	R4-3	X201B35
"	R4-3	X201N21
Smoking	RG-180	X201U18
Snowmobile	W11-6	X201J06
Snowmobiling	RS-070	X201W26
Snowshoeing	RS-080	X201V27
Soft Shoulder	W8-4	X201G10
South Cardinal Direction Auxiliary	M3-3	X201R02
South (Interstate) Cardinal Direction Auxiliary	M3-3	X201R06
Specific Services (Example)	NA	X201T15
Speed Hump	W17-1	X201G18
Speed Limit, 10 M.P.H.	R2-1	X201A06
Speed Limit, 15 M.P.H.	R2-1	X201A07
Speed Limit, 20 M.P.H.	R2-1	X201A08
Speed Limit, 25 M.P.H.	R2-1	X201A09
Speed Limit, 30 M.P.H.	R2-1	X201A10
Speed Limit, 35 M.P.H.	R2-1	X201A11
Speed Limit, 40 M.P.H.	R2-1	X201A12
Speed Limit, 45 M.P.H.	R2-1	X201A17

S-T

S

Name	MUTCD	UltSym
Speed Limit, 50 M.P.H.	R2-1	X201A18
Speed Limit, 55 M.P.H.	R2-1	X201A20
Speed Limit 50 M.P.H., Min. 30 M.P.H.	R2-1	X201A27
Speed Limit, 60 M.P.H.	R2-1	X201A21
Speed Limit, 65 M.P.H.	R2-1	X201A22
Speed Limit, 80 km/h	R2-1	X201A19
Speed Limit 80 km/h, Min. 30 km/h	R2-4a	X201A28
Speed Reduction	W3-5	X201G06
Speed Zone Ahead	R2-5c	X201A24
"	W3-5a	X201G33
"	W3-5a	X201G34
Spelunking	RL-070	X201V28
Square	NA	X201X16
Stable	RL-080	X201V29
State Police Monitor	D12-3	X201S30
State Route Marker	M1-6	X201Q32
State Route Sign	M1-5	X201Q27
Stay in Lane	R4-9	X201C03
Steep Hill (Caution Bicyclists)	W7-5	X201G26
Stop	R1-1	X201A01
Stop Ahead	W3-1	X201G01
"	W3-1	X201G03
Stop Here On Red	R10-6	X201M16
Stop Here When Flashing	R8-10	X201M15
Stop / Slow Paddle (Back)	NA	X201L14
Stop / Slow Paddle (Front)	NA	X201L13
Storage Space Between Tracks and Highway 30 Meters	W10-11a	X201L29
Storage Space Between Tracks and Highway 45 Meters	W10-11b	X201L31
Storage Space Between Tracks and Highway 100 Feet	W10-11a	X201L28
Storage Space Between Tracks and Highway 150 Feet	W10-11b	X201L30
Storage Space Symbol	W10-11	X201L26
Street Light	NA	X201X10
Street Name Sign	D-3	X201T20
Supplemental Plaque to Bicycle Route Sign	D1-1b	X201P10
"	D1-1b	X201P11
Surfing	RW-120	X201W13
Survey Crew	W21-6	X201K10
Swimming	RW-130	X201W14

T

Name	MUTCD	UltSym
Taxi Lane (Supplemental)	R3-5d	X201B11
Telephone	RM-150	X201V01
Temp Auxiliary	M4-7a	X201R16
Temporary Auxiliary	M4-7	X201R15
3 Tracks	R15-2	X201M06
Through Lane-Use Arrow, Pavement Marking	NA	X201Q01
T-Intersection Ahead	W2-4	X201H29
To Auxiliary	M4-5	X201R13
To Oncoming Traffic	R1-2a	X201A03
To Request Green Wait on Signal	R10-22	X201N35
To (Supplemental Plaque)	M4-13	X201P08
Tourist Information	D9-10	X201S07
Tourist Information Center (Supplemental)	NA	X201T34
Tourist Oriented Directional (Example)	E2-1A	X201T35
Tow-Away Zone	R7-201	X201C41
"	R7-201a	X201C42
Tracks Out Of Service	R8-9	X201M14
Traffic Circle	W16-12p	X201H31
Traffic Laws Photo Enforced	R10-18	X201A30
Trail	I-4	X201T32
Trail (Bicycle)	RL-090	X201V30
Trailer Camping	D9-3a	X201R36
Trailer Sanitary Station	RM-160	X201V02
Trail (Hiking)	RL-100	X201V31
Trail (Horse)	RL-110	X201V32
Trail (Interpretive, Auto)	RL-120	X201V33
Trail (Interpretive, Pedestrian)	RL-130	X201V34
Trail / Road (4 WD Vehicle)	RL-140	X201V35
Trail (Trail Bike)	RL-150	X201V36
Trains May Exceed 80 MPH	W10-8	X201L24
Trains May Exceed 130 km/h	W10-8	X201L25
Train Station	I-7	X201S24
Tramway	RL-160	X201V37
Trash Receptacle	D9-4	X201S02
Travel Info Call 511 (Logo)	D12-4	X201S32
Truck	RG-190	X201U19
Truck Crossing	W8-6	X201H35
"	W11-10	X201H40
Truck Escape Ramp	W7-4c	X201F31
Truck Lane 500 Feet	R4-6	X201B38
Trucks Lane 150 Meters	R4-6	X201B39
Truck Parking	D9-16	X201S17
Truck Route	R14-1	X201B36
Truck Route Auxiliary	M4-4	X201R12
Truck Speed Limit, 40 M.P.H.	R 2-2	X201A13
Truck Speed Limit, 60 km/h	R2-2	X201A14
Trucks Use Lower Gear	W7-2b	X201F37
Trucks Use Right Lane	R4-5	X201B37
Tubular Marker	NA	X201L02
"	NA	X201L03
Tunnel	RG-200	X201U20
Turn and Through Lane-Use Arrow, Pavement Marking	NA	X201Q03
Turn Lane-Use Arrow, Pavement Marking	NA	X201Q02
Turn Off 2-Way Radio	W22-2	X201K03
Two Arrow	W12-1	X201K12
Two Directions (Left and Right)	W1-7	X201H23
2 Hour Parking 8:30 AM to 5:30 PM	R7-108	X201C37
Two-way Left-turn Arrow, Lane-Use Control Signal	NA	X201Q07
Two Way Left Turn Only	R3-9b	X201B19
Two Way Traffic	W6-3	X201H21
"	W6-4	X201H22
Type 1 Object Marker	OM1-1	X201Q09
"	OM1-2	X201Q10
"	OM1-3	X201Q11
Type 2 Object Marker	OM2-1V	X201Q12
"	OM2-2V	X201Q13
"	OM2-1H	X201Q14
"	OM2-2H	X201Q15
Type 3 Barricade with Warning Light	NA	X201L09
Type 3 Object Marker	OM-3L	X201Q16
"	OM-3C	X201Q17
"	OM-3R	X201Q18

U-Y

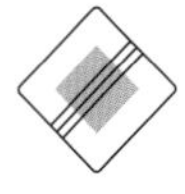

Highway Signs II: International (UNCRT)

2

Overview

Beyond the United States, the difficulty of a multiplicity of languages has led to the development of a pictorial sign system. The signs included in this collection originated in Holland, but represent the majority of signs used in Europe and most other countries. The Dutch highway sign system was chosen because it is among the most contemporary and well-designed.

Countries appear to have developed their own stylistic variations for some of the more illustrative symbols such as "Accident" and "Compulsory Horse Track", and in the way signs are formatted, including type fonts used. Signs that reflect localized conditions also appear, such as warning signs for reindeer or camel crossing. However, the basic message content of most sign systems is generally consistent with and based on the *Protocol on Road Signs and Signals* guideline as agreed upon by the United Nations Conference on Road and Motor Transports in Geneva in 1949 and revised in Vienna in 1968 (United Nations 1969)[1], amended with new rules for Europe in 1971, 1973 and 1993.

Below are acceptable variations from The Netherlands, Sweden, and Denmark of the same message with three related but different approaches to signal leaving a built-up area.

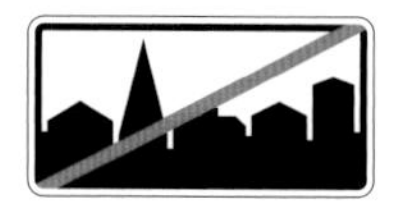

Similarly, although the Canadian road sign system closely adheres to the United States system, there are many specialized signs that impart the local flavor and attractions of that country, as the Canadian road sign samples demonstrate in the addendum to this volume on page 50. But the American/Canadian highway sign system relies heavily on language use in addition to pictorial symbols and is therefore much more difficult to navigate for foreign visitors, who may not understand what is being communicated in the native tongue. Unlike the United States, Canada has at least begun to conform to the universally accepted metric system of measurements for its signs.

Description

There are three classes of international highway signs: Danger Warning, Regulatory, and Informative.

Danger Warning Signs use a very distinctive red triangular shape, apex up, sometimes seen with the optional yellow diamond shape, as used in the United States.

Regulatory Signs are divided into Priority, Prohibitory, and Mandatory:

> Priority Signs have a variety of shapes including the standard American stop sign.

> Prohibitory Signs are round with a red rim and a white center in which various instruction symbols are displayed. All such signs should be taken as negative; i.e., no entry, no speed greater than X, no turn, no pedestrians, etc.

> Mandatory Signs are circular and blue in color.

> There are also special regulation signs that show miscellaneous rules. These signs are in general rectangular with either a blue base with a white foreground, or a light base with a dark foreground.[2]

Informative Signs are rectangular in shape. They are usually blue in color with a white and black symbol included in the center. If red is used, it must not be the dominant color.[3] They include facilities or service signs, direction, position or indication signs, and additional panels which may be attached to the main signs for more information.

Danger Warning Signs

X02**A**01
Roundabout

X02**A**02
Dangerous Bend (right)

X02**A**03
Dangerous Bend (left)

X02**A**04
Double Curve (right)

X02**A**05
Double Curve (left)

X02**A**06
Dangerous Intersection

X02**A**07
Intersection with Non-Priority Road

X02**A**08
Intersection with Non-Priority Road (left)

X02**A**09
Intersection with Non-Priority Road (right)

X02**A**10
Left Lane Ends

X02**A**11
Road Narrows

X02**A**12
Right Lane Ends

X02**A**13
Slippery When Wet

X02**A**14
Limited Visibility Due to Snow, Rain, or Fog

X02**A**15
Sleet or Snow

X02**A**16
Other Dangers

X02**A**17
Accident

X02**A**18
Heavy Traffic Possible Congestion

X02**A**19
Loose Gravel

X02**A**20
Cyclists Entering or Crossing

X02**A**21
Pedestrian Crossing

X02**A**22
Pedestrians

X02**A**23
Children at Play

X02**A**24
Road Works

X02**A**25
Wild Animal Crossing

X02**A**26
Domestic Animal Crossing

X02**A**27
Airfield / Low Flying Aircraft

X02**A**28
Possible Danger of Strong Cross-Wind

X02**A**29
Dangerous Descent

X02**A**30
Dangerous Ascent

X02**A**31
Uneven Road

X02**A**32
Falling Rocks

X02**A**33
Road Leads on to Canal or River Bank

X02**A**34
Swing Bridge

X02**A**35
Tunnel

X02**A**36
Two Way Traffic

X02**A**37
Light Signals Ahead

X02**A**38
Blinking Light

X02**A**39
Intersection with a Tramway Line

X02**A**40
Railway, Level Crossing without Gates

X02**A**41
Railway, Level Crossing with Gates

X02**A**42
Railroad Crossing, Single Track

Priority Signs

X02**B**01
Stop

X02**B**02
Give Way;
Yield

X02**B**03
Priority Over
Oncoming Traffic

X02**B**04
Oncoming Traffic
has Priority

X02**B**05
Priority Road

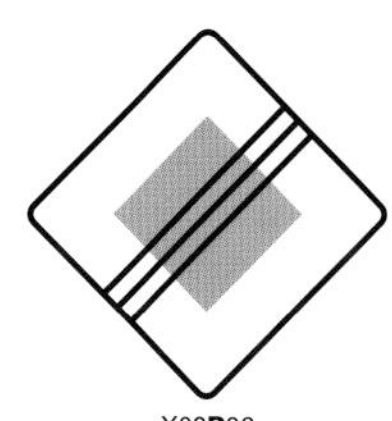
X02**B**06
End of Priority
Road

Prohibitory
Signs

X02**B**07
Maximum Speed Limit

X02**B**08
Maximum Speed Limit

X02**B**09
Maximum Speed Limit

X02**B**10
Maximum Speed Limit

X02**B**11
Maximum Speed Limit

X02**B**12
Maximum Speed Limit

X02**B**13
Maximum Speed Limit

X02**B**14
Maximum Speed Limit

X02**B**15
Maximum Speed Limit

X02**B**16
Maximum Speed Limit

X02**B**17
Maximum Speed Limit

X02**B**18
Maximum Speed Limit

X02**B**19
Maximum Speed Limit

X02**B**20
End High Speed Zone

X02**B**21
Advised Speed

X02**B**22
End Advised Speed

X02**B**23
Do Not Enter

X02**B**24
Closed to All Vehicles
in Both Directions

X02**B**25
Passing without
Stopping Prohibited

X02**B**26
Police; Passing without
Stopping Prohibited

X02**B**27
Customs; Passing without
Stopping Prohibited

X02**B**28
No Left Turn

X02**B**29
No Right Turn

X02**B**30
No U Turns

X02**B**31
No Passing Zone

X02**B**32
End of No Passing Zone

X02**B**33
Truck No Passing Zone

X02**B**34
End of Truck
No Passing Zone

X02**B**35
End All Previous
Restrictions

X02**B**36
Closed to Vehicles
with Dangerous Cargo

X02**B**37
Minimum Distance
(50 Meters)

X02**B**38
No Entry
Width Limit

X02**B**39
No Entry
Height Limit

X02**B**40
No Entry
Weight Limit

X02**B**41
No Entry
Weight Per Axle Limit

X02**B**42
No Entry
Length Limit

Prohibitory Signs continued

X02**C**01
No Bicycles or Vehicles for Disabled w/o Motor

X02**C**02
No Mopeds or Vehicles for Disabled w/ Motors

X02**C**03
No Bicycles, Mopeds, or Vehicles for the Disabled

X02**C**04
No Motorcycles

X02**C**05
Closed to Motor Vehicles w/ more than 2 Wheels

X02**C**06
No Motor Vehicles

X02**C**07
No Pedestrians

X02**C**08
No Trailers

X02**C**09
No Slow Agricultural or Motor Vehicles

X02**C**10
No Slow Vehicles, Bicycles or Horseback Riders

X02**C**11
No Trucks

X02**C**12
No Buses

Mandatory Signs

X02**C**13
Compulsory Footpath

X02**C**14
End Compulsory Footpath

X02**C**15
Compulsory Horse Track

X02**C**16
End Compulsory Horse Track

X02**C**17
Compulsory Cycle Track

X02**C**18
End Compulsory Cycle Track

X02**C**19
Snow Chains Compulsory

X02**C**20
Compulsory Roundabout

X02**C**21
Pass This Side (left)

X02**C**22
Pass This Side (right)

X02**C**23
Direction to be Followed (left)

X02**C**24
Direction to be Followed (right)

X02**C**25
Straight Ahead

X02**C**26
May Be Passed on Both Sides

X02**C**27
Left Turn

X02**C**28
Right Turn

X02**C**29
Straight Ahead or Left

X02**C**30
Straight Ahead or Right

Informative Signs

X02**C**31
Compulsory Right or Left Turn

X02**C**32
One Way (left)

X02**C**33
One Way (right)

X02**C**34
One Way Street

X02**C**35
Two Way Street

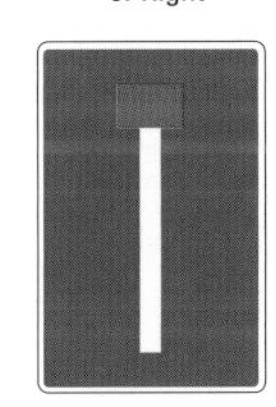
X02**C**36
No Through Road

X02**C**37
Lane Indicator

X02**C**38
Lane Indicator

X02**C**39
Lane Indicator

X02**C**40
Main Road Bends

X02**C**41
Roadway Coated with Ice

X02**C**42
Disabled

Informative Signs continued

X02**D**01
Highway

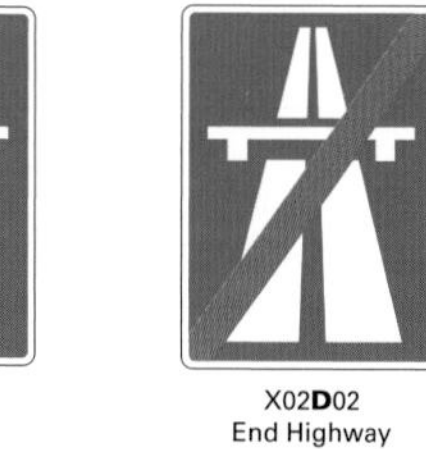
X02**D**02
End Highway

X02**D**03
Road for Motor Vehicles

X02**D**04
End of Road for Motor Vehicles

X02**D**05
Mountain Mail Route

X02**D**06
End of Mountain Mail Route

X02**D**07
Residential Area

X02**D**08
End of Residential Area

X02**D**09
Entering City limits

X02**D**10
Leaving City Limits

X02**D**11
Hospital

X02**D**12
Preferred Bike, Motorcycle Route

X02**D**13
Water Protection Zone

X02**D**14
Tunnel

X02**D**15
Camping Site

X02**D**16
Caravan / R.V. Site

X02**D**17
Telephone

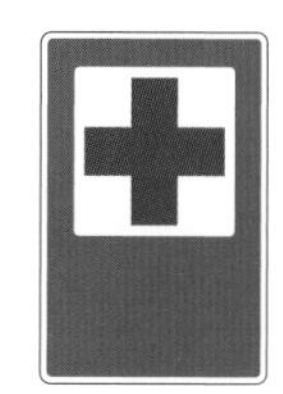
X02**D**18
First Aid

X02**D**19
Breakdown Service

X02**D**20
Filling Station

X02**D**21
Restaurant and Hotel / Motel

X02**D**22
Restaurant

X02**D**23
Refreshments / Cafeteria

X02**D**24
Information

X02**D**25
Direction Sign for Main road

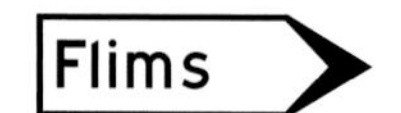

X02**D**26
Direction Sign for Minor Road

X02**D**27
Direction Sign for Approach to Highway

X02**D**28
Direction Sign for Detour / Alternate Route

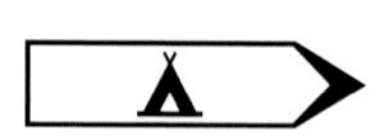
X02**D**29
Direction Sign for Camping Site

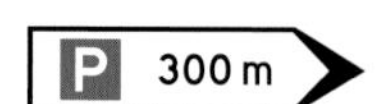

X02**D**30
Direction Sign for Parking Site

Regulatory Signs

X02**D**31
Parking Permitted

X02**D**32
Parking for Taxis Only

X02**D**33
Parking for the Disabled

X02**D**34
Loading and Unloading Only

X02**D**35
Parking Only for Vehicles Indicated on Sign

X02**D**36
Parking Fee

X02**D**37
No Parking

X02**D**38
Do Not Park Bicycles and Mopeds

X02**D**39
No Standing

X02**D**40
Parking Prohibited on Odd Days

X02**D**41
Parking Prohibited on Even Days

X02**D**42
Left Lane of Roundabout has Priority

International Distinguishing Signs for Vehicles

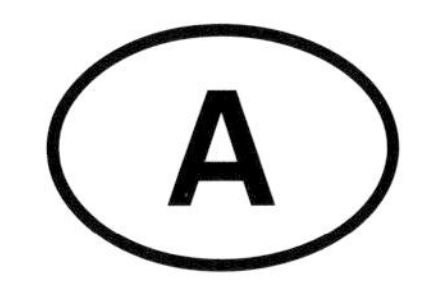

X02**E**01
Austria

AUS
X02**E**02
Australia

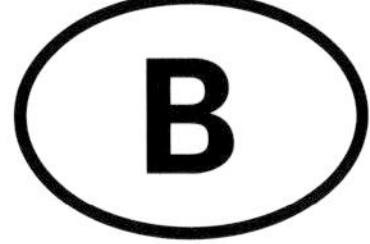

X02**E**03
Belgium

BG
X02**E**04
Bulgaria

BR
X02**E**05
Brazil

CDN
X02**E**06
Canada

CH
X02**E**07
Switzerland

CZ
X02**E**08
Czech Republic

D
X02**E**09
Germany

DK
X02**E**10
Denmark

E
X02**E**11
Spain
(incl. African Territories)

F
X02**E**12
France

FIN
X02**E**13
Finland

GB
X02**E**14
United Kingdom of
Great Britian and
Northern Ireland

GR
X02**E**15
Greece

H
X02**E**16
Hungary

HK
X02**E**17
Hong Kong

I
X02**E**18
Italy

IL
X02**E**19
Israel

IND
X02**E**20
India

IRL
X02**E**21
Ireland

IS
X02**E**22
Iceland

J
X02**E**23
Japan

L
X02**E**24
Luxembourg

MC
X02**E**25
Monaco

MEX
X02**E**26
Mexico

N
X02**E**27
Norway

NL
X02**E**28
Netherlands

P
X02**E**29
Portugal

PL
X02**E**30
Poland

X02**E**31
Argentina

RCH
X02**E**32
Chile

RO
X02**E**33
Romania

RP
X02**E**34
Philippines

RUS
X02**E**35
Russian Federation

S
X02**E**36
Sweden

X02**E**37
Slovakia

TR
X02**E**38
Turkey

X02**E**39
United States
of America

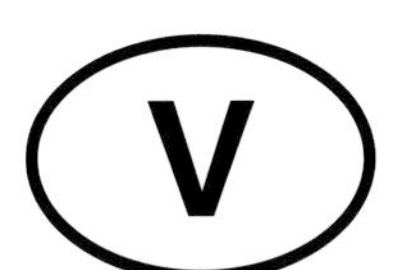

X02**E**40
Vatican City

X02**E**41
Venezuela

X02**E**42
South Africa

Addendum:
Miscellaneous
International
Road Signs
- Denmark

X02**F**01
Point of Interest
Scenic View

X02**F**02
Compulsory Sled Route

X02**F**03
Train Station

X02**F**04
Mountain Postal Route

X02**F**05
Highway Interchange

X02**F**06
Ferry, Port

- Sweden

X02**F**07
Danger: Wild Animal Crossing
Elk, Reindeer

X02**F**08
Danger: Ski Crossing

X02**F**09
Danger: Tram Crossing

X02**F**10
No Horse Drawn Vehicles

X02**F**11
Caution: Tractor Drawn Sled

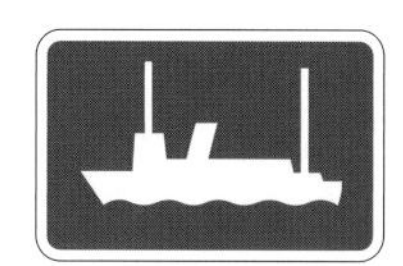

X02**F**12
Ferry, Port

- Canada

X02**F**13
No Stopping

X02**F**14
Bus and High Occupancy
Vehicles Lane

X02**F**15
New Regulation

X02**F**16
New Regulation, 30 km/h

X02**F**17
Danger: Sharp Turn or
Bend Ahead

X02**F**18
Warning: Survey Crew Ahead

X02**F**19
Warning: Fire Station
Ahead

X02**F**20
Warning: School Bus Stop
Ahead

X02**F**21
Warning: Draw Bridge
Ahead

X02**F**22
Warning: Cars and Bicycles
Share Road Ahead

X02**F**23
Warning: Construction
Vehicle Crossing

X02**F**24
Warning: Children Playing

X02**F**25
Warning: Turn Right
into Center Lane

X02**F**26
Warning: Wild Animal
Crossing, Moose

X02**F**27
Cul-de-Sac
Turnaround

X02**F**28
Seaplane Port

X02**F**29
Ferry, Port

X02**F**30
Highway Marker Shield
Trans-Canada Highway

X02**F**31
Highway Marker Shield
Provincial Highway, B.C.

X02**F**32
Highway Marker Shield
Crows Nest Highway, B.C.

X02**F**33
Highway Marker Shield
Yellowhead Route, B.C.

X02**F**34
Wildlife Area

X02**F**35
Visitor Info Right

X02**F**36
Viewpoint Ahead

X02**F**37
Whale Observing Area

X02**F**38
Museum

X02**F**39
Artisan

X02**F**40
Bed & Breakfast

X02**F**41
Think Metric
Maximum 60 MPH is
Maximum 100 km/h

X02**F**42
Thank You
Resume Speed

Symbol Signs: Recreational (SEGD)

3

Overview
In 1982 the U.S. Army Corps of Engineers contracted Danne & Blackburn Associates to design a sign standards program for their 4,500 recreation projects throughout the country. Because symbols would be an important part of the Corps sign program, they wanted the symbols to be easily integrated into all sign applications.

In an attempt to incorporate the existing Federal Recreation Symbols, it was found that many of the pictographic concepts were out of date and the overall system incomplete for current applications. It was decided to re-design the system in the graphic style of the AIGA Symbol Signs for Transportation Related Facilities, while adopting many of the pictographic concepts of the earlier National Park Service symbols. The goal was a system that would become an extension of these two existing and highly successful symbol programs, which already had substantial public acceptance and visual equity.

Fifteen of the 193 recreation symbols displayed in this volume have been adapted from the AIGA Symbol Signs for Transportation Related Facilities (see page 69). Note, however, that the design of these symbols has been modified to increase legibility when viewed at threshold, and for viewers with reduced visual acuity. The configuration of the border (figure, field and stroke width) for all symbols in the manual have been designed for viewing at a common distance. All symbols, except the prohibitions and several others, are presented in this book in both positive contrast with a light symbol in a dark field, and a negative contrast version with a dark symbol and border in a light field.

The symbols used as a prohibition have been altered (proportions or orientation changed) and are not interchangeable with the other formats. The prohibition layout shown places the symbol slash under the symbol, not over the symbol as is commonly done for simple symbols such as "No Smoking". This format is based on research done by Robert Dewer, a human factors engineer at the University of Calgary, that showed much greater understanding if a complex symbol is not broken apart by the large slash.

Displayed below are the four standard formats of the recreation symbols with a description of each. The border configuration and relation of symbol to border are sized proportionally and are the same regardless of the sign size.

Recreation This standard format with light figure and border format allows for systematic applications of symbols. These include grouped (multiple symbol) applications. When used with typography and arrows, the areas around the symbol (outside the border) may vary depending on application. A version without the outside border is shown for application to a sign with light color background.

Highway For highway applications the border abuts the edge of the sign, in compliance with Federal Highway Standards. These may be used on guide sign panels, suspended below guide sign panels, or used individually or ganged with arrows as guide signs. Symbols used on highway signs are referred to as recreational and cultural interest area signs. The groupings developed by the Federal Highway Administration for the symbols used on road signs is different for some symbols and uses a separate numbering system. Not all symbols identified in the FHWA are allowed for use on highway signs. Symbols for highway sign applications use a different border configuration.

Prohibition The red circle and slash graphic with a black symbol on a white field is the standard format for all prohibition signs. This color and graphic format allows for maximum contrast and legibility. Border formats will vary depending on application. Narrow border prohibitions are for placement on dark panels. When free-standing, the overall area is used as a larger white field with radius corners. Symbols placed on a panel with a dark background maintain the border when used in groups or individually. Single panels displaying symbols such as "No Radios" and "No Diving" adopt the full frame with radius corners.

Warning The diamond-shaped warning sign uses a square set on a 45° diagonal. This sign has a yellow background and a black symbol and border. Note: Warning symbols shown here are for non-highway applications. For highway warning signs refer to the federal *Manual on Uniform Traffic Control Devices*[1] (see page 11).

Credits

Principal designers on this project were Donald Meeker, Paul Singer, and Peter Reedijk. The initial effort was supported by George Tabb and Dan Hilemen at the Corps of Engineers. After the initial 80+ symbols were designed for the Corps, the Society for Environmental Graphic Design received a grant from the National Endowment for the Arts for the expansion and refinement of the system design for broad public use.

As part of the NEA/SEGD project, support was received from the National Park Service and Tom Geismar of Chermayeff & Geismar Inc. Geismar and the NPS laid the foundation for this project with their work on the design of the original Park Service recreation symbols in the '60s, and with Geismar's work directing the AIGA symbol sign project on which this effort builds.

Updates

Periodically, in order to keep pace with the expanding options for recreational activities, the National Park Service has asked Meeker & Associates to add new symbols to the original set. Donald Meeker, working with Christopher O'Hara, developed and added new symbols to the system, most recently in 2002. The latest symbols contain contemporary activity messages such as "In-Line Skating" and "Snowboarding". With the exception of the prohibitions and a few other symbols, all of the images are presented in both positive and negative contrast applications. In addition, a select subset of the symbols (51) were simplified and redrawn for use in the NPS mapping system (see pgs. 64-65). Not including duplicate positive versions, prohibitions, or the NPS mapping symbols, the current total of recreational symbols is 122.

'First Aid' Symbol Color Revision

In 1999, American Red Cross informed the author/designer Mies Hora that the Red Cross emblem is legally protected and requested that it be removed from *Official Signs & Icons*. The explanation is as follows: "The red cross symbol is *not* a generic symbol for emergency, health-care, first-aid or medical services, products, or personnel. While the Red Cross emblem is protected by federal and state trademark law, unfair competition law and anti-dilution law, it is also protected by criminal law. As a signatory to the Geneva Conventions, the United States Congress agreed to protect the Greek cross (red cross on a white ground) as an international humanitarian symbol and to delegate permission for its use to the American Red Cross. Generic use of the emblem jeopardizes the neutral status that is essential for the effective accomplishment of the Red Cross mission. Such unauthorized use also infringes the trademark rights of the American Red Cross."[2] In response, the color of the "First Aid" symbols on page 58 have been changed from red to "Safety Green", which according to *ANSI Z535.1-2002 Safety Color Code* is nearest to Pantone® color PMS 3415 C.

Accessibility Symbols

Organizations, both public and private, are working to be fully accessible to this country's 54 million citizens with disabilities, as well as to foreign visitors. Organizations that receive government funding are required to provide accessible programs and services under Sections 503 and 504 of the Rehabilitation Act of 1973. A more recent law, the 1990 Americans with Disability Act (ADA), extends accessibility provisions to the private sector in order to help guarantee persons with disabilities employment and the right to enter the economic, social and cultural mainstreams. The ADA goes well beyond federally funded organizations to encompass private sector entities that serve the public, including retail businesses, movie theaters, restaurants, and cultural organizations that do not receive federal support.

Any language accompanying the symbols should focus on the accommodation or service, not on who uses it. For example, "Ramped Entrance" may accompany the wheelchair symbol. This is important because not only do individuals in wheelchairs use ramps, but so do people with baby carriages, luggage, packages, etc. Language that fosters dignity is important too. For example, "Reserved Parking" or "Accessible Parking" may be used with the wheelchair symbol to indicate parking spaces designated for people with disabilities.[3]

The accessibility symbols displayed on page 65 are a response to the ADA. In 1992-93, Roger Whitehouse of Whitehouse & Co. developed the *SEGD Americans With Disabilities Act (ADA) White Paper*. One of the most requested publications that SEGD distributes, this paper defines the organization's official interpretation of the ADA as it relates to signage (www.SEGD.org).

As part of the SEGD White Paper, Whitehouse included updated versions of the four basic accessibility symbols, some of which were redrawn to make them compatible with the AIGA/DOT set. These included the wheelchair symbol (originally created together with Peter Reedijk when he was with Whitehouse & Company), the "Text Telephone" symbol, the "Hearing Impaired" symbol, and the "Volume Control Telephone" symbol. These symbols were afterwards made available on disk by SEGD. In 2004, while compiling symbols for *Official Signs & Icons 2*, the author and designer Mies Hora decided to update additional accessibility symbols and include them here for a comprehensive overview. Working together, Whitehouse and Hora revised and improved the "Hearing Impaired" symbol. The "Sight Impaired" and "Sign Language Interpretation" images, originally produced by the Graphic Artists Guild Foundation, were also redrawn and updated to visually conform with the SEGD Recreational symbol signs system. "Audio Description", "Closed Captioning", and "Open Captioning" symbols round out the accessibility symbol set.

About SEGD

Known as the Society for Environmental Graphic Design, the organization was founded in 1973. SEGD is an international design association with over 1,000 members who are involved in the design of graphic elements in the environment.

As EGD (Environmental Graphic Design) work involves many different design disciplines, SEGD members come from diverse backgrounds, such as graphic design, interior design, architecture, landscape architecture, and industrial design. The field is rapidly expanding and so is SEGD membership.

Membership is open to anyone working in EGD: designers, students, educators, in-house designers, artisans and fabricators. Twenty-five percent of SEGD's members are industry members – fabricators, suppliers and manufacturers. The organization is headquartered in Washington, DC, and represented locally by more than 20 regions run by Chapter Chairs.

SEGD's other activities include a national conference and expo, an annual Design Awards Program, and publications. Environmental Graphic Design embraces many design disciplines including graphic, architectural, interior, landscape, and industrial design, all concerned with the visual aspects of wayfinding, communicating identity and information, and shaping the idea of place. Some common examples of work by EGD practitioners include wayfinding systems, architectural graphics, signage, exhibit design, identity graphics, civic design, pictogram design, retail and store design, mapping, and themed environments. www.segd.org

Systems used to communicate specific information are described as follows:

Identification Confirms destinations, creates landmarks, helps establish recognition (street numbering, main entrance signs, public art).

Information Communicates knowledge concerning designations, facts, and circumstances (kiosks, symbols, directories).

Directional Guides users to destinations (airports, hospitals). The design and implementation of directional systems are often referred to as "wayfinding."

Interpretation Provides verbal and visual explanations of a particular topic or set of artifacts (exhibits).

Orientation Gives users a frame of reference within a particular environment (maps).

Regulatory Displays rules of conduct ("Stop" and "No Parking" signs).

Ornamentation Enhances or beautifies the environment (banners, architectural coloration, gateways).

Land Recreation

X203**A**01
Horse Trail
RS-064

X203**A**02
Motor Bike Trail
RS-065

X203**A**03
Bicycle Trail
RS-066

X203**A**04
Off-Road Vehicle
RS-067

X203**A**05
Hiking Trail
RS-068

X203**A**06
Playground
RS-069

X203**A**07
Horse Trail
RS-064

X203**A**08
Motor Bike Trail
RS-065

X203**A**09
Bicycle Trail
RS-066

X203**A**10
Off-Road Vehicle
RS-067

X203**A**11
Hiking Trail
RS-068

X203**A**12
Playground
RS-069

X203**A**13
Amphitheater
RS-070

X203**A**14
Hunting
RS-072

X203**A**15
Wildlife Viewing
RS-076

X203**A**16
Technical Rock Climbing
RS-081

X203**A**17
Climbing
RS-082

X203**A**18
Rock Collecting
RS-083

X203**A**19
Amphitheater
RS-070

X203**A**20
Hunting
RS-072

X203**A**21
Wildlife Viewing
RS-076

X203**A**22
Technical Rock Climbing
RS-081

X203**A**23
Climbing
RS-082

X203**A**24
Rock Collecting
RS-083

X203**A**25
Spelunking / Caves
RS-084

X203**A**26
All-Terrain Trail
RS-095

X203**A**27
Baseball
RS-096

X203**A**28
Exercise Fitness Area
RS-097

X203**A**29
Skateboarding
RS-098

X203**A**30
In-Line Skating
RS-099

X203**A**31
Spelunking / Caves
RS-084

X203**A**32
All-Terrain Trail
RS-095

X203**A**33
Baseball
RS-096

X203**A**34
Exercise Fitness Area
RS-097

X203**A**35
Skateboarding
RS-098

X203**A**36
In-Line Skating
RS-099

Note: All symbols and signs are available as fully editable vector image files: see page 238 or www.ultimatesymbol.com

Land Recreation continued

X203**B**01
Interpretive Trail / Auto
RS-064

X203**B**02
Interpretive Trail / Pedestrian
RS-065

X203**B**03
Archery
RS-066

X203**B**04
Hang Gliding
RS-068

X203**B**05
Golfing
RS-069

X203**B**06
Tennis
RS-070

X203**B**07
Interpretive Trail /Auto
RS-064

X203**B**08
Interpretive Trail / Pedestrian
RS-065

X203**B**09
Archery
RS-066

X203**B**10
Hang Gliding
RS-068

X203**B**11
Golfing
RS-069

X203**B**12
Tennis
RS-070

Winter Recreation

X203**B**13
C.C. Skiing
RS-046

X203**B**14
Downhill Skiing
RS-047

X203**B**15
Ski Jumping
RS-048

X203**B**16
Sledding
RS-049

X203**B**17
Ice Skating
RS-050

X203**B**18
Snowmobiling
RS-052

X203**B**19
C.C. Skiing
RS-046

X203**B**20
Downhill Skiing
RS-047

X203**B**21
Ski Jumping
RS-048

X203**B**22
Sledding
RS-049

X203**B**23
Ice Skating
RS-050

X203**B**24
Snowmobiling
RS-052

X203**B**25
Winter Rec. Area
RS-077

X203**B**26
Snow-Shoeing
RS-078

X203**B**27
Ice Fishing
RS-092

X203**B**28
Chair Lift / Ski Lift
RS-105

X203**B**29
Snowboarding
RS-106

X203**B**30
Winter Rec. Area
RS-077

X203**B**31
Snow-Shoeing
RS-078

X203**B**32
Ice Fishing
RS-092

X203**B**33
Chair Lift / Ski Lift
RS-105

X203**B**34
Snowboarding
RS-106

Water Recreation

X203**C**01
Fish Hatchery
RS-010

X203**C**02
Tour Boat
RS-087

X203**C**03
Marina
RS-053

X203**C**04
Boat Launch Ramp
RS-054

X203**C**05
Motorboating
RS-055

X203**C**06
Rowboating
RS-057

X203**C**07
Fish Hatchery
RS-010

X203**C**08
Tour Boat
RS-087

X203**C**09
Marina
RS-053

X203**C**10
Boat Launch Ramp
RS-054

X203**C**11
Motorboating
RS-055

X203**C**12
Rowboating
RS-057

X203**C**13
Waterskiing
RS-058

X203**C**14
Surfing
RS-059

X203**C**15
Swimming
RS-061

X203**C**16
Scuba Diving
RS-060

X203**C**17
Diving
RS-062

X203**C**18
Fishing Area
RS-063

X203**C**19
Waterskiing
RS-058

X203**C**20
Surfing
RS-059

X203**C**21
Swimming
RS-061

X203**C**22
Scuba Diving
RS-060

X203**C**23
Diving
RS-062

X203**C**24
Fishing Area
RS-063

X203**C**25
Canoeing
RS-079

X203**C**26
Wading
RS-088

X203**C**27
Fish Ladder
RS-089

X203**C**28
Fish Cleaning
RS-093

X203**C**29
Lifejackets
RS-094

X203**C**30
Seal Viewing
RS-106

X203**C**31
Canoeing
RS-079

X203**C**32
Wading
RS-088

X203**C**33
Fish Ladder
RS-089

X203**C**34
Fish Cleaning
RS-093

X203**C**35
Lifejackets
RS-094

X203**C**36
Seal Viewing
RS-106

Water Recreation continued

X203**D**01
Whale Viewing
RS-107

X203**D**02
Wind Surfing
RS-108

X203**D**03
Sailing
RS-056

X203**D**04
Hand Launch / Small Boat Launch, RS-029

X203**D**05
Kayaking
RS-030

X203**D**06
Fishing Pier
RS-032

X203**D**07
Whale Viewing
RS-107

X203**D**08
Wind Surfing
RS-108

X203**D**09
Sailing
RS-056

X203**D**10
Hand Launch / Small Boat Launch, RS-029

X203**D**11
Kayaking
RS-030

X203**D**12
Fishing Pier
RS-032

X203**D**13
Jet Ski-Personal Watercraft
RS-033

X203**D**14
Jet Ski-Personal Watercraft
RS-033

Services

X203**D**15
Drinking Water
RS-013

X203**D**16
Information
RS-014

X203**D**17
Ranger Station
RS-015

X203**D**18
Grocery Store
RS-020

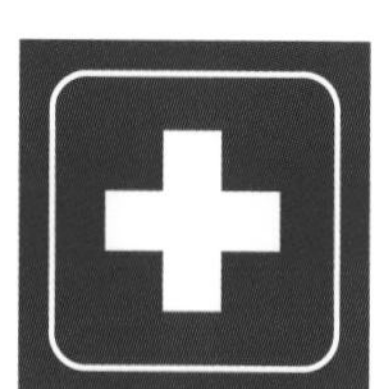
X203**D**19
First Aid
RS-024

X203**D**20
Telephone
RS-025

X203**D**21
Drinking Water
RS-013

X203**D**22
Information
RS-014

X203**D**23
Ranger Station
RS-015

X203**D**24
Grocery Store
RS-020

X203**D**25
First Aid
RS-024

X203**D**26
Telephone
RS-025

Services
continued

X203**E**01
Post Office
RS-026

X203**E**02
Mechanic
RS-027

X203**E**03
Airport
RS-029

X203**E**04
Lockers / Storage
RS-030

X203**E**05
Gas Station / Fuel
RS-032

X203**E**06
Vehicle Ferry
RS-033

X203**E**07
Post Office
RS-026

X203**E**08
Mechanic
RS-027

X203**E**09
Airport
RS-029

X203**E**10
Lockers / Storage
RS-030

X203**E**11
Gas Station / Fuel
RS-032

X203**E**12
Vehicle Ferry
RS-033

X203**E**13
Showers
RS-035

X203**E**14
Picnic Shelter
RS-039

X203**E**15
Sanitary Station
RS-041

X203**E**16
Trail Shelter
RS-043

X203**E**17
Picnic Site
RS-044

X203**E**18
Kennel
RS-045

X203**E**19
Showers
RS-035

X203**E**20
Picnic Shelter
RS-039

X203**E**21
Sanitary Station
RS-041

X203**E**22
Trail Shelter
RS-043

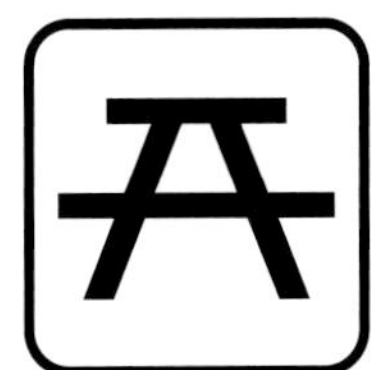
X203**E**23
Picnic Site
RS-044

X203**E**24
Kennel
RS-045

X203**E**25
Tramway
RS-071

X203**E**26
Stable
RS-073

X203**E**27
Laundromat
RS-085

X203**E**28
Litter Receptacle
RS-086

X203**E**29
Trash Dumpster
RS-091

X203**E**30
Theater
RS-109

X203**E**31
Tramway
RS-071

X203**E**32
Stable
RS-073

X203**E**33
Laundromat
RS-085

X203**E**34
Litter Receptacle
RS-086

X203**E**35
Trash Dumpster
RS-091

X203**E**36
Theater
RS-109

Services continued

X203**F01** Library RS-110

X203**F02** Firewood Cutting RS-112

X203**F03** Radiator Water RS-124

X203**F04** Hospital RS-201

X203**F05** Pack It In Pack It Out RS-139

X203**F06** Clean Up After Your Dog RS-140

X203**F07** Library RS-110

X203**F08** Firewood Cutting RS-112

X203**F09** Radiator Water RS-124

X203**F10** Pack It In Pack It Out RS-139

X203**F11** Clean Up After Your Dog RS-140

General

X203**F12** Smoking RS-002

X203**F13** Automobile RS-003

X203**F14** Trucks RS-004

X203**F15** Tunnel RS-005

X203**F16** Lookout Tower RS-006

X203**F17** Lighthouse RS-007

X203**F18** Smoking RS-002

X203**F19** Automobiles RS-003

X203**F20** Trucks RS-004

X203**F21** Tunnel RS-005

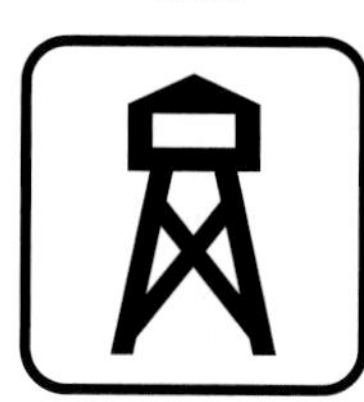
X203**F22** Lookout Tower RS-006

X203**F23** Lighthouse RS-007

X203**F24** Falling Rocks RS-008

X203**F25** Dam RS-009

X203**F26** Deer Viewing RS-011

X203**F27** Bear Viewing RS-012

X203**F28** Pedestrian Crossing RS-016

X203**F29** Pets on Leash RS-017

X203**F30** Falling Rocks RS-008

X203**F31** Dam RS-009

X203**F32** Deer Viewing RS-011

X203**F33** Bear Viewing RS-012

X203**F34** Pedestrian Crossing RS-016

X203**F35** Pets on Leash RS-017

General
continued

X203**G**01
Bus Stop
RS-031

X203**G**02
Viewing Area
RS-036

X203**G**03
Campfires
RS-042

X203**G**04
Point of Interest
RS-080

X203**G**05
Fire Extinguisher
RS-090

X203**G**06
Rattlesnakes
RS-099

X203**G**07
Bus Stop
RS-031

X203**G**08
Viewing Area
RS-036

X203**G**09
Campfires
RS-042

X203**G**10
Point of Interest
RS-080

X203**G**11
Fire Extinguisher
RS-090

X203**G**12
Rattlesnakes
RS-099

X203**G**13
Cans or Bottles
RS-101

X203**G**14
Snack Bar
RS-102

X203**G**15
Radios
RS-103

X203**G**16
Strollers
RS-111

X203**G**17
Sea Plane
RS-115

X203**G**18
Recycling Facility, Recycle
RS-200

X203**G**19
Cans or Bottles
RS-101

X203**G**20
Snack Bar
RS-102

X203**G**21
Radios
RS-103

X203**G**22
Strollers
RS-111

X203**G**23
Sea Plane
RS-115

X203**G**24
Wood Gathering
RS-120

X203**G**25
Stay on Boardwalk
RS-122

X203**G**26
Stay on Trail
RS-123

X203**G**27
Walk Your Bicycle
RS-136

X203**G**28
Wood Gathering
RS-120

X203**G**29
Stay on Boardwalk
RS-122

X203**G**30
Stay on Trail
RS-123

X203**G**31
Walk Your Bicycle
RS-136

Accommoda-
tions

X203**H**01
Lodging
RS-018

X203**H**02
Restaurant / Food
RS-019

X203**H**03
Men's Room
RS-021

X203**H**04
Restrooms
RS-022

X203**H**05
Women's Room
RS-023

X203**H**06
Wheelchair Accessible
RS-028

X203**H**07
Lodging
RS-018

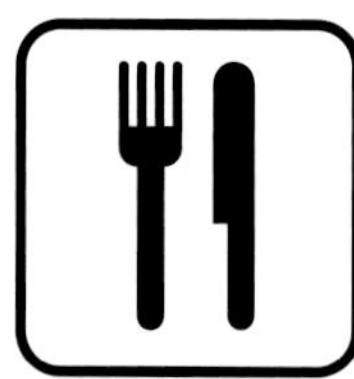

X203**H**08
Restaurant / Food
RS-019

X203**H**09
Men's Room
RS-021

X203**H**10
Restrooms
RS-022

X203**H**11
Women's Room
RS-023

X203**H**12
Parking
RS-034

X203**H**13
Sleeping Shelter
RS-037

X203**H**14
Campground
RS-038

X203**H**15
Trailer Site
RS-040

X203**H**16
Recreational Vehicle Site
RS-104

X203**H**17
Baby Changing Station
Men's Room RS-137

X203**H**18
Parking
RS-034

X203**H**19
Sleeping Shelter
RS-037

X203**H**20
Campground
RS-038

X203**H**21
Trailer Site
RS-040

X203**H**22
Recreational Vehicle Site
RS-104

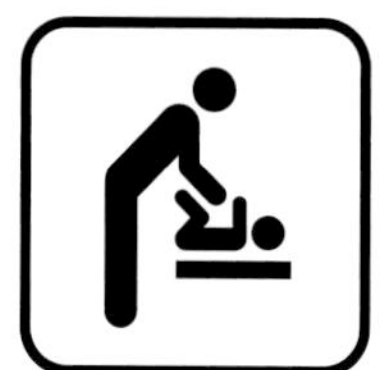

X203**H**23
Baby Changing Station
Men's Room RS-137

X203**H**24
Baby Changing Station
Women's Room RS-138113

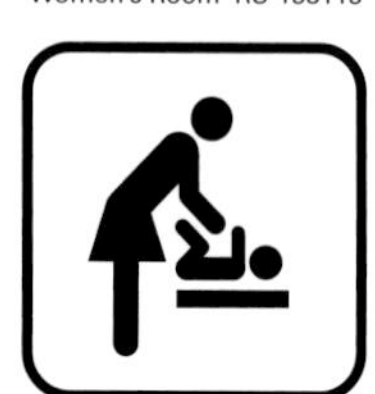

X203**H**25
Baby Changing Station
Women's Room RS-138113

Prohibition

X203**J**01
No Firearms
PS-001

X203**J**02
No Smoking
PS-002

X203**J**03
No Automobiles
PS-003

X203**J**04
No Trucks
PS-004

X203**J**05
Do Not Drink
PS-013

X203**J**06
No Trailers
PS-040

X203**J**07
No Campfires
PS-042

X203**J**08
No Picnics
PS-044

X203**J**09
No Downhill Skiing
PS-047

X203**J**10
No Ski Jumping
PS-048

X203**J**11
No Waterskiing
PS-058

X203**J**12
No Surfing
PS-059

X203**J**13
No Swimming
PS-061

X203**J**14
No Diving
PS-062

X203**J**15
No Hunting
PS-072

X203**J**16
No Tech. Rock Climbing
PS-081

X203**J**17
No Climbing
PS-082

X203**J**18
No Rock Collecting
PS-083

X203**J**19
No Litter
PS-086

X203**J**20
No Skateboarding
PS-098

X203**J**21
No Alcoholic Beverages
PS-100

X203**J**22
No Bottles or Cans
PS-101

X203**J**23
No Food or Drink
PS-102

X203**J**24
No Radios
PS-103

X203**J**25
No Hand Launch / Small Boat Launch PS-117

X203**J**26
No Wood Gathering
PS-120

X203**J**27
No Jet Ski / Personal Watercraft
PS-121

X203**J**28
Stay on Boardwalk
PS-122

X203**J**29
Do Not Step
PS-123

X203**J**30
Do Not Feed Animals
(General)
PS-130

X203**J**31
Do Not Feed Animals
(Ducks)
PS-131

X203**J**32
Do Not Feed Animals
(Squirrels)
PS-132

X203**J**33
Do Not Feed Animals
(Coyotes)
PS-133

X203**J**34
Do Not Feed Animals
(Deer)
PS-134

X203**J**35
Do Not Feed Animals
(Bears)
PS-135

X203**J**36
Do Not Cross
PS-016

Prohibition
continued

X203**K**01
No Pets
PS-017

X203**K**02
No Gasoline
PS-032

X203**K**03
No Parking
PS-034

X203**K**04
No Camping
PS-038

X203**K**05
No Sledding
PS-049

X203**K**06
No Skating
PS-050

X203**K**07
No Snowmobiling
PS-052

X203**K**08
No Boat Launching, Ramp
PS-054

X203**K**09
No Motorboats
PS-055

X203**K**10
No Fishing
PS-063

X203**K**11
No Horses
PS-064

X203**K**12
No Motor Biking
PS-065

X203**K**13
No Bicycling
PS-066

X203**K**14
No Off-Road Vehicles
PS-067

X203**K**15
No Wading
PS-088

X203**K**16
No Ice Fishing
PS-092

X203**K**17
No Fish Cleaning
PS-093

X203**K**18
No All-Terrain Vehicles
PS-095

X203**K**19
No Ball Playing
PS-096

X203**K**20
No Recreation Vehicles
PS-104

X203**K**21
No Baby Strollers
PS-111

X203**K**22
No Wood Chipping
PS-112

X203**K**23
No In-Line Skating
PS-125

X203**K**24
No Hang Gliding
PS-126

X203**K**25
No Snowboarding
PS-127

X203**K**26
No Golfing
PS-128

Addendum:
NPS Mapping
Symbols

X203**L**01
Horse Trail

X203**L**02
Motor Bike Trail

X203**L**03
Bicycle Trail

X203**L**04
4-Wheel-Drive Road

X203**L**05
Hiking Trail

X203**L**06
Amphitheater

X203**L**07
Cross-Country Skiing

X203**L**08
Skiing

X203**L**09
Sledding

X203**L**10
Ice Skating

X203**L**11
Snowmobiling

X203**L**12
Tour Boat

X203**L**13
Marina

X203**L**14
Boat Launch Ramp

X203**L**15
Boat Tour

X203**L**16
Swimming

X203**L**17
Scuba Diving

X203**L**18
Fishing Area

X203**L**19
Canoeing

X203**L**20
Sailing

X203**L**21
Drinking Water

X203**L**22
Visitor Information

X203**L**23
Ranger Station

X203**L**24
Grocery Store

X203**L**25
First Aid

X203**L**26
Telephone

X203**L**27
Post Office

X203**L**28
Air Transportation

X203**L**29
Gas Station

X203**L**30
Showers

X203**L**31
Sanitary Disposal
Station

X203**L**32
Shelter

X203**L**33
Picnic Site

X203**L**34
Stable

X203**L**35
Litter Disposal

X203**L**36
Bus Stop

Addendum:
NPS Mapping Symbols continued

X203**M**01
Open Fire Allowed

X203**M**02
Lodging

X203**M**03
Restaurant

X203**M**04
Restrooms

X203**M**05
Wheelchair Accessible
Handicapped Access, Disabled

X203**M**06
Parking

X203**M**07
Recreational Vehicle Site,
RV Camping

X203**M**08
Campground

X203**M**09
Pets on Leash

X203**M**10
Trailside Exhibit,
Interpretive Trail,
Pedestrian

X203**M**11
Radiator Water

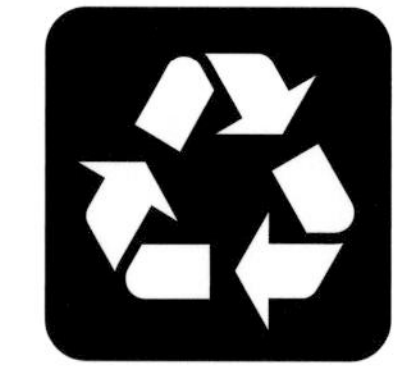
X203**M**12
Recycling Facility
Recycle

X203**M**13
Golf

X203**M**14
Hospital

Accessibility Symbols

X203**M**15
Wheelchair Accessible
Handicapped Access, Disabled

X203**M**16
Telecommunications
Device for the Deaf (TDD)

X203**M**17
Hearing Impaired
Access for Hearing Loss

X203**M**18
Volume Control
Telephone

X203**M**19
Access for the Sight
Impaired

X203**M**20
Sign Language
Interpretation

X203**M**21
Wheelchair Accessible
Handicapped Access, Disabled

X203**M**22
Telecommunications
Device for the Deaf (TDD)

X203**M**23
Hearing Impaired
Access for Hearing Loss

X203**M**24
Volume Control
Telephone

X203**M**25
Access for the Sight
Impaired

X203**M**26
Sign Language
Interpretation

X203**M**27
Audio Description

X203**M**28
Closed Captioning

X203**M**29
Open Captioning

X203**M**30
Audio Description

X203**M**31
Closed Captioning

X203**M**32
Open Captioning

Alphabetical Index: Recreational (SEGD)

A-N

Name	SEGD	UltSym
4-Wheel-Drive Road		X203L04
A		
Access for Hearing Loss		X203M18, X203M24
Access for the Sight, Impaired		X203M20, X203M26
Airport	RS-029	X203E03, X203E09
Air Transportation		X203L28
All-Terrain Trail	RS-095	X203A26, X203A32
Amphitheater	RS-070	X203A13, X203A19, X203L06
Archery	RS-066	X203B03, X203B09
Audio Description		X203M28, X203M31
Automobile	RS-003	X203F13, X203F19
B		
Baby Changing Station / Men's Room	RS-137	X203H17, X203H23
Baby Changing Station / Women's Room	RS-138113	X203H24, X203H25
Baseball	RS-096	X203A27, X203A33
Bear Viewing	RS-012	X203F27, X203F33
Bicycle Trail	RS-066	X203A03, X203A09, X203L03
Boat Launch		X203L14
Boat Launch Ramp	RS-054	X203C04, X203C10
Bottles or Cans	RS-101	X203G13, X203G19
Boat Tour		X203L15
Bus Stop	RS-031	X203G01, X203G07, X203L36
C		
Campfires	RS-042	X203G03, X203G09
Campground	RS-038	X203H14, X203H20, X203M08
Canoeing	RS-079	X203C25, X203C32, X203L19
Cans or Bottles	RS-101	X203G13, X203G19
Chair Lift / Ski Lift	RS-105	X203B28, X203B33
Clean Up After Your Dog	RS-140	X203F06, X203F11
Climbing	RS-082	X203A17, X203A23
Closed Captioning		X203M29, X203M32
Cross Country Skiing	RS-046	X203B13, X203B19, X203L07
D		
Dam	RS-009	X203F25, X203F31
Deer Viewing	RS-011	X203F26, X203F32
Diving	RS-062	X203C17, X203C23
Do Not Cross	PS-016	X203J36
Do Not Drink	PS-013	X203J05
Do Not Feed Animals (Bears)	PS-135	X203J35
Do Not Feed Animals (Coyotes)	PS-133	X203J33
Do Not Feed Animals (Deer)	PS-134	X203J34
Do Not Feed Animals (Ducks)	PS-131	X203J31
Do Not Feed Animals (General)	PS-130	X203J30
Do Not Feed Animals (Squirrels)	PS-132	X203J32
Do Not Step	PS-123	X203J29
Downhill Skiing	RS-047	X203B14, X203B20
Drinking Water	RS-013	X203D15, X203D21, X203L21
E		
Exercise Fitness Area	RS-097	X203A28 / X203A34
F		
Falling Rocks	RS-008	X203F24, X203F30
Fire Extinguisher	RS-090	X203G05, X203G11
Firewood Cutting	RS-112	X203F02, X203F08
First Aid	RS-024	X203D19, X203D25, X203L25
Fish Cleaning	RS-093	X203C28, X203C34
Fish Hatchery	RS-010	X203C01, X203C07
Fishing Area	RS-063	X203C18, X203C24, X203L18
Fishing Pier	RS-032	X203D06, X203D12
Fish Ladder	RS-089	X203C27, X203C33
Fitness / Exercise Area	RS-097	X203A28, X203A34
Food	RS-019	X203H02, X203H08
Fuel	RS-032	X203E05, X203E11

Name	SEGD	UltSym
G		
Gas Station	RS-032	X203E05, X203E11, X203L29
Golf		X203M14
Golfing	RS-069	X203B05, X203B11
Grocery Store	RS-020	X203D18, X203D24
H		
Hand Launch / Small Boat Launch	RS-029	X203D04, X203D10
Hang Gliding	RS-068	XO3B05, X203B11
Hearing Impaired		X203M18, X203M24
Hiking Trail	RS-068	X203A05, X203A11, X203L05
Horse Trail	RS-064	X203A01, X203A07, X203L01
Hospital	RS-201	X203F04, X203M15
Hunting	RS-072	X203A14, X203A20
I		
Ice Fishing	RS-092	X203B27, X203B32
Ice Skating	RS-050	X203B17, X203B23, X203L10
Information	RS-014	X203D16, X203D22
In-Line Skating	RS-099	X203A30, X203A36
Interpretation		X203M21, X203M27
Interpretive Trail / Auto	RS-064	X203B01, X203B07
Interpretive Trail / Pedestrian	RS-065	X203B02, X203B08
J		
Jet Ski / Personal Watercraft	RS-033	X203D13, X203D14
K		
Kayaking	RS-030	X203D05, X203D11
Kennel	RS-045	X203E18, X203E24
L		
Laundry / Laundromat	RS-085	X203E27, X203E33
Library	RS-110	X203F01, X203F07
Life Jackets	RS-094	X203C29, X203C35
Lighthouse	RS-007	X203F17, X203F23
Litter Disposal		X203L35
Litter Receptacle	RS-086	X203E28, X203E34
Lockers	RS-030	X203E04, X203E10
Lodging	RS-018	X203H01, X203H07, X203M02
Lookout Tower	RS-006	X203F16, X203F22
M		
Marina	RS-053	X203C03, X203C09, X203L13
Mechanic	RS-027	X203E02, X203E08
Men's Room	RS-021	X203H03, X203H09
Motor Bike Trail	RS-065	X203A02, X203A08, X203L02
Motorboating	RS-055	X203C05, X203C11
N		
No Alcoholic Beverages	PS-100	X203J21
No All-Terrain Vehicles	PS-095	X203K18
No Automobiles	PS-003	X203J03
No Baby Strollers	PS-111	X203K21
No Ball Playing	PS-096	X203K19
No Baseball	PS-096	X203K19
No Bicycle Riding	PS-066	X203K13
No Boat Launch Ramps	PS-054	X203K08
No Bottles or Cans	PS-101	X203J22
No Campfires	PS-042	X203J07
No Camping	PS-038	X203K04
No Cans or Bottles	PS-101	X203J22
No Climbing	PS-082	X203J17
No Diving	PS-062	X203J14
No Downhill Skiing	PS-047	X203J09
No Firearms	PS-001	X203J01
No Firewood Cutting	PS-112	X203K22
No Fish Cleaning	PS-093	X203K17
No Fishing	PS-063	X203K10

N-W

N

Name	SEGD	UltSym
No Food or Drinks	PS-102	X203J23
No Gas / Fuel	PS-032	X203K02
No Golfing	PS-128	X203K26
No Hand Gliding	PS-126	X203K24
No Hand Launch / Small Boat Launch	PS-117	X203J25
No Horses, Riding	PS-064	X203K11
No Hunting	PS-072	X203J15
No Ice Fishing	PS-092	X203K16
No Ice Skating	PS-050	X203K06
No In-Line Skating	PS-125	X203K23
No Jet Ski / Personal Watercraft	PS-121	X203J27
No Littering	PS-086	X203J19
No Motor Biking	PS-065	X203K12
No Motorboats	PS-055	X203K09
No Off-Road Vehicles	PS-067	X203K14
No Parking	PS-034	X203K03
No Pedestrian Crossing	PS-016	X203J36
No Pets	PS-017	X203K01
No Picnics	PS-044	X203J08
No Radios	PS-103	X203J24
No Recreational Vehicles	PS-104	X203K20
No Rock Collecting	PS-083	X203J18
No Skateboarding	PS-098	X203J20
No Skating	PS-050	X203K06
No Ski Jumping	PS-048	X203J10
No Sledding	PS-049	X203K05
No Smoking	PS-002	X203J02
No Snowboarding	PS-127	X203K25
No Snowmobiling	PS-052	X203K07
No Step	PS-123	X203J29
No Strollers	PS-111	X203K21
No Surfing	PS-059	X203J12
No Swimming	PS-061	X203J13
No Technical Rock Climbing	PS-081	X203J16
No Trailers	PS-040	X203J06
No Trucks	PS-004	X203J04
No Wading	PS-088	X203K15
No Waterskiing	PS-058	X203J11
No Wood Gathering	PS-120	X203J26
No Wood Chipping	PS-112	X203K22
NPS Mapping Symbols, Addendum	Pages	65-66

O

Name	SEGD	UltSym
Off-Road Vehicle	RS-067	X203A04, X203A10
Open Captioning		X203M30, X203M33
Open Fire Allowed		X203M01

P

Name	SEGD	UltSym
Pack It In Pack It Out	RS-139	X203F05, X203F10
Parking	RS-034	X203H12, X203H18
Parking		X203M06
Pedestrian Crossing	RS-016	X203F28, X203F34
Pets on Leash	RS-017	X203F29, X203F35, X203M09
Picnic Shelter	RS-039	X203E14, X203E20
Picnic Site	RS-044	X203E17, X203E23, X203L33
Playground	RS-069	X203A06, X203A12
Point of Interest	RS-080	X203G05, X203G11
Post Office	RS-026	X203E01, X203E07, X203L27

R

Name	SEGD	UltSym
Radiator Water	RS-124	X203F03, X203F09, X203M12
Radios	RS-103	X203G15, X203G21
Ranger Station	RS-015	X203D17, X203D23, X203L23
Rattlesnakes	RS-099	X203G06, X203G12
Recreational Vehicle Site	RS-104	X203H16, X203H22
Recycle / Recycling Facility	RS-200	X203G18, X203M13
Restaurant		X203M03
Restaurant / Food	RS-019	X203H02, X203H08
Restrooms	RS-022	X203H04, X203H10, X203M04
Rock Collecting	RS-083	X203A18, X203A24
Rowboating	RS-057	X203C06, X203C12
RV Camping		X203M07

S

Name	SEGD	UltSym
Sailing	RS-056	X203D03, X203D09, X203L20
Sanitary Disposal Station	RS-041	X203E15, X203E21, X203L31
Scuba Diving	RS-060	X203C16, X203C22, X203L17
Sea Plane	RS-115	X203G17, X203G23
Seal / Sea Lion Viewing	RS-106	X203C30, X203C36
Shelter		X203L32
Showers	RS-035	X203E13, X203E19, X203L30
Sign Language / Interpretation		X203M21, X203M27
Skateboarding	RS-098	X203A29, X203A35
Skiing		X203L08
Ski Jumping	RS-048	X203B15, X203B21
Sledding	RS-049	X203B16, X203B22, X203L09
Sleeping Shelter	RS-037	X203H13, X203H19
Smoking	RS-002	X203F12, X203F18
Snack Bar	RS-102	X203G14, X203G20
Snowboarding	RS-106	X203B29, X203B34
Snowmobiling	RS-052	X203B18, X203B24, X203L11
Snow-Shoeing	RS-078	X203B26, X203B31
Spelunking / Caves	RS-084	X203A25, X203A31
Stable	RS-073	X203E26, X203E32, X203L34
Stay On Boardwalk	PS-122	X203J28
"	RS-122	X203G26, X203G30
Stay On Trail	RS-123	X203G26, X203G30
Storage	RS-030	X203E04, X203E10
Store		X203L24
Strollers	RS-111	X203G16, X203G22
Surfing	RS-059	X203C14, X203C20
Swimming	RS-061	X203C15, X203C21, X203L16
Symbol of Access	RS-028	X203H06

T

Name	SEGD	UltSym
Technical Rock Climbing	RS-081	X203A16 / X203A22
Telecommunications Device for the Deaf (TDD)		X203M17, X203M23
Telephone	RS-025	X203D20, X203D26, X203L25
Tennis	RS-070	X203B06, X203B12
Theater	RS-109	X203E30, X203E36
Tour Boat	RS-087	X203C02, X203C08, X203L12
Trailer Site	RS-040	X203H15, X203H21
Trail Shelter	RS-043	X203E16, X203E22
Trailside Exhibit		X203M10
Tramway	RS-071	X203E25, X203E31
Trash Dumpster	RS-091	X203E29, X203E35
Trucks	RS-004	X203F14, X203F20
Tunnel	RS-005	X203F15, X203F21

V

Name	SEGD	UltSym
Vehicle Ferry	RS-033	X203E06, X203E12
Viewing Area	RS-036	X203G02, X203G08
Visitor Information		X203L22
Volume Control Telephone		X203M19, X203M25

W

Name	SEGD	UltSym
Wading	RS-088	X203C26, X203C32
Walk Your Bicycle	RS-136	X203G27, X203G31
Waterskiing	RS-058	X203C13, X203C19
Whale Viewing	RS-107	X203D01, X203D07
Wheelchair Accessible	RS-028	X203H06
Wheelchair Accessible (Mapping)		X203M05
Wheelchair Accessible		X203M16, X203M22
Wildlife Viewing	RS-076	X203A15, X203A21
Wind Surfing	RS-108	X203D02, X203D08
Winter Recreation Area	RS-077	X203B25, X203B30
Women's Room	RS-023	X203H05, X203H11
Wood Gathering	RS-120	X203G24, X203G28

Symbol Signs: Transportation I (AIGA / DOT)

4

Overview

In an attempt to bring some order to the proliferation of pictograms being developed by numerous organizations concerned with international travel, the American Institute of Graphic Arts (AIGA) in 1974 completed and submitted to the U.S. Department of Transportation (DOT) a report recommending the adoption of 34 symbol signs.

The report was favorably received, and the symbol signs were implemented and tested at various facilities throughout the United States. They also had impact internationally through features in design publications and news magazines, and on television. In addition, a Japanese reprint of the entire report was widely distributed.

In 1979 the AIGA completed a second study, which resulted in symbols for 16 additional messages, along with an expanded series of standards for background forms and shapes. Additional symbols were added in 1993, at which time several signs were updated to include symbols for the disabled.

Process and Credits

In order to maintain a consistent approach, all phases of the Symbol Signs study were carried out by essentially the same group of participants.

A committee of AIGA members had prime responsibility to review existing symbol systems in use around the world, to analyze the effectiveness of each, to recommend from this analysis a clear concept for each message area, and to continually review the actual design work and the preparation of guidelines. This AIGA Committee was composed of: Thomas H. Geismar (Chairman), Seymour Chwast, Rudolph deHarak, John Lees, and Massimo Vignelli.

Using a step-by-step procedure as the basis of evaluating symbols, three distinct dimensions were applied. The *semantic* dimension refers to the relationship of visual image to meaning: how well does this symbol represent the message? The *syntactic* dimension refers to the relationship of one visual image to another: how well does this symbol relate to other symbols? The *pragmatic* dimension refers to the relationship of a visual image to the user: can a person see the sign? Each existing symbol was analyzed independently by each committee member. In addition, each message group was discussed at some length by the whole committee, and the recommendations were arrived at as a joint decision of the group. Some decisions were easily made while others provoked considerable discussion.[1]

Following the AIGA Committee's recommendations for concepts, Roger Cook and Don Shanosky of Cook and Shanosky Associates, Inc., Princeton, NJ, designed and produced the symbols, spending considerable time to give a consistent graphic treatment to a diverse group of images.

Ken Resen worked on the development of the application guidelines, and the establishment of added guidelines based on field experience.

Under the guidance of Professor Alving Eisenman, a group of graphic design students and graduates from the Yale University School of Art acted as project coordinators, organizing masses of disparate information, designing the reports, and preparing all artwork for reproduction. Don and Karen Moyer performed these functions for the first report; Mark Ackley organized the analysis, and Juanita Dugdale designed the second report. Debora Trainer of the AIGA served as the project coordinator.

Throughout all the studies, William R. Myers, Director of the Office of Facilitation of the U.S. Department of Transportation, was not only a knowledgeable and determined client, but also a constant source of encouragement. It is only through his efforts that this project happened.[2]

Several key points were agreed upon:

> The effectiveness of symbols is fairly limited. They are most effective when they represent a service or concession and less effective when used to represent a process such as "Ticket Purchase".

> The symbols are fairly useless at a facility unless incorporated as part of an intelligent total sign system.

> It is more harmful to oversign than to undersign. Only those messages that are truly essential should be considered.

Addendum: Symbol Signs Aboard Commercial Aircraft

Additional symbols were created for use aboard commercial aircraft in the same style and format as the AIGA symbols. They provide a logical continuity and improved recognition as passengers move from the terminal to the aircraft.

Standards for Symbology and Graphic Signage Aboard Commercial Aircraft is a publication developed by the Transport Airworthiness Requirements Committee (TARC) of the Aerospace Industries Association (AIA), Washington, DC, the trade association for commercial aircraft manufacturers. The document number is TARC 82-29.[3]

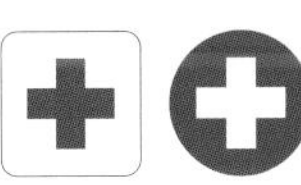

'First Aid' Symbol Color Revision

In 1999, American Red Cross informed the author/designer Mies Hora that the Red Cross emblem is legally protected and requested that it be removed from *Official Signs & Icons*. The explanation is as follows: "The red cross symbol is *not* a generic symbol for emergency, health-care, first-aid or medical services, products or personnel. While the Red Cross emblem is protected by federal and state trademark law, unfair competition law and anti-dilution law, it is also protected by criminal law. As a signatory to the Geneva Conventions, the United Sates Congress agreed to protect the Greek cross (red cross on a white ground) as an international humanitarian symbol and to delegate permission for its use to the American Red Cross. Generic use of the emblem jeopardizes the neutral status that is essential for the effective accomplishment of the Red Cross mission. Such unauthorized use also infringes the trademark rights of the American Red Cross."[4] In response, the color of the "First Aid" symbols on pages 72 and 76 has been changed from red to "Safety Green", which according to *ANSI Z535.1-2002 Safety Color Code* is nearest to Pantone® color PMS 3415 C.

About AIGA

The American Institute of Graphic Arts, the professional association for communication design, is committed to furthering excellence in communication design as a broadly defined discipline, strategic tool for business and cultural force. AIGA is the place design professionals turn to first to exchange ideas and information, participate in critical analysis, and research and advance education and ethical practice. AIGA sets the national agenda for the role of design in its economic, social, political, cultural and creative contexts. AIGA is the oldest and largest membership association for professionals engaged in the discipline, practice, and culture of designing. Founded as the American Institute of Graphic Arts in 1914 as a small, exclusive club, AIGA now represents more than 16,000 designers through national activities and local programs developed by 48 chapters and more than 150 student groups.

AIGA supports the interests of professionals, educators, and students who are engaged in the process of designing, regardless of where they are in the arc of their careers. The disciplines represented in the profession range from book and type design through the traditional communication design disciplines to the newer disciplines of interaction design, experience design, and motion graphics. In addition, AIGA supports the interests of those involved in designing from other disciplines, professions, and business who share designers' commitment to advancing understanding of the value of design.

Through the relationships members develop within the community of designers, the information they share and the standards they develop for the profession, AIGA helps the profession validate its own ethos and role in business and society, and actively communicates the value of design to both the business community and the public. AIGA serves as a hub of thought-leadership and activity for the designing community. The association is committed to stimulating thinking about design through conferences, competitions, exhibitions, publications and websites. AIGA inspires, educates and informs designers, helping them to realize their talents and to advocate the value of design among the media, the business community, public agencies and the general public. While AIGA was created to advance the design profession, its members now place a higher priority on AIGA's work in communicating the value of design to audiences outside the profession. www.aiga.org

International Symbol Signs System:

A
Standard Format
Figure in Symbol Field

B
Reversed Symbol Field

C
Circular Symbol Field

D
Reversed Circular
Symbol Field

E
Without Symbol Field

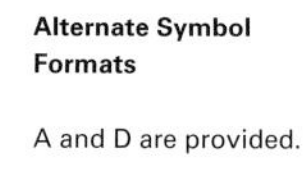

Alternate Symbol Formats

A and D are provided.

B and C are created from A and D.

Note: D includes 1-point rule for creation of C.

Public Services

X04**A**01
Telephone

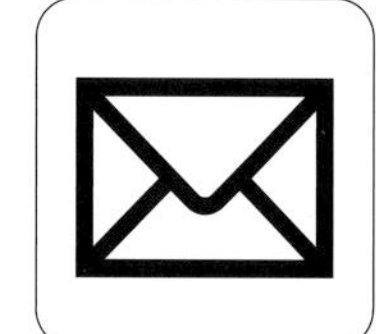

X04**A**02
Mail
Post Office

X04**A**03
Telegrams

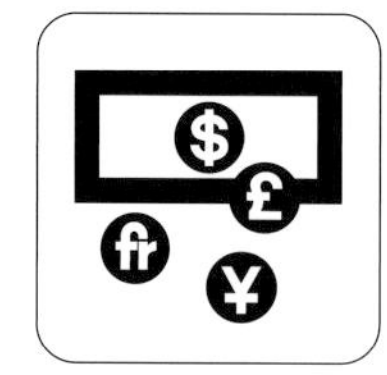

X04**A**04
Currency Exchange
Bank

X04**A**05
Cashier

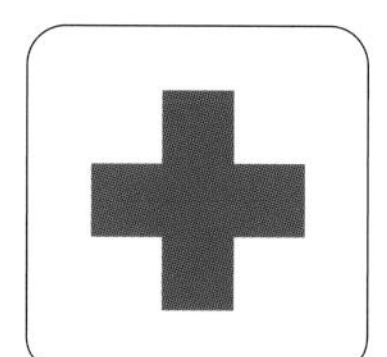

X04**A**06
First Aid

X04**A**07
Telephone

X04**A**08
Mail
Post Office

X04**A**09
Telegrams

X04**A**10
Currency Exchange
Bank

X04**A**11
Cashier

X04**A**12
First Aid

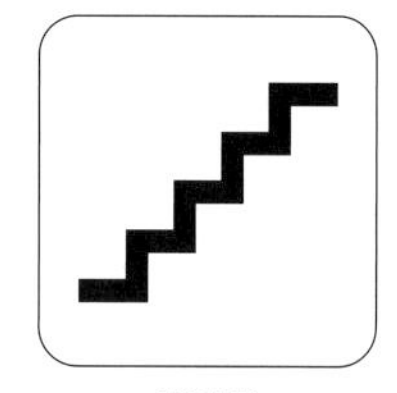

X04**A**13
Stairs

X04**A**14
Stairs, Up

X04**A**15
Stairs, Down

X04**A**16
Escalator

X04**A**17
Escalator, Up

X04**A**18
Escalator, Down

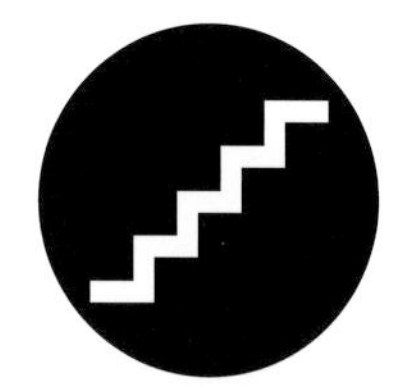

X04**A**19
Stairs

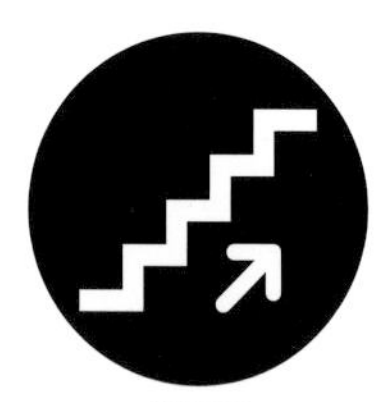

X04**A**20
Stairs, Up

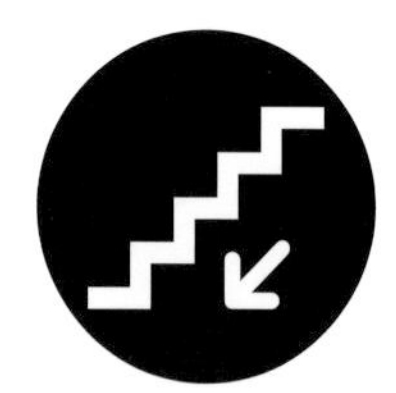

X04**A**21
Stairs, Down

X04**A**22
Escalator

X04**A**23
Escalator, Up

X04**A**24
Escalator, Down

X04**A**25
Lost and Found

X04**A**26
Coat Check

X04**A**27
Baggage Lockers

X04**A**28
Left Baggage

X04**A**29
Baggage Cart

X04**A**30
Lost and Found

X04**A**31
Coat Check

X04**A**32
Baggage Lockers

X04**A**33
Left Baggage

X04**A**34
Baggage Cart

Public
Services
continued

X04**B**01
Toilets, Men
Men

X04**B**02
Toilets, Women
Women

X04**B**03
Toilets

X04**B**04
Elevator

X04**B**05
Nursery

X04**B**06
Drinking Fountain
Drinking Water

X04**B**07
Toilets, Men
Men

X04**B**08
Toilets, Women
Women

X04**B**09
Toilets

X04**B**10
Elevator

X04**B**11
Nursery

X04**B**12
Drinking Fountain
Drinking Water

X04**B**13
Waiting Room
Lounge

X04**B**14
Information

X04**B**15
Hotel Information

X04**B**16
Air Transportation
Airport

X04**B**17
Heliport

X04**B**18
Taxi

X04**B**19
Waiting Room
Lounge

X04**B**20
Information

X04**B**21
Hotel Information

X04**B**22
Air Transportation
Airport

X04**B**23
Heliport

X04**B**24
Taxi

X04**B**25
Bus

X04**B**26
Ground Transportation

X04**B**27
Rail Transportation
Train(s)

X04**B**28
Water Transportation
Ship(s), Pier(s)

X04**B**29
Handicapped Access
Disabled

X04**B**30
Bus

X04**B**31
Ground Transportation

X04**B**32
Rail Transportation
Train(s)

X04**B**33
Water Transportation
Ship(s), Pier(s)

X04**B**34
Handicapped Access
Disabled

Note: All symbols and signs are available as fully editable vector image files: see page 238 or www.ultimatesymbol.com

Concessions

X04**C**01
Car Rental
Rent-a-Car

X04**C**02
Restaurant

X04**C**03
Coffee Shop
Snack Bar

X04**C**04
Bar
Cocktails

X04**C**05
Shops
News & Gifts

X04**C**06
Barber Shop
Beauty Salon, Hairdresser

X04**C**07
Car Rental
Rent-a-Car

X04**C**08
Restaurant

X04**C**09
Coffee Shop
Snack Bar

X04**C**10
Bar
Cocktails

X04**C**11
Shops
News & Gifts

X04**C**12
Barber Shop
Beauty Salon, Hairdresser

X04**C**13
Barber Shop

X04**C**14
Beauty Salon
Hairdresser

X04**C**15
Barber Shop

X04**C**16
Beauty Salon
Hairdresser

Processing Activities

X04**C**17
Ticket Purchase

X04**C**18
Baggage Check-in
Baggage Claim

X04**C**19
Customs

X04**C**20
Immigration

X04**C**21
Departing Flights

X04**C**22
Connecting Flights

X04**C**23
Ticket Purchase

X04**C**24
Baggage Check-in
Baggage Claim

X04**C**25
Customs

X04**C**26
Immigration

X04**C**27
Departing Flights

X04**C**28
Connecting Flights

X04**C**29
Arriving Flights
Passenger Pick-Up

X04**C**30
Arriving Flights
Passenger Pick-Up

Regulations

Directional Arrows

Addendum:
Symbol Signs
Aboard
Commercial
Aircraft

X04**E**01
Smoking Permitted

X04**E**02
No Smoking

X04**E**03
Ash Tray

X04**E**04
No Smoking
Positive and Negative

X04**E**05
No Cigarette Disposal

X04**E**06
Smoking Permitted

X04**E**07
Attendant Call
Unisex Version

X04**E**08
Attendant Call
Female Version

X04**E**09
Attendant Call
Small Button Version

X04**E**10
Do Not Sit Here

X04**E**11
Return to Seat

X04**E**12
Fasten Seat Belt

X04**E**13
Seat Position Indicator

X04**E**14
Seat Position Indicator

X04**E**15
Lavatory

X04**E**16
Lavatories Occupied

X04**E**17
Handicapped
Accommodated

X04**E**18
Please Lock Door

X04**E**19
Occupied

X04**E**20
Vacant

X04**E**21
Waste Disposal

X04**E**22
No Waste Disposal

X04**E**23
Sanitary Napkins

X04**E**24
Razor Blade Disposal

X04**E**25
Diaper Changing
Table

X04**E**26
Toilet Seat Covers

X04**E**27
Fire Extinguisher

X04**E**28
Life Raft

X04**E**29
Oxygen

X04**E**30
First Aid Kit

X04**E**31
Flashlight

X04**E**32
Battery - Emergency
Power Pack

X04**E**33
Air Sick Bags

X04**E**34
Reading Light

X04**E**35
Megaphone

X04**E**36
No Stowage

X04**E**37
Electrical Outlet

Symbol Signs: Transportation II (TCRP / DOT)

5

Overview

In response to the Americans with Disabilities Act (ADA), new symbols were designed for the Transit Facility Signing and Graphics in addition to the international symbols from the American Institute of Graphic Arts (AIGA) and Society of Environmental Graphic Design (SEGD).

The symbols encourage safe, secure, and efficient movement of passengers to and through transit facilities. Riders need graphic information to formulate an action plan concerning wayfinding in an unfamiliar environment. The graphic information they need is a comprehensible signage system of directional, regulatory, and identification messages.

Basic guidelines have been developed to provide:
> An understanding of the needs of the users
> Principles of wayfinding
> Copy style
> Size
> Terminology
> Consistent symbols,
> Colors,
> Shapes, and
> Placement of signs

Development & Evaluation

1. Existing signing practices were surveyed and tested in more than 30 transit properties that allowed a survey and documentation of their signage practices, many of whom also provided us samples of their graphics. These included airports, bus terminals, subway lines, and train and ferry terminals around the country and Canada.
2. A search was made of current literature and sign standards.
3. Preliminary sketches were developed and existing symbols were adopted, new symbols were created, and alterations were made in proportions for overall consistency and unity.
4. Symbols of the American Institute of Graphic Arts (AIGA), Society of Environmental Graphic Design (SEGD), and new designs by graphic designers were tested by transit riders and non-riders, and disability focus groups. Many organizations played an important role in the evaluation of the candidate signs and symbols, including: Self Help for Hard of Hearing People, Inwood House Independent Living Center, The Center for Unique Learners, American Bus Association, The American Public Transit Association, Alexandria City Public Schools, The Lighthouse for the Blind, Volunteers for Visually Handicapped, Iona House, and National Electric Sign Association.
5. Symbols were tested in various print sizes at various mounting heights and viewing distances.
6. Visual signs and symbols and tactile signs were field tested. A test was made at a Southeastern Pennsylvania Transportation Authority (SEPTA) station in Philadelphia. SEPTA coordinated the signing and field testing conducted at the Fern Rock Transportation Center with more than 40 signs during the summer of 1995.

7. Guidelines were developed for transit facility signing and graphics which include:
(a) Signing philosophy and principles of wayfinding,
(b) User groups with disabilities, representing individuals with visual, mobility, cognitive, and hearing impairments,
(c) Wayfinding design and trip segment techniques,
(d) Standard terminology and message hierarchy,
(e) Signage design,
(f) Transit facility symbols, arrows, and graphic applications,
(g) Electronic visual information,
(h) Material selection and preparation,
(i) Consultant selection and compensation, bidding procedures and recommendations,
(j) Booklet and CD or disk with more than 50 symbols with three different versions.

Several individuals in the sign industry made technical contributions that have added greatly to the technical content of the manual.

The guideline's manual was made available in early 1997. For more information, contact J.L.Ortiz at 212.875.1380. An excerpt from the manual illustrating symbol applications appears on pages 80-81.

Credits
Design and Development: KRW, Inc. and advisory panel, in association with Jose Luis Ortiz and assisted by Andrew Brenits.

Commissioned in 1994 by The Transportation Research Board's Transit Cooperative Research Program (TCRP).

2005 Update: 'First Aid' Symbol Color Revision
In 1999, American Red Cross informed the author and designer Mies Hora that the Red Cross emblem is legally protected and requested that it be removed from *Official Signs & Icons*. The explanation is as follows: "The red cross symbol is *not* a generic symbol for emergency, health-care, first-aid or medical services, products or personnel. While the Red Cross emblem is protected by federal and state trademark law, unfair competition law and anti-dilution law, it is also protected by crimina law. As a signatory to the Geneva Conventions, the United Sates Congress agreed to protect the Greek cross (red cross on a white ground) as an international humanitarian symbol and to delegate permission for its use to the American Red Cross. Generic use of the emblem jeopardizes the neutral status that is essential for the effective accomplishment of the Red Cross mission. Such unauthorized use also infringes the trademark rights of the American Red Cross."[1]

In response, the color of the "First Aid" symbols on pages 81-84 has been changed from red to "Safety Green", which according to *ANSI Z535.1-2002 Safety Color Code* is nearest to Pantone® color PMS 3415 C.

Sign Structure

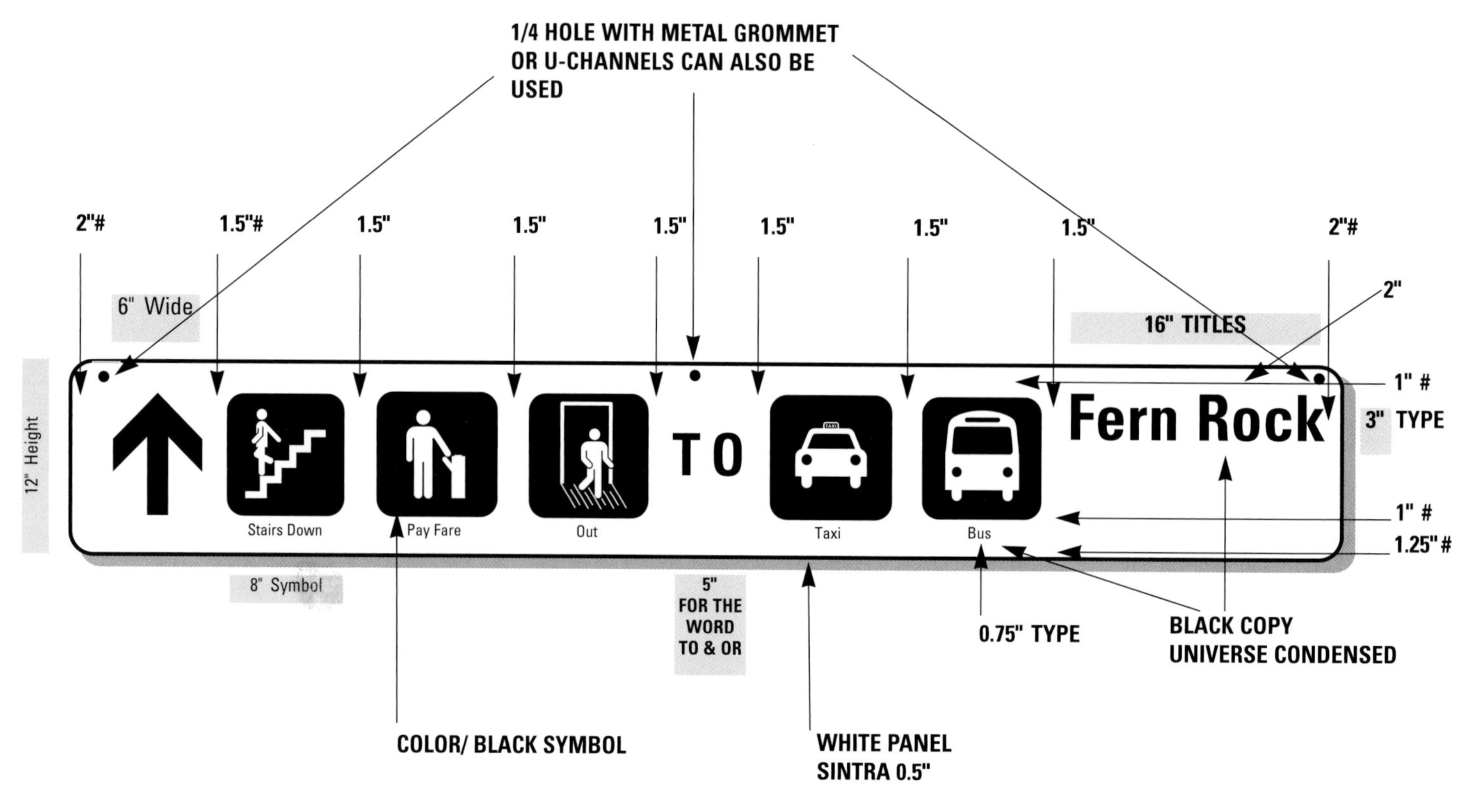

General specifications for Philadelphia signage:

The height is 12".

The width varies depending on the titles (type).

The width could vary from 0.5" to 0.75".

The size of the symbols are 8".

The arrows are 7" wide (horizontal) & 6" wide (vertical).

The size of the type is 3" high, open spacing, for the name of the destination.

All symbols, letters and arrows are cut outs from vinyl, mounted on Sintra 0.5 or Komacel 0.5".

Mounting holes should be a minimum distance of 1" from the edge with metal grommet.

U-Channels can also be used for signs larger the 36".

Trip A

Location

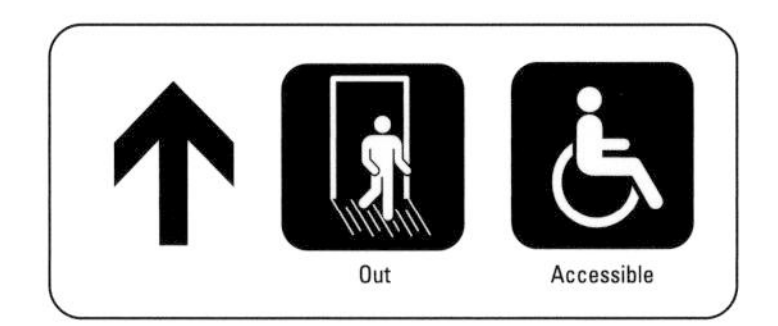

On platform perpendicular to tracks

On platform by stairs

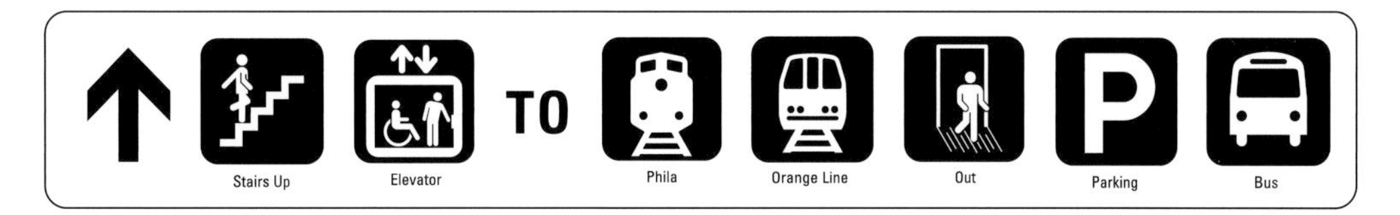

On platform perpendicular to tracks

Next to elevator

On platform

At the top of the stairs Mezzanine level

Individual Signs (various locations)

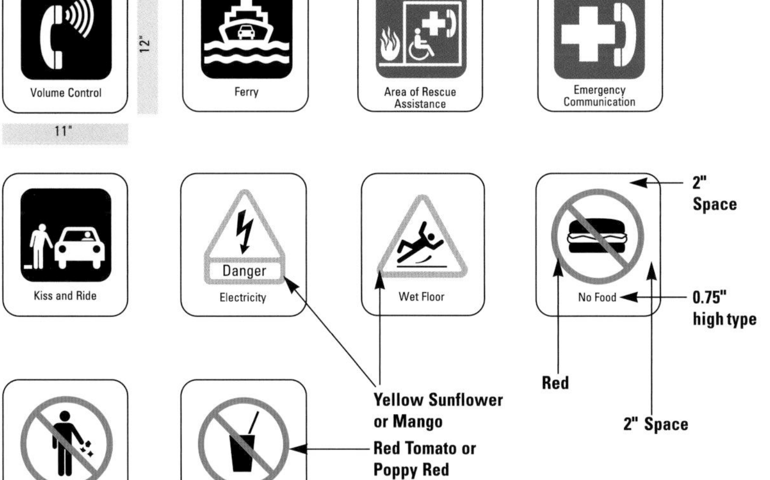

The size of the symbols names is 0.75" high, open space.

The height of the sign is 12" by 11" width.

The size of the symbols are 7".

All symbols and letters are cut outs from black vinyl (red & black for the prohibition symbols and yellow & black for the safety symbols).

Mounted on Sintra 0.5".

Transit Facility Symbol Signs: Public Services

X05**A**01
Out / Exit

X05**A**02
Information

X05**A**03
Wheelchair Accessible
Disabled

X05**A**04
Escalator

X05**A**05
Stairs Up

X05**A**06
Stairs Down

X05**A**07
Out / Exit

X05**A**08
Information

X05**A**09
Wheelchair Accessible
Disabled

X05**A**10
Escalator

X05**A**11
Stairs Up

X05**A**12
Stairs Down

X05**A**13
Elevator

X05**A**14
Men

X05**A**15
Women

X05**A**16
Toilets

X05**A**17
Drinking Fountain

X05**A**18
Litter

X05**A**19
Elevator

X05**A**20
Men

X05**A**21
Women

X05**A**22
Toilets

X05**A**23
Drinking Fountain

X05**A**24
Litter

X05**A**25
Telephone

X05**A**26
Text Telephone

X05**A**27
Volume Control

X05**A**28
Hearing Assistance

X05**A**29
First Aid

X05**A**30
Lost and Found

X05**A**31
Telephone

X05**A**32
Text Telephone

X05**A**33
Volume Control

X05**A**34
Hearing Assistance

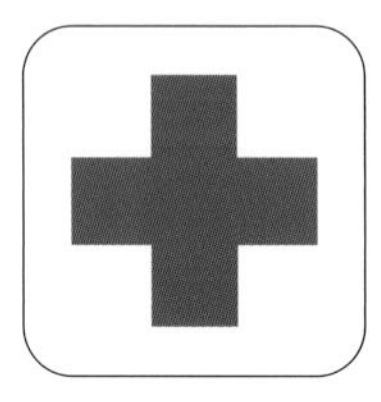
X05**A**35
First Aid

X05**A**36
Lost and Found

Note: All symbols and signs are available as fully editable vector image files: see page 238 or www.ultimatesymbol.com

Public
Services
continued

X05**B**01
Lockers

X05**B**02
Smoking

X05**B**03
Fire Extinguisher

X05**B**04
Taxi

X05**B**05
Bus

X05**B**06
Ferry

X05**B**07
Lockers

X05**B**08
Smoking

X05**B**09
Fire Extinguisher

X05**B**10
Taxi

X05**B**11
Bus

X05**B**12
Ferry

X05**B**13
Car Rental

X05**B**14
Bicycle

X05**B**15
Motorcycle

X05**B**16
Parking

X05**B**17
Mail

X05**B**18
Recycle

X05**B**19
Car Rental

X05**B**20
Bicycle

X05**B**21
Motorcycle

X05**B**22
Parking

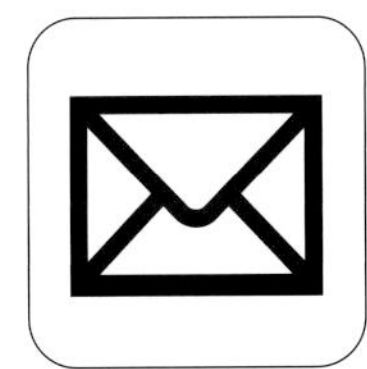

X05**B**23
Mail

X05**B**24
Recycle

X05**B**25
Pay Fare

X05**B**26
Ramp

X05**B**27
Light Rail

X05**B**28
Commuter Rail

X05**B**29
Rapid Rail

X05**B**30
Area of Rescue
Assistance

X05**B**31
Pay Fare

X05**B**32
Ramp

X05**B**33
Light Rail

X05**B**34
Commuter Rail

X05**B**35
Rapid rail

X05**B**36
Area of Rescue
Assistance

Public Services continued

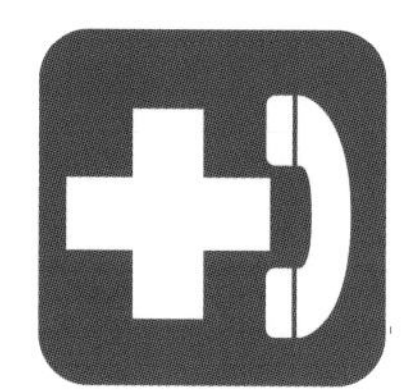
X05**C**01
Emergency Communication

X05**C**02
Drop Off / Pick Up Area

X05**C**03
Bus Bays

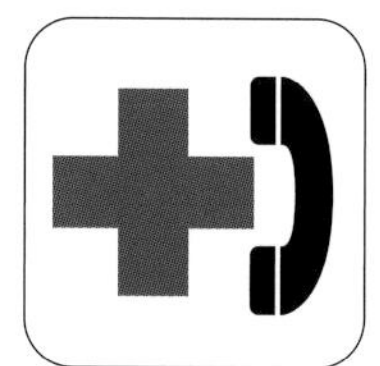
X05**C**04
Emergency Communication

X05**C**05
Drop Off / Pick Up Area

X05**C**06
Bus Bays

Prohibitions

X05**C**07
No Radios

X05**C**08
No Food

X05**C**09
No Litter

X05**C**10
No Drinks

X05**C**11
No Radio, Food Drinks, Litter

X05**C**12
No Smoking

Warning

X05**C**13
Wet Floor

X05**C**14
Electricity

X05**C**15
Fire

X05**C**16
Walk

Directional Arrows

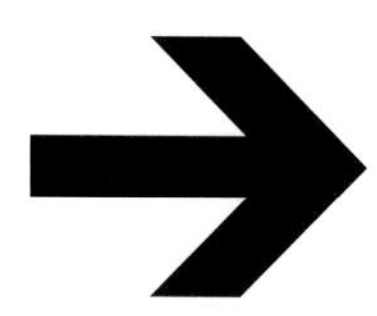
X05**C**17
Pointed Arrow, Right

X05**C**18
Pointed Arrow, Up

X05**C**19
Pointed Arrow, Reverse Direction

Hospitality Symbol Signs System (APEC)

Overview

Despite an increasingly interconnected global economy, until now, no internationally accepted or comprehensive reference symbol set for travel and hotels had been created by a governmental or commercial agency for several decades. The result is that accommodation firms design their own varied (and branded) visual communications for many of the same activities and facilities, sometimes basing them on outdated source material.

Often, though visually pleasing, some of these symbol signs, when carefully tested, are correctly interpreted by less than 50% of the public. The semantic, syntactic, and pragmatic aspects of symbol sign messaging are not given sufficient consideration before application in the field. Where agreement on symbol content and meaning is lacking, there is inconsistent messaging, reduced comprehension by various constituencies, and additional confusion for all but the most sophisticated traveler. Improving visual communications is an important means of fulfilling the needs of travelers and guests, while encouraging and strengthening the tourist/accommodation industry worldwide.

In 1999, Ultimate Symbol Inc. decided to take up the challenge of creating an international symbol signs system for hospitality oriented uses that is an extension of, and that meets the same high standards as the existing AIGA/Department of Transportation and SEGD recreational symbol signs systems.

The new symbol signs relate to the above-mentioned systems in format, scale, proportion, style, execution, and overall effectiveness, while using an up-to-date understanding of wayfinding realities based on experience and the particular needs of the international lodging industry.

Rather than endure the lengthy delays required to obtain government and/or commercial grants for this substantial undertaking, Ultimate Symbol Inc. chose to underwrite the whole project.

Mission Statement

> Create a universal symbol signs system for the travel & accommodation sectors that is comprehensive, rigorously tested, and internationally accepted.
> Create a non-mandatory, up-to-date reference work with the potential to inform future as well as current sign implementations.
> Provide simple, low-cost documentation and hi-res source material/artwork for accurate reproduction and easy dissemination.
> Publicize the new system globally through endorsements of participating organizations and by posting on the world wide web.
> Commence contact between nations, agencies, companies, designers, and sign-makers so that new needs are acted on more quickly as they arise.

Phase I: Data Collection

Collection of data and samples of existing symbols and symbol sets: during the first of three years, symbols for each message content were solicited from every imaginable source (U.S., foreign, current, and old), and collated by an in-house team. The resulting compilation of symbols was reviewed by the Hospitality Advisory Committee, which is comprised of a group of top designers working in the sign communications field today (see list, page 87). Specifically requested were lists from tourist-oriented industries (see Participating Organizations, page 87) of symbols that were deemed essential for wayfinding in today's rapidly changing and technologically oriented public spaces, such as "Modem Hookup, Email Access". A core group of 64 new messages emerged whose primary content was hospitality related. Those messages were then rounded out by adding symbols already available from the National Park Service recreational and AIGA/DOT sets (see Volumes 3 and 4) that were appropriate for this system as well, such as "Water Skiing" and "Taxi".

Phase II: Design/Review

After getting comments from the Committee and refining the list of prospective symbols and essential message content, the design team developed clear sketches for each type of symbol content. The result was a fairly tight symbol set. The process has been flexible and evolutionary, with deletions, contributions, and new ideas continually occurring. The design/review process was repeated many times over the three year period.

Phase III: Testing & Evaluation

During the second year, the symbol signs were tested by having various constituencies answer a questionnaire. By the end of the process more than 1,200 people were asked to identify the symbols and describe their meaning. These included senior citizens, non-U.S. guests sitting at hotel bars, adult-ed community college students, design college students, design professionals, and participating tourist organizations, including employees of the American Hotel and Lodging Association (AHLA). In addition, the total membership of the SEGD rated the individual symbols as either Excellent (easy to understand), Okay (but needs work) or Poor (not clear, redesign).

After each group's responses were evaluated, alterations were made to symbols with poor ratings and the questionnaire updated before testing the next group. Some groups were tested twice to ascertain whether there was increased comprehension (in most cases there was).

The Advisory Committee was asked to review new symbol changes more than a dozen times. The current symbol set has been reviewed and refined to such a degree that there are very few questions outstanding as to what a symbol means and its intended message. Comprehension rates now exceed 80% overall. There are several exceptions, such as the "Meeting Point" symbol, which will gain acceptance and improved comprehension with continuous use.

The latest updates to the symbol set were in response to studying and conforming to the Asia Pacific Economic Cooperation (APEC) Tourism Working Group (TWG) document: *Standardization of Symbols for Visitor Signage in the APEC Region.*

Phase IV: Production & Dissemination

The completed symbol signs system is available in hi-res Mac/PC EPS format with accompanying documentation on the world wide web for download and will also be made available as a separate CD with booklet. In addition, a press release will be sent to every major publication and mailers delivered to select industry groups. Coordination will continue with participating organizations by web links, articles for publications/newsletters, and industry conference presentations.

A Work In Progress

The system published in this book includes 220 symbols, most of which are presented in both positive and negative contrast applications. The set will be revised periodically and will a remain a work in progress, as it is certain that new symbol content, and messaging needs will arise over time. You are encouraged to forward ideas, content and any new symbols that come to your attention that may be relevant to this area of research to Mies Hora at www.ultimatesymbol.com.

Participating Organizations

The following are among the organizations that were asked to review the proposed symbols, comment, and inform their constituents about the completed symbol signs system:

Air Transport Association (ATA)
Airport Council International (ACI)
American Association of Airport Executives (AAAE)
American Automobile Association (AAA)
American Bus Association (ABA)
American Hotel and Lodging Association (AHLA)
American Public Transit Association (APTA)
American Recreation Coalition (ARC)
AMTRAK
Asia Pacific Economic Cooperation (APEC)
Association of American Railroads (AAR)
Lodging Magazine
Railway Progress Institute (RPI)
Society of Environmental Graphic Design (SEGD)
Travel Industry Association of America (TIAA)

Hospitality Advisory Committee

Roger Cook, Thomas H. Geismar, Mies Hora (Chair), Donald T. Meeker, Paul Singer, and Lance Wyman. The committee included Kenneth F. Hine, President of Global Consultants, Inc., former CEO and Director General of the International Hotel & Restaurant Association, Paris, and former President and CEO of the American Hotel & Lodging Association (AHLA). Special thanks go to Douglas Viehland, former President of the AHLA Foundation, for his thoughtful support.

Project Design Team

Mies Hora, Project Coordinator/Designer
Chris O'Hara, Designer
Chisa Yagi, Design Assistant
Emily Flynn, Design Assistant

Public Services

X206**A**01
Women's Restroom

X206**A**02
Men's Restroom

X206**A**03
Restrooms

X206**A**04
Nursery

X206**A**05
Diaper Changing Table
Male

X206**A**06
Diaper Changing Table
Female

X206**A**07
Women's Restroom

X206**A**08
Men's Restroom

X206**A**09
Restrooms

X206**A**10
Nursery

X206**A**11
Diaper Changing Table
Male

X206**A**12
Diaper Changing Table
Female

X206**A**13
Strollers

X206**A**14
Elevator

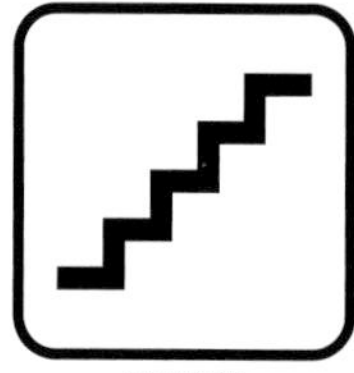
X206**A**15
Stairs

X206**A**16
Escalator

X206**A**17
Escalator Up

X206**A**18
Escalator Down

X206**A**19
Strollers

X206**A**20
Elevator

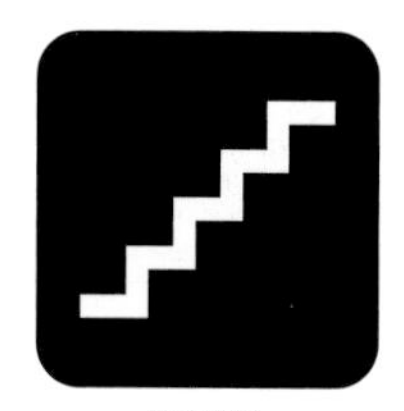
X206**A**21
Stairs

X206**A**22
Escalator

X206**A**23
Escalator Up

X206**A**24
Escalator Down

X206**A**25
Telephone

X206**A**26
Fax

X206**A**27
Mail

X206**A**28
Business Center
Fax Copies Deliveries

X206**A**29
Automatic Teller
Machine (ATM)

X206**A**30
Currency Exchange

X206**A**31
Telephone

X206**A**32
Fax

X206**A**33
Mail

X206**A**34
Business Center
Fax Copies Deliveries

X206**A**35
Automatic Teller
Machine (ATM)

X206**A**36
Currency Exchange

Note: All symbols and signs are available as fully editable vector image files: see page 238 or www.ultimatesymbol.com

Public
Services
continued

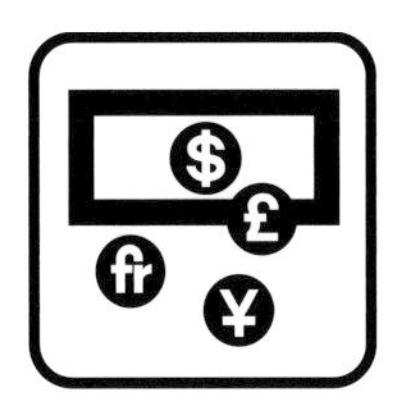
X206**B**01
Currency Exchange

X206**B**02
Lost and Found

X206**B**03
Baggage Lockers

X206**B**04
Room Safe
Safe Deposit Box

X206**B**05
Dry Cleaning

X206**B**06
Ice

X206**B**07
Currency Exchange

X206**B**08
Lost and Found

X206**B**09
Baggage Lockers

X206**B**10
Room Safe
Safe Deposit Box

X206**B**11
Dry Cleaning

X206**B**12
Ice

X206**B**13
Vending Machine

X206**B**14
Drinking Fountain

X206**B**15
Drinking Water

X206**B**16
Litter Disposal
Trash

X206**B**17
Laundry

X206**B**18
Kennel

X206**B**19
Vending Machine

X206**B**20
Drinking Fountain

X206**B**21
Drinking Water

X206**B**22
Litter Disposal
Trash

X206**B**23
Laundry

X206**B**24
Kennel

X206**B**25
Meeting Place

X206**B**26
Public Health

X206**B**27
Parking

X206**B**28
Taxi

X206**B**29
Bus

X206**B**30
Ground
Transportation

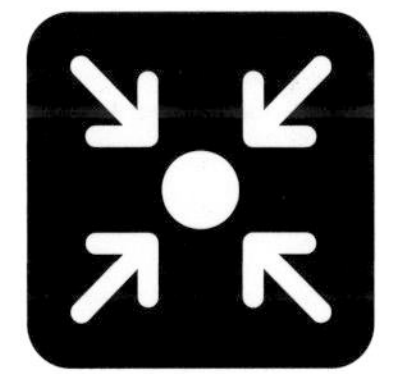
X206**B**31
Meeting Place

X206**B**32
Public Health

X206**B**33
Parking

X206**B**34
Taxi

X206**B**35
Bus

X206**B**36
Ground
Transportation

Public Services continued

X206**C**01
Courtesy Van
Shuttle

X206**C**02
Gas Station

X206**C**03
Mechanic
Maintenance

X206**C**04
Air Transportation
Airport

X206**C**05
Heliport

X206**C**06
Water Transportation
Ship(s), Pier(s)

X206**C**07
Courtesy Van
Shuttle

X206**C**08
Gas Station

X206**C**09
Mechanic
Maintenance

X206**C**10
Air Transportation
Airport

X206**C**11
Heliport

X206**C**12
Water Transportation
Ship(s), Pier(s)

X206**C**13
Rail Transportation
Train(s)

X206**C**14
Rail Transportation
Train(s)

Concessions

X206**C**15
Restaurant

X206**C**16
Coffee Shop
Tea Room

X206**C**17
Snack Bar

X206**C**18
Bar
Cocktails

X206**C**19
Barber Shop
Beauty Salon

X206**C**20
Shoe Shine

X206**C**21
Restaurant

X206**C**22
Coffee Shop
Tea Room

X206**C**23
Snack Bar

X206**C**24
Bar
Cocktails

X206**C**25
Barber Shop
Beauty Salon

X206**C**26
Shoe Shine

Concessions continued

X206**D**01 Florist

X206**D**02 Shops News & Gifts

X206**D**03 Movie Theater Cinema

X206**D**04 Play Theater

X206**D**05 Pharmacy Drug Store

X206**D**06 Car Rental Rent-a-Car

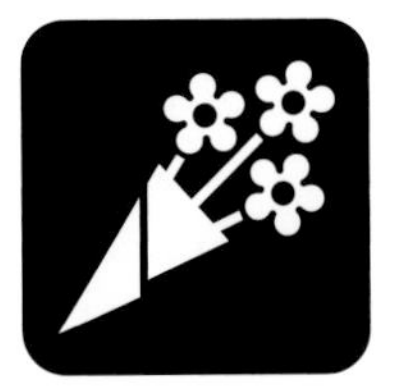
X206**D**07 Florist

X206**D**08 Shops News & Gifts

X206**D**09 Movie Theater Cinema

X206**D**10 Play Theater

X206**D**11 Pharmacy Drug Store

X206**D**12 Car Rental Rent-a-Car

Information

X206**D**13 Hotel

X206**D**14 Bedrooms Lodging / Accommodations

X206**D**15 Hotel Information

X206**D**16 Hotel Reservations

X206**D**17 Check-in Registration Front Desk

X206**D**18 Information

X206**D**19 Hotel

X206**D**20 Bedrooms Lodging / Accommodations

X206**D**21 Hotel Information

X206**D**22 Hotel Reservations

X206**D**23 Check-in Registration Front Desk

X206**D**24 Information

X206**D**25 Room Key Return

X206**D**26 Bellman Bell Woman

X206**D**27 Room Service

X206**D**28 House Keeping

X206**D**29 House Phone

X206**D**30 Tourist Information

X206**D**31 Room Key Return

X206**D**32 Bellman Bell Woman

X206**D**33 Room Service

X206**D**34 House Keeping

X206**D**35 House Phone

Information continued

X206**E**01
Electrical Outlet

X206**E**02
Light Switch

X206**E**03
Used Razor Blades

X206**E**04
Thermostat

X206**E**05
In-room Hair Dryer
Hi-Wattage Plug

X206**E**06
Baggage Claim
Check In

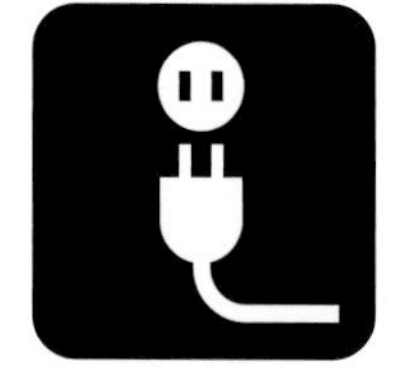
X206**E**07
Electrical Outlet

X206**E**08
Light Switch

X206**E**09
Used Razor Blades

X206**E**10
Thermostat

X206**E**11
In-room Hair Dryer
Hi-Wattage Plug

X206**E**12
Baggage Claim
Check In

X206**E**13
Ticket Purchase

X206**E**14
Conference Room
Meeting Room

X206**E**15
Modem Hookup
Email Access

X206**E**16
Ticket Purchase

X206**E**17
Conference Room
Meeting Room

X206**E**18
Modem Hookup
Email Access

Recreation

X206**E**19
TV Lounge

X206**E**20
Exercise Area
Gym

X206**E**21
Sauna, Steam, Spa

X206**E**22
Shower

X206**E**23
Swimming
Pool

X206**E**24
Snorkeling

X206**E**25
TV Lounge

X206**E**26
Exercise Area
Gym

X206**E**27
Sauna, Steam, Spa

X206**E**28
Shower

X206**E**29
Swimming
Pool

X206**E**30
Snorkeling

Recreation
continued

X206**F**01
Scuba Diving

X206**F**02
Canoeing

X206**F**03
Sail Boating

X206**F**04
Motor Boating

X206**F**05
Water Skiing

X206**F**06
Marina

X206**F**07
Scuba Diving

X206**F**08
Canoeing

X206**F**09
Sail Boating

X206**F**10
Motor Boating

X206**F**11
Water Skiing

X206**F**12
Marina

X206**F**13
Fishing

X206**F**14
Tennis

X206**F**15
Golf

X206**F**16
Hiking Trail

X206**F**17
Bicycle Trail

X206**F**18
Horse Trail

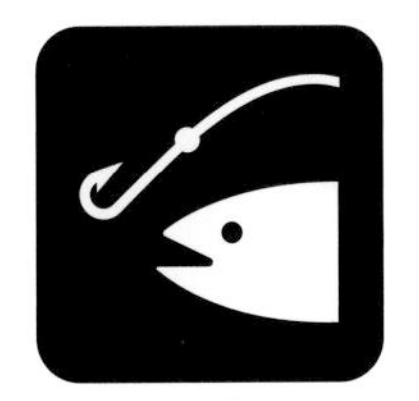
X206**F**19
Fishing

X206**F**20
Tennis

X206**F**21
Golf

X206**F**22
Hiking Trail

X206**F**23
Bicycle Trail

X206**F**24
Horse Trail

X206**F**25
Stable

X206**F**26
Hunting

X206**F**27
Skiing

X206**F**28
Ice Skating

X206**F**29
Snowmobiling

X206**F**30
Playground

X206**F**31
Stable

X206**F**32
Hunting

X206**F**33
Skiing

X206**F**34
Ice Skating

X206**F**35
Snowmobiling

X206**F**36
Playground

Recreation
continued

X206**G**01
Play Room
Day Care

X206**G**02
Game Room
Arcade

X206**G**03
Night Club
Dancing

X206**G**04
Casino
Gambling

X206**G**05
Very Important Person
Lounge

X206**G**06
Play Room
Day Care

X206**G**07
Game Room
Arcade

X206**G**08
Night Club
Dancing

X206**G**09
Casino
Gambling

X206**G**10
Very Important Person
Lounge

Accessibility
ADA

X206**G**11
Hearing Impaired
Access for Hearing Loss

X206**G**12
TDD
Text Telephone

X206**G**13
Telephone Volume
Control

X206**G**14
Accessibility

X206**G**15
Accessibility Ramp

X206**G**16
Accessibility Shower

X206**G**17
Hearing Impaired
Access for Hearing Loss

X206**G**18
TDD
Text Telephone

X206**G**19
Telephone Volume
Control

X206**G**20
Accessibility

X206**G**21
Accessibility Ramp

X206**G**22
Accessibility Shower

X206**G**23
Accessibility Telephone

X206**G**24
Accessibility Telephone

Safety

X206**H**01
First Aid Station

X206**H**02
First Aid Kit

X206**H**03
Stretcher

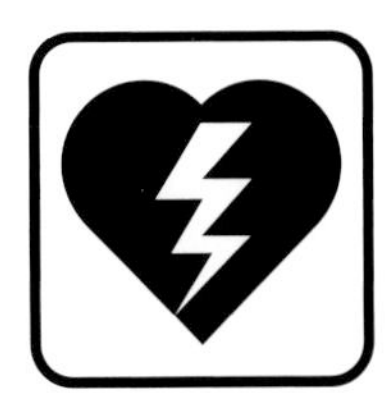
X206**H**04
Defibrillator

X206**H**05
Emergency Exit
Right

X206**H**06
Emergency Exit
Left

X206**H**07
First Aid Station

X206**H**08
First Aid Kit

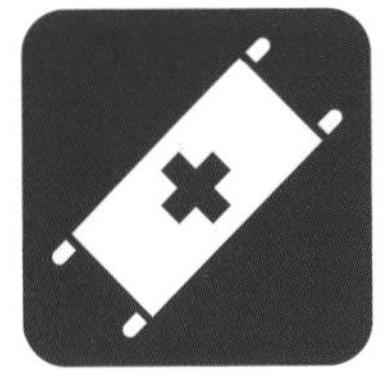
X206**H**09
Stretcher

X206**H**10
Defibrillator

X206**H**11
Emergency Exit
Right

X206**H**12
Emergency Exit
Left

X206**H**13
Break to Obtain
Access

X206**H**14
Life Preserver

X206**H**15
Emergency Flashlight

X206**H**16
Hospital

X206**H**17
Emergency Alarm
Fire Alarm

X206**H**18
Break to Obtain
Access

X206**H**19
Life Preserver

X206**H**20
Emergency Flashlight

X206**H**21
Emergency Alarm
Fire Alarm

Fire
Emergency

X206**H**22
Fire Extinguisher

X206**H**23
Fire Hose

X206**H**24
Emergency Ladder
Fire Escape

X206**H**25
Fire Ax

X206**H**26
Fire Phone

X206**H**27
In Case of Fire
Use Stair

X206**H**28
Fire Extinguisher

X206**H**29
Fire Hose

X206**H**30
Emergency Ladder
Fire Escape

X206**H**31
Fire Ax

X206**H**32
Fire Phone

X206**H**33
In Case of Fire
Use Stair

Warning

X206**J**01
Warning
Attention!

X206**J**02
High Voltage, Electrocution,
Shock or Burn

X206**J**03
Wet Paint

X206**J**04
Caution Slippery

X206**J**05
Watch Step Down

X206**J**06
Watch Step Up

X206**J**07
Difficult Swimming
Conditions; Use Caution

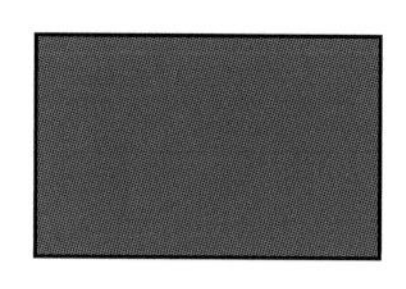
X206**J**08
Safety Beach Flag
Safe to Swim

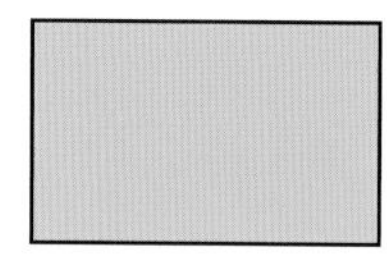
X206**J**09
Caution Beach Flag
Care Needed

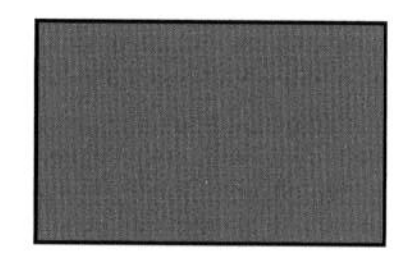
X206**J**10
Danger Beach Flag
Do Not Swim

Prohibition

X206**J**11
No Swimming

X206**J**12
No Diving

X206**J**13
No Fishing

X206**J**14
No Anchoring

X206**J**15
No Cell Phones

X206**J**16
No Glassware
No Breakables Allowed

X206**J**17
No Parking

X206**J**18
No Horn Blowing

X206**J**19
No Bicycling

X206**J**20
No Running

X206**J**21
No Skate Boarding

X206**J**22
No Bare Feet

X206**J**23
No Pets

X206**J**24
No Food Allowed

X206**J**25
No Smoking

X206**J**26
Open Fire Prohibited

X206**J**27
Out Of Order
Do Not Use

X206**J**28
No Entry
Occupied

Regulations

X206**J**29
Smoking
Smoking Area

X206**J**30
Quiet

X206**J**31
Pets on Leash

X206**J**32
No Entry
U.S. Roads Only

X206**J**33
Smoking
Smoking Area

X206**J**34
Quiet

X206**J**35
Pets on Leash

Telephone Symbols

X206**K**01
Front Desk

X206**K**02
Phone Messages

X206**K**03
Bellman
Bell Woman

X206**K**04
House Keeping

X206**K**05
Room Service

X206**K**06
Valet Laundry

X206**K**07
Front Desk

X206**K**08
Phone Messages

X206**K**09
Bellman
Bell Woman

X206**K**10
House Keeping

X206**K**11
Room Service

X206**K**12
Valet Laundry

X206**K**13
Wake-up Call

X206**K**14
Business Center
Fax Copies Deliveries

X206**K**15
Hotel Operator

X206**K**16
Long Distance Calls

X206**K**17
Local Calls

X206**K**18
Room to Room Calls
Guest Rooms

X206**K**19
Wake-up Call

X206**K**20
Business Center
Fax Copies Deliveries

X206**K**21
Hotel Operator

X206**K**22
Long Distance Calls

X206**K**23
Local Calls

X206**K**24
Room to Room Calls
Guest Rooms

X206**K**25
Barber Shop,
Beauty Salon, Hairdresser

X206**K**26
Exercise Area
Gym

X206**K**27
Shops
News & Gifts

X206**K**28
Barber Shop,
Beauty Salon, Hairdresser

X206**K**29
Exercise Area
Gym

X206**K**30
Shops
News & Gifts

Directional Arrows

X206**L**01 Arrow Down
X206**L**02 Arrow Left Down
X206**L**03 Arrow Right Down
X206**L**04 Arrow Left
X206**L**05 Arrow Right
X206**L**06 Arrow Right Up

X206**L**07 Arrow Down
X206**L**08 Arrow Left Down
X206**L**09 Arrow Right Down
X206**L**10 Arrow Left
X206**L**11 Arrow Right
X206**L**12 Arrow Right Up

X206**L**13 Arrow Up
X206**L**14 Arrow Left Up

X206**L**15 Arrow Up
X206**L**16 Arrow Left Up

Locator Numerals

X206**L**17 1
X206**L**18 2
X206**L**19 3
X206**L**20 4
X206**L**21 5
X206**L**22 6

X206**L**23 1
X206**L**24 2
X206**L**25 3
X206**L**26 4
X206**L**27 5
X206**L**28 6

Locator
Numerals
continued

Locator
Alphabet

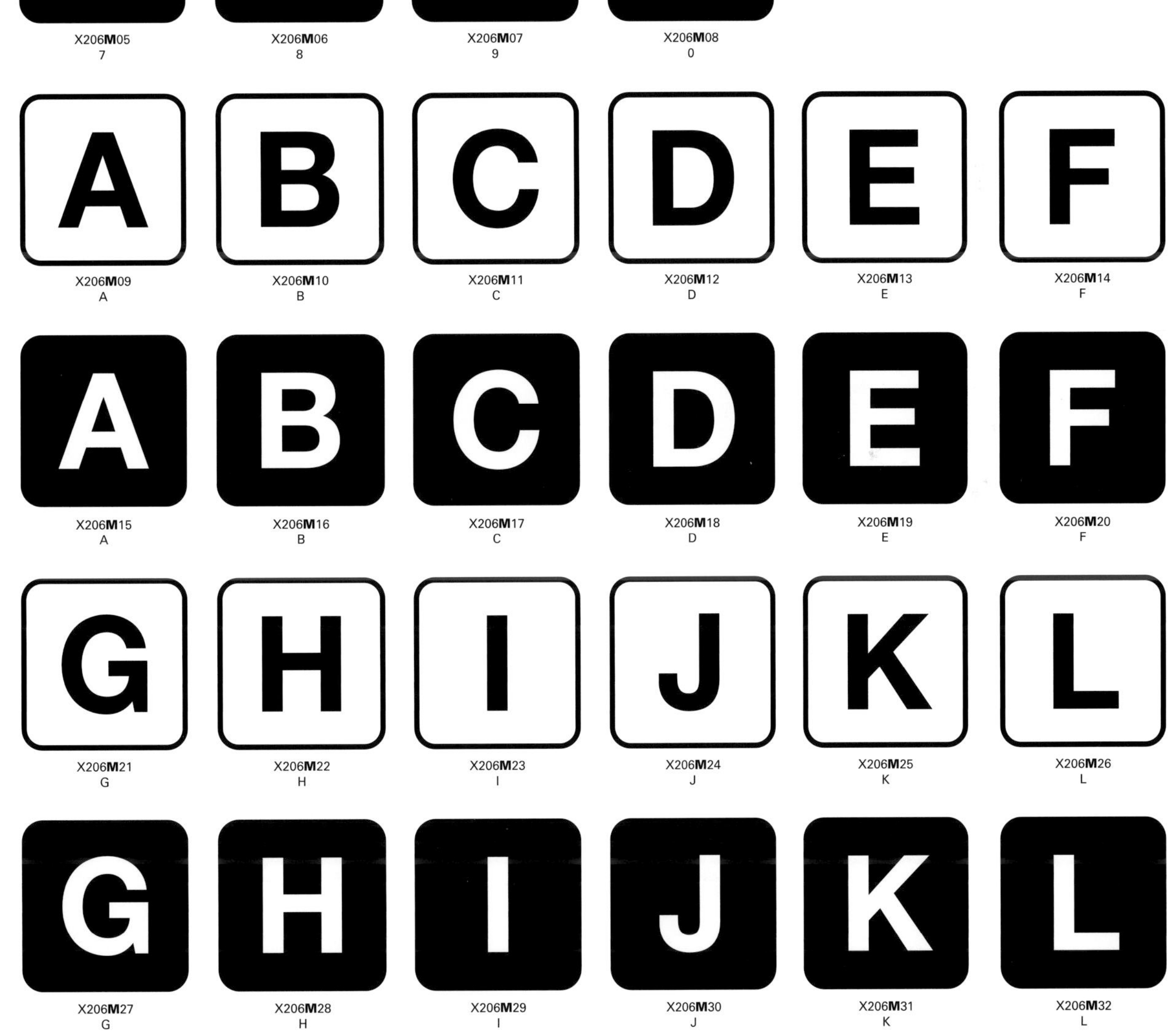

Locator
Alphabet
continued

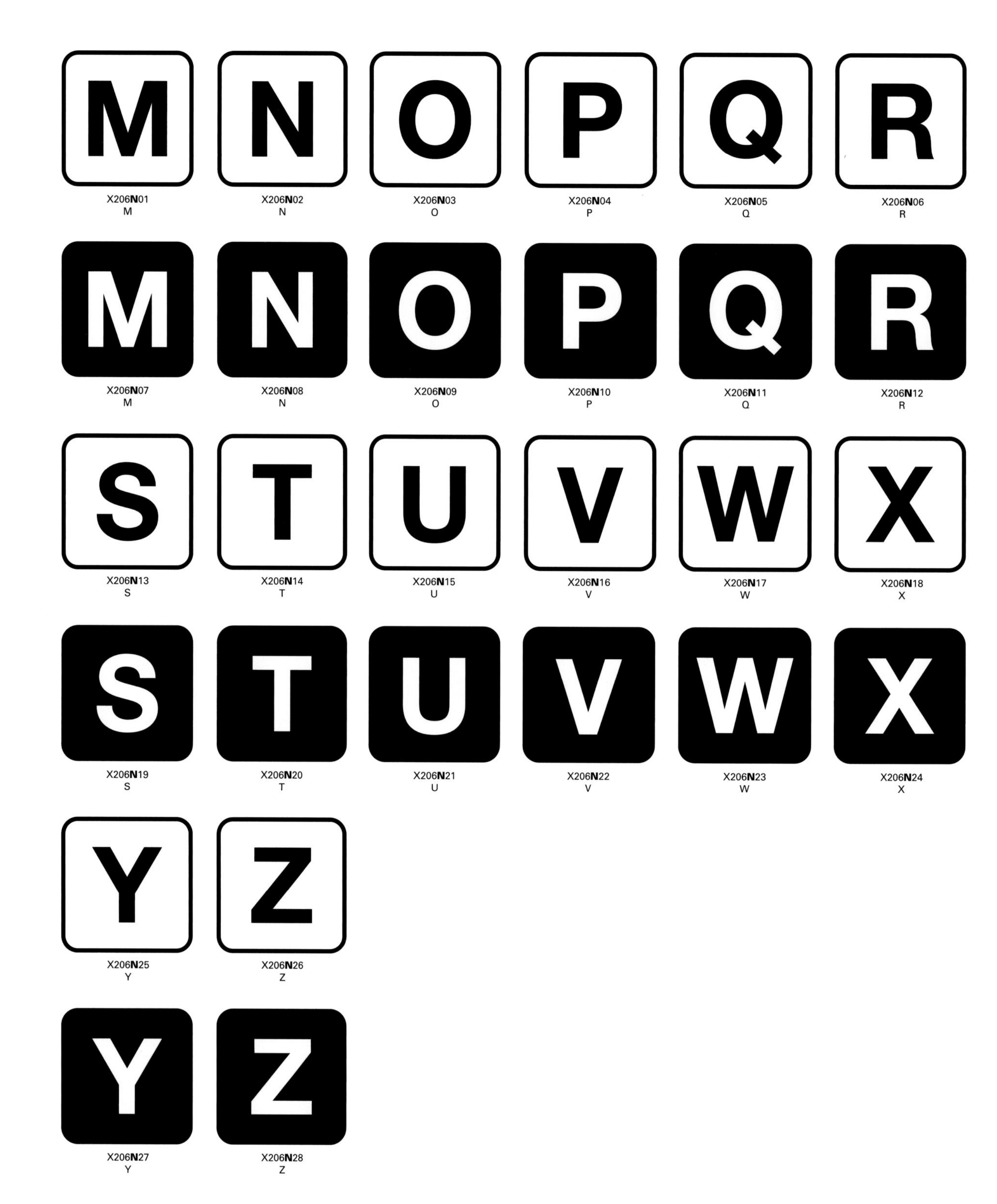

X206**N**01 M
X206**N**02 N
X206**N**03 O
X206**N**04 P
X206**N**05 Q
X206**N**06 R
X206**N**07 M
X206**N**08 N
X206**N**09 O
X206**N**10 P
X206**N**11 Q
X206**N**12 R
X206**N**13 S
X206**N**14 T
X206**N**15 U
X206**N**16 V
X206**N**17 W
X206**N**18 X
X206**N**19 S
X206**N**20 T
X206**N**21 U
X206**N**22 V
X206**N**23 W
X206**N**24 X
X206**N**25 Y
X206**N**26 Z
X206**N**27 Y
X206**N**28 Z

Safety Symbols Labeling (DOT / ANSI / ISO)

7

Overview

Like the development of most modern symbol and sign systems, safety symbol standardization is an evolutionary process that never ceases. Progress is driven by the review, revision, and publication at regular intervals of national and international guidelines or standards. Standardization strives to consolidate information about rapidly changing technologies and respond to the need for clearer communications in an era of marketplace globalization. In the realm of hazardous materials and workplace and product safety, that increasingly means the development of non-verbal, visual symbol systems that can easily be understood in multi-cultural/multi-lingual, emergency, and hazardous environments.

The materials collected, developed, and presented in this volume provide a clearly organized, comprehensive perspective on the current state of safety symbols, signs, and labels.

HazMat Labels

Hazardous materials labels alert handlers of the hazards associated with a package's contents. When accidents occur, labels aid in hazard and material identification for an appropriate response to the emergency. Fortunately, millions of packages containing hazardous materials are transported daily throughout the world and reach their destinations uneventfully. In addition to strict international shipping standards and the diligent care of shippers and carriers, the HazMat labels that are affixed to packages play a significant role in this success.

The framework that made this high level of safe transport possible, thereby protecting public safety, the environment, and property, are international standards, such as the United Nations (UN) recommendations for the transportation of dangerous goods, and national standards. In the United States, the U.S. Department of Transportation (DOT) developed the Hazardous Material Transportation Regulations (HMR) to promote the safe transportation of hazardous materials. (In international commerce, hazardous materials are referred to as dangerous goods.)

DOT labels are 100 mm X 100 mm square on point labels. Each DOT label corresponds to a DOT Hazard Class or Division Number (see page108). A label for the material's primary hazard displays the Hazard Class/ Division number on the bottom corner. Their design is federally regulated. DOT placards (not displayed in this book) are very similar to labels, but larger in size (273 mm x 273 mm). They are placed on bulk packages and transport vehicles.[1]

Safety Symbols, Signs and Labeling

Safety symbols, signs, and labels aid manufacturers and alert operators, consumers, and other exposed people in the general public to risks, instruct them on how to avoid hazards, inform of the consequence of interaction with the hazard, and convey the severity of the hazard. Also, since many accidents are the result of impulsive actions, a safety label/sign can remind people of open and obvious hazards that might otherwise have caused them injury.

American standards on equipment and products sold in the United States are produced by the American National Standards Institute. Built on the Z35 and Z53 standards published in the early 1970s, the new ANSI Z535 Series was approved in 1991, revised in 1998 and again as of July 1, 2002, and now includes five separate standards:

Z535.1 Safety Color Code
Z535.2 Environmental and Facility Safety Signs
Z535.3 Criteria for Safety symbols
Z535.4 Product Safety Signs and Labels
Z535.5 Safety Tags and Barricade Types (for Temporary Hazards)

For international standards, the primary general standard concerning safety signs is International Organization for Standarization's ISO 3864, which is under the responsibility of ISO Technical Committee 145 (TC 145). Though other product specific ANSI, ISO, and IEC standards exist (as well as several UL and NEMA standards), the principle standards to review for developing the vast majority of product safety labels continue to be ANSI Z535.4 and the ISO 3864-2 standard.

While these standards provide guidelines for symbol creation and use, interestingly, they are voluntary and not a legal requirement. In practice, however, the standards are essentially mandatory. From a legal point of view, product manufacturers have a legal "duty to warn" about hazards associated with the use or maintenance of their products. Part of this legal requirement is the duty to "meet or exceed" standards. The ANSI Z535 standards are held up in U.S. courts as the standards benchmark to "meet or exceed." [2]

A strong legal argument can be made that safety labels are more adequate if they contain well-drawn symbols because such safety labels have the ability to communicate hazard information quickly and serve to remind persons of hazards with which they are already familiar. Where word messages can be ignored, symbols stand out and are seen, distinct from the clutter of text information that we confront on a regular basis.

Often the standards themselves display only limited symbol examples or universally recognized "referents" or image content (the literal description of the elements of the sign/symbol)[3] along with general design issues and suggestions. Concerning a specific symbol, it is best to use a symbol that has acceptance in a standard when the symbol is appropriate to the hazard information being conveyed. Generally, there is license to find and use a different symbol or to create a new symbol when a particular symbol does not clearly match the hazard.

Harmonization

One problem that has arisen is that the international (ISO) and American (ANSI) standards are not always consistent. The bringing together of various standards requirements so that a given set of symbols or standards are unified is called "harmonization". The technical review committees that revise the standards are working continuously to harmonize specifications so that there are fewer export/import problems for manufacturers in the global marketplace, as well as to encourage broader comprehension of a "universal" set of images/messages worldwide for the general public. Although optional, the ISO standards have the advantage of recognizing that symbols alone have the ability to communicate across language barriers, whereas the American standards still specify the use of symbols and worded messages for safety signs.

ISO 3864 safety symbols come in three categories:
1. Warning: Yellow warning triangle with black graphical symbol surrounded by a black band.
2. Prohibition: Red circle with 45 degree angled slash on black graphical symbol, indicating a prohibited action to avoid the hazard.
3. Mandatory Action: Blue solid circle with white (reverse) graphical symbol, indicating an action to take to avoid a hazard.

ANSI Z535.3 adds an additional category:
4: Information: Black symbol on a white field in a square or rectangular background, for general safety or fire safety information and equipment.

In the U.S., either an ISO formatted symbol or a non-ISO formatted symbol (i.e., a black symbol that does not appear in a color international surround shape) may be used in a safety sign along with the appropriate verbal message. In some cases using multiple symbols is advised to communicate both the hazard description and the hazard avoidance information.[4]

Signal Word (Hazard Severity) Panels
A signal word panel (the orange panel in the example above) is comprised of a signal word, the corresponding background color, and in cases of personal injury hazard, the general warning sign. *Signal word* is defined as the word or words that call attention to the safety sign and designate a degree or level of hazard.[4] Signal word panels in several languages can be found on page 117.

The signal words for product safety signs are:
1. DANGER: Indicates an imminently hazardous situation which, if not avoided, will result in death or serious injury. This signal word is to be limited to the most extreme situations. Panel color: Safety Red.
2. WARNING: Indicates a potentially hazardous situation which, if not avoided, could result in death or serious injury. Panel color: Safety Orange.
3. CAUTION: Indicates a potentially hazardous situation which, if not avoided, may result in minor or moderate injury. It may also be used to alert against unsafe practices. Panel color: Safety Yellow.[4]

The safety alert symbol is the triangle with an exclamation mark that is used next to the signal word. In the vocabulary of ANSI Z535 signage, this symbol indicates that a possible personal (human) injury hazard exists. The ISO 3864-2 standard refers to this as the "general warning sign". This yellow safety alert symbol is the general warning sign W001 specified in ISO 7010.[5] The process of harmonization between the ISO and ANSI standards continues, and the use of the ISO yellow safety alert symbol on most signal word panels has already begun to replace other, older options.

Safety Symbol and Sign Colors
Colors used in safety symbols and signs are specified in the standards, the most current being *ANSI Z535.1-2002: Safety Color Code.* Color coding is used to convey and reinforce different safety messages. To simplify the specification of safety signs, the nearest PMS (Pantone®) colors have been assigned to the safety colors:

Color	PMS	Meaning
Safety Red	485 C	Danger Prohibition Stop
Safety Orange	152 C	Warning
Safety Yellow	109 C	Caution
Safety Blue	287 C	Mandatory Action
Safety Green	3415 C	Safe Condition
Safety Purple	253 C	Regulation
Safety Brown	168 C	Regulation
Safety Grey	430 C	Regulation
Safety Black	Process Black	Regulation
Safety White	White	Regulation

Developing a Comprehensive Safety Symbol System
There were many hurdles to compiling an up-to-date collection of the often requested safety symbols for *Official Signs & Icons 2.0*. Following the usual procedure used throughout this book of collecting and reviewing available symbols, it became obvious that there is not yet an "official" system of safety symbols in wide use that meets the diverse needs of the marketplace.

As has been mentioned, while encouraged, the ANSI and ISO symbol standards do not require the use of the basic, but crudely drawn symbol examples that are provided. What is agreed is that the image content is more important than the formalities of the artwork. While the existing standards provide voluntary graphic guidelines, they also make clear that it is advisable to utilize or develop safety symbols that are designed, wherever possible, as elements of a consistent visual system.

Indeed, careful research of old as well as recent foreign and American symbols revealed that there are many different visual approaches in use today to communicate hazards. Development of the most up-to-date and comprehensive symbol systems in use is largely being undertaken by commercial sign-making firms for obvious reasons, although with varying degrees of success.

There have been some important, if limited, advances in safety symbol development. In 1995, Van Nostrand Reinhold published *Safety Symbol Art* by Nora Olgyay.[3] In it, she analyzed contemporary ANSI and ISO standards and developed a set of 40 symbols which were then comprehension tested and refined. The resulting symbol system, while borne of good intentions and nicely realized, has been hampered by being too general for use in the many specific situations encountered in the marketplace, as well as by a lack of effective distribution and promotion. More than a decade later, the Olgyay symbols are not widely utilized or seen on most commercially manufactured safety signs and labels. Although she refers in her book to "SEGD Safety Symbol Art", the SEGD does not acknowledge any official affiliation with her, nor does it offer her safety symbol art to its membership through its network of resources.

The ambitious goal of the compilation presented in this book is to provide a baseline set of image content messages that will communicate a broad selection of hazard messages, while conforming to the latest internationally recognized safety standards. The intent is to make available a visually consistent, harmonized system of symbols that can be used on labels and signs both in the United States and abroad.

After choosing the image content, symbols from both international and American sources were carefully organized into a logical system. Many symbols were then graphically refined to conform with the well-established design style of the AIGA/DOT Transportation Symbol Signs System (page 69) and the NPS Recreational Symbols (page 51). Symbol design lessons learned and advances made as a result of Olgyay's symbol comprehension testing were taken into account and used where applicable. Certain widely accepted symbols were left intact because through long and continuous use, they are already highly recognizable *de facto* standards.

In order to provide this new collection of safety symbols, which was derived from disparate sources, with a unifying graphic consistency as is suggested in ANSI Z535.3, a "middle-of-the-road" graphic approach was developed. Symbols with weak proportions, over-abundant detail, or that were poorly rendered were simplified and tuned up. Dated and illustrative aspects were brought up to date using a modern visual vernacular.

However, rather than force image content messages into an extreme, overly simplified, or abstract style to achieve a uniformity of design, symbol elements were either retained if visually successful, refined if not, or completely reconceived if the message warranted it.

For example, the mandatory action personal protective equipment symbols on pages 113-114 were completely reconceptualized and designed for maximum comprehension. In particular, for headgear, a 3/4 view of a human head was developed to enhance recognition factors and clearly communicate the many types of equipment in use, whereas the conventional frontal view and the "profile head" mentioned in the standard are not well-suited to convey the complexity of the multiple image content messages of the protective head gear without compromising individuation (there are 14 variations).

The "Dust Respirator" symbol (above left) is from an old ISO set. While fairly clear, it is dated, poorly rendered and very illustrative in design. Nora Olgyay's reductive design from 1995 (center) is simpler and more graphic, but suffers from being unnecessarily abstract. The symbol (right) developed for the new system in this book (page 113) displays a dimensionality that is easily comprehended, illustrative, yet symbolic and contemporary in design. Another set of examples with similar characteristics is shown below: ANSI (left), Olgyay (center) and Hora (right). What hinders the two versions of "Eye Wash" on the left is the assumption of an

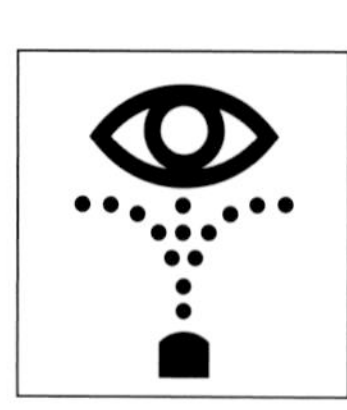

accompanying worded message panel to provide clarity for what might otherwise be mistaken as some type of drinking fountain, unlike the design on the right, which is an update of a concept by the late Paul Aurthur. Yet ISO-formatted safety signs do not require words and indeed are designed to function completely non-verbally due to the language barriers encountered among nations outside the U.S. Furthermore, language based safety issues are becoming more prevalent as immigrants and foreign-nationals continue to join the American workforce in large numbers and to consume our products and services locally.

The complete system presented in this volume is comprised of 50 hazard warnings, 35 mandatory actions, 41 prohibitions, and 41 general safety symbols including referential objects. Hazard warning symbols are presented in the ISO-formatted yellow triangle with black band, in the ANSI format of black symbol on a white rectangular field, as well as without a surround shape for use as needed. Mandatory actions are also provided both in the ISO-formatted solid blue circle and as optional black positive symbols for use in other applications. Like the SEGD recreational prohibition symbols in Chapter 3, the approach taken with safety prohibitions places the symbol slash under the symbol, not over the symbol as is commonly done for simple symbols such as "No Smoking". This format is based on research done by Robert Dewer, a human factors engineer at the University of Calgary, that showed much greater understanding if a complex symbol is not broken apart by the large slash.

It is important to recognize that the symbols displayed here, while state of the art for 2005, will inevitably be superseded over time as the international standards continue to evolve and new safety requirements and equipment emerge on the world scene.

Credits

In preparing this new safety symbol system, I would like to acknowledge the symbol development history and work of Donald Meeker, Lance Wyman, and Roger Cook, whose influence on my process cannot be underestimated. I credit Christopher O'Hara, whose deep knowledge of sign systems, advanced illustration skills, and smart design sense made it feasible to shape an amorphous mass of data into an intelligent symbol system. Thanks also belong to my design interns, Meng-Yen Pan and Elizabeth Sweeney.

WHMIS Symbols

The Workplace Hazardous Materials Information System (WHMIS) is Canada's hazard communication standard. The key elements of the system are cautionary labelling of containers of WHMIS "controlled products", the provision of material safety data sheets (MSDSs), and worker education programs. The Controlled Products Regulations (CPR) establish a national standard for the classification of hazardous workplace materials. In addition to setting out criteria for biohazards, chemical and acute hazards, the regulations specify criteria for chronic health hazards including mutagenicity, carcinogenicity, embryo and reproductive toxicity, respiratory tract and skin sensitization.[6] The WHMIS symbols are on page 118.

Mr. Yuck Symbol

Developed to alert children of dangerous or toxic materials in homes, the green, animated "Mr. Yuck" symbol has been in existence for decades. It has proven to be more easily understood and responded to by children than the standard "skull and bones" symbols. Its original provenance is unknown, but various variations of it can be found on a number of poison awareness related sites.

Target Organs and Systems

The fourteen images on page 118 were developed to bring attention to specific organs or aspects of body systems that might be targeted by a particular hazard or remedy.

Freight Container Packaging Imprints

Ubiquitous, these imprints come in many graphic styles and formats. There does not appear to be a complete "official" set beyond what individual companies develop for their own use. A sample selection of some the most commonly seen symbols can be found starting on page 119.

About ANSI

Founded in 1918, the American National Standards Institute (ANSI) is a private, non-profit organization that administers and coordinates the U.S. voluntary standardization and conformity assessment system. The Institute's mission is to enhance both the global competitiveness of U.S. business and the U.S. quality of life by promoting and facilitating voluntary consensus standards and conformity assessment systems, and safeguarding their integrity. www.ansi.org

About ISO

International Organization for Standardization (ISO) is a network of the national standards institutes of 150 countries, on the basis of one member per country, with a Central Secretariat in Geneva, Switzerland, that coordinates the system. Developing technical consensus on this international scale is a major operation. In all, there are some 3,000 ISO technical groups (technical committees, subcommittees, working groups, etc.) in which some 50,000 experts participate annually to develop ISO standards.

ISO develops only those standards for which there is a market requirement. The work is carried out by experts on loan from the industrial, technical, and business sectors that have asked for the standards, and that subsequently put them to use. These experts may be joined by others with relevant knowledge, such as representatives of government agencies, consumer organizations, academia, and testing laboratories. www.iso.org

Hazardous Materials (HazMat) D.O.T. Labeling

- Class 1: Explosives
- Class 2: Gases
- Class 3: Flammable Liquids
- Class 4: Flammable Solids
- Class 5: Oxidizing Substances & Organic Peroxide
- Class 6: Toxic & Infectious Substances
- Class 7: Radioactive Materials
- Class 8: Corrosives
- Class 9: Misc. Dangerous Goods

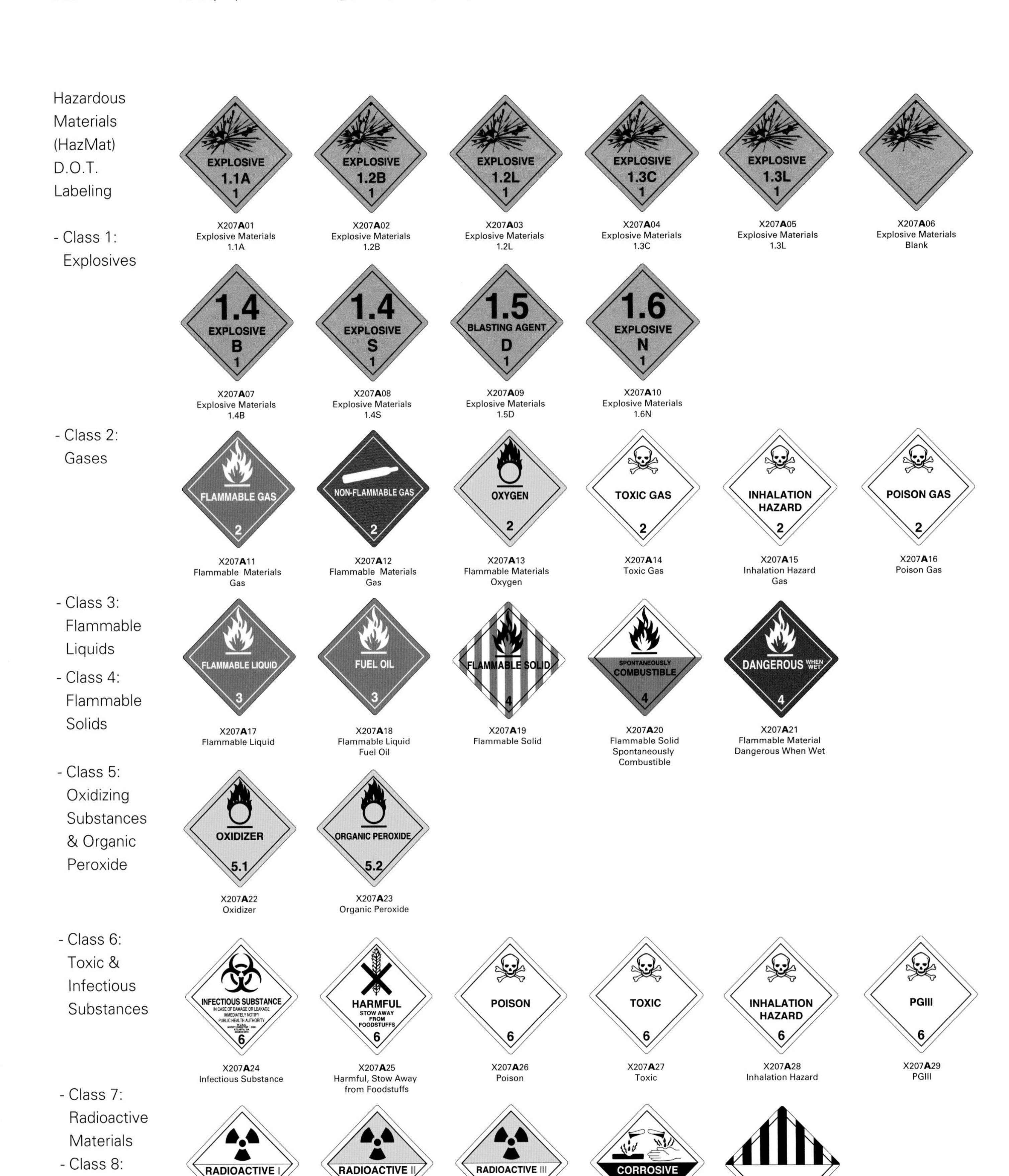

X207**A**01 Explosive Materials 1.1A

X207**A**02 Explosive Materials 1.2B

X207**A**03 Explosive Materials 1.2L

X207**A**04 Explosive Materials 1.3C

X207**A**05 Explosive Materials 1.3L

X207**A**06 Explosive Materials Blank

X207**A**07 Explosive Materials 1.4B

X207**A**08 Explosive Materials 1.4S

X207**A**09 Explosive Materials 1.5D

X207**A**10 Explosive Materials 1.6N

X207**A**11 Flammable Materials Gas

X207**A**12 Flammable Materials Gas

X207**A**13 Flammable Materials Oxygen

X207**A**14 Toxic Gas

X207**A**15 Inhalation Hazard Gas

X207**A**16 Poison Gas

X207**A**17 Flammable Liquid

X207**A**18 Flammable Liquid Fuel Oil

X207**A**19 Flammable Solid

X207**A**20 Flammable Solid Spontaneously Combustible

X207**A**21 Flammable Material Dangerous When Wet

X207**A**22 Oxidizer

X207**A**23 Organic Peroxide

X207**A**24 Infectious Substance

X207**A**25 Harmful, Stow Away from Foodstuffs

X207**A**26 Poison

X207**A**27 Toxic

X207**A**28 Inhalation Hazard

X207**A**29 PGIII

X207**A**30 Radioactive I

X207**A**31 Radioactive II

X207**A**32 Radioactive III

X207**A**33 Class 8 Corrosive Materials

X207**A**34 Class 9 Misc. Dangerous Goods

General Hazards

X207**B**01
General Danger

X207**B**02
General Danger

X207**B**03
General Danger

X207**B**04
Non-Ionizing Radiation
Radio Frequency Energy

X207**B**05
Non-Ionizing Radiation
Radio Frequency Energy

X207**B**06
Non-Ionizing Radiation
Radio Frequency Energy

X207**B**07
Voltage, Arc Flash, Shock
(see ISO alternate pg. 112)

X207**B**08
Voltage, Arc Flash, Shock
(see ISO alternate pg. 112)

X207**B**09
Voltage, Arc Flash, Shock
(see ISO alternate pg. 112)

X207**B**10
Laser
LED Radiation

X207**B**11
Laser
LED Radiation

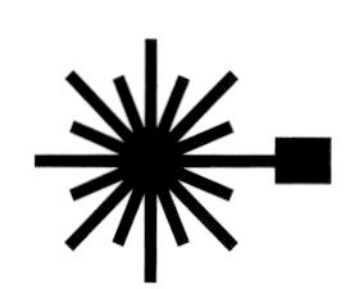
X207**B**12
Laser
LED Radiation

X207**B**13
Electrostatic Sensitive
Device

X207**B**14
Electrostatic Sensitive
Device

X207**B**15
Electrostatic Sensitive
Device

X207**B**16
Fire, Flammable
(see ISO alternate pg. 112)

X207**B**17
Fire, Flammable
(see ISO alternate pg. 112)

X207**B**18
Fire, Flammable
(see ISO alternate pg. 112)

X207**B**19
Biohazard

X207**B**20
Biohazard

X207**B**21
Biohazard

X207**B**22
Oxidizer
(see ISO alternate pg. 112)

X207**B**23
Oxidizer
(see ISO alternate pg. 112)

X207**B**24
Oxidizer
(see ISO alternate pg. 112)

X207**B**25
Poison
Infectious, Lethal

X207**B**26
Poison
Infectious, Lethal

X207**B**27
Poison
Infectious, Lethal

X207**B**28
Freezing Hazard
Frostbite

X207**B**29
Freezing Hazard
Frostbite

X207**B**30
Freezing Hazard
Frostbite

X207**B**31
Cancer Causing
Carcinogenic

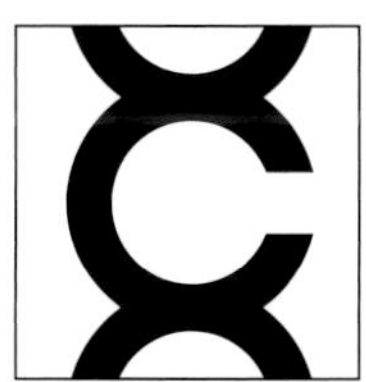
X207**B**32
Cancer Causing
Carcinogenic

X207**B**33
Cancer Causing
Carcinogenic

X207**B**34
Burn Hazard
Hot Surface

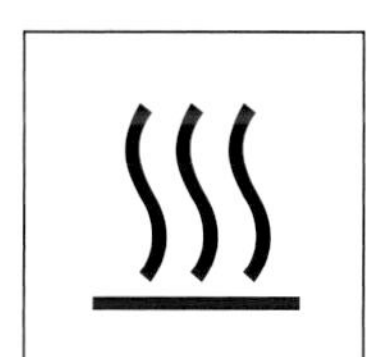
X207**B**35
Burn Hazard
Hot Surface

X207**B**36
Burn Hazard
Hot Surface

X207**B**37
Radiation
X-Rays

X207**B**38
Radiation
X-Rays

X207**B**39
Radiation
X-Rays

X207**B**40
Burn Hazard
Hot Stock, Steam or Liquid

X207**B**41
Burn Hazard
Hot Stock, Steam or Liquid

X207**B**42
Burn Hazard
Hot Stock, Steam or Liquid

General
Hazards
continued

X207**C**01
Explosive Materials

X207**C**02
Explosive Materials

X207**C**03
Explosive Materials

X207**C**04
Trip

X207**C**05
Trip

X207**C**06
Trip

X207**C**07
Explosion
Arc Flash

X207**C**08
Explosion
Arc Flash

X207**C**09
Explosion
Arc Flash

X207**C**10
Slip

X207**C**11
Slip

X207**C**12
Slip

X207**C**13
UV Light

X207**C**14
UV Light

X207**C**15
UV Light

X207**C**16
Fall

X207**C**17
Fall

X207**C**18
Fall

X207**C**19
Bright Light
Avoid Exposure

X207**C**20
Bright Light
Avoid Exposure

X207**C**21
Bright Light
Avoid Exposure

X207**C**22
Low Object; Head Hazard

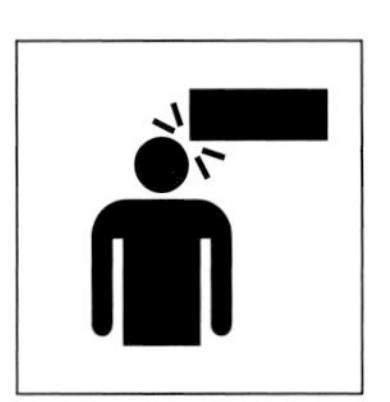
X207**C**23
Low Object; Head Hazard

X207**C**24
Low Object; Head Hazard

X207**C**25
Strong Magnetic Field

X207**C**26
Strong Magnetic Field

X207**C**27
Strong Magnetic Field

X207**C**28
Lift Hazard
Heavy Object

X207**C**29
Lift Hazard
Heavy Object

X207**C**30
Lift Hazard
Heavy Object

X207**C**31
Automatic Start-up

X207**C**32
Automatic Start-up

X207**C**33
Automatic Start-up

X207**C**34
Tip Over Hazard

X207**C**35
Tip Over Hazard

X207**C**36
Tip Over Hazard

X207**C**37
Forklift

X207**C**38
Forklift

X207**C**39
Forklift

X207**C**40
Body Crush
Force From Above

X207**C**41
Body Crush
Force From Above

X207**C**42
Body Crush
Force From Above

General Hazards continued

X207**D**01
Crush / Impact Hazard
Foot

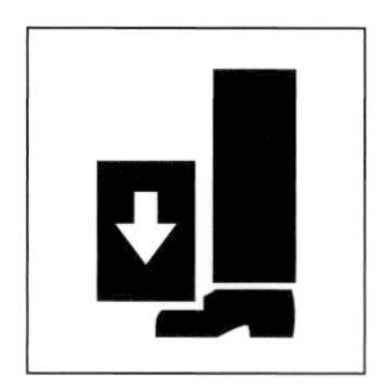
X207**D**02
Crush / Impact Hazard
Foot

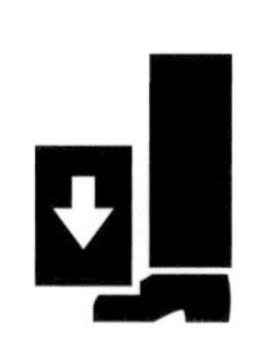
X207**D**03
Crush / Impact Hazard
Foot

X207**D**04
Pinch / Entanglement
Gear / Chain Drive

X207**D**05
Pinch / Entanglement
Gear / Chain Drive

X207**D**06
Pinch / Entanglement
Gear / Chain Drive

X207**D**07
Crush / Impact
Moving Parts Can
Crush & Cut

X207**D**08
Crush / Impact
Moving Parts Can Crush & Cut

X207**D**09
Crush / Impact
Moving Parts Can
Crush & Cut

X207**D**10
Cut / Sever
Rotating Blade / Saw

X207**D**11
Cut / Sever
Rotating Blade / Saw

X207**D**12
Cut / Sever
Rotating Blade / Saw

X207**D**13
Cut / Sever / Shear
Sharp Blade

X207**D**14
Cut / Sever / Shear
Sharp Blade

X207**D**15
Cut / Sever / Shear
Sharp Blade

X207**D**16
Cut / Sever
Rotating Blade / Screw

X207**D**17
Cut / Sever
Rotating Blade / Screw

X207**D**18
Cut / Sever
Rotating Blade / Screw

X207**D**19
Cut / Puncture
Sharp Blade / Point

X207**D**20
Cut / Puncture
Sharp Blade / Point

X207**D**21
Cut / Puncture
Sharp Blade / Point

X207**D**22
Hot Surface
Burn Hazard

X207**D**23
Hot Surface
Burn Hazard

X207**D**24
Hot Surface
Burn Hazard

X207**D**25
Pinch Rollers

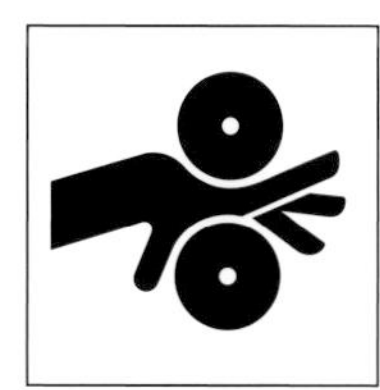
X207**D**26
Pinch Rollers

X207**D**27
Pinch Rollers

X207**D**28
Skin Puncture
Pressurized Air / Water Jet

X207**D**29
Skin Puncture
Pressurized Air / Water Jet

X207**D**30
Skin Puncture
Pressurized Air / Water Jet

X207**D**31
Pinch / Entanglement / Crush
Gears

X207**D**32
Pinch / Entanglement / Crush
Gears

X207**D**33
Pinch / Entanglement / Crush
Gears

X207**D**34
Corrosive

X207**D**35
Corrosive

X207**D**36
Corrosive

X207**D**37
Pinch / Entanglement Roller
Belt Drive / Shear Point

X207**D**38
Pinch / Entanglement Roller
Belt Drive / Shear Point

X207**D**39
Pinch / Entanglement Roller
Belt Drive / Shear Point

X207**D**40
Corrosive

X207**D**41
Corrosive

X207**D**42
Corrosive

General Hazards continued

X207**E**01
Corrosive H_20_5

X207**E**02
Corrosive H_20_5

X207**E**03
Corrosive H_20_5

X207**E**04
Voltage, Body Shock, Electrocution
Electric Shock or Burn

X207**E**05
Voltage, Body Shock, Electrocution
Electric Shock or Burn

X207**E**06
Voltage, Body Shock, Electrocution
Electric Shock or Burn

X207**E**07
Ingestion Hazard
Hazardous Liquid

X207**E**08
Ingestion Hazard
Hazardous Liquid

X207**E**09
Ingestion Hazard
Hazardous Liquid

X207**E**10
Voltage Hazard, Electrocution
Electric Shock or Burn

X207**E**11
Voltage Hazard, Electrocution
Electric Shock or Burn

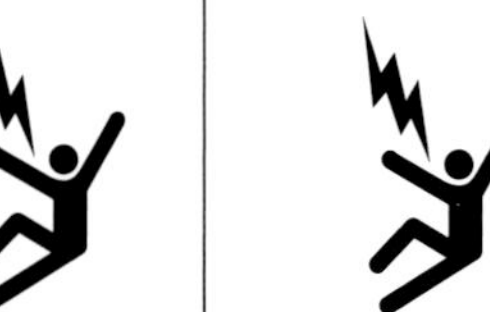
X207**E**12
Voltage Hazard, Electrocution
Electric Shock or Burn

X207**E**13
Inhalation Hazard
Hazardous Gas in Area

X207**E**14
Inhalation Hazard
Hazardous Gas in Area

X207**E**15
Inhalation Hazard
Hazardous Gas in Area

X207**E**16
Voltage Hazard
Shock in the Box

X207**E**17
Voltage Hazard
Shock in the Box

X207**E**18
Voltage Hazard
Shock in the Box

X207**E**19
Voltage, Hand Shock, Electrocution
Electric Shock or Burn

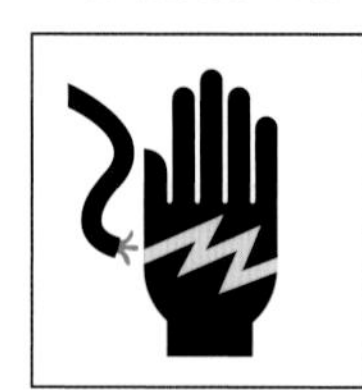
X207**E**20
Voltage, Hand Shock, Electrocution
Electric Shock or Burn

X207**E**21
Voltage, Hand Shock, Electrocution
Electric Shock or Burn

X207**E**22
Voltage Hazard
Electric Meter Shock

X207**E**23
Voltage Hazard
Electric Meter Shock

X207**E**24
Voltage Hazard
Electric Meter Shock

Addendum: Original ISO Versions

X207**E**25
Voltage Hazard, Electrocution
Electric Shock or Burn
(see alternate pg. 109)

X207**B**26
Poison
Infectious, Lethal
(see alternate pg. 109)

X207**E**27
Fire, Flammable
(see alternate pg. 109)

X207**E**28
Oxidizer
(see alternate pg. 109)

X207**B**29
Explosive Materials
(see alternate pg. 110)

Note: All symbols and signs are available as fully editable vector image files: see page 238 or www.ultimatesymbol.com

Mandatory Actions

Personal Protective Equipment

X207**F**01
Wear Safety Glasses

X207**F**02
Safety Glasses

X207**F**03
Safety Glasses

X207**F**04
Wear Hearing Protection

X207**F**05
Hearing Protection

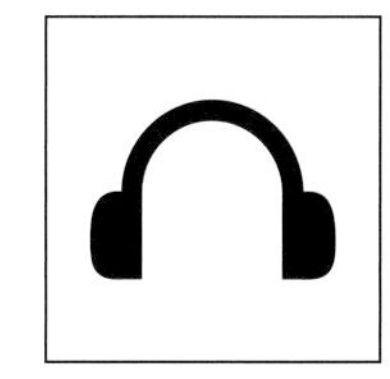
X207**F**06
Hearing Protection

X207**F**07
Wear Safety Goggles

X207**F**08
Safety Goggles

X207**F**09
Safety Goggles

X207**F**10
Wear Head Protection
Hard Hat / Helmet

X207**F**11
Head Protection
Hard Hat / Helmet

X207**F**12
Head Protection
Hard Hat / Helmet

X207**F**13
Wear Full-Face Shield

X207**F**14
Full-Face Shield

X207**F**15
Full-Face Shield

X207**F**16
Wear Eye & Ear Protection

X207**F**17
Eye & Ear Protection

X207**F**18
Wear Dust Respirator

X207**F**19
Dust Respirator

X207**F**20
Dust Respirator

X207**F**21
Wear Head & Eye Protection
Hard Hat & Goggles

X207**F**22
Head & Eye Protection,
Hard Hat & Goggles

X207**F**23
Wear Vapor Respirator

X207**F**24
Vapor Respirator

X207**F**25
Vapor Respirator

X207**F**26
Wear Head & Ear
Protection

X207**F**27
Wear Head & Ear
Protection

X207**F**28
Wear Full-Face Respirator

X207**F**29
Full-Face Respirator

X207**F**30
Full-Face Respirator

X207**F**31
Wear Eye, Ear &
Head Protection

X207**F**32
Eye, Ear &
Head Protection

X207**F**33
Wear Air Line Respirator

X207**F**34
Air Line Respirator

X207**F**35
Air Line Respirator

X207**F**36
Wear Full-Face Respirator
& Head Protection

X207**F**37
Full-Face Respirator
& Head Protection

Mandatory
Actions
continued

X207**G**01
Wear Foot Protection
Construction Boot (Steel Toe)

X207**G**02
Foot Protection
Construction Boot (Steel Toe)

X207**G**03
Wear Body Harness

X207**G**04
Body Harness

X207**G**05
Switch Off Before
Beginning Work

X207**G**06
Switch Off Before
Beginning Work

X207**G**07
Wear Foot Protection
Chemical Boots

X207**G**08
Foot Protection
Chemical Boots

X207**G**09
Two Person Lift
Heavy Object

X207**G**10
Two Person Lift
Heavy Object

X207**G**11
Unplug Before Opening

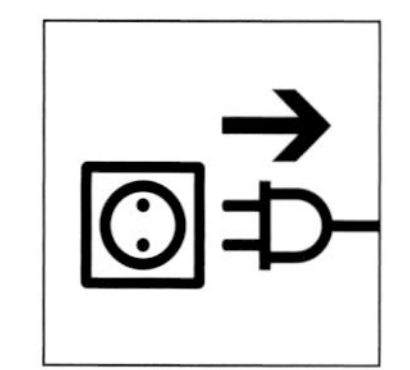
X207**G**12
Unplug Before Opening

X207**G**13
Wear Hand Protection
Safety Gloves

X207**G**14
Hand Protection
Safety Gloves

X207**G**15
Consult Service Manual

X207**G**16
Consult Service Manual

X207**G**17
Insert Safety Lock Before
Getting In Hazardous Area

X207**G**18
Insert Safety Lock Before
Getting In Hazardous Area

X207**G**19
Wear Hand Protection
Chemical Gloves

X207**G**20
Hand Protection
Chemical Gloves

X207**G**21
Consult Operator's Manual

X207**G**22
Consult Operator's Manual

X207**G**23
Lock Out
Electrical Power

X207**G**24
Lock Out
Electrical Power

X207**G**25
Wear Body Protection
Apron

X207**G**26
Body Protection
Apron

X207**G**27
Forklift Point
(Right)

X207**G**28
Forklift Point
(Right)

X207**G**29
Lock Out in
De-Energized State

X207**G**30
Lock Out in
De-Energized State

X207**G**31
Wear Body Suit

X207**G**32
Body Suit

X207**G**33
Forklift Point
(Left)

X207**G**34
Forklift Point
(Left)

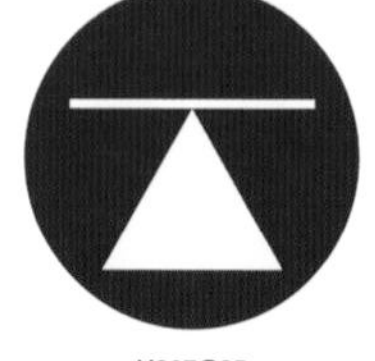
X207**G**35
Center of Gravity

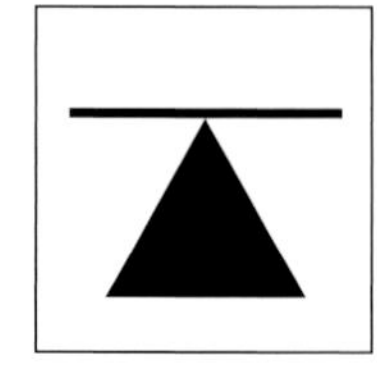
X207**G**36
Center of Gravity

X207**G**37
Wear Full Body Suit

X207**G**38
Full Body Suit

X207**G**39
Lift Point

X207**G**40
Lift Point

X207**G**41
General Mandatory
Action

X207**G**42
General Mandatory
Action

Prohibited Actions

X207**H**01
Do Not Smoke
No Smoking

X207**H**02
No Open Flames

X207**H**03
No Fire

X207**H**04
No Extinguishing with Water

X207**H**05
Do Not Touch

X207**H**06
Do Not Turn Off (Switch)

X207**H**07
Do Not Turn Off (Button)

X207**H**08
Do Not Remove Plug

X207**H**09
Do Not Switch

X207**H**10
No Liquid Near Plug

X207**H**11
Do Not Operate With Guard Removed

X207**H**12
Do Not Operate With Guard Removed, Gears Beneath

X207**H**13
No Way Out

X207**H**14
Do Not Close Door

X207**H**15
Do Not Enter, Confined Space

X207**H**16
No Welding

X207**H**17
No Digging

X207**H**18
No Digging
Underground Electrical Cable

X207**H**19
Do Not Dig
Do Not Use Back Hoe

X207**H**20
No Drilling

X207**H**21
No Littering

X207**H**22
No Food or Drink

X207**H**23
No Cans or Bottles

X207**H**24
Do Not Drink Water

X207**H**25
No Dumping (Drain)

X207**H**26
No Pacemaker Wearers

X207**H**27
No Cell Phones or Radio Transmitters

X207**H**28
No Cross Walk

X207**H**29
No Cars

X207**H**30
No Trucks

X207**H**31
No Lift Point
Do Not Lift with Hook

X207**H**32
No Fork Lift

X207**H**33
Overhead Power Lines

X207**H**34
Do Not Enter

X207**H**35
Do Not Enter
No Entry

X207**H**36
No People Allowed

X207**H**37
Stay Clear

X207**H**38
No Access for Unauthorized Persons

X207**H**39
Do Not Step

X207**H**40
Do Not Stand Here

X207**H**41
General Prohibition

General Safety Information and Referential Objects

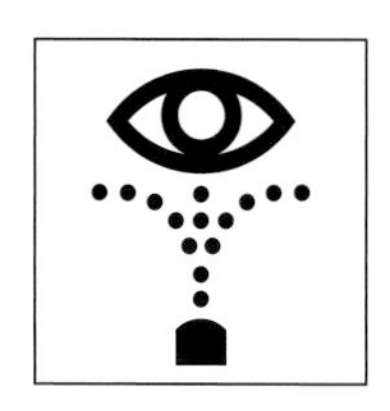
X207**J**01
Eye Wash

X207**J**02
Safety Shower

X207**J**03
Wash Hands

X207**J**04
First Aid Station

X207**J**05
Stretcher

X207**J**06
First Aid Kit

X207**J**07
Fire Extinguisher

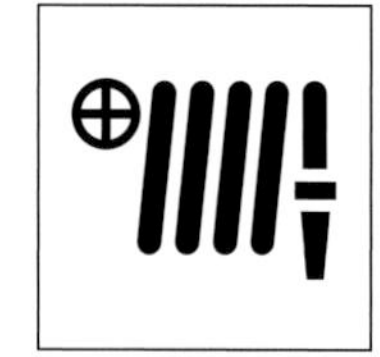
X207**J**08
Fire Hose

X207**J**09
Fire Ax

X207**J**10
Fire Hydrant
Fire Plug

X207**J**11
Fire Alarm

X207**J**12
Fire Door

X207**J**13
Fire Exit (Left)

X207**J**14
Fire Exit (Right)

X207**J**15
Use Stairs In Case Of Fire

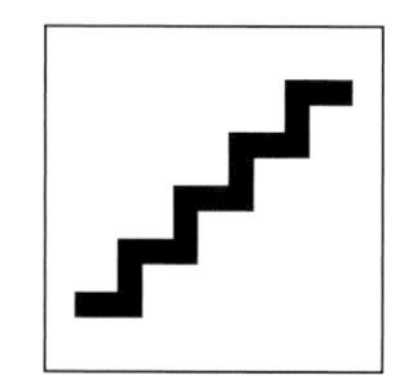
X207**J**16
Stairs

X207**J**17
Emergency Exit (Left)
This Way Out

X207**J**18
Emergency Exit (Right)
This Way Out

X207**J**19
Low Height

X207**J**20
Confined Space

X207**J**21
Keep Area Clean

X207**J**22
Watch For
Oncoming Traffic

X207**J**23
Welding

X207**J**24
Needle Disposal
Deposit Syringes Here

X207**J**25
Security Guard

X207**J**26
Guard Station

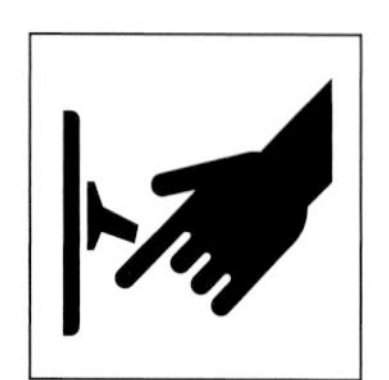
X207**J**27
Switch

X207**J**28
Button

X207**J**29
Poisonous Gas
Dead Bird

X207**J**30
Type B / Type BF Applied Part
IEC 60417 / ISO 7000

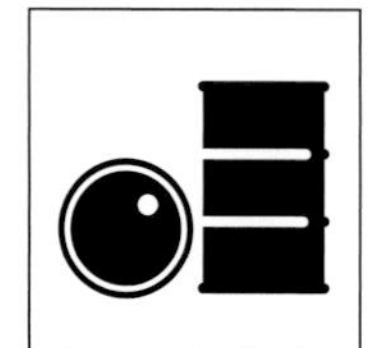
X207**J**31
Barrel

X207**J**32
Pressurized Gas

X207**J**33
Pressurized Gas Bottles

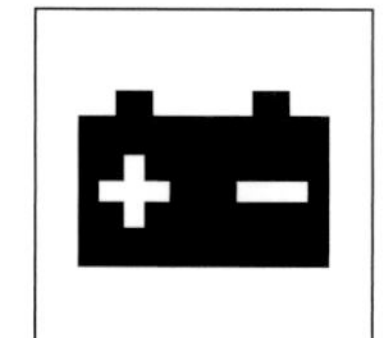
X207**J**34
Battery

X207**J**35
Digging
Back Hoe

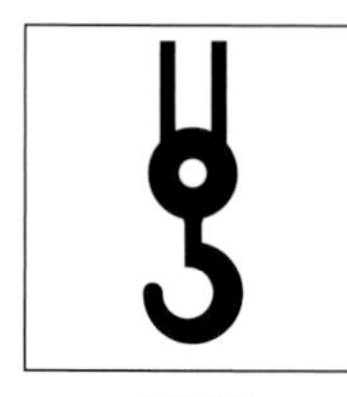
X207**J**36
Lift
Hook

X207**J**37
Overhead Power Lines

X207**J**38
Smoking

X207**J**39
Sparks

X207**J**40
Drain

X207**J**41
This Way Out

Signal Word Panels

- English

X207**K**01
Danger

X207**K**02
Warning

X207**K**03
Caution

X207**K**04
Caution
Non-Personal Injury

X207**K**05
Notice

X207**K**06
Safety Instructions

- Spanish

X207**K**07
Peligro
(Danger)

X207**K**08
Advertencia
(Warning)

X207**K**09
Atención
(Caution)

X207**K**10
Atención
(Caution)
Non-Personal Injury

X207**K**11
Aviso
(Notice)

X207**K**12
Instrucciones De Seguridad
(Safety Instructions)

- German

X207**K**13
Gefahr
(Danger)

X207**K**14
Warnung
(Warning)

X207**K**15
Vorsicht
(Caution)

X207**K**16
Vorsicht
(Caution)
Non-Personal Injury

X207**K**17
Nachright
(Notice)

X207**K**18
Sicherheit-Svorschriften
(Safety Instructions)

- Italian

X207**K**19
Pericolo
(Danger)

X207**K**20
Avvertenza
(Warning)

X207**K**21
Attenzione
(Caution)

X207**K**22
Attenzione
(Caution)
Non-Personal Injury

X207**K**23
Avviso
(Notice)

X207**K**24
Istruzioni di Sicurezza
(Safety Instructions)

Arrows as defined by ISO 11684

X207**K**25
Motion of Components

X207**K**26
Motion of Components
(Left)

X207**K**27
Motion of Components
(Right)

X207**K**28
Exertion of Pressure
or Force (Left)

X207**K**29
Exertion of Pressure
or Force (Right)

X207**K**30
Motion of Entire Objects
Such as Machines

X207**K**31
Motion of Entire Objects
Such as Machines (Left)

X207**K**32
Motion of Entire Objects
Such as Machines (Right)

X207**K**33
Motion of Falling or Flying
Objects Such as Machines

X207**K**34
Keep Safe Distance
From Hazard

General Directionals

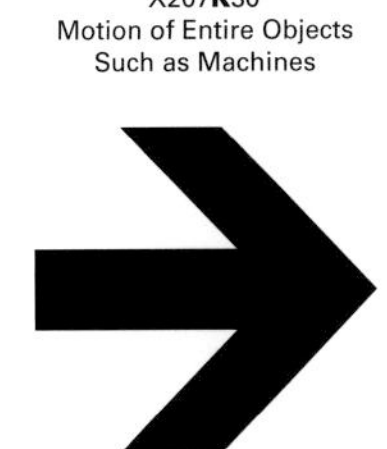

X207**K**35
Arrow Right

X207**K**36
Arrow Upper Right

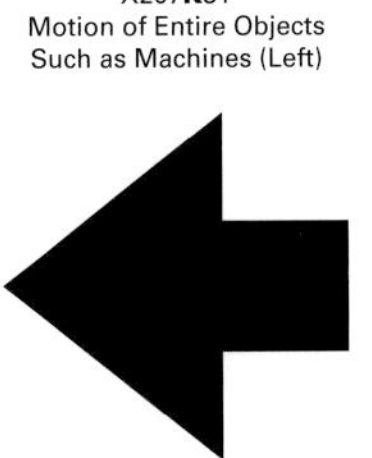

X207**K**37
Arrow Left

X207**K**38
Arrow Right

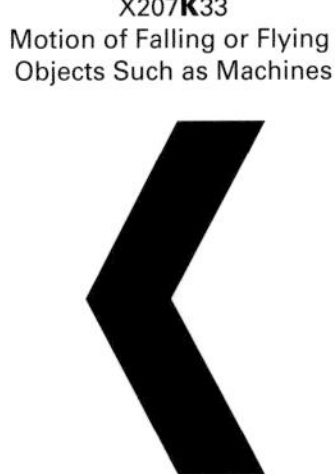

X207**K**39
Arrow Left

X207**K**40
Arrow Right

WHMIS Hazards (Canadian)

X207**L**01
Compressed Gases

X207**L**02
Flammable and Combustible Materials

X207**L**03
Oxidizing Materials

X207**L**04
Poisonous and Infectious Materials

X207**L**05
Materials Causing Other Toxic Effects

X207**L**06
Biohazardous Infectious Materials

X207**L**07
Corrosive Materials

X207**L**08
Dangerously Reactive Materials

NFPA Special Hazards

ACID

X207**L**09
Acid

ALK

X207**L**10
Alkali
Base

COR

X207**L**11
Corrosive

OX

X207**L**12
Oxidizer

RAD

X207**L**13
Radioactive

X207**L**14
Water Reactive
Use No Water

Toxic / Poison Warning

X207**L**15
"Mr Yuck", Child's Warning for Dangerous Substances in Home

Target Organs & Systems

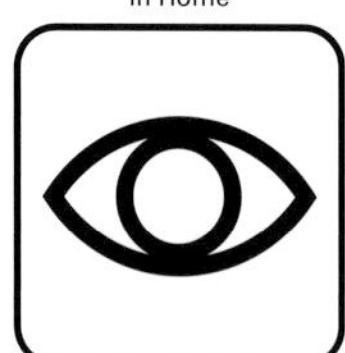
X207**L**16
Sight
Eyes

X207**L**17
Nervous System
Brain

X207**L**18
Liver

X207**L**19
Skin
Hand

X207**L**20
Cardiovascular
Heart

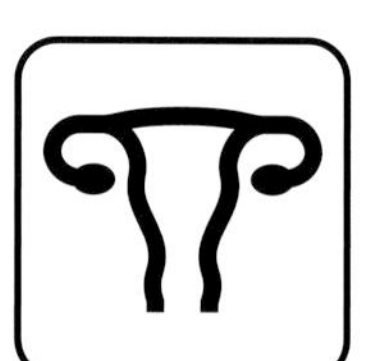
X207**L**21
Reproductive
Uterus

X207**L**22
Blood

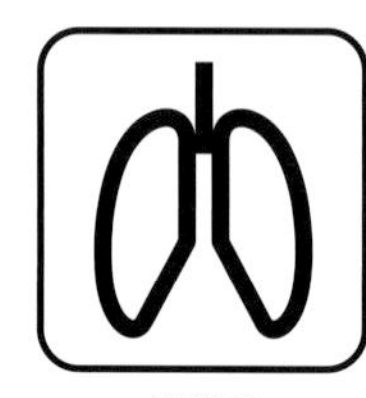
X207**L**23
Respiratory
Lungs

X207**L**24
Renal
Kidney

X207**L**25
Bone Marrow
Bone

X207**L**26
Sinus
Nose and Throat

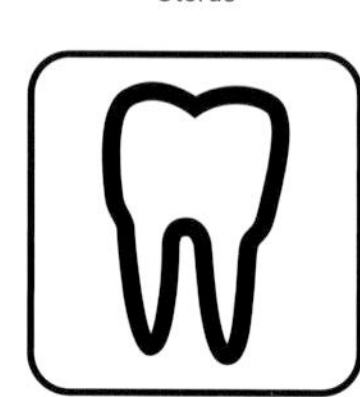
X207**L**27
Dental
Tooth

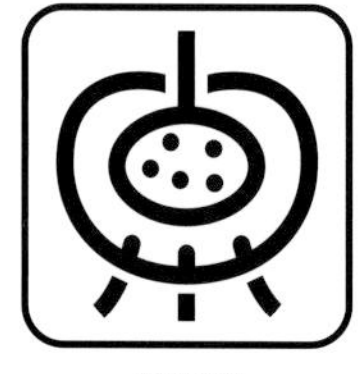
X207**L**28
Endocrine
Gland

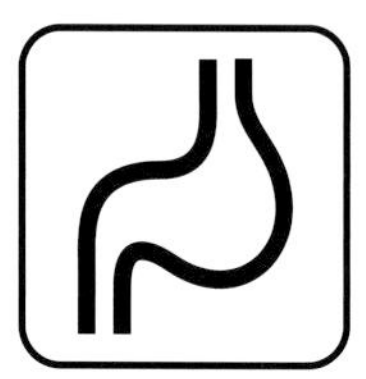
X207**L**29
Digestive
Stomach

Freight
Container
Packaging
Imprints

X207**M**01
Keep Dry

X207**M**02
Fragile

X207**M**03
Fragile

X207**M**04
Handle with Care

X207**M**05
Poison

X207**M**06
Use No Hooks

X207**M**07
Keep Dry

X207**M**08
Fragile

X207**M**09
Magnetized

X207**M**10
Handle with Care

X207**M**11
Poison

X207**M**12
Use No Hooks

X207**M**13
Keep Dry

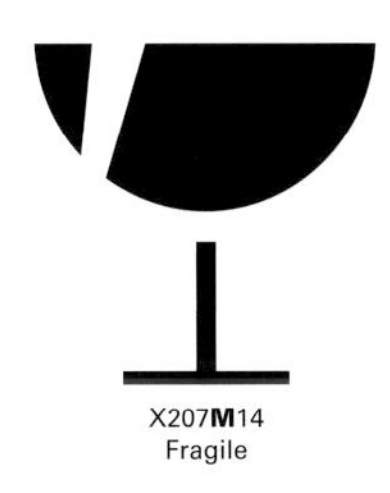
X207**M**14
Fragile

X207**M**15
Magnetized

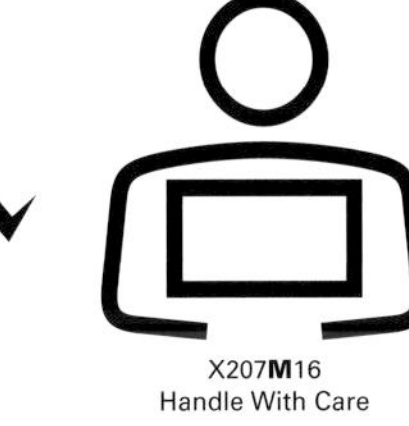
X207**M**16
Handle With Care

X207**M**17
Noxious

X207**M**18
Dangerous

X207**M**19
Keep Dry

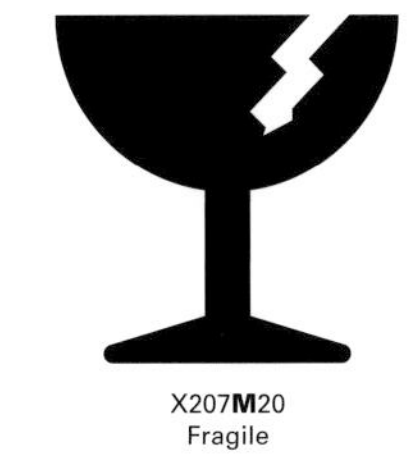
X207**M**20
Fragile

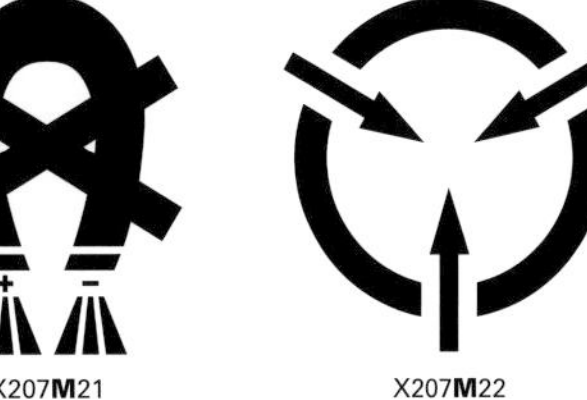
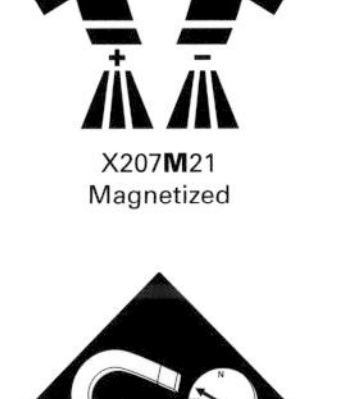
X207**M**21
Magnetized

X207**M**22
Electrostatic Sensitive

X207**M**23
Biohazard

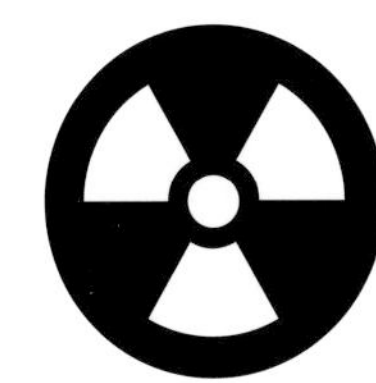

X207**M**24
Radioactive

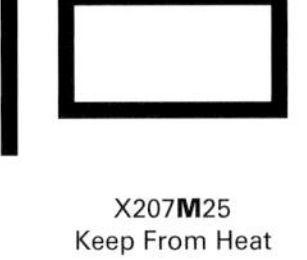
X207**M**25
Keep From Heat

X207**M**26
Fragile

X207**M**27
Magnetized Material

X207**M**28
Static Sensitive

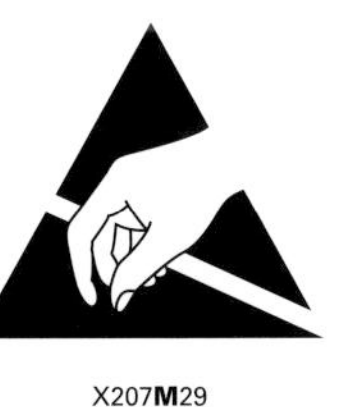
X207**M**29
Static Electricity Hazard
Do Not Touch

X207**M**30
Keep Frozen
Keep Cool

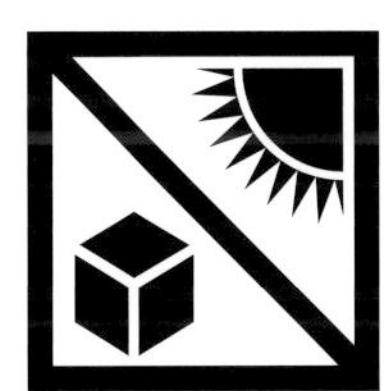
X207**M**31
Keep From Heat

X207**M**32
Keep From heat

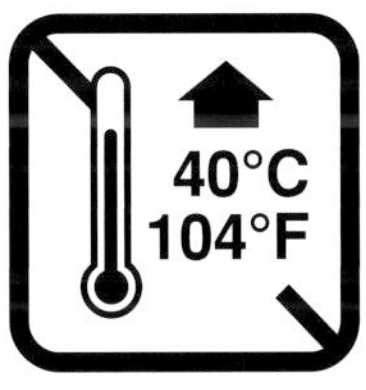

X207**M**33
Keep From Heat

X207**M**34
Keep From Heat

X207**M**35
Keep From Cold

X207**M**36
Do Not Freeze

Freight
Container
Packaging
Imprints
continued

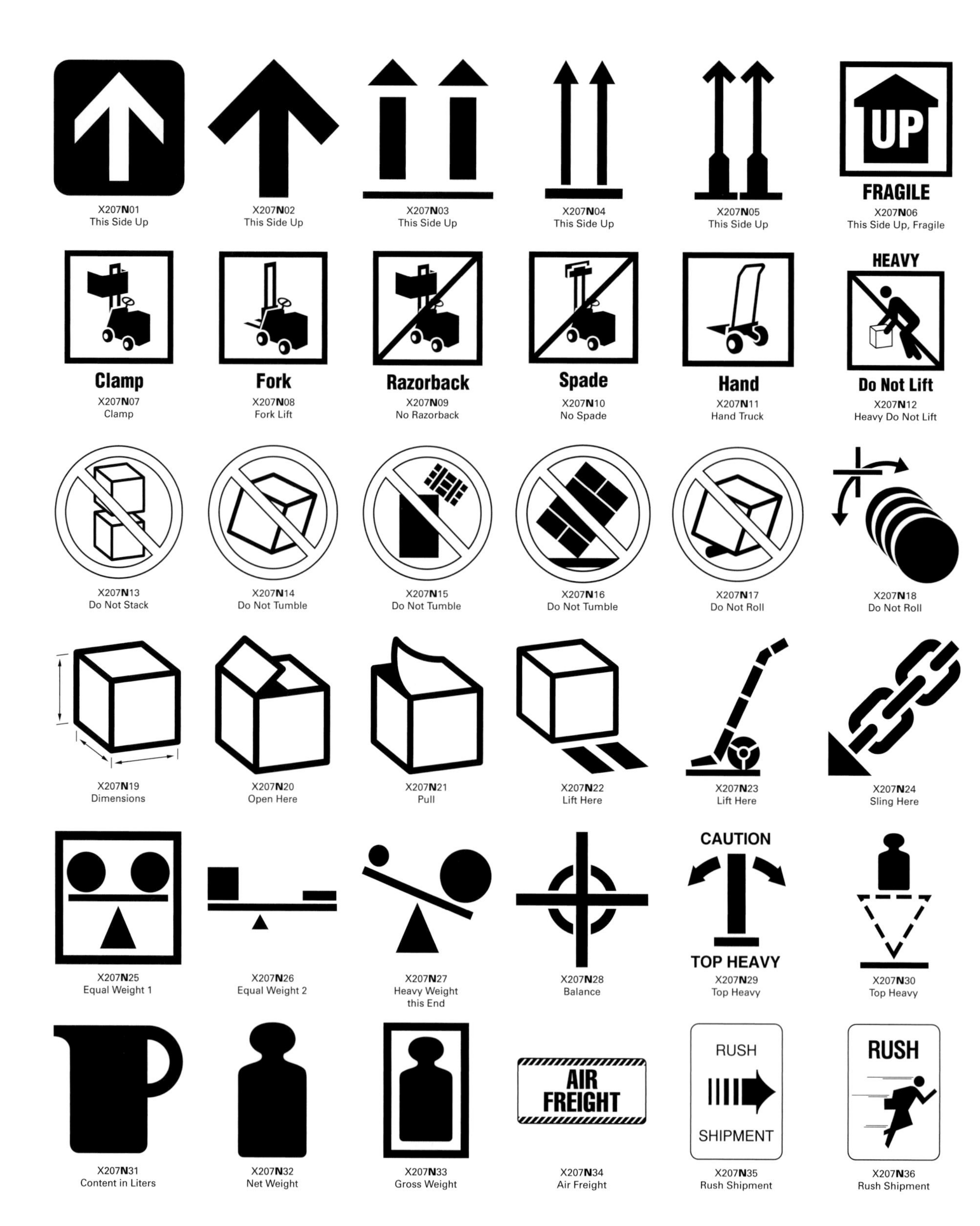

X207N01 This Side Up
X207N02 This Side Up
X207N03 This Side Up
X207N04 This Side Up
X207N05 This Side Up
X207N06 This Side Up, Fragile
X207N07 Clamp
X207N08 Fork Lift
X207N09 No Razorback
X207N10 No Spade
X207N11 Hand Truck
X207N12 Heavy Do Not Lift
X207N13 Do Not Stack
X207N14 Do Not Tumble
X207N15 Do Not Tumble
X207N16 Do Not Tumble
X207N17 Do Not Roll
X207N18 Do Not Roll
X207N19 Dimensions
X207N20 Open Here
X207N21 Pull
X207N22 Lift Here
X207N23 Lift Here
X207N24 Sling Here
X207N25 Equal Weight 1
X207N26 Equal Weight 2
X207N27 Heavy Weight this End
X207N28 Balance
X207N29 Top Heavy
X207N30 Top Heavy
X207N31 Content in Liters
X207N32 Net Weight
X207N33 Gross Weight
X207N34 Air Freight
X207N35 Rush Shipment
X207N36 Rush Shipment

Freight
Container
Packaging
Imprints
continued

X207**P**01
Made In U.S.A.

X207**P**02
Made In U.S.A.

X207**P**03
Proudly Made
In the USA

X207**P**04
Made In America

X207**P**05
Packed with Pride
in the U.S.A.

X207**P**06
Made In Canada

X207**P**07
Made In Canada

X207**P**08
Photographic Material

X207**P**09
Live Animals

X207**P**10
Live Animals

X207**P**11
Marine Pollutant

X207**P**12
Harmful, Tow Away
from Foodstuffs

X207**P**13
Perishable

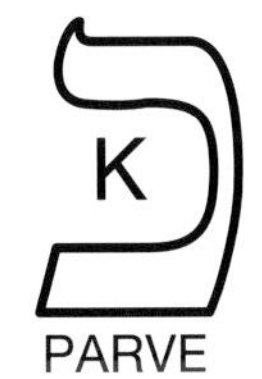

X207**P**14
Kosher Parve

X207**P**15
Kosher Parve

X207**P**16
Kosher

X207**P**17
Kosher U

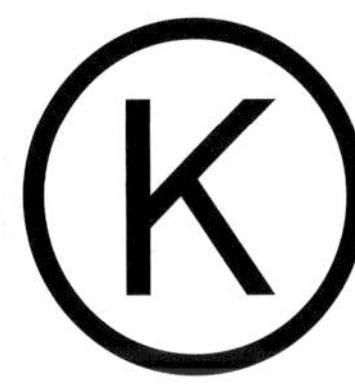

X207**P**18
Kosher K

X207**P**19
Irradiated

X207**P**20
No Cholesterol
Vegetable Oil

X207**P**21
No Cholesterol

X207**P**22
No Lard

X207**P**23
No Tropical Oils

X207**P**24
Microwaveable

X207**P**25
Stacking Limit

X207**P**26
Stacking Limit
Stack No More Than 1

X207**P**27
Stacking Limit
Stack No More Than 2

X207**P**28
Stacking Limit
Stack No More Than 3

X207**P**29
Stacking Limit
Stack No More Than 4

X207**P**30
Stacking Limit
Stack No More Than 5

X207**P**31
Stacking Limit

X207**P**32
Stacking Limit
Stack No More Than 1

X207**P**33
Stacking Limit
Stack No More Than 2

X207**P**34
Stacking Limit
Stack No More Than 3

X207**P**35
Stacking Limit
Stack No More Than 4

X207**P**36
Stacking Limit
Stack No More Than 5

Freight
Container
Packaging
Imprints
continued

X207Q01
Stacking Limit
Stack No More Than 6

X207Q02
Stacking Limit
Stack No More Than 7

X207Q03
Stacking Limit
Stack No More Than 8

X207Q04
Stacking Limit
Stack No More Than 9

X207Q05
Stacking Limit
Stack No More Than 10

X207Q06
Stacking Limit
Stack No More Than 11

6

X207Q07
Stacking Limit
Stack No More Than 6

7

X207Q08
Stacking Limit
Stack No More Than 7

8

X207Q09
Stacking Limit
Stack No More Than 8

9

X207Q10
Stacking Limit
Stack No More Than 9

10

X207Q11
Stacking Limit
Stack No More Than 10

11

X207Q12
Stacking Limit
Stack No More Than 11

X207Q13
Stacking Limit
Stack No More Than 12

12

X207Q14
Stacking Limit
Stack No More Than 12

International Icons I: Computer Electronic (ISO / IEC / JEITA)

Overview
As technology becomes more complex, users and consumers are becoming more aware of their dependence on products whose design and construction they may not understand. Reassurance is needed that products are reliable and will meet expectations in terms of performance, safety, durability, and other criteria. International standards provide a reference framework, or a common technological language, between suppliers and their customers, which facilitates communication, trade, and the global transfer of technology.

Organizations such as ISO (International Organization for Standardization), IEC (International Electrotechnical Commission) and JEITA (Japan Electronics and Information Technology Industries Association) develop the technical agreements provide the framework for compatible technology worldwide. As non-governmental organizations, they have no legal authority to enforce implementation, regulate, or legislate, therefore the standards are voluntary.

A certain percentage of standards – mainly those concerned with health, safety, or the environment – has been adopted in some countries as part of their regulatory framework, or is referred to in legislation for which it serves as the technical basis. Such adoptions are sovereign decisions by the regulatory authorities or governments of the countries concerned. Although international standards are voluntary, they may become a market requirement, as has happened in the case of quality management systems, or dimensions of freight containers and bank cards.[1]

Specific groups of symbols collected both in this volume (Computer Electronic) and in *Volume 9: Mechanical Labeling* (see page 153) are culled from company specifications, from screen icons in general use on the internet, or commercial sources of logos and certifications. The majority, however, are derived and interpreted from international standards.

Organizing the Symbols
To make the vast number of symbols in these two volumes easier to assimilate and find, they have been organized into categories such as Computer, Audio, etc. In actuality, international standards overlap and often assign different symbol numbers to the same message content. The symbols were therefore "harmonized" into a rational system, combining material from various sources to compile a comprehensive and systematic set. The alphabetical indexes at the end of each volume display, wherever possible, the assigned numbers for the symbols from the different standards. It should be noted that international standards are continuously being updated and revised. To ensure complete accuracy for a particular message content, it is recommended that the latest appropriate standard be obtained and reviewed.

Rendering the Message Content
As in most standards, it is the message content that is the key element being agreed upon and published, not the final rendering. The symbols are intended to be interpreted within guidelines and adapted for use in varying reproduction processes, such as printing, hot stamping, and injection molding. Tim K. Murphy, a former member of a corporate symbol standards technical committee employed by a major computer manufacturer, was helpful in providing the general criteria and guidance used for the development and production of the electronic and mechanical labeling symbols in this book.

Symbol Search and Creation Once the need for a symbol is recognized, a clear and unambiguous definition of the function or status that the symbol will represent must be developed. When corporate standards lack the appropriate symbol, international standards should be searched and implemented according to design principles described in ISO 3641-1. Failing this search, other sources may be referenced and/or a new symbol may be created. It is possible that no symbol is an adequate substitute for the appropriate verbiage.

Application Line weights, spacing, and other syntactic qualities are kept consistent. Although these symbols are designed to provide flexibility in application, variances in substrate, placement options, and other factors may require special attention. The integrity of the

symbol and symbol family should not be sacrificed to meet those needs. Symbol originals are drawn on the ISO 75 mm grid (left, not shown full size) with a nominal height dimension of 50 mm. Line weights are 4 mm for most symbols with a second weight of 7 mm to differentiate elements as needed. The recommended nominal size of the finished symbol in use is 7 mm in height (below left).

For further information regarding symbol modification, refer to ISO 3164-1 or IEC 416.[2]

Credits

The designer/illustrator Michael Wong diligently and accurately rendered the bulk of the symbols in Volumes 8 and 9. This was accomplished using Adobe Illustrator on a Macintosh over a period of more than a year. Heartfelt thanks also go to Stephen Letsch for his perseverance in helping to harmonize and index the symbols, and to Tim Murphy for his generous gift of time, resources, and guidance.

About ISO

The International Organization for Standardization (ISO) is a network of the national standards institutes of 150 countries, on the basis of one member per country, with a Central Secretariat in Geneva, Switzerland, that coordinates the system. Developing technical consensus on this international scale is a major operation. In all, there are some 3,000 ISO technical groups (technical committees, subcommittees, working groups, etc.) in which some 50,000 experts participate annually to develop ISO standards.

ISO develops only those standards for which there is a market requirement. The work is carried out by experts on loan from the industrial, technical, and business sectors that have asked for the standards, and that subsequently put them to use. These experts may be joined by others with relevant knowledge, such as representatives of government agencies, consumer organizations, academia, and testing laboratories. ISO collaborates closely with the IEC on all matters of electrotechnical standardization. www.iso.org

About IEC

The International Electrotechnical Commission (IEC) is the primary global organization that prepares and publishes international standards for all electrical, electronic and related technologies. These serve as a basis for national standardization and as references when drafting international tenders and contracts.

The IEC charter embraces all electrotechnologies including electronics, magnetics and electromagnetics, electroacoustics, multimedia, telecommunication, and energy production and distribution, as well as associated general disciplines such as terminology and symbols, electromagnetic compatibility, measurement and performance, dependability, design and development, safety, and the environment. Put simply, a component or system manufactured to IEC standards and manufactured in country A can be sold and used in countries B through to Z. www.iec.ch

About JEITA

The Japan Electronics and Information Technology Industries Association (JEITA) was formed on November 1, 2000, through the merger of the Electronic Industries Association of Japan (EIAJ) and Japan Electronic Industries Development Association (JEIDA). JEITA is a new industry organization in Japan with activities covering both the electronics and information technology (IT) fields.

EIAJ was founded in 1948 as a non-profit national trade organization to develop Japan's electronics industry and represent its views. Important issues include advancing international technical standardization, supporting the creation of emerging markets such as home information appliances, fostering technological development, and establishing and enhancing international industrial cooperation. www.jeita.or.jp

Computer

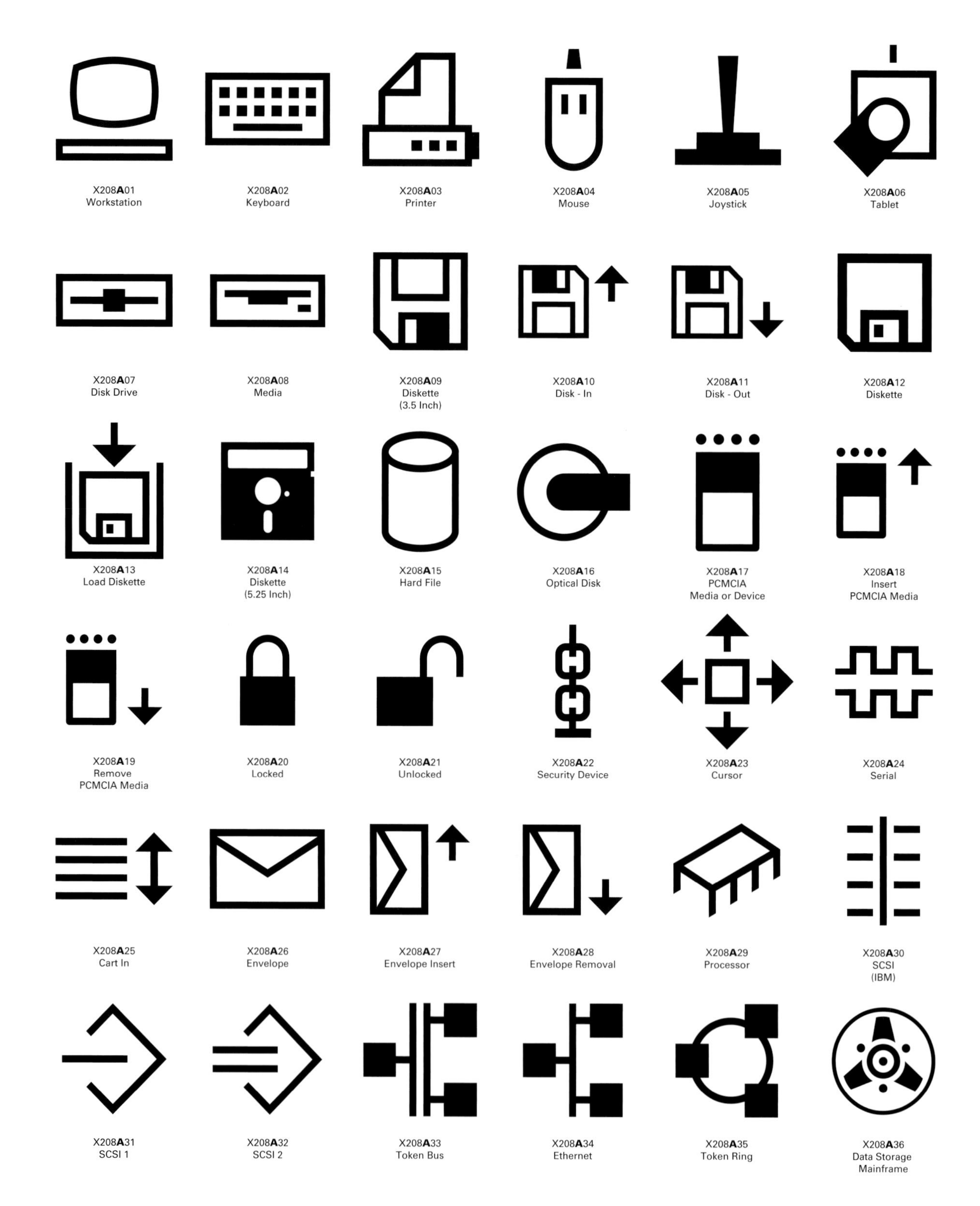

Note: All symbols and signs are available as fully editable vector image files: see page 238 or www.ultimatesymbol.com

General
IN
OUT
IN
OUT
X208B01
Apple 1
X208B02
Apple 2
X208B03
Command
X208B04
Volume Off
X208B05
Volume Minimum
X208B06
Volume Medium
X208B07
Volume Full
X208B08
PS/2/ Serial
X208B09
USB Connection
X208B10
Firewire
X208B11
VGA Port
X208B12
Modem
X208B13
Mic
X208B14
Mic On
X208B15
Mic/ Live Recording
X208B16
Headphones
X208B17
Brightness
X208B18
Contrast
X208B19
Camera 1
X208B20
Camera 2
X208B21
Camera In
X208B22
Camera Out
X208B23
S Camera In
X208B24
S Camera Out
Screen Icons
X208B25
Text Tool
Cursor
X208B26
Pointer Tool
X208B27
Direct Selection
X208B28
Magnifying Tool
X208B29
Enlarge
X208B30
Reduce
X208B31
Timer
X208B32
Trash
Trash Can
X208B33
Error, Bomb, Crash
X208B34
E-Cart
Shopping Cart
X208B35
Disc
X208B36
Discs
X208B37
Timer
Hourglass
X208B38
Mailbox
X208B39
Mailbox
Outgoing Mail, Mail to Send
X208B40
Mailbox Empty
X208B41
Mailbox
You Have Mail
X208B42
Save File(s)
Filing Cabinet

Screen Icons continued

Audio

Audio
continued

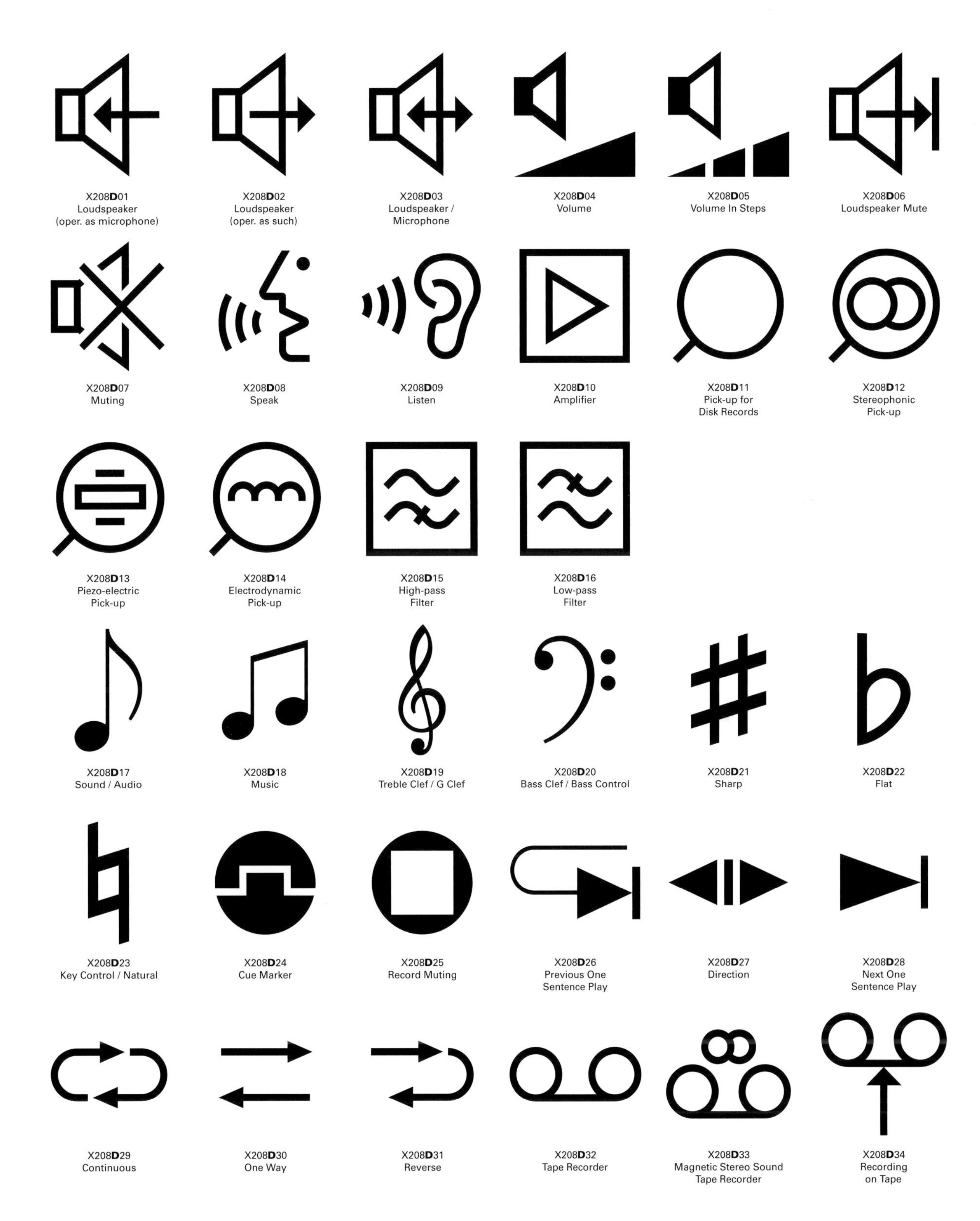

Audio
continued

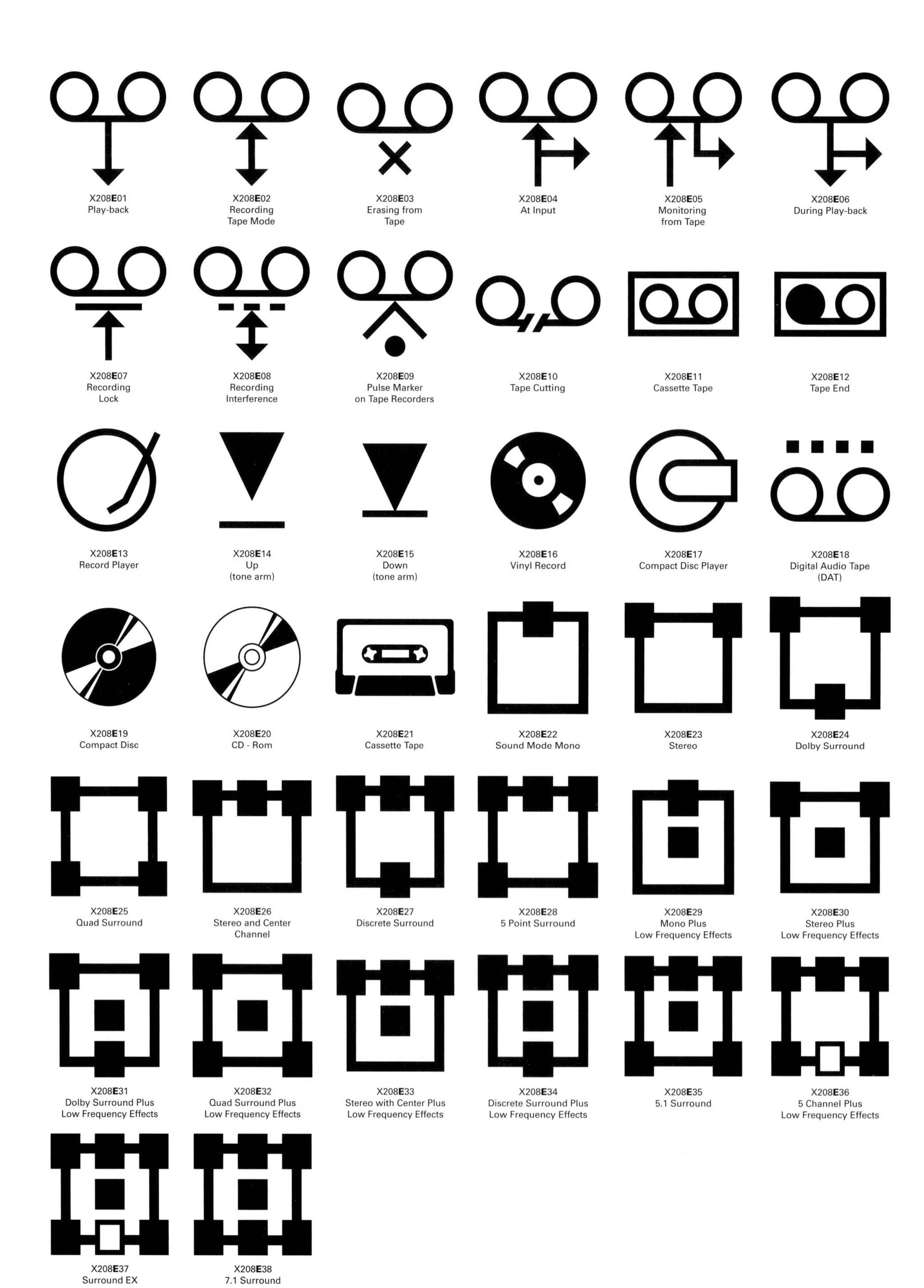

Video

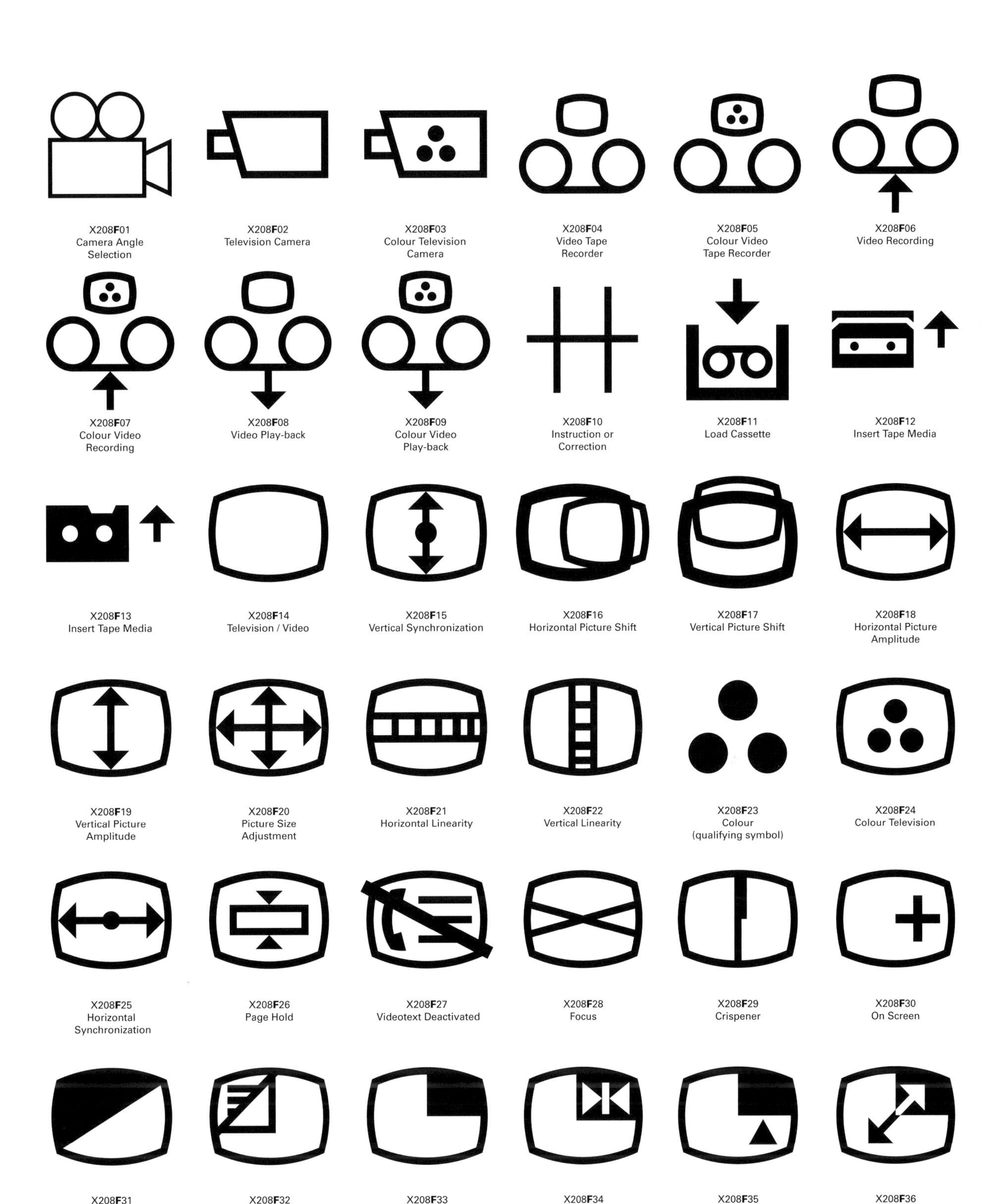

X208**F**01 Camera Angle Selection

X208**F**02 Television Camera

X208**F**03 Colour Television Camera

X208**F**04 Video Tape Recorder

X208**F**05 Colour Video Tape Recorder

X208**F**06 Video Recording

X208**F**07 Colour Video Recording

X208**F**08 Video Play-back

X208**F**09 Colour Video Play-back

X208**F**10 Instruction or Correction

X208**F**11 Load Cassette

X208**F**12 Insert Tape Media

X208**F**13 Insert Tape Media

X208**F**14 Television / Video

X208**F**15 Vertical Synchronization

X208**F**16 Horizontal Picture Shift

X208**F**17 Vertical Picture Shift

X208**F**18 Horizontal Picture Amplitude

X208**F**19 Vertical Picture Amplitude

X208**F**20 Picture Size Adjustment

X208**F**21 Horizontal Linearity

X208**F**22 Vertical Linearity

X208**F**23 Colour (qualifying symbol)

X208**F**24 Colour Television

X208**F**25 Horizontal Synchronization

X208**F**26 Page Hold

X208**F**27 Videotext Deactivated

X208**F**28 Focus

X208**F**29 Crispener

X208**F**30 On Screen

X208**F**31 Temporary Inactive Attributes

X208**F**32 Reveal

X208**F**33 Picture-in-Picture Mode

X208**F**34 Picture-in-Picture Freeze

X208**F**35 Selection of Picture-in-Picture

X208**F**36 Picture-in-Picture Swap

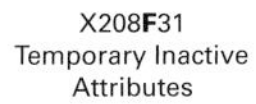

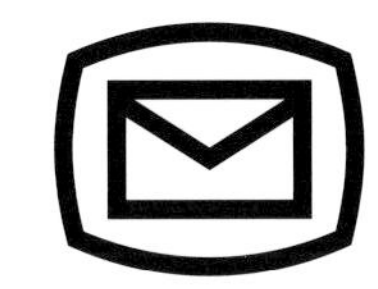

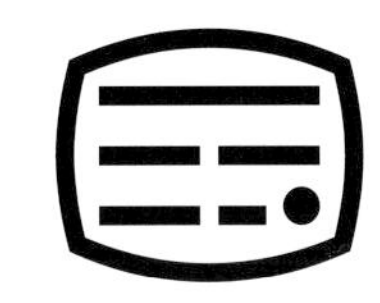

X208**F**37 Picture-in-Picture Shift

X208**F**38 Freezed Picture

X208**F**39 Multi Image Display

X208**F**40 Billing Information

X208**F**41 Message Service

X208**F**42 End of Data Entry

Video
continued

Video
continued

X208**H**01
Teletext Mode

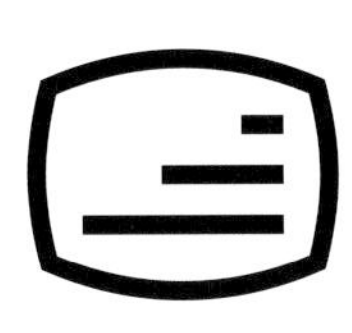

X208**H**02
TV & Text Mixed

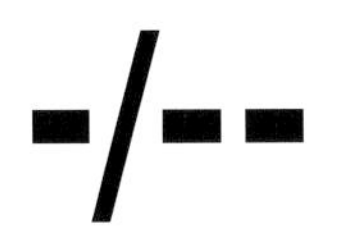

X208**H**03
One or Multi Digit Selection

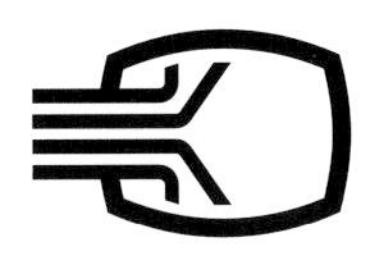

X208**H**04
CATV Mode

X208**H**05
Videodisc Player

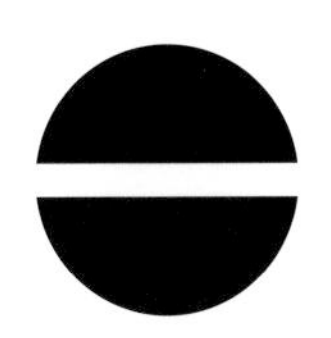

X208**H**06
Audio Dubbing

X208**H**07
Insert

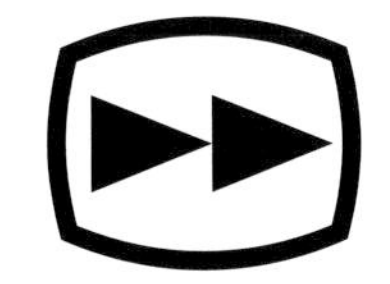

X208**H**08
Cue / Review

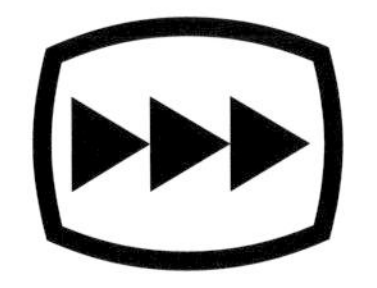

X208**H**09
Fast Cue / Fast Review

X208**H**10
Video Head Clogged

X208**H**11
Dew / Moisture

X208**H**12
Rec Review

X208**H**13
Tracking

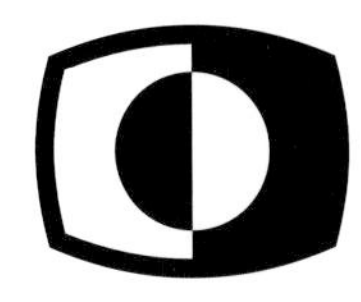

X208**H**14
Nega / Posi Reversal

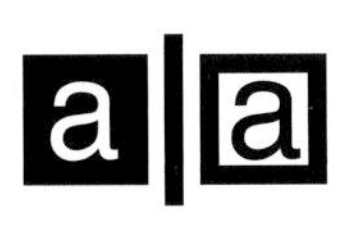

X208**H**15
Reverse

X208**H**16
LCD Monitor

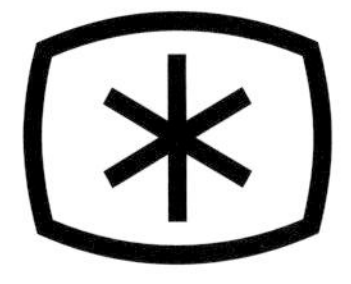

X208**H**17
Initiator

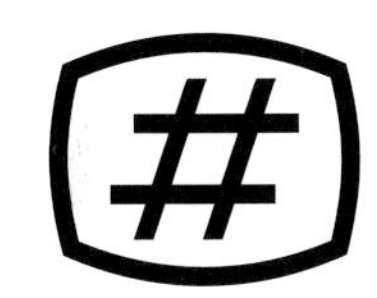

X208**H**18
Terminator

X208**H**19
Clear Screen

X208**H**20
Scrolling

X208**H**21
Page # Down

X208**H**22
Page # Up

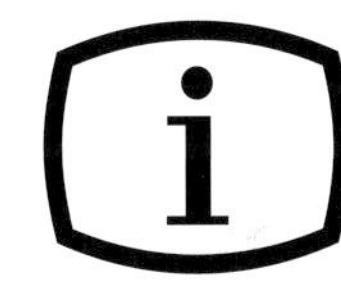

X208**H**23
Help

X208**H**24
Additional Information

X208**H**25
Main Index Page

X208**H**26
Application Assistance

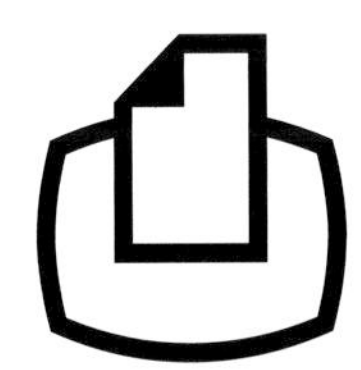

X208**H**27
Print Screen

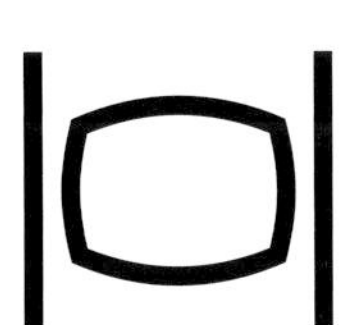

X208**H**28
Television Monitor

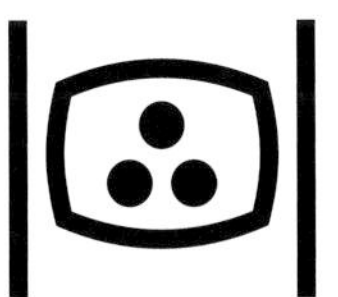

X208**H**29
Colour Television Monitor

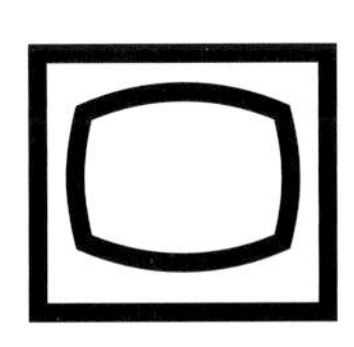

X208**H**30
Television Receiver

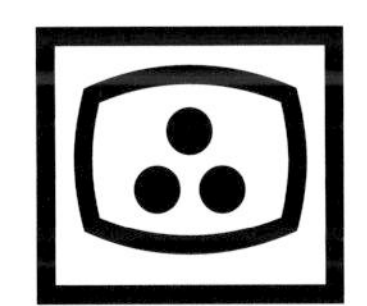

X208**H**31
Colour Television Receiver

X208**H**32
Normal Aspect

X208**H**33
Reversal Right to Left

X208**H**34
Inverted Top to Bottom

X208**H**35
Inverted Top to Bottom & Reversal Right to Left

X208**H**36
Cancelled Screen

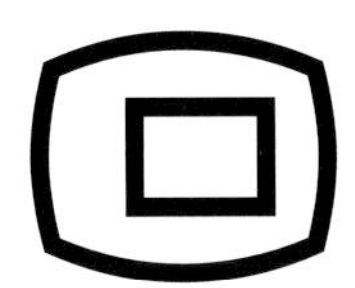

X208**H**37
System Status Display

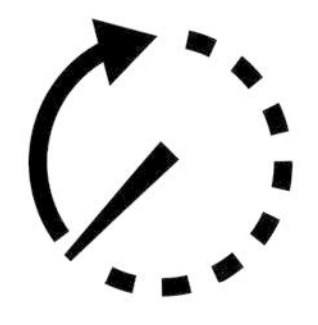

X208**H**38
Remaining Time Display

X208**H**39
Elapsed Time Display

X208**H**40
Single Frame Shot

Camera

Power Indicators

Action
Status

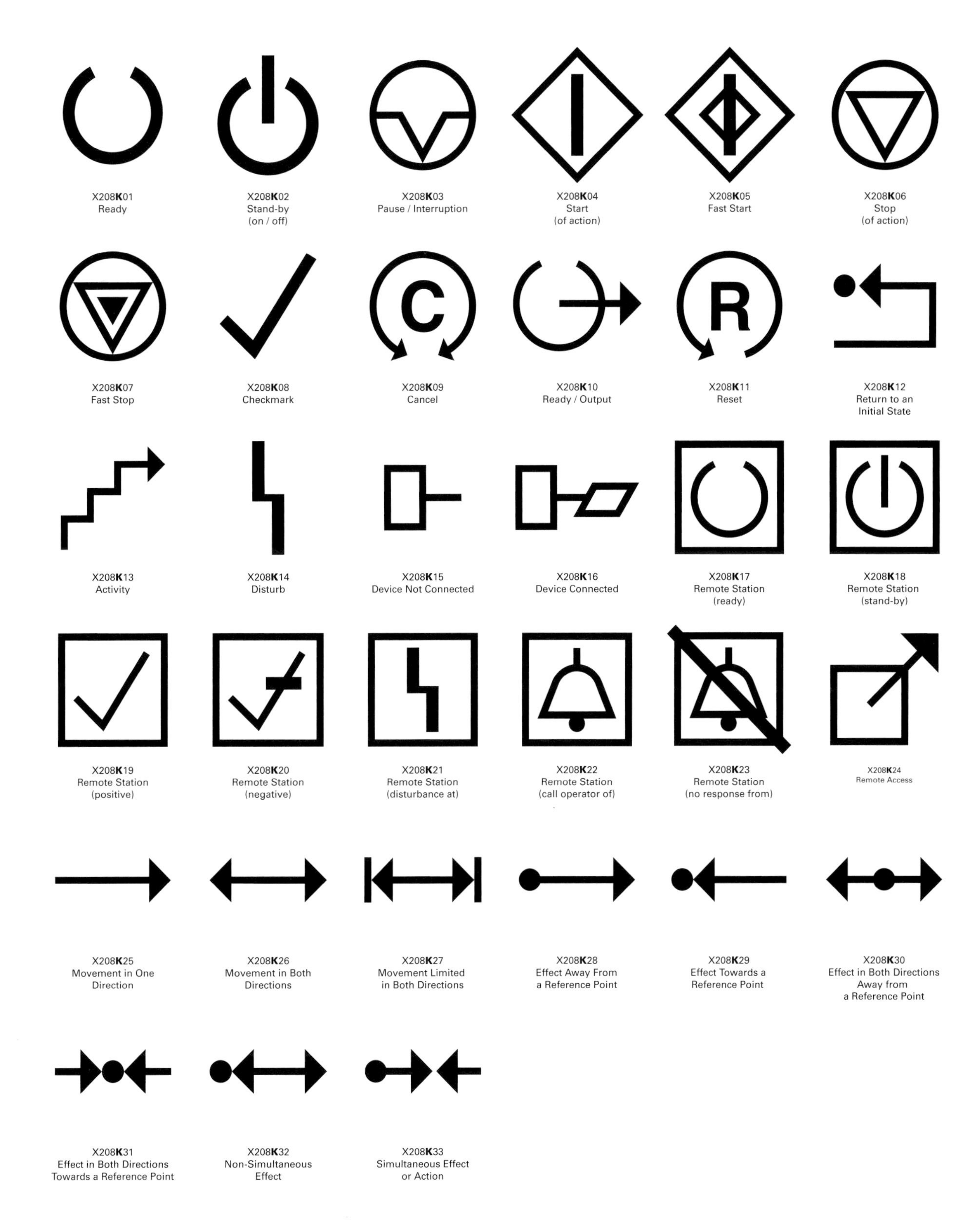

Controls

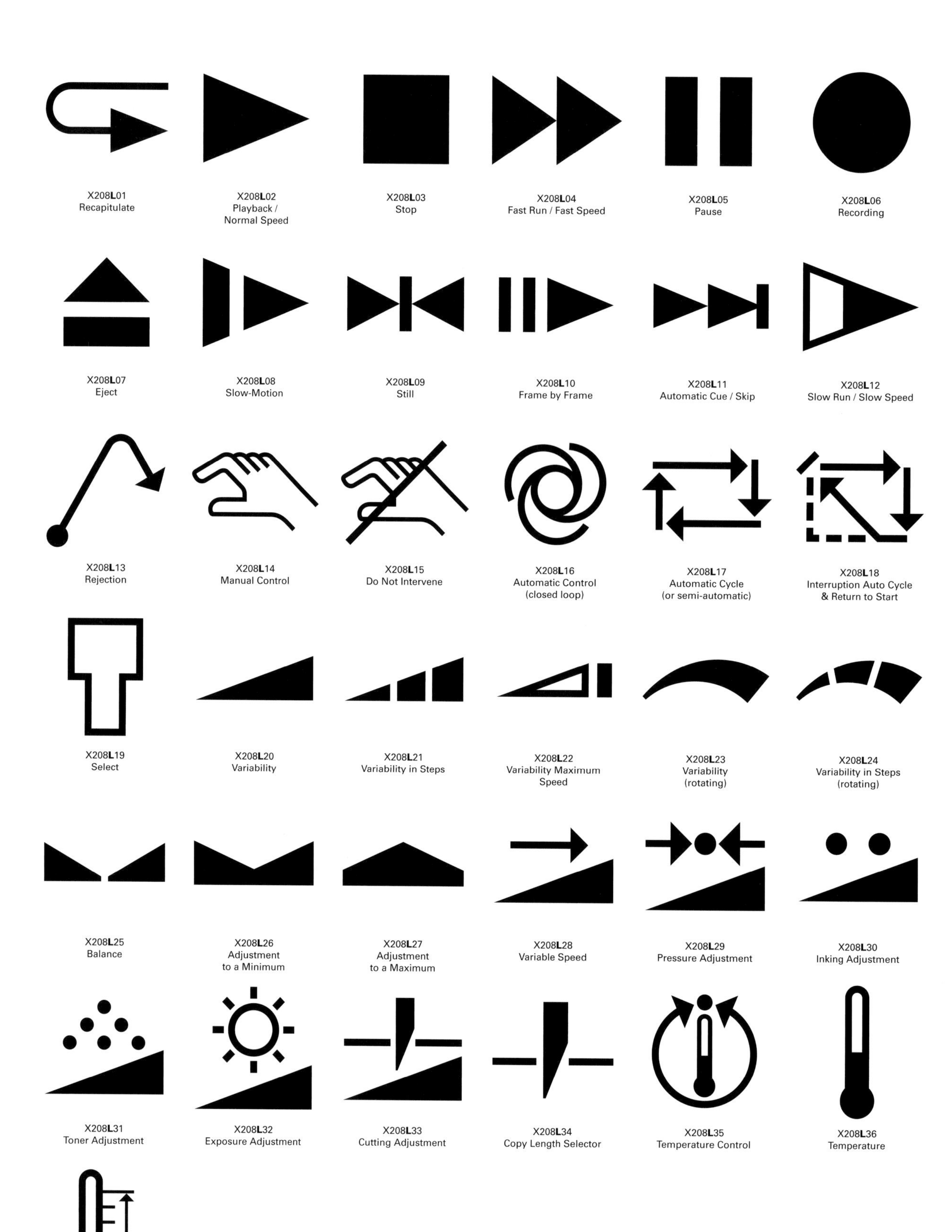
X208L01
Recapitulate
X208L02
Playback /
Normal Speed
X208L03
Stop
X208L04
Fast Run / Fast Speed
X208L05
Pause
X208L06
Recording
X208L07
Eject
X208L08
Slow-Motion
X208L09
Still
X208L10
Frame by Frame
X208L11
Automatic Cue / Skip
X208L12
Slow Run / Slow Speed
X208L13
Rejection
X208L14
Manual Control
X208L15
Do Not Intervene
X208L16
Automatic Control
(closed loop)
X208L17
Automatic Cycle
(or semi-automatic)
X208L18
Interruption Auto Cycle
& Return to Start
X208L19
Select
X208L20
Variability
X208L21
Variability in Steps
X208L22
Variability Maximum
Speed
X208L23
Variability
(rotating)
X208L24
Variability in Steps
(rotating)
X208L25
Balance
X208L26
Adjustment
to a Minimum
X208L27
Adjustment
to a Maximum
X208L28
Variable Speed
X208L29
Pressure Adjustment
X208L30
Inking Adjustment
X208L31
Toner Adjustment
X208L32
Exposure Adjustment
X208L33
Cutting Adjustment
X208L34
Copy Length Selector
X208L35
Temperature Control
X208L36
Temperature
X208L37
Temperature Range

Light / Exposure Controls

Switches

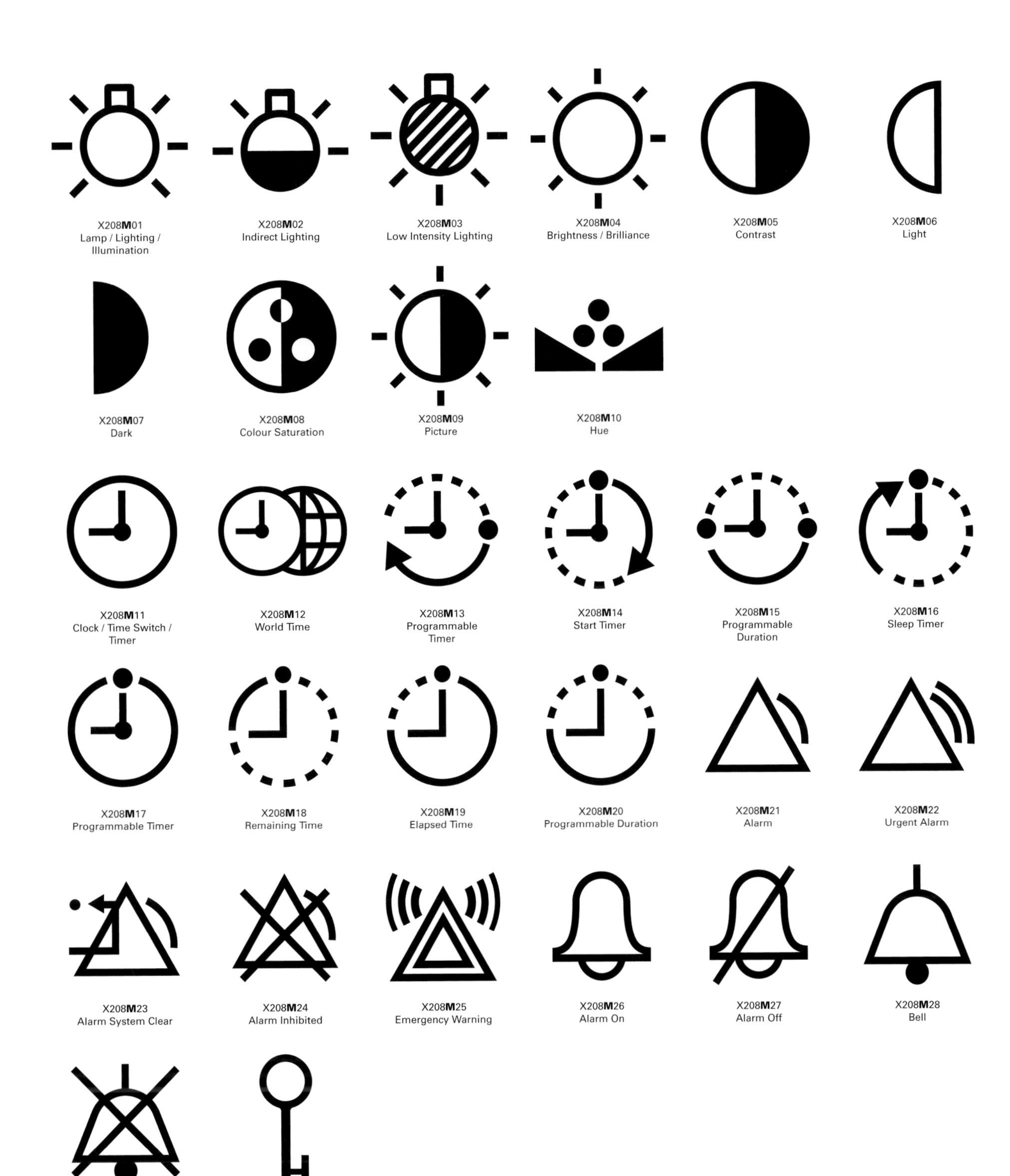

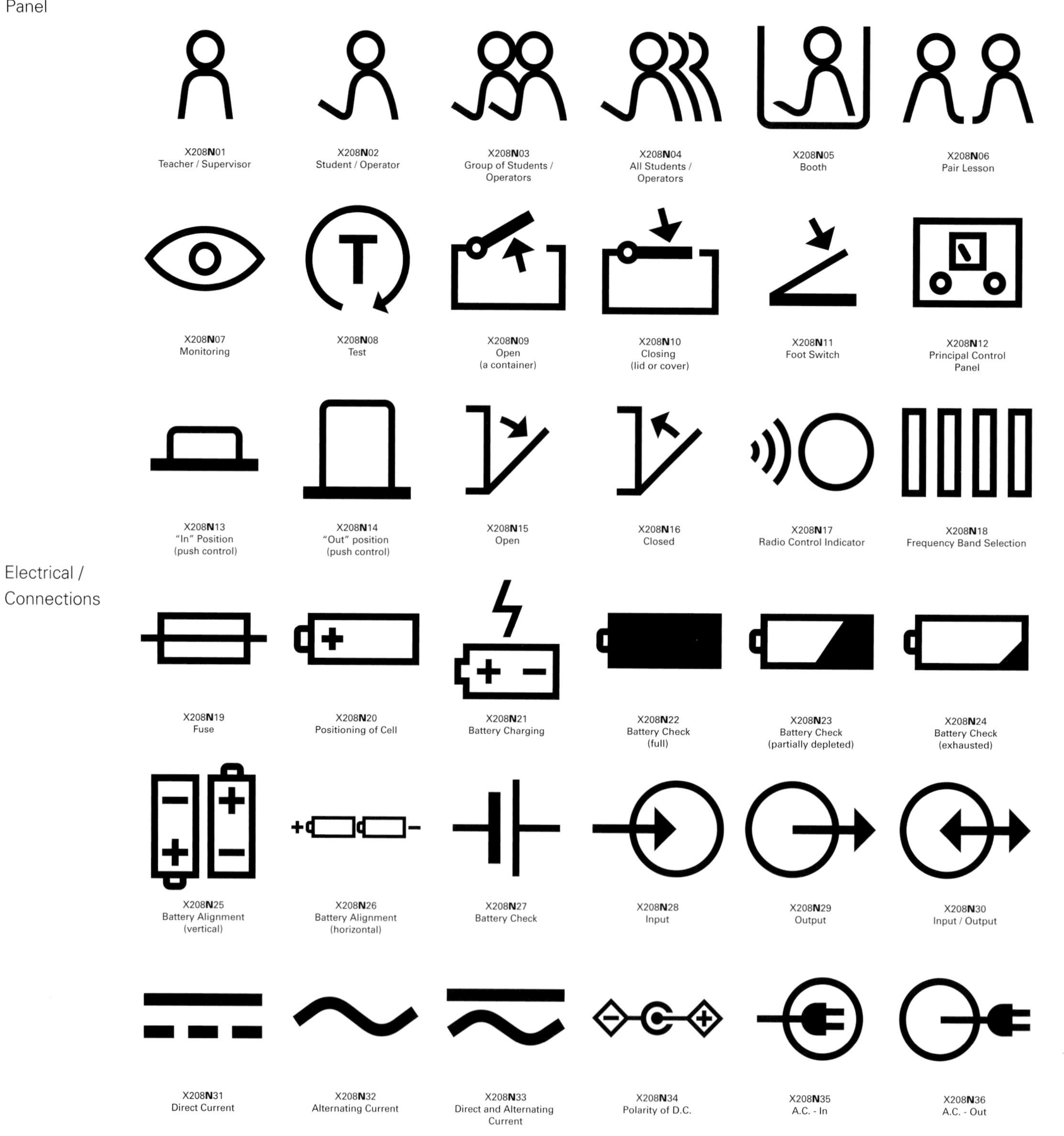

Note: All symbols and signs are available as fully editable vector image files: see page 238 or www.ultimatesymbol.com

Electrical / Connections continued

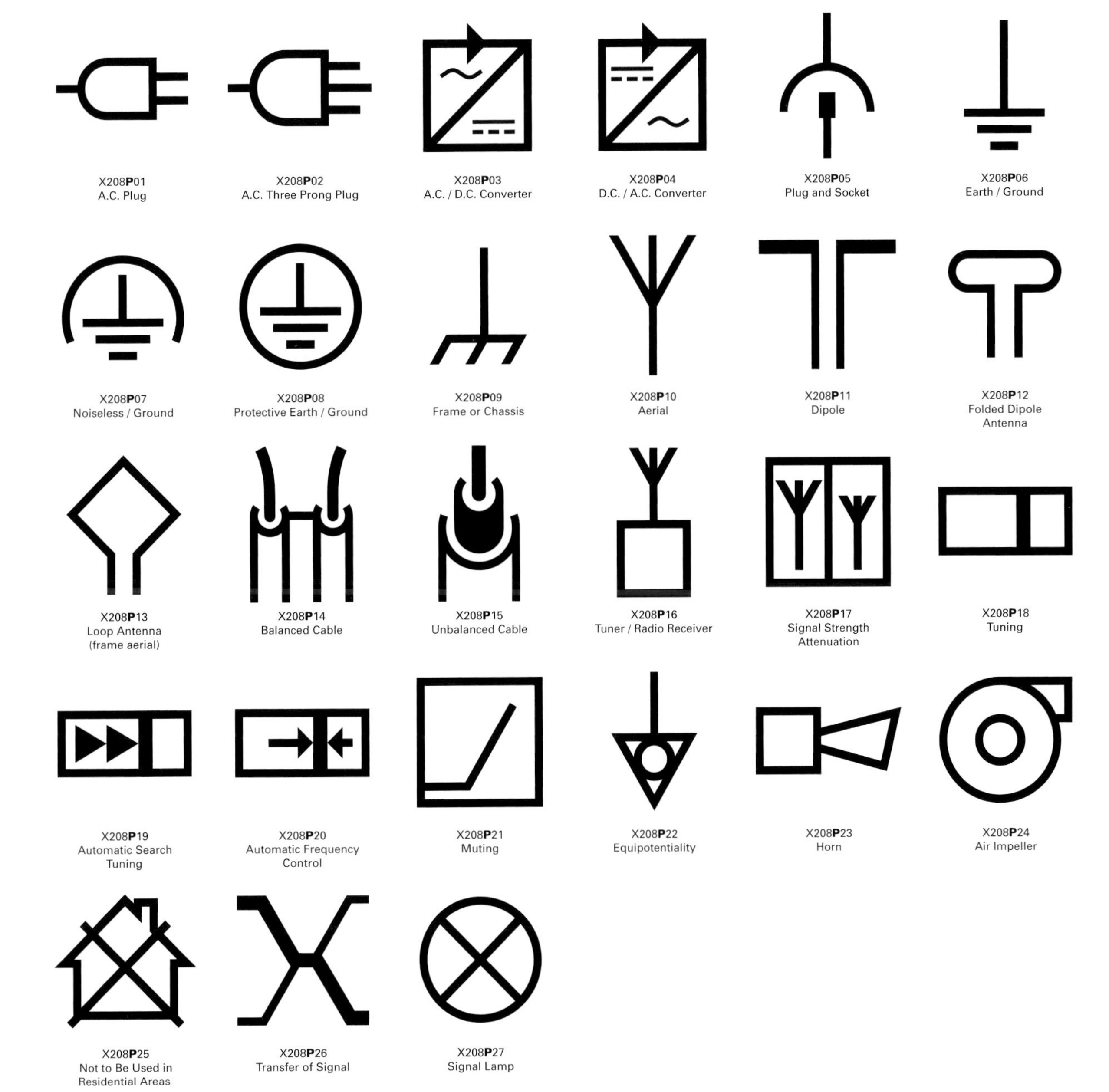

Storage

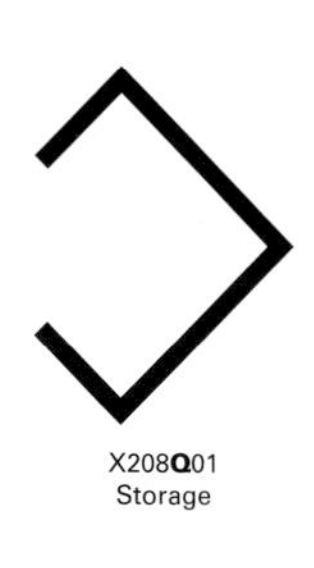
X208Q01
Storage

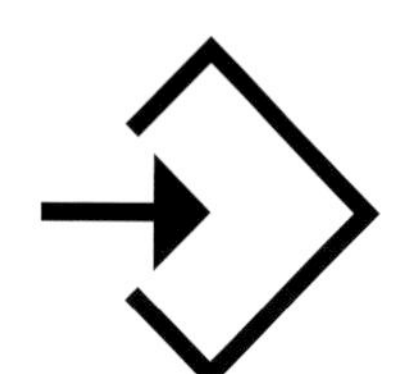
X208Q02
Enter / Write Data Into Storage

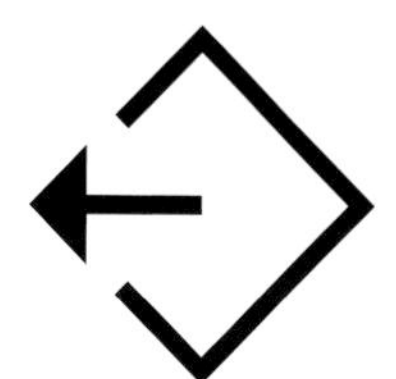
X208Q03
Read Data From Storage

X208Q04
Write and Read Data From Storage

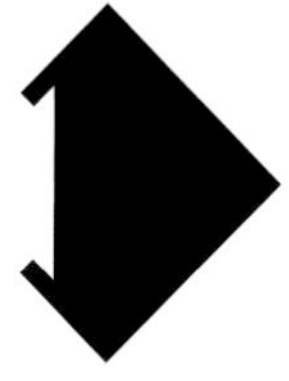
X208Q05
Memory / Storage Full

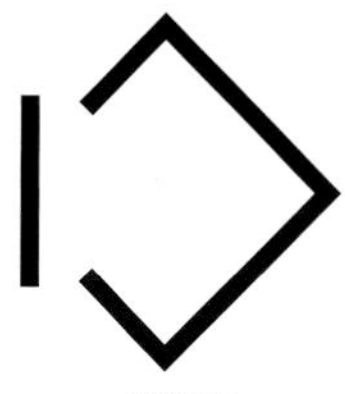
X208Q06
Storage Mode Finished

X208Q07
Data Activity

Manuals

X208Q08
Read Operator's Manual

X208Q09
Operation Instructions

X208Q10
Handbook

General

X208Q11
Telephone / Telephone Adapter

X208Q12
Telephone Disconnected

X208Q13
Telephone

X208Q14
Off Hook

X208Q15
Off Hook

X208Q16
Telephone Voice Communication

X208Q17
Magnetic Card (In)

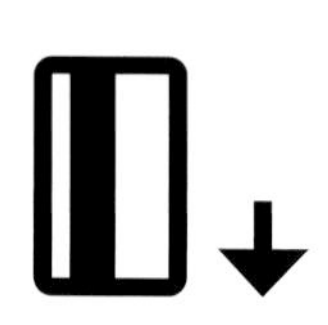
X208Q18
Magnetic Card (Out)

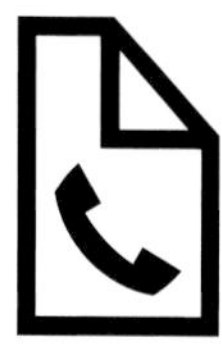
X208Q19
Facsimile / Fax

X208Q20
Printer

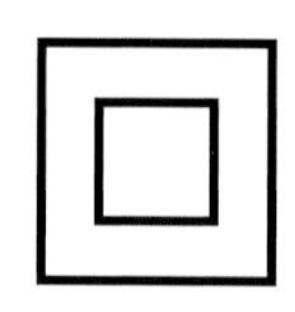
X208Q21
Class II Equipment

X208Q22
Test Voltage

X208Q23
Class III Equipment

Logos
- Labeling

X208**R**01
Mac 1

X208**R**02
Mac 2

X208**R**03
Mac 3

X208**R**04
Mac OS 1

X208**R**05
Mac OS 2

X208**R**06
For Mac

X208**R**07
For Windows

X208**R**08
Adobe PostScript

X208**R**09
Quicktime

X208**R**10
Quicktime

X208**R**11
Shockwave

X208**R**12
Flash

X208**R**13
Real

X208**R**14
USB 1

X208**R**15
USB 2

X208**R**16
Firewire 1

X208**R**17
Firewire 2

X208**R**18
High Density

- Media

X208**R**19
Compact Disc

X208**R**20
Data Storage

X208**R**21
Digital Data

X208**R**22
Recordable

X208**R**23
Rewritable

X208**R**24
DVD

X208**R**25
DVD Rom 1

X208**R**26
DVD Rom 2

X208**R**27
DVD Rom 3

X208**R**28
DVD-R1

X208**R**29
DVD-R2

X208**R**30
DVD-R3

X208**R**31
DVD-RAM

X208**R**32
DVD-R/RAM

X208**R**33
ROM/RAM

X208**R**34
MiniDisc 1

X208**R**35
MiniDisc 2

X208**R**36
MiniDisc 3

X208**R**37
MiniDisc 4

Logos
- Video / Interactive Photo

X208**S**01
DVD-Video 1

X208**S**02
DVD-Video 2

X208**S**03
DVD Video 3

X208**S**04
DVD-Video/Audio

X208**S**05
DVD-ROM/Video

X208**S**06
DVD-Digital Video

X208**S**07
CD Video

X208**S**08
Hi 8

8

X208**S**09
Eight/8

VHS

X208**S**10
VHS

VHS C

X208**S**11
VHS C

X208**S**12
D VHS

DIGITAL S

X208**S**13
Digital S

X208**S**14
VHS/HiFi

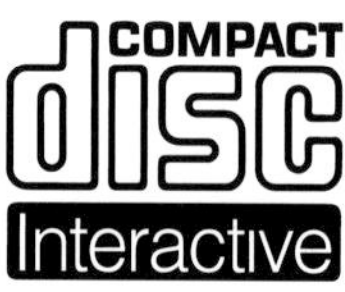

X208**S**15
Compact Disc
Interactive

X208**S**16
Compact Disc
Interactive

X208**S**17
Copy Protected

X208**S**18
Widescreen 16:9

X208**S**19
CD Extra 1

X208**S**20
CD Extra 2

X208**S**21
Compact Disc
Photo

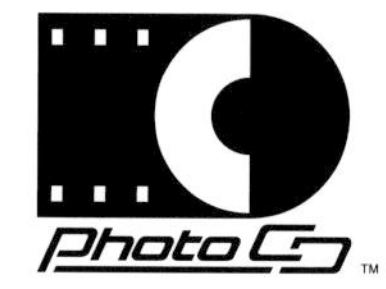

X208**S**22
Photo CD

- Audio

X208**S**23
Digital Audio

X208**S**24
Digital Audio Plus

X208**S**25
Recordable

X208**S**26
Text

X208**S**27
Graphics

X208**S**28
Extended Graphics

X208**S**29
Midi

X208**S**30
Super Audio CD

X208**S**31
DVD-Audio

Microsoft® HDCD®

X208**S**32
Microsoft HDCD

X208**S**33
Dolby

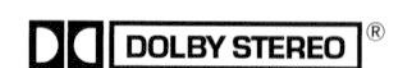

X208**S**34
Dolby Stereo

Logos
- Audio
  continued

X208**T**01
Dolby System

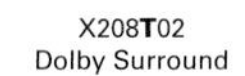

X208**T**02
Dolby Surround

X208**T**03
Dolby Surround

X208**T**04
Dolby Digital

X208**T**05
Dolby Surround
Pro Logic

X208**T**06
Dolby Surround
Pro Logic II

X208**T**07
Dolby Type-B
Noise Reduction

X208**T**08
Dolby Type-S
Noise Reduction

X208**T**09
Dolby HX Pro Headroom
Extension Type-B

X208**T**10
Dolby HX Pro Headroom
Extension Type-S

X208**T**11
Dolby Headphones

X208**T**12
Sony Dynamic
Digital Surround

Sony Dynamic
Digital Sound™

X208**T**13
Sony Dynamic
Digital Surround

X208**T**14
Digital Cinema

X208**T**15
DBX

X208**T**16
THX

THX®

X208**T**17
THX

X208**T**18
DTS
Digital Theater Surround

X208**T**19
DTS
Digital Theater Surround

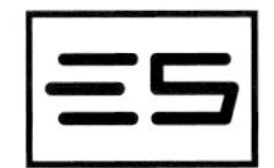

X208**T**20
ES
Extended Surround

X208**T**21
ES
Extended Surround

X208**T**22
Digital Audio

X208**T**23
Digital Sound

X208**T**24
MLP
Meridian Lossless
Packing

X208**T**25
AAD
Analog Analog Digital

X208**T**26
AAD
Analog Analog Digital

X208**T**27
ADD
Analog Digital Digital

X208**T**28
ADD
Analog Digital Digital

X208**T**29
DDD
Digital Digital Digital

X208**T**30
DDD
Digital Digital Digital

X208**T**31
Parental Advisory
Explicit Lyrics

MPAA Film Ratings

X208**U**01
General Audiences

X208**U**02
Parental Guidance Suggested

X208**U**03
Parents Strongly Cautioned

X208**U**04
Restricted

NC-17 is not available from the MPAA

V-Chip Rating System USTV

X208**U**05
TV-Y

X208**U**06
TV-Y7

X208**U**07
TV-Y7-FV

X208**U**08
TV-G

X208**U**09
TV-PG

X208**U**10
TV-14

X208**U**11
TV-MA

V-Chip Rating System Canadian-English

X208**U**12
C

X208**U**13
C8

X208**U**14
G

X208**U**15
PG

X208**U**16
14+

X208**U**17
18+

Testing and Certification Agencies

X208**U**18
ASTA, U.K.

X208**U**19
CEBEC, Comité Electotechnique Belge

X208**U**20
CE, Consultants Europe

X208**U**21
CSA, Canadian Standards Association Small Registered

X208**U**22
CSA, Canadian Standards Association Large Registered

X208**U**23
CSA, Canadian Standards Association Canadian/US Markets

X208**U**24
CCEE
China Commission for Conformity Certification

X208**U**25
CCIB, China Commodity Inspection Bureau

X208**U**26
ACA, C-Tick Australian Communications Authority

X208**U**27
DEMKO, Danmarks Elektriske Materiel Kontrollanatalten Denmark

X208**U**28
DENTORI, T-Mark Japan

X208**U**29
ETL, Electrical Testing Laboratories

Testing and Certification Agencies continued

X208**V**01
FCC, Federal Communications Commission USA

X208**V**02
GS Mark
Geprüfte Sicherheit
Germany

X208**V**03
GS Mark
Geprüfte Sicherheit
Germany

X208**V**04
GS Mark, Geprüfte Sicherheit; Germany

X208**V**05
GS Mark, Geprüfte Sicherheit; Germany

X208**V**06
IMQ
Italy

X208**V**07
IRAM, Instituto Argentino de Normalización Argentina

X208**V**08
KEMA KEUR, Keuring van Electrotechnische Materialen - Netherlands

X208**V**09
NF, Normes Françaises
France

X208**V**10
NEMKO, Norges Elektriske Materiellkontroll, Norway

X208**V**11
NOM, Normas Oficiales Mexicanas, Mexico

X208**V**12
NOM, Normas Oficiales Mexicanas, Mexico

X208**V**13
OVE, Österreichischer Verband für Elektrotechnik; Austria

X208**V**14
GOST, Gosudarstvenne Komitet Standartov
Russia

X208**V**15
SETI, Sähkötarkastuskeskus Elinspektions Centalen
Finland

X208**V**16
SEMKO, Svenska Electriska Materiel Kontrollanatalten
Sweden

X208**V**17
SAA, Standards Association of Australia

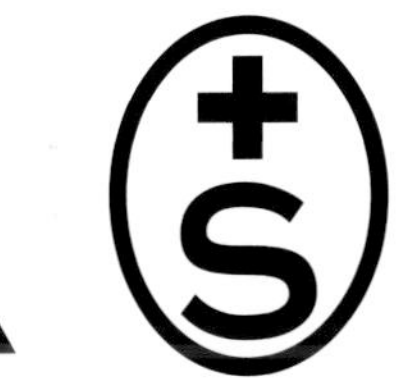

X208**V**18
SEV, Schweizerischer Elektrotechnischer Verein
Switzerland

X208**V**19
SII, Standards Institution of Israel

X208**V**20
UL Recognized Components

X208**V**21
UL Recognized Components

X208**V**22
TÜV, TÜV Rheinland
Canadian/US Compliance

X208**V**23
TÜV, TÜV Rheinland
Berlin Brandenburg

X208**V**24
TÜV, TÜV Rheinland
S-Mark; Japan

X208**V**25
TÜV, TÜV Rheinland
Ergonomics Approved

X208**V**26
TÜV, TÜV Rheinland
Product Safety
EMV/EMC

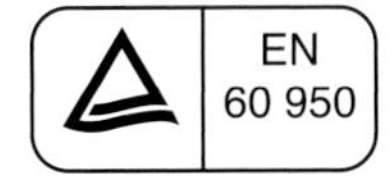

X208**V**27
TÜV, TÜV Rheinland

X208**V**28
UL, Underwriters Laboratories USA

X208**V**29
UL, Underwriters Laboratories Registered
USA

X20**V**30
UL, Underwriters Laboratories GS Mark
Europe

X208**V**31
UTE, Union Technique del l'Electricité
France

X208**V**32
VCCI, Voluntary Control Council for Interference
Japan

X208**V**33
VDE, Verband Deutscher Electrotechniker
Germany

0-C

0-9

Name	IEC	ISO	EIAJ	UltSym
5 Point Surround				X208E28
5.1 Surround				X208E35
5 Channel + Low Frequency Effects				X208E36
7.1 Surround				X208E38
8 / Eight				X208S09
16:9 Widescreen				X208S18

A

Name	IEC	ISO	EIAJ	UltSym
AAD Analog Analog Digital				X208T25
"				X208T26
A.C. In				X208N35
A.C. Out				X208N36
A.C. Plug			1106	X208P01
A.C. / D.C. Converter, Rectifier, Substitute Power Supply	5003			X208P03
ACA, C-Tick Australian Communications Authority				X208U26
A.C. Three Prong Plug				X208P02
Activity				X208K13
ADD Analog Digital Digital				X208T27
"				X208T28
Amplifier				X208D10
Adjustment to a Maximum	5147			X208L27
Adjustment to a Minimum	5146			X208L26
Adobe PostScript				X208R08
Adobe Portable Doc. File (PDF)				X208C11
Aerial / Antenna	5039		1209	X208P10
Air Impeller	5015			X208P24
Alarm			1254	X208M21
Alarm Inhibited				X208M24
Alarm Off				X208M27
Alarm On				X208M26
Alarm System Clear				X208M23
All Students, Operators	5190		7105	X208N04
Alternating Current	5032		1109	X208N32
Amplifier	5084			X208D10
Analog Analog Digital AAD				X208T25
"				X208T26
Analog Digital Digital ADD				X208T27
"				X208T28
Antenna / Aerial	5039		1209	X208P10
Apple				X208B01
"				X208B02
Application Assistance	5289			X208H26
ASTA, U.K.				X208U18
At Input				X208E04
Audio Dubbing			3103	X208H06
Automatic Control (Closed Loop)		0017	1203	X208L16
Automatic Cue, Skip			1251	X208L11
Automatic Cycle (or Semi)		0026		X208L17
Automatic Frequency Control	5046			X208P20
Automatic Search Tuning			1219	X208P19

B

Name	IEC	ISO	EIAJ	UltSym
Balance	5072		1215	X208L25
Balanced Cable			1212	X208P14
Bass Control / Bass Clef	5038		1217	X208D20
Battery Alignment (Horizontal)				X208N26
Battery Alignment (Vertical)				X208N25
Battery Charging				X208N21
Battery Check	5001			X208N27
Battery Check (Exhausted)			1112	X208N24
Battery Check (Full)			1112	X208N22
Battery Check (Partially Depleted)			1112	X208N23
Battery Eliminator / A.C. / D.C. Converter	5003			X208P03
Bell	5013			X208M28
Bell Cancel				X208M29
Bidirectional			6107	X208C34
Bidirectional Microphone	5074			X208C30
Bilingual / Dual			1235	X208C27
Billing Information	1960			X208F40
Booth			7106	X208N05
Bow, Horizontal				X208G09
Bow, Vertical				X208G10
Bright Outdoors			3112	X208J02
Brightness	5056		2103	X208B17
Brightness / Brilliance	5056			X208M04

C

Name	IEC	ISO	EIAJ	UltSym
Camera				X208B19
"				X208B20
"				X208J01
Camera Angle Selection				X208F01
Camera In				X208B21
Camera Out				X208B22
Cancel				X208K09
Cancelled Screen				X208H36
Cart In				X208A25
Cassette Tape		1238		X208E11
"				X208E21
CATV Mode		2122		X208H04
CCEE, China Commission for Conformity Certification				X208U24
CCIB, China Commodity Inspection Bureau				X208U25
CD-Rom				X208E20
CD / DVD				X208C15
CD Video				X208S07
CD Extra				X208S19
"				X208S20
CEBEC, Comité Electotechnique Belge				X208U19
CE, Consultants Europe				X208U20
Ceramic Piezo-electric Pick-up	5088			X208D13
Chassis or Frame	5020		1207	X208P09
Checkmark				X208K08
Class II Equipment	5172			X208Q21
Class III Equipment				X208Q23
Clear Screen	2024			X208H19
Clipboard				X208C01
Clock, Time Switch, Timer	5184		1301	X208M11
Closed				X208N16
Close-up			3126	X208J23
Closing (Lid or Cover)		0025		X208N10
Cloudy / Rainy Outdoors			3115	X208J05
Color Video Input / RGB		2110		X208G26
Color Video Input/Output / RGB		2111		X208G28
Color Video Output / RGB		2109		X208G27
Colour (Qualifying Symbol)	5048			X208F23
Colour Saturation	5058		2105	X208M08
Colour Television	5050			X208F24

C-D

Name	IEC	ISO	EIAJ	UltSym
Colour Television Camera	5117			X208F03
Colour Television Monitor	5052			X208H29
Colour Television Receiver	5054			X208H31
Colour Video Play-back	5123			X208F09
Colour Video Recording	5121			X208F07
Colour Video Tape Recorder	5119			X208F05
Command				X208B03
Compact Disc Player			4102	X208E17
Compact Disc				X208R19
"				X208E19
Compact Disc Interactive				X208S15
"				X208S16
Continuous	5108			X208D29
Contrast	5057		2104	X208M05
Convergence - Horizontal				X208G06
Convergence - Vertical				X208G05
Copy				X208C04
Copy Length Selector		0683		X208L34
Copy Protected				X208S17
Counter Light Control			3129	X208J26
Crispener	5059		2108	X208F29
Crystal or Ceramic Piezo-electric Pick-up	5088			X208D13
CSA, Canadian Standards Association Small Registered				X208U21
CSA, Canadian Standards Association Large Registered				X208U22
CSA, Canadian Standards Association Canadian / US Markets				X208U23
Cue, Review			3105	X208H08
Cue Marker			5103	X208D24
Current, Direct	5031		1108	X208N31
Cursor				X208A23
Cutting Adjustment	1981			X208L33

D

Name	IEC	ISO	EIAJ	UltSym
DDD Digital Digital Digital				X208T29
"				X208T30
Dark	2166			X208M07
Data Activity				X208Q07
Data Storage				X208R20
Data Storage Mainframe				X208A36
DBX				X208T15
D.C. / A.C. Converter				X208P04
DEMKO, Danmarks Elektriske Materiel Kontrollanatalten Denmark				X208U27
DENTORI, T-Mark Japan				X208U28
Device Connected				X208K16
Device Not Connected				X208K15
Dew, Moisture			3107	X208H11
Digital Audio				X208S23
"				X208T22
Digital Audio Plus				X208S24
Digital Audio Tape (DAT)			5109	X208E18
Digital Cinema				X208T14
Digital Data				X208R21
Digital Digital Digital, DDD				X208T29
"				X208T30
Digital S				X208S13
Digital Sound				X208T23
Dipole	5040		1210	X208P11

Name	IEC	ISO	EIAJ	UltSym
Direct and Alternating Current, Both	5033		1110	X208N33
Direct Current	5031		1108	X208N31
Direct Selection				X208B27
Direction			5105	X208D27
Direction Tilt Correction				X208G16
Disc				X208B35
Discrete Surround				X208E27
Discrete Surround Plus Low Frequency Effects				X208E34
Discs				X208B36
Disk - In				X208A10
Disk - Out				X208A11
Disk Drive				X208A07
Diskette				X208A12
Diskette (3.5 Inch)				X208A09
Diskette (5.25 Inch)				X208A14
Disturb				X208K14
Dolby Surround				X208E24
Dolby Surround Plus Low Frequency Effects				X208E31
Do Not Operate / Intervene	1627			X208L15
Document		15		X208C06
Document Copy				X208C07
Dolby				X208S33
Dolby Digital				X208T04
Dolby HX Pro Headroom Extension Type-B				X208T09
Dolby HX Pro Headroom Extension Type-S				X208T10
Dolby Headphones				X208T11
Dolby Stereo				X208S34
Dolby Surround				X208T02
"				X208T03
Dolby Surround Pro Logic				X208T05
Dolby Surround Pro Logic II				X208T06
Dolby System				X208T01
Dolby Type-B Noise Reduction				X208T07
Dolby Type-S Noise Reduction				X208T08
Down (Tone Arm)			4104	X208E15
DTS Digital Theater Surround				X208T18
"				X208T19
During Play-back, Monitoring				X208E06
DVD				X208R24
DVD Audio				X208S31
DVD-Digital Video				X208S06
DVD R1				X208R28
DVD R2				X208R29
DVD R3				X208R30
DVD RAM				X208R31
DVD R / RAM				X208R32
DVD Rom				X208R25
"				X208R26
"				X208R27
DVD ROM / Video				X208S05
DVD-Video				X208S01
"				X208S02
"				X208S03
DVD Video / Audio				X208S04
D VHS				X208S12

E-H

I-M

I

Name	IEC	ISO	EIAJ	UltSym
Illumination / Lamp / Light	5012		1252	X208M01
Image Formation Plane		3130		X208J27
IMQ, Italy				X208V06
Incandescent Lamp Indoors			3113	X208J03
Indirect Lighting	5320			X208M02
Initiator	1963			X208H17
Inking Adjustment	1980			X208L30
"In" Position Of Bistable Push Control	5268		1205	X208N13
Input	5034			X208N28
Input / Output				X208N30
Insert			3104	X208H07
Insert PCMCIA Media or Device				X208A18
Insert Tape Media				X208F12
"				X208F13
Instruction or Correction	5105			X208F10
Interactive Videotext Deactivated	1957			X208F27
Interruption/Pause	5111			X208K03
Interruption of Automatic Cycle & Return to Start Position		0427		X208L18
Inverted Top to Bottom				X208H34
Inverted Top to Bottom & Reversal Right to Left				X208H35
IRAM, Instituto Argentino de Normalización Argentina				X208V07
Iris Diaphragm: Closed	5324		3118	X208J15
Iris Diaphragm: Open	5323		3117	X208J14
Iris Lock			3119	X208J16

J

Name	IEC	ISO	EIAJ	UltSym
Joystick				X208A05

K

Name	IEC	ISO	EIAJ	UltSym
KEMA KEUR, Keuring van Electrotechnische Materialen - Netherlands				X208V08
Keyboard				X208A02
Key Control / Natural				X208D23
Keystone, Horizontal				X208G11
Keystone, Vertical				X208G12
Key Switch of Key Fastener		0517		X208M30

L

Name	IEC	ISO	EIAJ	UltSym
Lamp / Lighting / Illumination	5012		1252	X208M01
LCD Monitor				X208H16
Light	2165			X208M06
Lighting / Lamp / Illumination	5012		1252	X208M01
Line Select				X208G01
Link / Security				X208C18
Listen	5211			X208D09
Load Cassette	1948			X208F11
Load Diskette	1947			X208A13
Locked				X208A20
Long Distance (Zone Focus)			3125	X208J22
Loop Antenna (U.S.A.)	5042			X208P13
Loop Antenna (Frame Aerial)	5042			X208P13
Loudness			1220	X208C42
Loudspeaker	5080		6101	X208C41
Loudspeaker / Microphone	5081			X208D03
Loudspeaker Mute				X208D06
Loudspeaker in Operation as a Microphone	5126			X208D01
Loudspeaker in Operation as Such	5127			X208D02
Low Intensity Lighting	5321			X208M03
Low Light Mode				X208J08
Low-pass Filter	5092			X208D16

M

Name	IEC	ISO	EIAJ	UltSym
Mac				X208R01
"				X208R02
"				X208R03
Mac OS				X208R04
"				X208R05
Magnetic Card - In				X208Q17
Magnetic Card - Out				X208Q18
Magnetic Stereo Sound Tape Recorder	5094		5102	X208D33
Magneto Electrodynamic Pick-up	5089			X208D14
Magnifying Tool				X208B28
Mailbox				X208B38
" , Empty				X208B40
" , Outgoing Mail				X208B39
" , You Have Mail				X208B41
Main Index Page				X208H25
Manual Control		0096	1204	X208L14
Media				X208A08
Memory / Storage Full	1946			X208Q05
Menu				X208G03
Meridian Lossless Packing, MLP				X208T24
Message Service	1961			X208F41
Mic				X208B13
Mic On				X208B14
Mic / Live Recording				X208B15
Microphone	5082		6102	X208C19
"				X208C21
"				X208C22
Microsoft HDCD				X208S32
Middle Distance (Zone Focus)			3124	X208J21
Midi				X208S29
MiniDisc				X208R34
"				X208R35
"				X208R36
"				X208R37
Moire'				X208G18
Monitoring	2030			X208N07
Monitoring at the Input during Recording on Tape	5098			X208E04
Monitoring during Play-back or Reading from Tape	5100			X208E06
Monitoring from Tape after Recording on Tape	5099			X208E05
Monophonic	5070		1236	X208C24
Mono Plus Low Frequency Effects				X208E29
Mouse				X208A04
"				X208C16
Movement in Both Directions	5023			X208K26
Movement in One Direction	5022			X208K25
Movement limited in Both Directions	5024			X208K27
Multi Image Display			2129	X208F39
Multiple Documents				X208C08
Multiplex TV Sound			2102	X208G04
Music	5085		1240	X208D18
Muting				X208D07
"	5047			X208P21

N-R

N

Name	IEC	ISO	EIAJ	UltSym
NEMKO, Norges Elektriske Materiellkontroll, Norway				X208V10
NF, Normes Françaises France				X208V09
Nega / Posi Reversal	5411		3110	X208H14
Next One Sentence Play				X208D28
Night Portrait Mode				X208J07
Noiseless (Clean) Earth / Ground	5018			X208P07
NOM, Normas Oficiales Mexicanas Mexico				X208V11
"				X208V12
Non-simultaneous Effect or Action Away from and Towards a Reference Point	5029			X208K32
Normal Aspect				X208H32
Normal Speed / Playback	5107		1242	X208L02
Not to Be Used in Residential Areas	5109			X208P25

O

Name	IEC	ISO	EIAJ	UltSym
Off (power)	5008		1103	X208J31
"Off" Part of an Equipment	5265			X208J35
Off Hook				X208Q14
"				X208Q15
Omnidirectional			6106	X208C33
Omnidirectional Microphone	5073			X208C29
On (power)	5007		1102	X208J30
On / Off (Push Button)	5011			X208J33
On / Off (Push-push)	5010		1104	X208J32
On / Off, Stand-by	5009			X208K02
"On" Part of an Equipment	5264			X208J34
On Screen			2116	X208F30
One or Multi-digit Selection			2121	X208H03
One Way			5106	X208D30
Open				X208N15
Open Folder				X208C03
Open (a Container)	0024			X208N09
Operation Instructions	1641			X208Q09
Optical Disk				X208A16
"Out" Position (Push Control)	5269		1206	X208N14
Output	5035			X208N29
OVE, Österreichischer Verband für Elektrotechnik Austria				X208V13

P

Name	IEC	ISO	EIAJ	UltSym
Page, Paper				X208C05
Page # Down				X208H21
Page # Up				X208H22
Page Hold	5290			X208F26
Pair Lesson			7103	X208N06
Parental Advisory Explicit Lyrics				X208T31
Parental Guidance Suggested				X208U02
Parents Strongly Cautioned				X208U03
Pause			1245	X208L05
Pause / Interruption	5111			X208K03
PCMCIA Media or Device				X208A17
PDF (Portable Document File)				X208C11
Photo CD				X208S22
Pick-up for Disk Records	5086			X208D11
Picture			2107	X208M09
Picture-in-Picture Freeze			2124	X208F34
Picture-in-Picture Mode	5291		2123	X208F33
Picture-in-Picture Shift			2127	X208F37
Picture-in-Picture Swap			2126	X208F36
Picture Rotation Adjustment				X208G15
Picture Size Adjustment	5067			X208F20
Piezo-electric Pick-up, Crystal Or Ceramic	5088			X208D13
Pincussion, Horizontal				X208G07
Pincussion, Vertical				X208G08
Plane of Sensitized Material: Judge Plane				X208J28
Playback			1242	X208E01
Playback / Normal Speed				X208L02
Play-back or Reading from Tape	5096			X208E01
Plug and Socket		0354		X208P05
Plug Connection, General		0354		X208P05
Pointer Tool				X208B26
Polarity of D.C. Input and Output Terminals (Unified Polarity Type)			1113	X208N34
Positioning of Cell	5002		1111	X208N20
Power Supply				X208J38
Pressure Adjustment	1979			X208L29
Prevention of Camera				X208J10
Previous One Sentence Play				X208D26
Principal Control Panel	5263			X208N12
Print, Printing				X208C04
Print Screen	2027			X208H27
Printer				X208A03
"				X208Q20
Processor				X208A29
Programmable Duration			1305	X208M15
"				X208M20
Programmable Timer	5440		1302	X208M13
"				X208M17
Protective Earth / Ground	5019		1208	X208P08
PS / 2 / Serial				X208B08
Pulse Marker on Tape Recorders	5102			X208E09
Purity				X208G17

Q

Name	IEC	ISO	EIAJ	UltSym
Quad Surround				X208E25
Quad Surround Plus Low Frequency Effects				X208E32
Quicktime				X208R09
"				X208R10

R

Name	IEC	ISO	EIAJ	UltSym
Radio Control Indicator				X208N17
Radio Receiver / Tuner	5043			X208P16
Read Data from Store	1026			X208Q03
Read Operator's Manual	0790			X208Q08
Reading / Recording Interference				X208E08
Reading / Recording Tape Mode				X208E02
Ready		1140		X208K01
Ready (to Proceed) / Checkmark	0422			X208K08
Ready / Output				X208K10
Real				X208R13
Rec review			3108	X208H12
Recapitulate	5125		1241	X208L01
Recordable				X208R22
"				X208S25
Record Muting			5104	X208D25
Record Player			4101	X208E13
Recorder, Tape	5093			X208D32
Recording			1246	X208L06
Recording Interference / Reading				X208E08

R-T

Name	IEC	ISO	EIAJ	UltSym
Recording Lock on Tape Recorders	5101			X208E07
Recording on Tape	5095			X208D34
Recording Tape Mode				X208E02
Red-Eye Reduction				X208J11
Reduce				X208B30
Rejection	5113			X208L13
Remaining Time Display			1303	X208H38
Remaining Time				X208M18
Remote Access				X208K24
Remote Station Ready	1937			X208K17
Remote Station Stand-By	1938			X208K18
Remote Station, Positive Acknowledgement of	1940			X208K19
Remote Station, Negative Acknowledgement of	1941			X208K20
Remote Station, Disturbance at	1939			X208K21
Remote Station, Call Operator of	1950			X208K22
Remote Station, No Operator Response from	1951			X208K23
Remove PCMCIA media or device				X208A19
Reset				X208K11
Restricted				X208U04
Return to an Initial State	5495			X208K12
Reveal	1959			X208F32
Reversal Right to Left				X208H33
Reverse			5107	X208D31
"				X208H15
Rewritable				X208R23
RGB / Color Video Input			2110	X208G26
RGB / Color Video Input / Output			2111	X208G28
RGB / Color Video Output			2109	X208G27
ROM / RAM				X208R33
Rumble Filter (See: High-pass Filter)	5091			X208D15

S

Name	IEC	ISO	EIAJ	UltSym
S Camera In				X208B23
S Camera Out				X208B24
S Video Input			1226	X208G23
S Video Input / Output			1227	X208G24
S Video Output			1225	X208G22
Satellite Mode			2120	X208G25
Save Files				X208B42
Scrolling	2025			X208H20
SCSI				X208A31
"				X208A32
SCSI (IBM)				X208A30
Security / Link				X208C18
Security Device				X208A22
Select	1996			X208L19
Selection of Picture-in-Picture				X208F35
Self Timer Shutter				X208J29
SEMKO, Svenska Electriska Materiel Kontrollanatalten Sweden				X208V16
Serial				X208A24
SETI, Sähkötarkastuskeskus Elinspektions Centalen Finland				X208V15
SEV, Schweizerischer Elektro-technischer Verein Switzerland				X208V18
Sharp				X208D21
Shockwave				X208R11
Short Distance (Zone Focus)			3123	X208J20
Signal Lamp	5115			X208P27
Signal Strength Attenuation (Local / Distant)	5044			X208P17
Simultaneous Effect or Action Away from and Towards a Reference Point	5030			X208K33
Single Frame Shot			3132	X208H40
Skew				X208G13
"				X208G14
Sleep Timer				X208M16
Slow-motion			1248	X208L08
Slow Run, Slow Speed	5124		1248	X208L12
Sony Dynamic Digital Surround				X208T12
"				X208T13
Sound / Audio	5182		1202	X208D17
Sound & Language Selection				X208C22
Sound Mode Mono				X208E28
Source Selection of Picture-in-Picture			2125	X208F35
Spatial Sound Effect			1237	X208C26
Speak	5210			X208D08
Sport Mode				X208J09
Squelch (U.S.A.) / Muting	5047			X208P21
SSA, Standards Association of Australia				X208V17
Stand-by (On / Off)	5009		1105	X208K02
Stand-by or Preparatory State for a Part of Equipment	5266			X208J36
Start (of Action)	5104		3131	X208K04
Start Timer				X208M14
Stereo				X208E23
Stereo and Center Channel				X208E26
Stereophonic	5071		1234	X208C25
Stereophonic Headphones	5078			X208C39
Stereophonic Microphone	5083		6105	X208C32
Stereophonic Pick-up for Disk Records	5087			X208D12
Stereo Plus Low Frequency Effects				X208E30
Stereo with Center Plus Low Frequency Effects				X208E33
Still			1249	X208L09
Stop			1243	X208L03
Stop (of Action)	5110			X208K06
Storage	0987			X208Q01
Storage / Store Mode Finished	5460			X208Q06
Student / Operator	5188		7102	X208N02
Studio Microphone			6104	X208C23
Subtitle, Caption				X208G02
Super Audio CD				X208S30
Surround EX				X208E37
System Status Display				X208H37

T

Name	IEC	ISO	EIAJ	UltSym
Tablet				X208A06
Tape Cutting	5103			X208E10
Tape End			1239	X208E12
Tape Recorder	5093		5101	X208D32
Teacher, Supervisor	5187		7101	X208N01
Tele			3128	X208J25
Telephone	5090			X208Q13
Telephone / Telephone Adapter	5090			X208Q11
Telephone Disconnected	1949			X208Q12
Telephone Voice Communication				X208Q16
Teletext Mode			2119	X208H01

T-W

Name	IEC	ISO	EIAJ	UltSym
Television Camera	5116		3111	X208F02
Television Monitor	5051		2101	X208H28
Television Receiver	5053			X208H30
Television / Video	5049		1201	X208F14
Temperature				X208L36
Temperature Control	0175			X208L35
Temperature Range				X208L37
Temporary Inactive Attributes, Disable Attributes	1958			X208F31
Terminator	1964			X208H18
Test				X208N08
Test Voltage				X208Q22
Text				X208S26
Text Document				X208C06
Text Tool				X208B25
Three Component Video In				X208G30
Three Component Video Input / Output				X208G32
Three Component Video Output				X208G31
Three Component Signal				X208G29
THX				X208T16
"				X208T17
Timer				X208B31
" , Hourglass				X208B37
Timer, Clock, Time Switch	5184	1301		X208M11
Token Bus				X208A33
Token Ring				X208A35
Toner Adjustment		0676		X208L31
Trackball Mouse				X208C17
Tracking			3109	X208H13
Transfer of Signal	5112			X208P26
Trash				X208B32
Treble Control / G or Treble Clef	5037		1216	X208D19
True-Type Font				X208C10
Tuner / Radio Receiver	5043			X208P16
Tuning	5045		1218	X208P18
TÜV, TÜV Rheinland				X208V27
TÜV, TÜV Rheinland Berlin Brandenburg				X208V23
TÜV, TÜV Rheinland Canadian/ US Compliance				X208V22
TÜV, TÜV Rheinland Ergonomics Approved				X208V25
TÜV, TÜV Rheinland Product Safety EMV/EMC				X208V26
TÜV, TÜV Rheinland S-Mark Japan				X208V24
TV & Text Mode				X208H02
Twilight Outdoors			3116	X208J06
Two Component Video Input				X208G33
Two Component Video Input / Output				X208G35
Two Component Video Output				X208G34

U

Name	IEC	ISO	EIAJ	UltSym
UL Recognized Components				X208V20
"				X208V21
UL, Underwriters Laboratories USA				X208V28
UL, Underwriters Laboratories GS Mark Europe				X208V30
UL, Underwriters Laboratories Registered USA				X208V29
Unbalanced Cable			1213	X208P15
UTEL, Union Technique del l'Electricité France				X208V31
Unidirectional			6108	X208C31
Unidirectional or Cardioid Microphone	5075			X208C25
Unlocked				X208A21
Up (Tone Arm)			4103	X208E14
Urgent Alarm				X208M22
USB				X208R14
"				X208R15
USB Connection				X208B09

V

Name	IEC	ISO	EIAJ	UltSym
VGA Port				X208B11
Variable Speed	1943			X208L28
Variability	5004		1214	X208L20
Variability, for Rotating Movement	1364			X208L23
Variability in Steps	5181			X208L21
Variability in Steps, for Rotating Movement	2164			X208L24
Variability Maximum Speed				X208L22
VCCI, Voluntary Control Council for Interference Japan				X208V32
VDE, Verband Deutscher Electrotechniker Germany				X208V33
Vertical Bow				X208G10
Vertical Keystone				X208G12
Vertical Linearity	5069			X208F22
Vertical Picture Amplitude	5066		2115	X208F19
Vertical Picture Shift	5064		2118	X208F17
Vertical Pincussion				X208G08
Vertical Synchronization	5062		2113	X208F15
Very Short Distance			3122	X208J19
VHS				X208S10
VHS C				X208S11
VHS / HiFi				X208S14
Video / Television	5049			X208F14
Video Data				X208G36
Video Disc Player			3102	X208H05
Video Head Clogged			3106	X208H10
Video Input			1223	X208G20
Video Input / Output			1224	X208G21
Video Output			1222	X208G19
Video Play-back	5122			X208F08
Video Recording	5120			X208F06
Video Tape Recorder	5118		3101	X208F04
Videotext Deactivated				X208F27
Vinyl Record				X208E16
Volume	5004		1214	X208D04
Volume in Steps				X208D05
Volume Off				X208B04
Volume Minimum				X208B05
Volume Medium				X208B06
Volume Full				X208B07

W

Name	IEC	ISO	EIAJ	UltSym
White Balance			3121	X208J18
Wide			3127	X208J24
Widescreen 16:9				X208S18
Window / Screen				X208C14
Workstation				X208A01
World Time				X208M12
Write and Read Data from Store	1107		1233	X208Q04

International Icons II: Mechanical Labeling (ISO / IEC)

9

Automotive
- Lighting and Signalling Devices

X209**A**01
High (Main) Beam

X209**A**02
Low (Dipped) Beam

X209**A**03
Headlamp Cleaner

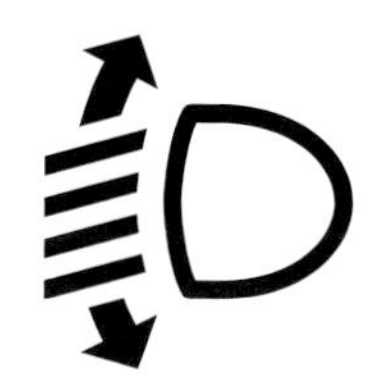
X209**A**04
Headlight Leveling Manual Control

X209**A**05
Front Fog Light

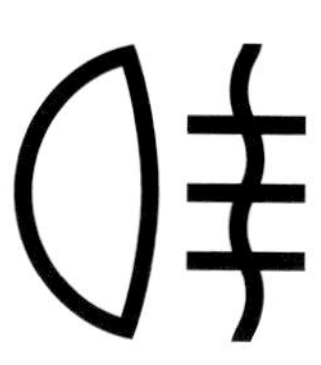
X209**A**06
Rear Fog Light

X209**A**07
Long-Range Light

X209**A**08
Parking Lights

X209**A**09
Position (Side) Lights

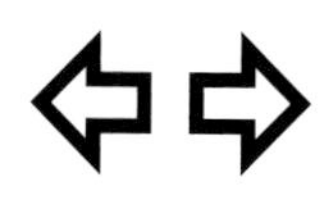
X209**A**10
Turn Signals

X209**A**11
Hazard Warning

X209**A**12
Horn

X209**A**13
Interior Compartment Illumination

X209**A**14
Beacon

X209**A**15
Dashboard Light Dimmer

- Braking System

X209**A**16
Brake Failure

X209**A**17
Parking Brake

X209**A**18
Failure Of Anti-Lock Brake System

X209**A**19
Worn Brake Linings

X209**A**20
Brake Fluid Level

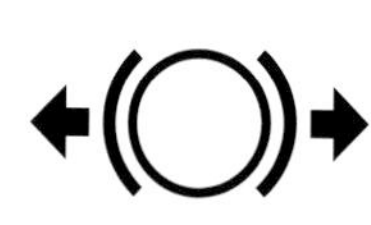
X209**A**21
Spring Brake Release

- Visibility

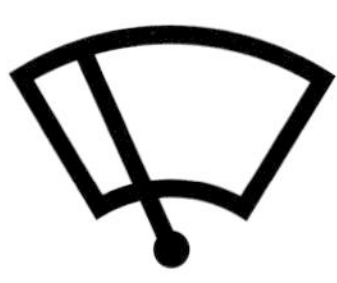
X209**A**22
Windscreen Wiper

X209**A**23
Windscreen Wiper – Intermittent

X209**A**24
Windscreen Washer

X209**A**25
Windscreen Washer And Wiper

X209**A**26
Windscreen Washer Fluid Level

X209**A**27
Windscreen Demisting And Defrosting

X209**A**28
Rear Window Wiper

X209**A**29
Rear Window Wiper – Intermittent

X209**A**30
Rear Window Washer

X209**A**31
Rear Window Wiper And Washer

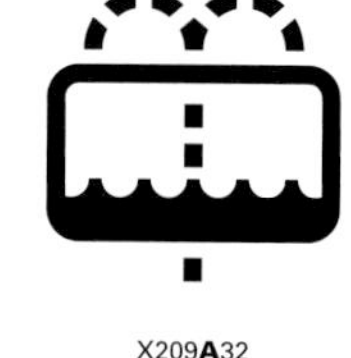
X209**A**32
Level of Rear Window Washer Fluid

X209**A**33
Rear Window Demisting And Defrosting

X209**A**34
Side Window Demisting And Defrosting

X209**A**35
Exterior Rear View Mirror Adjustment, Horizontal Type

X209**A**36
Exterior Rear View Mirror Adjustment, Vertical Type

X209**A**37
Exterior Rear View Mirror Heating, Horizontal Type

X209**A**38
Exterior Rear View Mirror Heating, Vertical Type

Automotive continued
- Cab Environment

X209**B**01
Air-Conditioning System

X209**B**02
Ventilating Fan

X209**B**03
Ventilating Fan

X209**B**04
Interior Heating

X209**B**05
Upper Air Outlet

X209**B**06
Lower Air Outlet

X209**B**07
Upper Air Outlet And Lower Air Outlet

X209**B**08
Fresh Air

X209**B**09
Fresh Air

X209**B**10
Recirculated Air

X209**B**11
Recirculated Air

X209**B**12
Window Lift – Power Operated

X209**B**13
Seat Adjustment – Longitudinal

X209**B**14
Seat-Back Recline Adjustment

X209**B**15
Seat Height Adjustment – Cushion Front

X209**B**16
Seat Height Adjustment – Cushion Rear

X209**B**17
Headrest Height Adjustment

X209**B**18
Heated Seat

X209**B**19
Lighter

- Engine

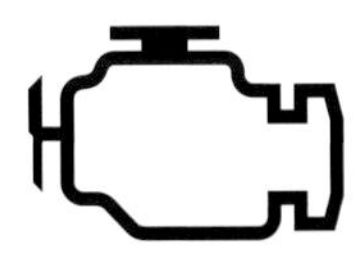
X209**B**20
Engine

X209**B**21
Engine Failure

X209**B**22
Engine Coolant

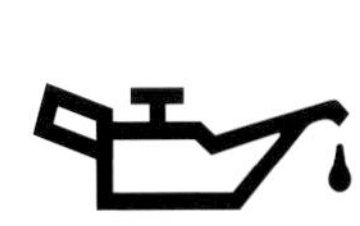
X209**B**23
Engine Oil

X209**B**24
Engine Oil Temperature

X209**B**25
Engine Oil Level

X209**B**26
Engine Oil Filter

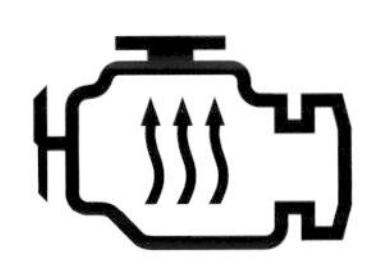
X209**B**27
Engine Heating

X209**B**28
Electronic Diesel Control

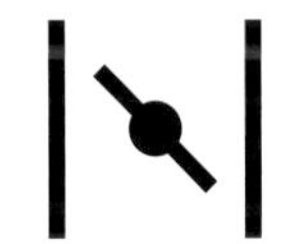
X209**B**29
Choke

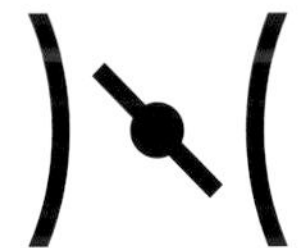
X209**B**30
Hand Throttle

X209**B**31
Engine Start

X209**B**32
Engine Shut-Off

X209**B**33
Engine Coolant Level

Automotive continued
- Fuel System

X209**C**01
Fuel

X209**C**02
Fuel

X209**C**03
Unleaded Fuel

X209**C**04
Fuel Economy

- Transmission

X209**C**05
Park (Automatic Transmission)

X209**C**06
Reverse (Automatic Transmission)

X209**C**07
Neutral (Automatic Transmission)

X209**C**08
Drive (Automatic Transmission)

X209**C**09
Transmission Failure

- Power Drive

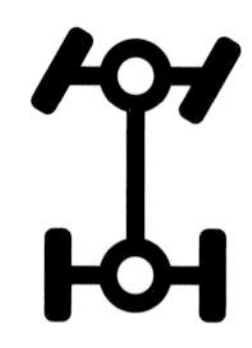

X209**C**10
All Wheel Drive 4x4

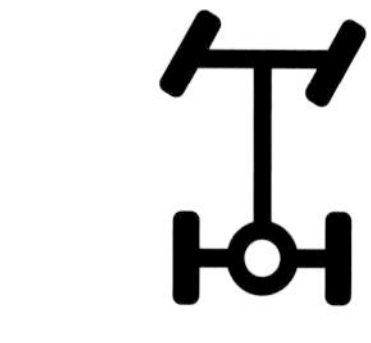

X209**C**11
Rear Axle Drive 4x4

X209**C**12
Front Axle Drive 4x4

- Vehicle Handling and Cruise Control

X209**C**13
Steering Fluid Level

X209**C**14
Steering Failure

- Active and Passive Safety Systems

X209**C**15
Seat Belt

X209**C**16
Seat Belt

X209**C**17
Airbag

X209**C**18
Child Seat Prohibition

X209**C**19
Door(s) Ajar

X209**C**20
Door(s) Ajar

- Security

X209**C**21
Bonnet (Front Hood)

X209**C**22
Bonnet (Front Hood)

X209**C**23
Boot (Rear Trunk)

X209**C**24
Boot (Rear Trunk)

X209**C**25
Door Lock Control

- Electric Functions

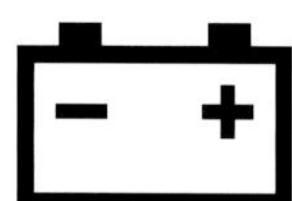

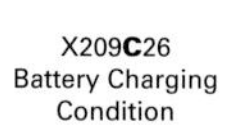

X209**C**26
Battery Charging Condition

X209**C**27
Battery Failure

X209**C**28
Battery Fluid Level

X209**C**29
Battery Shut-Off

Home
Utility

Note: All symbols and signs are available as fully editable vector image files: see page 238 or www.ultimatesymbol.com

Home Utility
continued

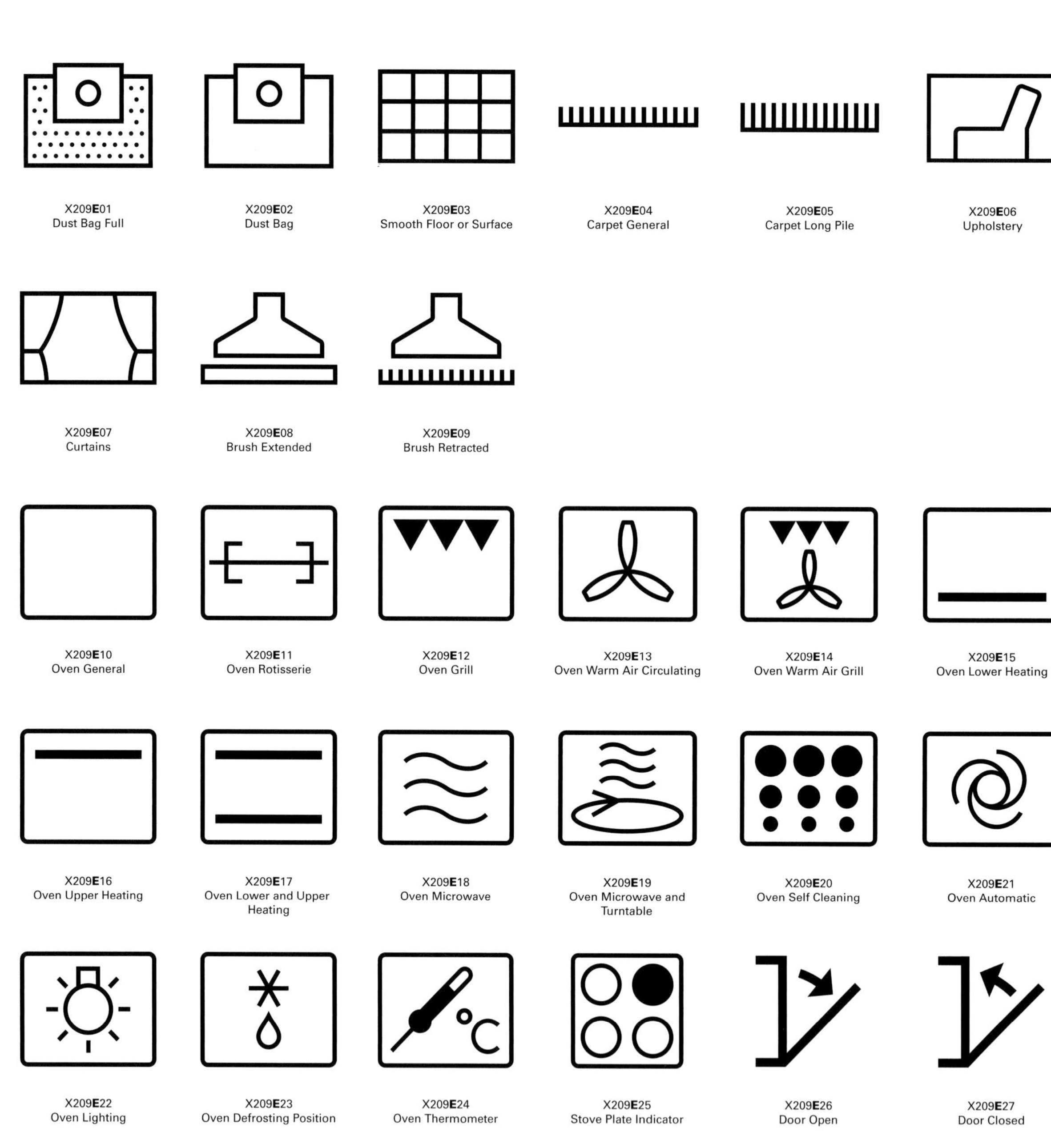

X209**E**01 Dust Bag Full

X209**E**02 Dust Bag

X209**E**03 Smooth Floor or Surface

X209**E**04 Carpet General

X209**E**05 Carpet Long Pile

X209**E**06 Upholstery

X209**E**07 Curtains

X209**E**08 Brush Extended

X209**E**09 Brush Retracted

X209**E**10 Oven General

X209**E**11 Oven Rotisserie

X209**E**12 Oven Grill

X209**E**13 Oven Warm Air Circulating

X209**E**14 Oven Warm Air Grill

X209**E**15 Oven Lower Heating

X209**E**16 Oven Upper Heating

X209**E**17 Oven Lower and Upper Heating

X209**E**18 Oven Microwave

X209**E**19 Oven Microwave and Turntable

X209**E**20 Oven Self Cleaning

X209**E**21 Oven Automatic

X209**E**22 Oven Lighting

X209**E**23 Oven Defrosting Position

X209**E**24 Oven Thermometer

X209**E**25 Stove Plate Indicator

X209**E**26 Door Open

X209**E**27 Door Closed

X209**E**28 Intermediate Rinsing

X209**E**29 Oven Warming

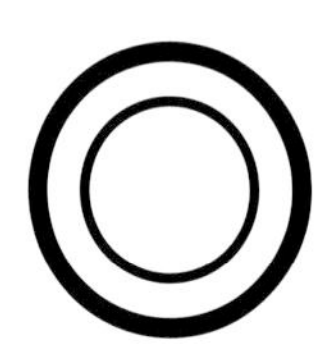

X209**E**30 Cooking Zone Central

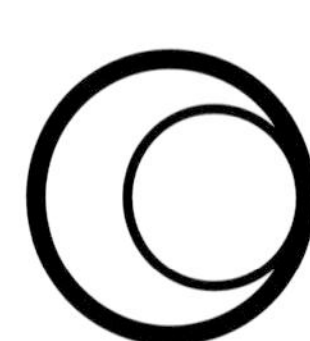

X209**E**31 Cooking Zone Eccentric

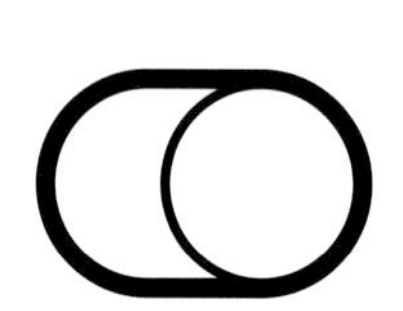

X209**E**32 Cooking Zone Oval

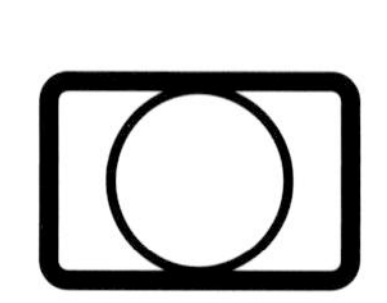

X209**E**33 Cooking Zone Bilateral

Care Labeling

X209**F**01
Hand Wash

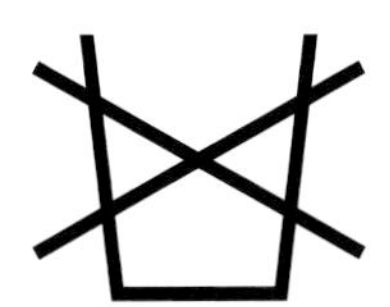

X209**F**02
Do Not Wash

X209**F**03
Maximum Temperature
95°C

X209**F**04
Max. Temp. 60°C / Reduce
Mechanical Action

X209**F**05
Max. Temp. 40° C /
Greatly Reduce
Mechanical Action

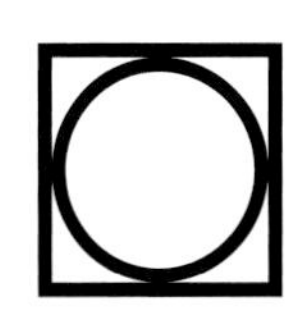

X209**F**06
Tumble Dry

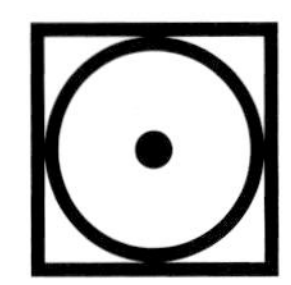

X209**F**07
Tumble Dry
(low heat)

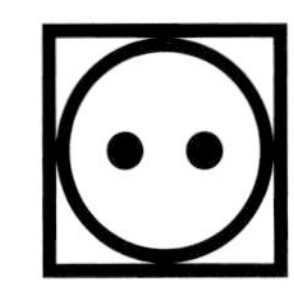

X209**F**08
Tumble Dry
(high heat)

X209**F**09
"Drip" Dry

X209**F**10
Hang to dry

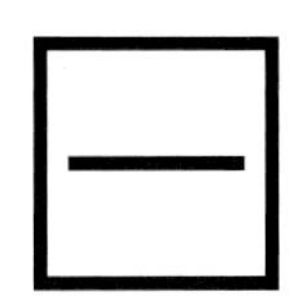

X209**F**11
Dry Flat

X209**F**12
Iron

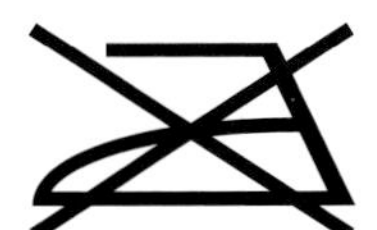

X209**F**13
Do Not Iron

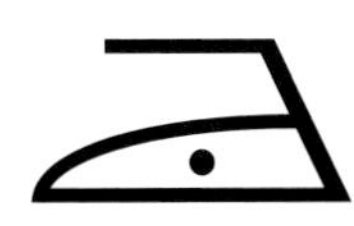

X209**F**14
Cool
(120°C / 248°F)

X209**F**15
Warm
(160°C / 320°F)

X209**F**16
Hot
(210°C / 410°F)

X209**F**17
Bleach

X209**F**18
Do Not Use
Chlorine Bleach

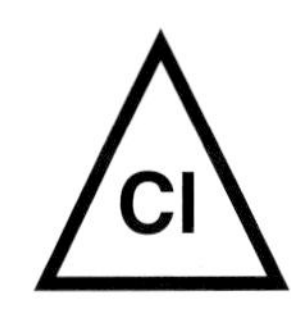

X209**F**19
Chlorine Bleach

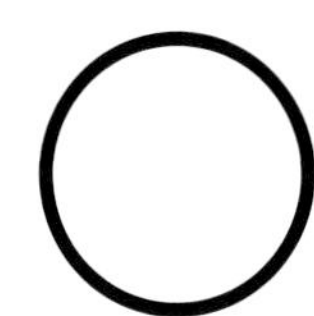

X209**F**20
Dry Clean

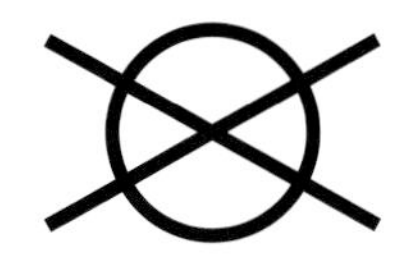

X209**F**21
Do Not Dry Clean

X209**F**22
Dry Clean In
Any Solvent

X209**F**23
Use Fluorocarbon
Solvent Only or Petroleum

X209**F**24
Dry Clean Except
Trichloroethylene

Photocopier

X209**F**25
Single-Sided Original

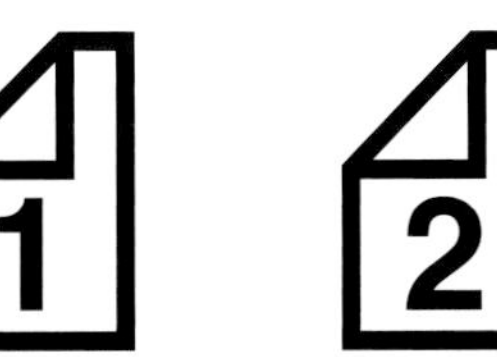

X209**F**26
Double-Sided Original

X209**F**27
Copies in Duplex

X209**F**28
Reduction 2

X209**F**29
Photo Original

X209**F**30
Bound Original

X209**F**31
Double Original

X209**F**32
Missed Original

X209**F**33
Single-Sided Copy

X209**F**34
Double-Sided Copy

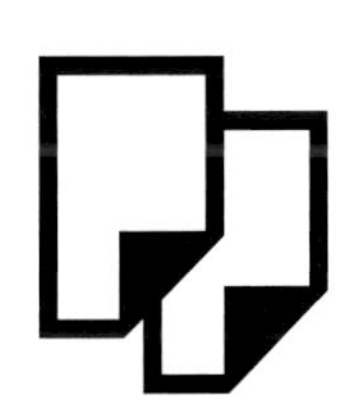

X209**F**35
Double Copy Fault

X209**F**36
Missed Copy Fault

Photocopier
continued

Document
Binding
and Folding

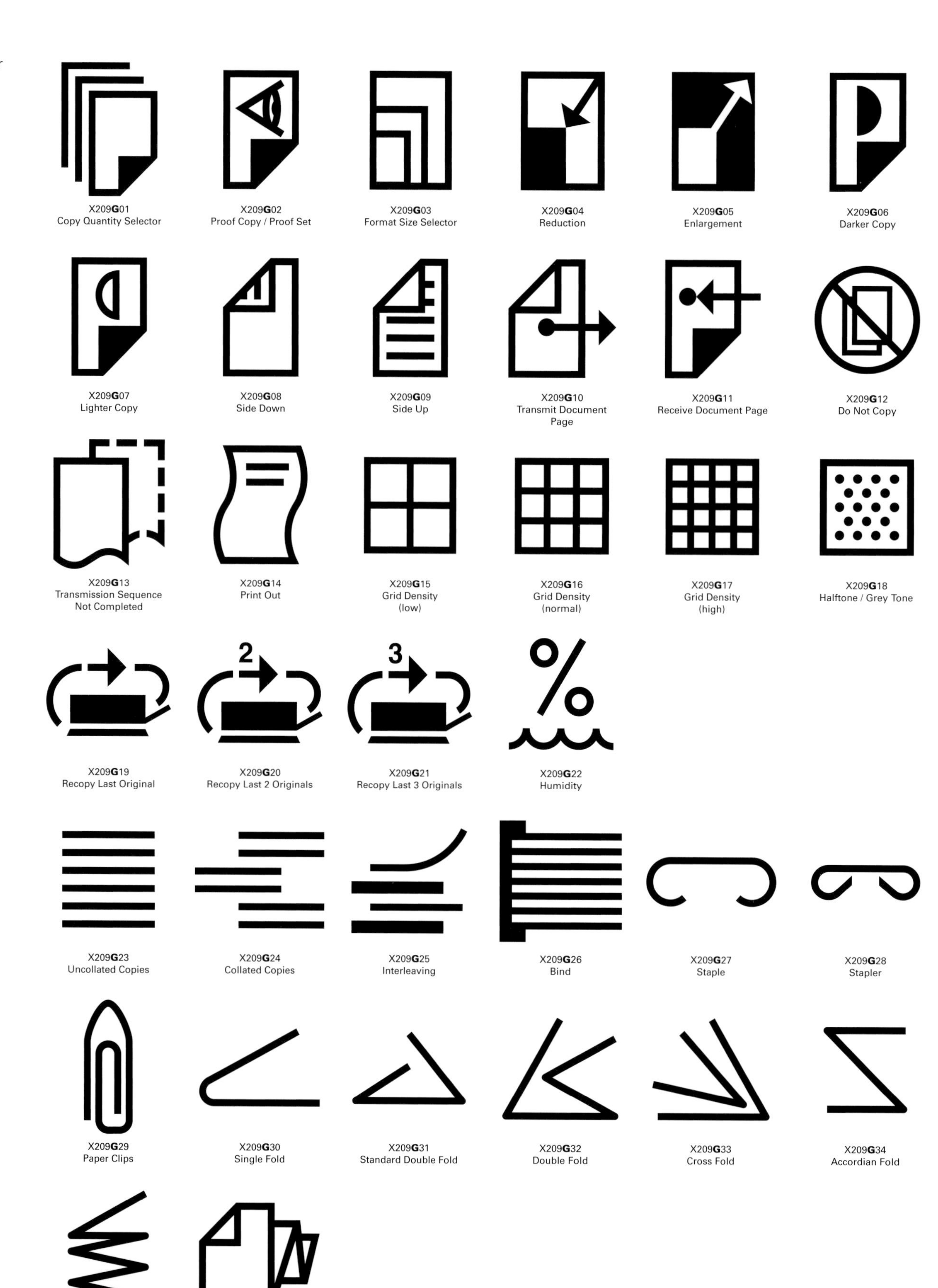

X209**G**01 Copy Quantity Selector
X209**G**02 Proof Copy / Proof Set
X209**G**03 Format Size Selector
X209**G**04 Reduction
X209**G**05 Enlargement
X209**G**06 Darker Copy
X209**G**07 Lighter Copy
X209**G**08 Side Down
X209**G**09 Side Up
X209**G**10 Transmit Document Page
X209**G**11 Receive Document Page
X209**G**12 Do Not Copy
X209**G**13 Transmission Sequence Not Completed
X209**G**14 Print Out
X209**G**15 Grid Density (low)
X209**G**16 Grid Density (normal)
X209**G**17 Grid Density (high)
X209**G**18 Halftone / Grey Tone
X209**G**19 Recopy Last Original
X209**G**20 Recopy Last 2 Originals
X209**G**21 Recopy Last 3 Originals
X209**G**22 Humidity
X209**G**23 Uncollated Copies
X209**G**24 Collated Copies
X209**G**25 Interleaving
X209**G**26 Bind
X209**G**27 Staple
X209**G**28 Stapler
X209**G**29 Paper Clips
X209**G**30 Single Fold
X209**G**31 Standard Double Fold
X209**G**32 Double Fold
X209**G**33 Cross Fold
X209**G**34 Accordian Fold
X209**G**35 Fan Fold (continuous stationery)
X209**G**36 Fan Fold

Photocopier (Mechanical)

Photocopier (Mechanical) continued

X209**J**01 Paper Thickness (thin)

X209**J**02 Paper Thickness (thick)

X209**J**03 Friction Pressure

X209**J**04 Paper Carrier Closed

X209**J**05 Paper Carrier Open

X209**J**06 Remove Used Master Container

X209**J**07 Close Cover

X209**J**08 Remove Original

X209**J**09 Insert Original

X209**J**10 Add Dry Toner

X209**J**11 Toner saver

X209**J**12 Add Ink

X209**J**13 Add Liquid Toner

X209**J**14 Add Liquid Dispersant

X209**J**15 Add Liquid Developer

X209**J**16 Add Water

X209**J**17 Start Moistening

X209**J**18 Stop Moistening

X209**J**19 Counter

X209**J**20 Key Counter

X209**J**21 Alternate Language

X209**J**22 Interrupt

X209**J**23 Call For Key Operator

X209**J**24 Call For Maintenance

Postal Meter

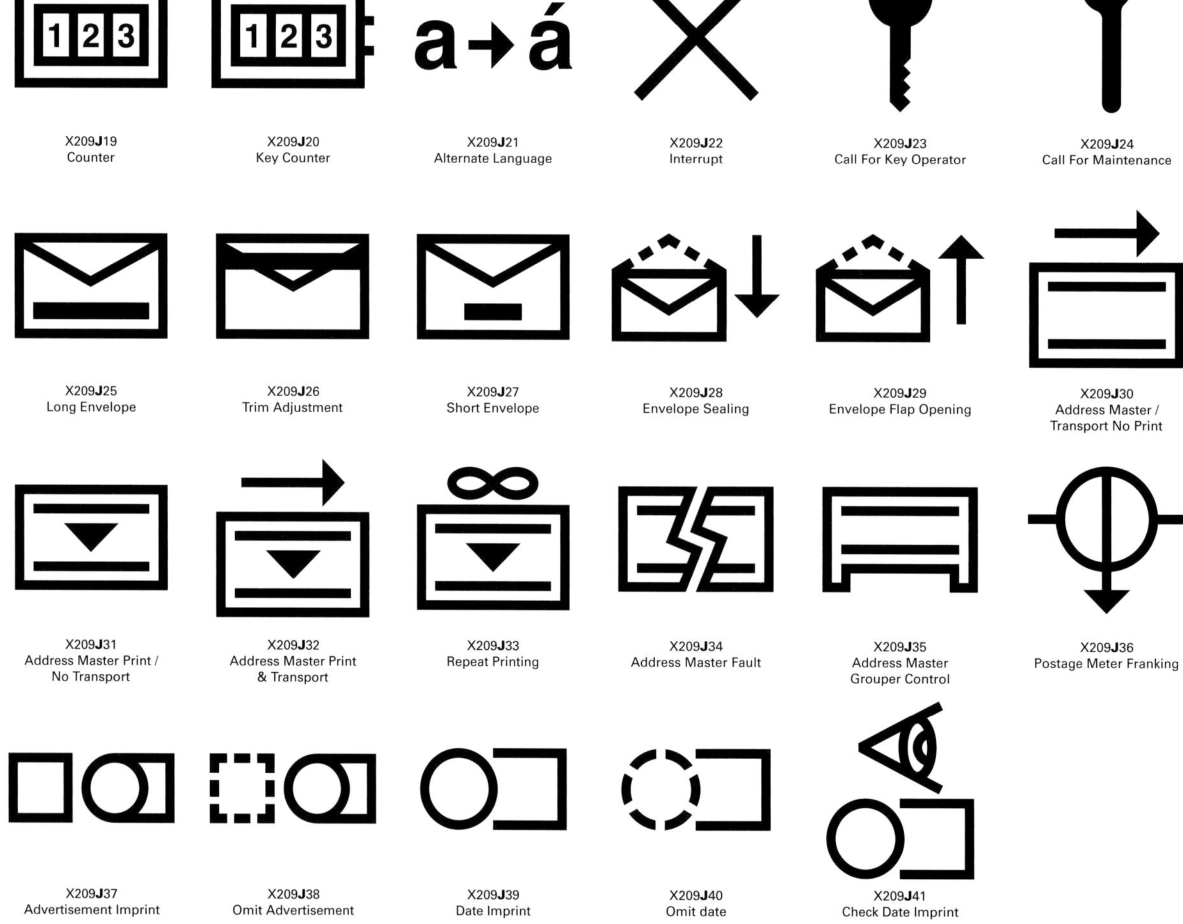

X209**J**25 Long Envelope

X209**J**26 Trim Adjustment

X209**J**27 Short Envelope

X209**J**28 Envelope Sealing

X209**J**29 Envelope Flap Opening

X209**J**30 Address Master / Transport No Print

X209**J**31 Address Master Print / No Transport

X209**J**32 Address Master Print & Transport

X209**J**33 Repeat Printing

X209**J**34 Address Master Fault

X209**J**35 Address Master Grouper Control

X209**J**36 Postage Meter Franking

X209**J**37 Advertisement Imprint

X209**J**38 Omit Advertisement

X209**J**39 Date Imprint

X209**J**40 Omit date

X209**J**41 Check Date Imprint

Commands (Keyboard)

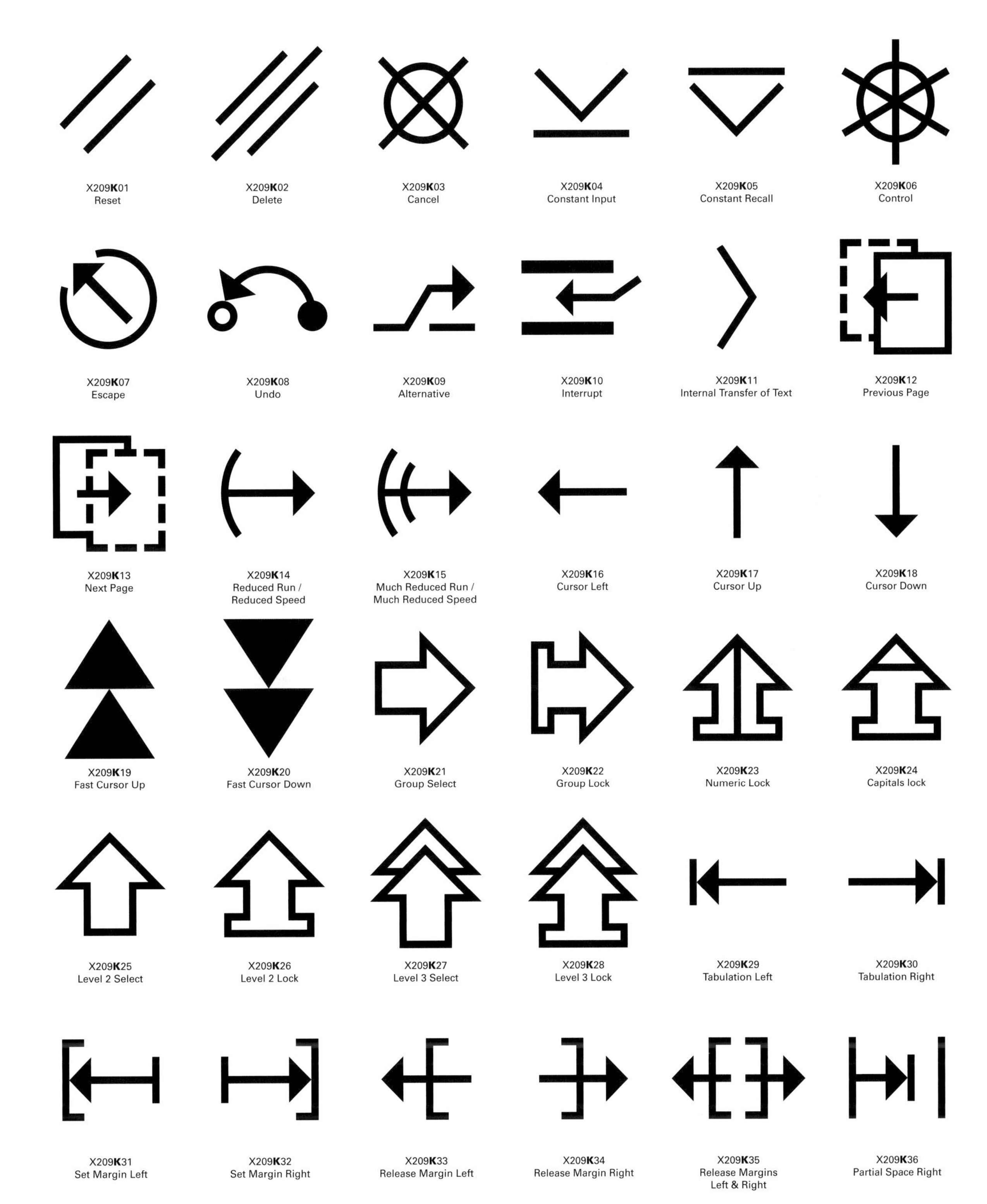

Commands (Keyboard) continued

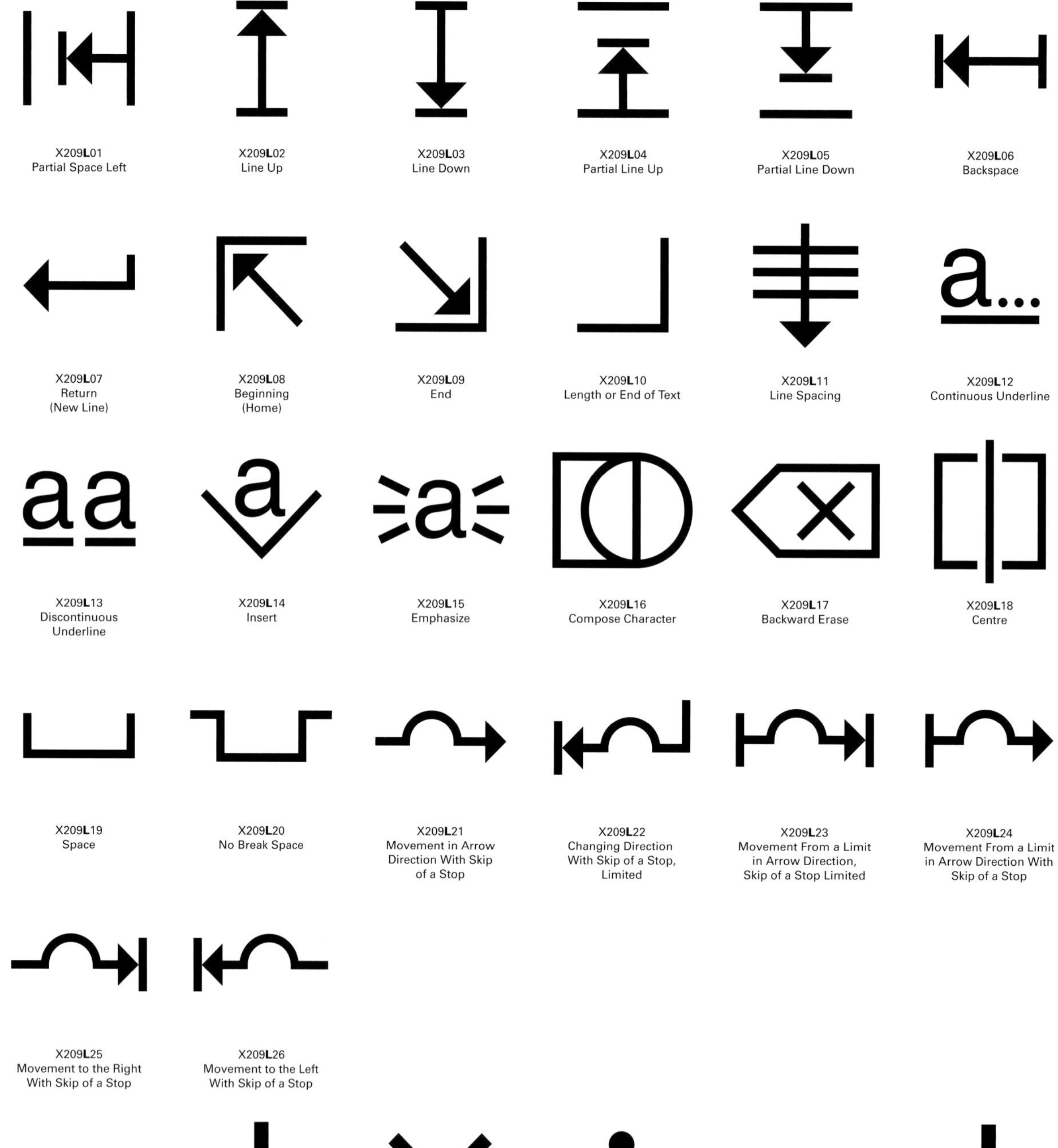

X209**L**01
Partial Space Left

X209**L**02
Line Up

X209**L**03
Line Down

X209**L**04
Partial Line Up

X209**L**05
Partial Line Down

X209**L**06
Backspace

X209**L**07
Return
(New Line)

X209**L**08
Beginning
(Home)

X209**L**09
End

X209**L**10
Length or End of Text

X209**L**11
Line Spacing

X209**L**12
Continuous Underline

X209**L**13
Discontinuous
Underline

X209**L**14
Insert

X209**L**15
Emphasize

X209**L**16
Compose Character

X209**L**17
Backward Erase

X209**L**18
Centre

X209**L**19
Space

X209**L**20
No Break Space

X209**L**21
Movement in Arrow
Direction With Skip
of a Stop

X209**L**22
Changing Direction
With Skip of a Stop,
Limited

X209**L**23
Movement From a Limit
in Arrow Direction,
Skip of a Stop Limited

X209**L**24
Movement From a Limit
in Arrow Direction With
Skip of a Stop

X209**L**25
Movement to the Right
With Skip of a Stop

X209**L**26
Movement to the Left
With Skip of a Stop

Mathematical

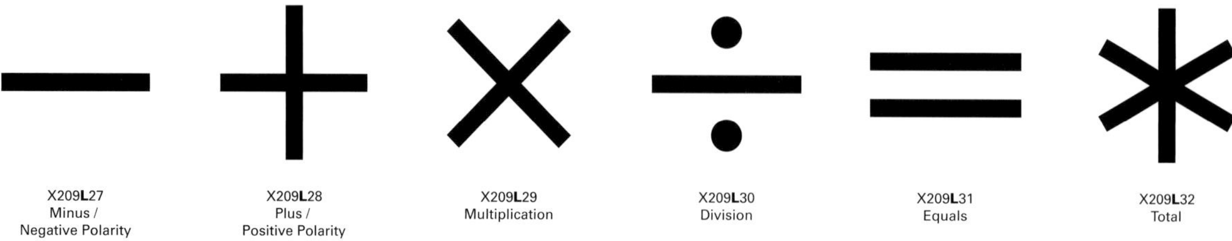

X209**L**27
Minus /
Negative Polarity

X209**L**28
Plus /
Positive Polarity

X209**L**29
Multiplication

X209**L**30
Division

X209**L**31
Equals

X209**L**32
Total

X209**L**33
Square Root

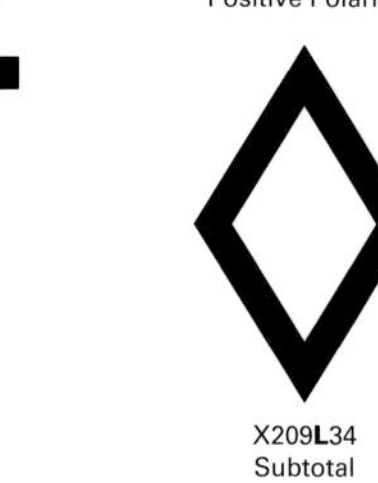

X209**L**34
Subtotal

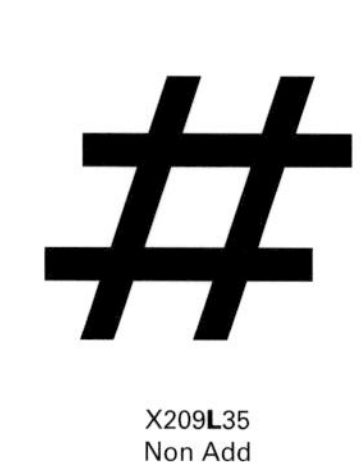

X209**L**35
Non Add

Flowchart

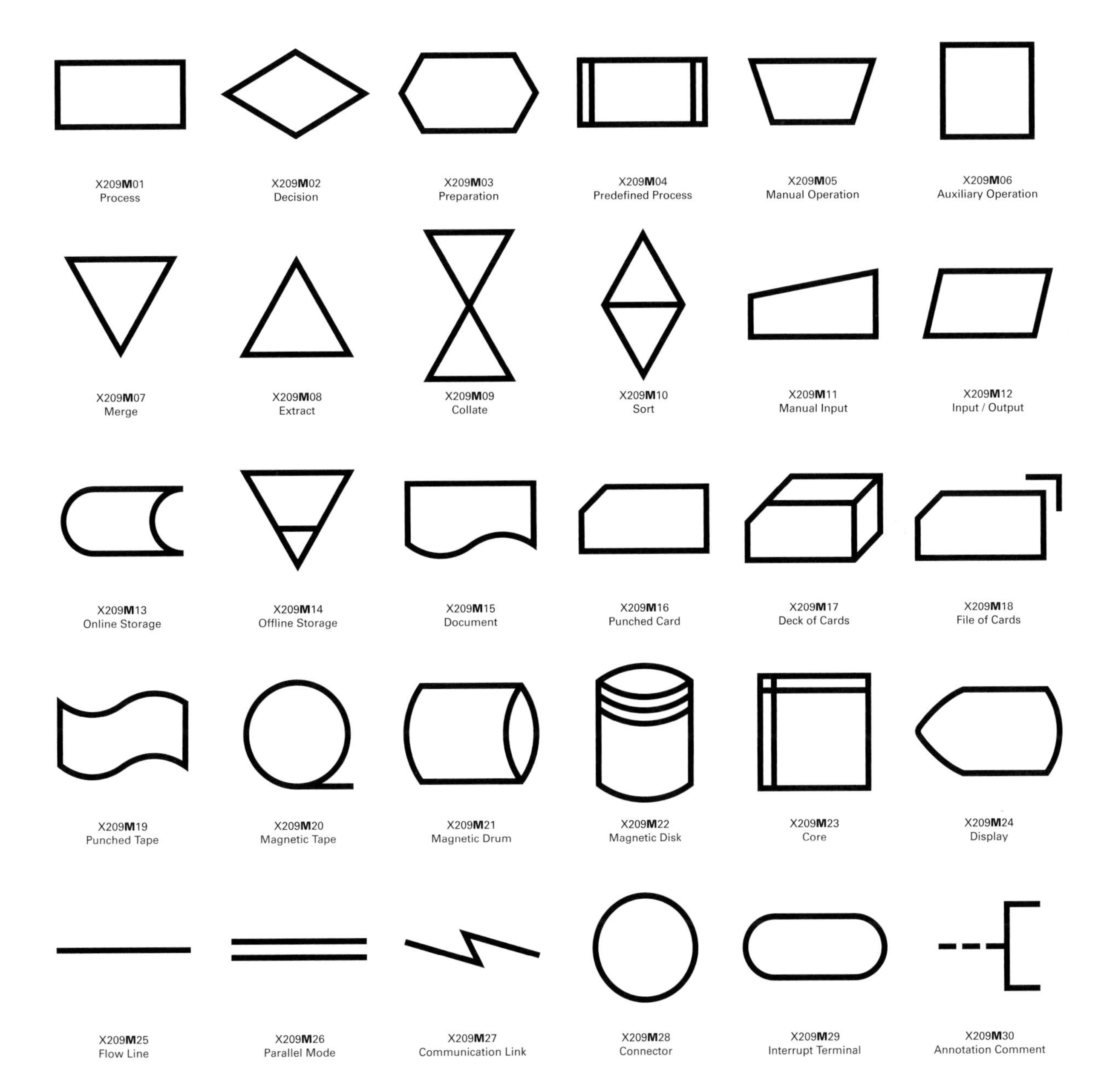
X209M01
Process
X209M02
Decision
X209M03
Preparation
X209M04
Predefined Process
X209M05
Manual Operation
X209M06
Auxiliary Operation
X209M07
Merge
X209M08
Extract
X209M09
Collate
X209M10
Sort
X209M11
Manual Input
X209M12
Input / Output
X209M13
Online Storage
X209M14
Offline Storage
X209M15
Document
X209M16
Punched Card
X209M17
Deck of Cards
X209M18
File of Cards
X209M19
Punched Tape
X209M20
Magnetic Tape
X209M21
Magnetic Drum
X209M22
Magnetic Disk
X209M23
Core
X209M24
Display
X209M25
Flow Line
X209M26
Parallel Mode
X209M27
Communication Link
X209M28
Connector
X209M29
Interrupt Terminal
X209M30
Annotation Comment

Telecommunication

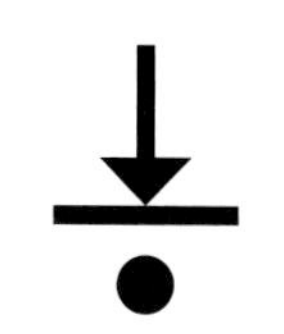

X209**N**01
Incoming Calls Barred

X209**N**02
Repeat Last Call

X209**N**03
No Reply Diversion

X209**N**04
Enquiry Call

X209**N**05
Call Waiting

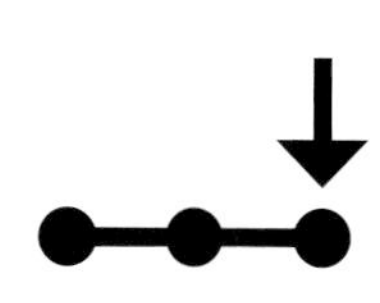

X209**N**06
Call Pick-up

X209**N**07
Disconnect

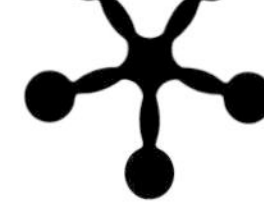

X209**N**08
Conference

X209**N**09
Parked (Held) Call

X209**N**10
Transfer (Call)

X209**N**11
Short Code Dialing

X209**N**12
Basic Diversion

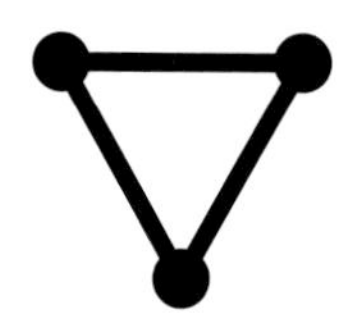

X209**N**13
Three-Party Call

X209**N**14
Call-Back

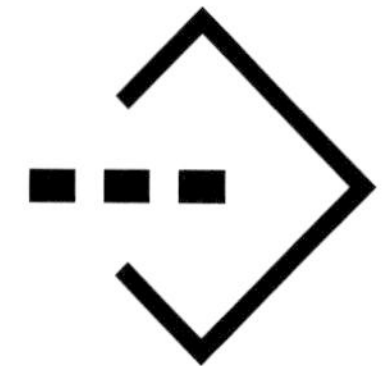

X209**N**15
Enter Subscriber Data
Into Local Memory

X209**N**16
Interchange

X209**N**17
Modem

Telex

X209**N**18
Who Are You?

X209**N**19
I am

General

X209**N**20
Repeat

X209**N**21
Clear

X209**N**22
Information

X209**N**23
Information

X209**N**24
Registered

X209**N**25
Trademark

X209**N**26
Copyright

X209**N**27
Link-Okay

X209**N**28
Okay

X209**N**29
Prohibit

X209**N**30
Recycling

X209**N**31
Handicap Access

X209**N**32
Caution, Attention,
See Instructions for Use

X209**N**33
Electrostatic Sensitive
Devices

X209**N**34
Dangerous Voltage

X209**N**35
Radiation of
Laser Beam

X209**N**36
Magnet

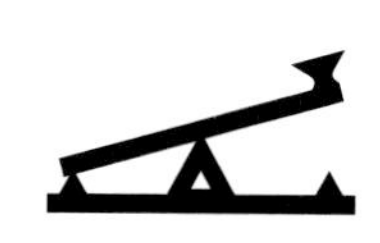

X209**N**37
Morse Key

Medical Devices

X209**P**01
Category AP Equipment

X209**P**02
Category AP Equipment

X209**P**03
Category APG Equipment

X209**P**04
Category APG Equipment

X209**P**05
Type B Equipment

X209**P**06
Type BF Equipment

X209**P**07
Type CF Equipment

X209**P**08
Non-ionizing Radiation

X209**P**09
Use By

X209**P**10
Do Not Reuse

X209**P**11
Batch Code

X209**P**12
Reference Symbol

X209**P**13
Serial Number

X209**P**14
Control

X209**P**15
Negative Control

X209**P**16
Positive Control

X209**P**17
Sterile

X209**P**18
Sterilization Using Aseptic Processing

X209**P**19
Sterilization Using Ethylene Oxide

X209**P**20
Sterilization Using Irradiation

X209**P**21
Sterilization Using Steam or Dry Heat

X209**P**22
Three-phase Alternating Current

X209**P**23
Three-phase Alternating Current with Natural Conductor

X209**P**24
Connection Point for Natural Conductor on Permanently Installed Equipment

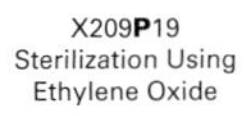

X209**P**25
Protected Against Dripping Water

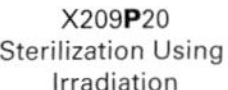

X209**P**26
Protected Against Splashing Water

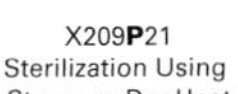

X209**P**27
Protected Against the Effects of Immersion

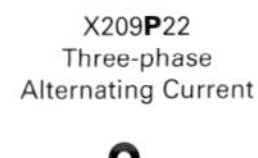
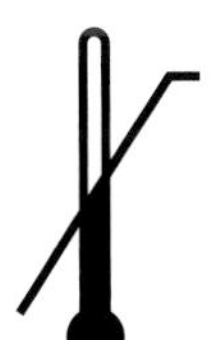

X209**P**28
Upper Limit of Temperature

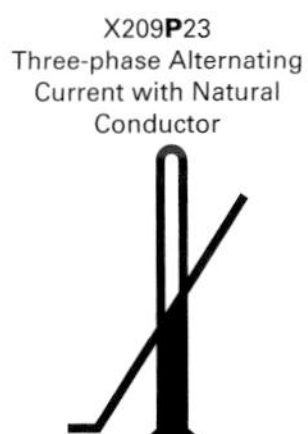

X209**P**29
Lower Limit of Temperature

X209**P**30
Temperature Limitation

X209**P**31
Date of Manufacture

X209**P**32
Keep Dry

X209**P**33
Consult Operating Instructions

X209**P**34
Attention, See Instructions for Use, Caution

X209**P**35
Fragile, Handle with Care

X209**P**36
Keep Away From Sunlight

X209**P**37
Protect from Heat and Radioactive Sources

A-C

A

Name	IEC	ISO	EIAJ	UltSym
Accordion Fold	2006			X209G34
Add Dry Toner		0720		X209J10
Add Ink		0721		X209J12
Add Liquid Developer (Premix)		0724		X209J15
Add Liquid Dispersant		0723		X209J14
Add Liquid Toner		0722		X209J13
Add Roll Paper (Material)		0719		X209H16
Add Sheet Paper (Material)		0718		X209H14
Add Water		0725		X209J16
Additional Sheet Paper Supply		0687		X209H12
Address Master Fault	1986			X209J34
Address Master Grouper Control	1987			X209J35
Address Master, Transport No Print	1982			X209J30
Address Master Print, No Transport	1984			X209J31
Address Master Print And Transport	1983			X209J32
Adjust Stop		0701		X209H27
Advertisement Imprint	1990			X209J37
Air-Conditioning System		0027		X209B01
Airbag		2108		X209C17
All Wheel Drive 4x4			1203	X209C10
Alternate Language				X209J21
Alternate Sheet Paper Supply		0688		X209H13
Alternative	2105			X209K09
Annotation Comment		30		X209M30
Attention, See Instructions for Use, Caution	348			X209P34
Automatic-Original / Master Feed		0675		X209H32
Auxiliary Operation		06		X209M06

B

Name	IEC	ISO	EIAJ	UltSym
Backspace	2037			X209L06
Backward Erase	2023			X209L17
Badly Soiled Items, Cooking Utensils	5294			X209D13
Basic Diversion	5499			X209N12
Batch Code				X209P11
Battery Charging Condition		0247		X209C26
Battery Failure			2456	X209C27
Battery Fluid Level			2455	X209C28
Battery Shut-off			2063	X209C29
Beacon			1141	X209A14
Beginning (Home)	2031			X209L08
Bind	0704			X209G26
Blanket Cleaning		0706		X209H02
Blanket Inking		0666		X209H01
Bleach				X209F17
Bonnet (Front Hood)		0241		X209C21
"		0241		X209C22
Boot (Rear Trunk)		0242		X209C23
"		0242		X209C24
Bound Original		0671		X209F30
Brake Failure		0239		X209A16
Brake Fluid Level		1401		X209A20
Brush Extended				X209E08
Brush Retracted				X209E09

C

Name	IEC	ISO	EIAJ	UltSym
Call-back	5501			X209N14
Call for Key Operator (Assistance)		0716		X209J23
Call for Maintenance		0717		X209J24
Call Pick-up	5508			X209N06
Call Waiting	5507			X209N05
Cancel, General	5503			X209K03
Capitals Lock	2010			X209K24
Carpet General				X209E04
Carpet Long Pile				X209E05
Category AP Equipment	0207			X209P01
"				X209P02
Category APG Equipment				X209P03
"	0208			X209P04
Caution, Attention, See Instructions for use	0434			X209N32
Centre	2022			X209L18
Changing Direction with Skip of a Stop, Limited				X209L22
Check Date Imprint	1994			X209J41
Check Auto Document Feed				X209H33
Child Seat Prohibition				X209C18
Chlorine Bleach May Be Used				X209F19
Choke (Cold Starting Aid)		0243		X209B29
Clear				X209N21
Close Cover				X209J07
Collate		09		X209M09
Collated Copies, Sets		1133		X209G24
Communication Link		27		X209M27
Compose Character	2021			X209L16
Conference	5250			X209N08
Connector		28		X209M28
Connection Point for Natural Conductor on Permanently Installed Equipment				X209P24
Constant Input	1972			X209K04
Constant Recall	1973			X209K05
Consult Operating Instructions				X209P33
Continuous Underline	2018			X209L12
Control	2028			X209K06
"				X209P14
Cooking Zone Bilateral				X209E33
Cooking Zone Central				X209E30
Cooking Zone Eccentric				X209E31
Cooking Zone Oval				X209E32
Cool (120° C / 248° F)				X209F14
Copies in Duplex				X209F27
Copy Quantity Selector		0681		X209G01
Copyright				X209N26
Core		23		X209M23
Counter		0695		X209J19
Cross Fold	2007			X209G33
Cursor Down	5107			X209K18
Cursor Left	5107			X209K16
Cursor Up	5107			X209K17
Curtains				X209E07

D-H

D

Name	IEC	ISO	EIAJ	UltSym
Darker Copy		0678		X209G06
Dashboard Light Dimmer				X209A15
Date of Manufacture				X209P31
Date Imprint	1992			X209J39
Dangerous Voltage	5036			X209N34
Decision		02		X209M02
Deck of Cards		17		X209M17
Delete	1028			X209K02
Delicate Items	5297			X209D16
Detector		0708		X209H06
Disconnect	5509			X209N07
Discontinuous Underline	2019			X209L13
Display		24		X209M24
Division	0655			X209L30
Do Not Copy				X209G12
Do Not Dry Clean				X209F21
Do Not Iron				X209F13
Do Not Use Chlorine Bleach				X209F18
Do Not Wash				X209F02
Do Not Reuse		1051		X209P10
Document				X209M15
Door(s) Ajar		2239		X209C19
"		2239		X209C20
Door Closed				X209E27
Door Lock Control		0638		X209C25
Door Open				X209E26
Double Copy Fault	0711			X209F35
Double Fold	2005			X209G32
Double Original		0709		X209F31
Double Sided Copy		0670		X209F34
Double Sided Original		0668		X209F26
Draining	5236			X209D11
"Drip" Dry, Hang Soaking Wet				X209F09
Drive (Automatic Transmission)				X209C08
Dry Clean				X209F20
Dry Clean in Any Solvent				X209F22
Dry Clean Except Trichloroethylene				X209F24
Dry Flat After Removing Excess Water				X209F11
Drying Or Warming Operation	5237			X209D12
Dust Bag				X209E02
Dust Bag Full				X209E01

E

Name	IEC	ISO	EIAJ	UltSym
Electric Shaver Outlet	5225			X209D01
Electronic Diesel Control		2424		X209B28
Electrostatic Sensitive Devices	5134			X209N33
Elevator Switch				X209H19
Emphasize	2020			X209L15
Empty Bin Available	1988			X209H09
Empty Sorter		0698		X209H23
End	2032			X209L09
Engine		0640		X209B20
Engine Coolant (Temperature)		0246		X209B22
Engine Coolant Level		2429		X209B33
Engine Failure		2423		X209B21
Engine Heating		2422		X209B27
Engine Oil		0248		X209B23
Engine Oil Filter		2428		X209B26
Engine Oil Level		2427		X209B25
Engine Oil Temperature		2426		X209B24
Engine Start		2425		X209B31
Engine Shut-off		1180		X209B32
Enlargement		0680		X209G05
Enquiry Call	5506			X209N04
Enter / Return (New Line)				X209L07
Enter Subscriber Data into Local Memory	5251			X209N15
Envelope Flap Opening	2000			X209J29
Envelope Sealing	1999			X209J28
Equals	0652			X209L31
Escape	2029			X209K07
Extract		08		X209M08
Exterior Rear View Mirror Adjustment, Horizontal Type		1427		X209A35
Exterior Rear View Mirror Adjustment, Vertical Type		2469		X209A36
Exterior Rear View Mirror Heating, Horizontal Type		1426		X209A37
Exterior Rear View Mirror Heating, Vertical Type		2470		X209A38

F

Name	IEC	ISO	EIAJ	UltSym
Failure of Anti-lock Break System		1407		X209A18
Fan Fold				X209G36
Fan Fold (Continuous Stationery)			1139	X209G35
Fast Cursor Up	5108			X209K19
Fast Cursor Down	5108			X209K20
File of Cards		18		X209M18
Flow Line		25		X209M25
Format Size Selector		0682		X209G03
Fragile, Handle with Care				X209P35
Fresh Air		2485		X209B08
"		2485		X209B09
Friction Pressure		0693		X209J03
Front Axle Drive 4x4		1416		X209C12
Front Fog Light		0633		X209A05
Fuel		0245		X209C01
"		0245		X209C02
Fuel Economy		0641		X209C04
Fuel Level		0245		X209C01
Fuel, unleaded		0237		X209C03

G

Name	IEC	ISO	EIAJ	UltSym
General Cancel	5503			X209K03
Grid Density, High	1977			X209G17
Grid Density, Low	1975			X209G15
Grid Density, Normal	1976			X209G16
Group Lock	1862			X209K22
Group Select	0251			X209K21

H

Name	IEC	ISO	EIAJ	UltSym
Halftone / Grey Tone	1978			X209G18
Hand Throttle		1367		X209B30
Hand Wash				X209F01
Handicap Access				X209N31
Hang to Dry				X209F10
Hazard Warning		0085		X209A11
Headlamp Cleaner		0250		X209A03
Headlight Leveling Manual Control		0151		X209A04
Headrest Height Adjustment		1433		X209B17
Heated Seat		0649		X209B18
High (Main) Beam		0082		X209A01
High Water Level	5234			X209D09

H-N

Name	IEC	ISO	EIAJ	UltSym
Horn		0244		X209A12
Hot (210° C / 410° F)				X209F16
Humidity				X209G22
I				
I Am	1955			X209N19
Imprint Tape	1998			X209H05
Incoming Calls Barred	5502			X209N01
Information				X209N22
"				X209N23
Ink Prime	1995			X209H04
Ink Roller Cleaning	0707			X209H03
Input / Output		12		X209M12
Insert	2017			X209L14
Insert Original		0672		X209J09
Insert Paper	1944			X209H29
Interchange	5292			X209N16
Interior Compartment Illumination		1421		X209A13
Interior Heating		0637		X209B04
Interleaving		0699		X209G25
Intermediate Rinsing				X209E28
Internal Transfer of Text	1974			X209K11
Interrupt		1131		X209K10
"				X209J22
Interrupt Terminal		29		X209M29
Iron				X209F12
K				
Keep Away from Sunlight				X209P36
Keep Dry				X209P32
Key Counter		0696		X209J20
L				
Length or End of Text	5106			X209L10
Level 2 Lock	2011			X209K26
Level 2 Select	1861			X209K25
Level 3 Lock	2014			X209K28
Level 3 Select	2013			X209K27
Level of Rear Window Washer Fluid		1423		X209A32
Lighter		0620		X209B19
Lighter Copy		0677		X209G07
Lightly Soiled Items	5296			X209D15
Line Down	2036			X209L03
Line Spacing	0658			X209L11
Line Up	2035			X209L02
Link - Okay				X209N27
Long Envelope	2002			X209J25
Long Range Light		0639		X209A07
Low Beam (Dipped Beam)		0083		X209A02
Low Water Level	5235			X209D10
Lower Air Outlet		1866		X209B06
Lower Limit of Temperature				X209P29

Name	IEC	ISO	EIAJ	UltSym
M				
Magnet				X209N36
Magnetic Di		22		X209M22
Magnetic Drum		21		X209M21
Magnetic Tape		20		X209M20
Main Wash	5227			X209D03
Manual Feed Tray or Control				X209H35
Manual Input		11		X209M11
Manual Operation		05		X209M05
Maximum Temperature (95° C / 203° F)				X209F03
Maximum Temperature. Greatly Reduce Mechanical Action (40° C / 104° F)				X209F05
Maximum Temperature. Reduce Mechanical Action (60° C / 140° F)				X209F04
Merge		07		X209M07
Minus, Negative Polarity	5006			X209L27
Missed Copy Fault	0712			X209F36
Missed Original		0710		X209F32
Modem		5262		X209N17
Morse Key	5213			X209N37
Movement from a Limit in Arrow Direction with Skip of a Stop, Limited	0934			X209L23
Movement from a Limit in Arrow Direction with Skip of a Stop	0933			X209L24
Movement in Arrow Direction with Skip of a Stop	0936			X209L21
Movement to the Left with Skip of a Stop, Limited Column Skip Left	0932			X209L26
Movement to the Right with Skip of a Stop, Limited Column Skip Right	0931			X209L25
Movement with Changing Direction with Skip of a Stop, Limited	0935			X209L22
Much Reduced Run, Much Reduced Speed	0528			X209K15
Multiplication	0654			X209L29
N				
Neutral (Automatic Transmission)				X209C07
Negative Control				X209P15
Negative Polarity / Minus	5006			X209L27
Next Page	2034			X209K13
No Bin in Position	1989			X209H10
No Break Space	2016			X209L20
No Reply Diversion	5505			X209N03
Non Add	0657			X209L35
Non-ionizing Radiation				X209P08
Normally Soiled Items	5295			X209D14
Numeric Lock	2012			X209K23

O-R

O

Name	IEC	ISO	EIAJ	UltSym
Offline Storage		14		X209M14
O.K. / Okay				X209N28
Omit Advertisement	1991			X209J38
Omit Date	1993			X209J40
Online Storage		13		X209M13
Opening of Boot or Rear Deck		0242		X209C23
"		0242		X209C24
Opening of Front Hood or Bonnet		0241		X209C21
"		0241		X209C22
Operation, Drying or Warming	5237			X209D12
Oven Automatic				X209E21
Oven Defrosting Position				X209E23
Oven General				X209E10
Oven Grill				X209E12
Oven Lighting				X209E22
Oven Lower and Upper Heating				X209E17
Oven Lower Heating				X209E15
Oven Microwave				X209E18
Oven Microwave and Turntable				X209E19
Oven Rotisserie				X209E11
Oven Self Cleaning				X209E20
Oven Thermometer				X209E24
Oven Upper Heating				X209E16
Oven Warm Air Circulating				X209E13
Oven Warm Air Grill				X209E14
Oven Warming				X209E29

P

Name	IEC	ISO	EIAJ	UltSym
Paper Carrier Closed	1971			X209J04
Paper Carrier Open	1970			X209J05
Paper Clips		1134		X209G29
Paper Jam		0713		X209H30
Paper Jam in Original Feeder		0715		X209H34
Paper Jam in Sorter		0714		X209H24
Paper Platform (Feedboard), Lower	0691			X209H18
Paper Platform (Feedboard), Raise	0690			X209H17
Paper (Material) Thickness, Thick		0684		X209J02
Paper (Material) Thickness, Thin		0685		X209J01
Parallel Mode		26		X209M26
Park (Automatic Transmission)				X209C05
Parked (Held) Call	5252			X209N09
Parking Brake		0238		X209A17
Parking Lights		0240		X209A08
Position (Side) Lights				X209A09
Partial Line Down	2039			X209L05
Partial Line Up	2038			X209L04
Partial Space Left	2040			X209L01
Partial Space Right	2041			X209K36
Photo Original		1137		X209F29
Plus, Positive Polarity	5005			X209L28
Positive Polarity, Plus	5005			X209L28
Position (Side) Lights			0456	X209A09
Positive Control				X209P16
Postage Meter Franking	1997			X209J36
Predefined Process		04		X209M04
Preparation		03		X209M03
Pressure Rollers		0551		X209H36
Previous Page	2033			X209K12
Prewash	5226			X209D02
Primary Sheet Paper Supply		0686		X209H11
Print Out	0793			X209G14
Process		01		X209M01
Prohibit				X209N29
Proof Copy, Proof Set		0692		X209G02
Protected Against Dripping Water				X209P25
Protected Against Splashing Water				X209P26
Protected Against the Effects of Immersion				X209P27
Protect from Heat and Radioactive Sources				X209P37
Provision for the Disabled	0100			X209N31
Punched Card		16		X209M16
Punched Tape		19		X209M19

R

Name	IEC	ISO	EIAJ	UltSym
Radiation of Laser Beam, Laser Apperatures	5152			X209N35
Rear Axle Drive 4x4		1417		X209C11
Rear Fog Light		0634		X209A06
Rear Window Demisting and Defrosting		0636		X209A33
Rear Window Washer		0099		X209A30
Rear Window Wiper		0097		X209A28
Rear Window Wiper and Washer		0098		X209A31
Rear Window Wiper - Intermittent		1424		X209A29
Receive Document Page	1966			X209G11
Recirculated Air		2486		X209B10
"		2486		X209B11
Recopy Last Original				X209G19
Recopy Last 2 Originals				X209G20
Recopy Last 3 Originals				X209G21
Recycling, General	1135			X209N30
Reduced Run, Reduced Speed		0527		X209K14
Reduction		0679		X209G04
"				X209F28
Reference Symbol				X209P12
Registered				X209N24
Release Margin Left	2044			X209K33
Release Margin Right	2045			X209K34
Release Margins Left and Right	2046			X209K35
Remove Copies		0700		X209H25
Remove Original		0673		X209J08
Remove Paper	1944			X209H28
Remove Used Master Container		1138		X209J06
Repeat				X209N20
Repeat Last Call	5504			X209N02
Repeat Printing from One Address Master	1985			X209J33
Reset		1027		X209K01
Return (New Line) / Enter	0651			X209L07
Reverse (Automatic Transmission)				X209C06
Rinsing	5228			X209D04
Rolly Paper (Material) Supply		0689		X209H15

S-W

Signals Braille (ADA)

10

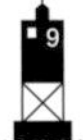

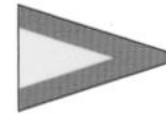

Overview

Throughout human history, ingenious ways of communicating non-verbally have been devised. To bridge whatever separates people, be it distance or physical impairment, messages are delivered through any and all means available. Body language, touch, thrown objects, fire, smoke, light, color, movement, electric pulses, alpha-numeric systems – all become useful when conveying information. This volume gathers together the most highly developed and successful messaging systems of the previous two centuries. Relating letters, numerals, signal flags, semaphores, Morse Code, sign language, and Braille to one another highlights the considerable problem solving that has been brought to bear on humanity's desire to communicate in varied situations and against all odds. With the exception of Morse Code, all are still in official use today despite the rapid advance of new technologies.

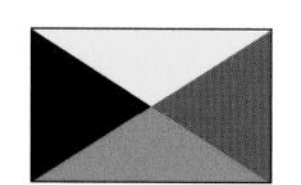

Signal Flags

International Marine Signal Flags are used by ships at sea. They can be used to spell out short messages, or more commonly, used individually or in combinations they have special meanings.[1] There are 68 different flags and pennants in a U.S. Navy flagbag that are used to make literally thousands of signals. These signals are used by NATO ships, for everything from asking to pick up mail, to tactical maneuvering signals. Flag signals, or Flaghoists, are used for military and civilian communications. Signals unique to the Navy are used when communicating with other U.S. Navy or allied forces. When communicating with all other vessels, the *International Code of Signals* is used. The code/answer pennant precedes all signals in international code.[2] One letter or number off could make up a whole new signal, so a Signalman must be able to recognize any of these flags without hesitation or uncertainty at a moment's notice. Strung end to end and hung bow to stern from the rigging, they are used to dress the ship for ceremonial and festive occasions.

Semaphore Flag Signaling System

The Semaphore [Greek: sema (*sign*), -phore (*bearer*)] flag signaling system is an alphanumeric signaling system based on the waving of a pair of handheld flags in a particular pattern.[3] The flags are usually square, red and yellow, divided diagonally with the red portion in the upper hoist. The flags are held, arms extended, in various positions representing each of the letters of the alphabet. The pattern resembles a clock face divided into eight positions: up, down, out, high, low, for each of the left and right hands (LH and RH). Six letters require the hand to be brought across the body so that both flags are on the same side.

History

Both the ancient Greeks and Romans are known to have signaled over short distances with torches and flags.[4] The telescope, invented in about 1600, greatly increased the range of such systems. Originally called in French "telegraphie", [tele (*distant*), -graphie (*writing*)], semaphore telegraph was first developed by Claude Chappe, a French engineer, as a shutter system for the French Army in the late 18th century. It was a huge rectangular frame with 6 shutters in it, in 2 columns of 3. The positions of the open and closed shutters related to letters of the alphabet. Coincidentally, the basis of the Braille cell, independently developed more than 30 years later by Louis Braille, was a similar design using 2 columns of 3.

In 1793, Chappe introduced a less cumbersome and more visible semaphore, using large wooden arms to spell out words and messages that could carry a message 230 km (144 mi) from Lille to Paris in two minutes – an idea that delighted Napoleon Bonaparte. He constructed a series of towers about 8 to 16 km (5 to 10 mi) apart and within sight of each other. On each tower was mounted a large horizontal beam, called a regulator, with two smaller wings, called indicators, mounted at the ends, seemingly mimicking a person with wide-outstretched arms, holding a signal flag in each hand. The angles of the indicators, and independently also the position of the large regulator beam, could be varied in increments of 45 degrees, sufficient for the encoding of hundreds of symbols. A telescope was located at each tower so that an operator could relay the beam-arm signals.[5]

S. F. Morse's electric telegraph supplanted Chappe's semaphore for long-distance signaling by the mid-1840s. However, Hutton Gregory, a telegraph engineer on the British railroads, modified Chappe's system by employing moving metal arms or rows of lights, mounted on towers, to signal trains. The railway semaphore is still in use. Semaphores also remain in use for maritime communications and in the U.S. Navy.

International Morse Code

The International Morse Code is a system of dots and dashes that can be used to send messages by a flash lamp, telegraph key, or other rhythmic device such as a tapping finger. As a telegraph key is moved up and down, it makes or breaks an electric circuit and transmits a signal as a series of electric pulses. The telegraph was invented by Samuel Morse in 1837. In the International Morse Code, each letter or number is represented by a combination of dashes and dots. A dash is equal to three dots in duration. A famous Morse Code signal signifies distress: dot dot dot dash dash dash dot dot dot (SOS).

History

The electric telegraph makes use of the relationship between magnetism and electricity. During the early 1790s, the Italian scientist Alessandro Volta invented an electrochemical cell that made a steady source of electric current available. In 1820, the Danish physicist Hans Christian Oersted discovered that an electric current will cause a magnetized needle to move. This principle is the basis of the telegraph, in which a current is varied systematically according to a code. In 1825 the British electrician William Sturgeon invented the electromagnet. The physicists William F. Cooke and Charles Wheatstone, working together in Great Britain, and the American inventor Samuel Morse used these discoveries to develop the telegraph.

Samuel F. B. Morse (1791-1872) was a painter and founder of the National Academy of Design. In 1832, while on a ship returning from Europe, he conceived the basic idea of an electromagnetic telegraph. Experiments with various kinds of electrical instruments and codes resulted in a demonstration of a working telegraph set in 1836, and introduction of the circuit relay. This made transmission possible for any distance. With his creation of the American Morse Code, the historic message, "What hath God wrought?" was successfully sent from Washington to Baltimore. Morse's partner, Alfred Vail, very likely assisted in the development of the code and the instruments used to transmit and receive it. In the United States, the Morse telegraph was successful for a number of reasons, including its simple operation and its relatively low cost. By 1851, the country had over 50 telegraph companies, though most telegraph business was controlled by the Magnetic Telegraph Company, which held the Morse patents.

The Morse Code used in those days differed greatly from that which is used today. Morse Code originated on telegraph lines and the original users did not listen to tones but instead to the clicking sounds created by sounders. They used the *American Morse Code* as opposed to today's *International Morse*. When sending dahs (Morse code is composed of dits or short key closures, and dahs or longer key closures), the user simply sent two close-together dits. This was created by using a conventional code key. With the advent of radio communications the international Morse became more widespread. Users of the international Morse created dahs with a longer key closure, instead of two close-spaced dits.

In more recent times, the user can employ keyers that electronically create dits and dahs. Lambic keyers have a memory so that the user can operate a mechanical "paddle" quicker than the keying rate of the keyer. This makes for very comfortable and nearly effortless keying. Today experienced operators copy received text without the need to write as they receive, and when transmitting, can easily converse at 20 to 30 words per minute. Searchlights and various other types of lights are still used to "flash" a variety of other ships, civilian and naval, from foreign countries around the world. Morse Code will always remain a viable means of providing highly reliable communications during difficult communication conditions or when the more sophisticated wireless technologies available fail.

When considered as a standard for information encoding, Morse Code had a successful lifespan that has not yet been surpassed by any other electronic encoding scheme. Morse Code was used as an international standard for maritime communication until 1999, when it was replaced by the *Global Maritime Distress Safety System.*[6] When the French navy ceased using Morse code in 1997, the final message transmitted was "Calling all. This is our last cry before our eternal silence."

American Sign Language

American Sign Language (ASL) is a linguistically complete, complex visual-spatial language that employs signs made with the hands and other movements, including facial expressions and postures of the body. It is the first language of many deaf North Americans, and one of several communication options available to deaf people. ASL is said to be the fourth most commonly used language in the United States. It is the native language of many deaf men and women, as well as some hearing children born into deaf families.

History

The exact beginnings of ASL are not clear. Many people believe that ASL came mostly from French Sign Language (FSL). Others claim that the foundation for ASL existed before FSL was introduced in America in 1817. It was in that year that a French teacher named Laurent Clerc, brought to the United States by Thomas Gallaudet, founded the first school for the deaf in Hartford, Connecticut. Clerc began teaching FSL to Americans, though many of his students were already fluent in their own forms of local, natural sign language. Today's ASL likely contains some of this early American signing. Which language had more to do with the formation of modern ASL is difficult to prove. Modern ASL and FSL share some elements, including a substantial amount of vocabulary. However, they are not mutually comprehensible.

ASL Linguistics

No one form of sign language is universal. Different sign languages are used in different countries. For example, British Sign Language (BSL) differs notably from ASL. Just as with other languages, specific ways of expressing ideas in ASL vary as much as ASL users themselves do. ASL users may choose from synonyms to express common words. ASL also allows for regional usage and jargon, just as certain English words are spoken differently in different parts of the country. Ethnicity, age, and gender are a few more factors that affect ASL usage and contribute to its variety.

Even though ASL is used in America, it is a language that shares no grammatical similarities to English and should not be considered in any way to be a broken, mimed, or gestural form of English. It contains all the fundamental features a language needs to function on its own – it has its own rules for grammar, punctuation, and sentence order. In terms of syntax, for example, ASL has a topic-comment syntax, while English uses subject-object-verb. In fact, in terms of syntax, ASL shares more with spoken Japanese than it does with English.

Every language expresses its features differently; ASL is no exception. Unlike spoken languages where there is just one serial stream of phonemes (utterances), sign languages can have multiple things going on at the same time. This multiple segmentation makes it an exciting language for linguists to study and a frustrating language for hearing people to learn. ASL has its own morphology (rules for the creation of words), phonetics (rules for handshapes), and grammar that are very unlike those found in spoken languages.[7]

In spoken language, the different sounds created by words and tones of voice (intonation) are the most important devices used to communicate. Sign language is based on the idea that sight is the most useful tool a deaf person has to communicate and receive information. Thus, ASL uses hand shape, position, and movement; body movements; gestures; facial expressions; and other visual cues to form its words. Sometimes, ASL users may ask a question by tilting their bodies forward while signaling with their eyes and eyebrows. Like any language, fluency in ASL often happens only after a long period of study and practice.

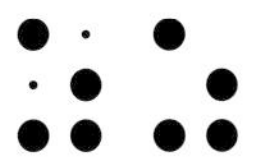

Braille

Braille is a system of touch reading and writing for blind persons in which raised dots represent the letters of the alphabet. It contains equivalents for punctuation marks, and provides symbols to show letter groupings.

Braille is read by gently gliding the hand or hands from left to right over paper or other materials that have been embossed with lines of Braille code. Both hands are usually involved in the reading process, and reading is generally done with the index fingers. The average reading speed is about 125 words per minute, but greater speeds of up to 200 words per minute are possible.

Various other methods had been attempted over the years to enable blind people to read, many of them raised versions of print letters. It is generally accepted that the Braille system has succeeded because it is based on a rational sequence of signs devised for the fingertips, rather than imitating signs devised for the eyes. In addition, Braille can be written by blind people and can be used for any notation that follows an accepted sequence, such as numerals, musical notes, or chemical tables. For notetaking, a pointed instrument is used to punch out the dots on paper held in a metal slate. The readable raised dots appear on the other side of the paper.

The Braille System

The basis of the Braille system is known as a Braille "cell". Each Braille character or cell is made up of 6 dot positions, arranged in a rectangle comprising 2 columns of 3 dots each. A dot may be raised at any of the 6 positions, or any combination. Counting the space, in which no dots are raised, there are 64 such combinations (that is, 2 to the 6th power). The basis of the various Braille codes for the world's natural languages is a straightforward assignment of most of the dot patterns to letters of the alphabet, punctuation marks, and other symbols. This is done with a certain consistency, quite often with reference to Louis Braille's original assignments, to the extent possible given the great variety of alphabets, accent marks, vocalization marks, etc. that are in use.

A natural question is what the Braille cells mean. However, the cells have no intrinsic meanings; since there is only one standard Braille alphabet, the cells mean different things depending on which Braille code is in use: math, music, Japanese, etc. The most common code in the United States is literary Braille or, more accurately, standard English Braille American Edition (EBAE).

Because the 64 distinct characters are never enough to cover all possible print signs and their variants, it is necessary to use multi-character sequences for some purposes. Often this is accomplished by using certain characters as "prefixes" or "indicators" that affect the meaning of subsequent cells. For example, in English a dot-6 before a letter indicates that the letter is a capital, whereas otherwise it is understood to be lower case.

For another example, dots 3-4-5-6, called the "numeric indicator", causes certain following letters (a through j) to be reinterpreted as digits. Dot height, cell size, and cell spacing are always uniform, and so many significant characteristics of the text, such as italics used for emphasis, must be handled by such indicators in Braille. An exception is that formatting, such as the centering of main headings, is commonly used in Braille in much the same way, and for most of the same purposes, as in print.

The size of the Braille cell is such that only about 25 lines of about 40 cells each – that is, 1,000 characters – can fit on a page of the usual size, which is about 11 inches wide by 11 or 12 inches deep. This contrasts with the 3,500 or so characters that will fit on a standard, smaller, typed page.[8]

The alphabet and punctuation marks are almost all the same assignments that Louis Braille made in the original French. There is also now some use of 8-dot Braille, formed by adding a dot position to each column, for certain special purposes, especially those related to computer access. However, due to cell size and other considerations, 6-dot Braille still seems to represent the best balance for general reading purposes.

Just as sighted people invented shorthand, blind people use a contracted version of Braille that is space saving and allows for more rapid reading and writing. These "contractions" substitute shorter sequences for the full spelling of commonly occurring letter groups. For example,"the" is usually just one character in English Braille, not only in the definite article but also in words such as "lather" and "chrysan- themum". However, that contraction is not used in words such as "motheaten" or "sweetheart", because of the way those words are constructed or pronounced. In other words, phonetics does play a role in modern Braille – but not so as to compromise an accurate representation of spelling. Wherever the Braille character for "the" appears, the reader can be sure that it stands for exactly those three letters and not some other sequence that may sound the same. When contractions are used, the Braille is called "Grade 2" in contrast to "Grade 1" transcriptions, where all words are spelled out letter-for-letter. In English, which has 189 contractions, almost all Braille is Grade 2.

Braille is produced in a number of ways. It can be transcribed from the original printed text on a machine that resembles a typewriter. The Braille writer has six keys which correspond to the six dots of the Braille cell. Computers are also used to transcribe and reproduce Braille texts. The electronic revolution is changing the way Braille is produced, stored and retrieved, making it easier to use in the work place. Braille readers use refreshable Braille displays as computer monitors. A refreshable Braille display, or RBD, produces Braille by raising and lowering pins in response to an electronic signal. RBDs make transitory Braille possible. RBDs can display digital information, including that from the internet, as ASCII characters in Braille; thus either Computer Braille Code – which maps standard print characters one-to-one to the Braille cells – or transcribed Braille can be displayed. RBDs also add a new modality for deaf-blind persons to communicate in real time. Braille-adapted devices such as watches, games, playing cards, and thermometers are examples of some of the practical and recreational uses of Braille.[9]

Specifying Braille

Many designers and fabricators may be unfamiliar with Braille and how it should be specified and used. Braille Grade 1 and Grade 2 (Grade 2 Braille is required for ADA signage) are generally similar, with the exception that Grade 2 Braille, as mentioned above, includes additional characters and character combinations that represent contractions of certain words and word components, such as "the" and "ation". Consequently, considerable care must be taken to translate Braille Grade 2 correctly, using either a computer-based or other translation program. It is also recommended that a Braille proofreader approve all final artwork.

Braille is read with the pad of the finger, not the very tip, so no obstructions such as dimensional frames or decorative features should prevent the finger from lying flat against the sign face. The form of the dots should ideally be distinct "mounds" rather than sharp-edged "cylinders" and should feel smooth but well-defined when the finger scans them with light pressure. Braille only exists in one size. The center point of dots within a cell should be .09" apart, should be separated from adjacent cells by .245" horizontally, and by .4" vertically to the center point of the top line on the next line.[9]

History

This system of writing and reading used by many blind people was invented almost 200 years ago. While several types of written communication systems were tried during a ten-year period beginning in 1825, the one invented by a blind teenager was adopted. Some modifications have been made to it over the years, but the Braille code in use today is virtually the same as it was in 1834.

Louis Braille was born January 4, 1809, in a small village near Paris. His father, Simon Renee Braille, was a harness and saddle maker who often used sharp tools in his work. While playing in his father's shop when he was three, Louis injured his eye on an awl. In spite of good care, infection set in and soon left him completely blind. There is an English word, *brail*, which describes a rope used in sailing and is derived from a 15th century French word *braiel*, meaning "strap". It seems reasonable to speculate that the family name was probably derived from an ancestor's similar occupation.[10] When Louis grew to school age, he was allowed to sit in the classroom to learn by listening. Louis was very bright and creative, and when he was ten, he was sent to the Royal Institution for Blind Youth in Paris. There too, most instruction was oral, but there were a few books in a kind of raised print developed by the school's founder. Although frustrated by the large, bulky books and slow reading of the tactile characters, he did well at his studies and dreamed of a better way. At that time, the raised letters were made by pressing shaped copper wire onto paper, but there was no way for blind people to write for themselves.

While a student, he began to use his creativity to invent an easy and quick way for blind people to read and write. Louis heard of a system of raised dots developed by a French army captain, Charles Barbier de la Serre. Barbier originally created a code of raised dots and dashes as a way to allow soldiers to write and read messages at night without using a light that might give away their positions. He later adapted the system, called "sonography", and presented it to the Institution for Blind Youth, hoping that it would be officially adopted there. It was based on phonetics and consisted of groups of 12 dots arranged in 2 columns of 6 dots each. Louis realized the potential in Barbier's tactile dot concept and began immediately to develop his own simplified system that we know today as Braille. He based his code on the normal alphabet and reduced the number of dots by half.

In October 1824, Louis, just 15 years old, unveiled his new alphabet. He had found 63 ways to use a six-dot cell (though some dashes were still included). His new alphabet was received enthusiastically by the other students and by the school's new director, Dr. Pignier, who ordered the special slates Louis had designed from Captain Barbier's original one. Gabriel Gauthier, Louis' best friend, was probably the very first person ever to read Braille.[11]

Louis Braille published the first Braille book in 1829, *Method of Writing Words, Music, and Plain Songs by Means of Dots, for Use by the Blind and Arranged for Them.* In 1837, he added symbols for math and music. Although Louis Braille went on to become a beloved and respected teacher, was encouraged in his research, and continued to believe in the value of his work, his system of reading and writing with raised dots was nevertheless not very widely accepted in his own time. Louis Braille died of tuberculosis on January 6, 1852.

His system survived, and in 1854, France adopted Braille as its official communications system for blind people. The Braille system spread to Switzerland soon after but encountered tremendous resistance in England, Germany and America, and often for the same reason: Braille's seeming opacity to the sighted because of its lack of resemblance to print. In 1860, the first American institution to adopt Braille was the Missouri School for the Blind, located in St. Louis, but the United States only fully came to the use of Braille in the 20th century.

A later Braille reader, Helen Keller, wrote: "Braille has been a most precious aid to me in many ways. It made my going to college possible – it was the only method by which I could take notes of lectures. All my examination papers were copied for me in this system. I use Braille as a spider uses its web – to catch thoughts that flit across my mind for speeches, messages, and manuscripts." [12]

Despite the fact that the Braille dots still do not resemble print letters (a complaint often heard to this day), it has been adapted to nearly every language on earth and remains the major medium of literacy for blind people throughout the world. Debunking the myth that Braille is somehow "too difficult" for the sighted to learn, sighted transcribers have long been a primary source of textbooks for blind students. Thousands of these volunteers learned Braille as an avocation and churned out books one cell at a time from kitchen tables and bedroom offices everywhere for many years with little fanfare. Their efforts in the United States have, if anything, expanded over the last decade with the coming of the computer age and the mainstreaming of blind students in public schools.

Whether through software translators or direct entry, Braille turned out to be extraordinarily well suited to computer-assisted production due to its elegance and efficiency. Braille displays for navigating and reading computer text in real time have become increasingly affordable and reliable as well. Thus, computers created an unprecedented and continuing explosion in the amount of Braille published and read throughout the world.

	Signal Flags	Semaphores	Morse Code	ASL (American Sign Language)	Braille Reader	Braille Touch
A	X210**A**01 Alfa Diver Down, Keep Clear Undergoing Speed Trial (Unstationary)	X210**A**02 A and 1	X210**A**03 A	X210**A**04 A	X210**A**05 A	X210**A**06 A
B	X210**A**07 Bravo Dangerous Cargo	X210**A**08 B and 2	X210**A**09 B	X210**A**10 B	X210**A**11 B	X210**A**12 B
C	X210**A**13 Charlie Yes, Affirmative (with 'N' = Distress)	X210**A**14 C and 3	X210**A**15 C	X210**A**16 C	X210**A**17 C	X210**A**18 C
D	X210**A**19 Delta Keep Clear Maneuvering with Difficulty	X210**A**20 D and 4	X210**A**21 D	X210**A**22 D	X210**A**23 D	X210**A**24 D
E	X210**A**25 Echo Altering Course to Starboard	X210**A**26 E and 5	X210**A**27 E	X210**A**28 E	X210**A**29 E	X210**A**30 E
F	X210**A**31 Foxtrot Disabled, Communicate	X210**A**32 F and 6	X210**A**33 F	X210**A**34 F	X210**A**35 F	X210**A**36 F
G	X210**A**37 Golf Require a Pilot, Hauling Nets	X210**A**38 G and 7	X210**A**39 G	X210**A**40 G	X210**A**41 G	X210**A**42 G

	Signal Flags	Semaphores	Morse Code	ASL (American Sign Language)	Braille Reader	Braille Touch
H	X210**B**01 Hotel Pilot on Board	X210**B**02 H and 8	X210**B**03 H	X210**B**04 H	X210**B**05 H	X210**B**06 H
I	X210**B**07 India Altering Course to Port	X210**B**08 I and 9	X210**B**09 I	X210**B**10 I	X210**B**11 I	X210**B**12 I
J	X210**B**13 Juliett On fire, Keep Clear Going to Send Message	X210**B**14 J	X210**B**15 J	X210**B**16 J	X210**B**17 J	X210**B**18 J
K	X210**B**19 Kilo Stop Instantly	X210**B**20 K and 0	X210**B**21 K	X210**B**22 K	X210**B**23 K	X210**B**24 K
L	X210**B**25 Lima Stop Important Communication	X210**B**26 L	X210**B**27 L	X210**B**28 L	X210**B**29 L	X210**B**30 L
M	X210**B**31 Mike I Am Stopped Doctor on Board	X210**B**32 M	X210**B**33 M	X210**B**34 M	X210**B**35 M	X210**B**36 M
N	X210**B**37 November No, Negative (with 'C' = Distress)	X210**B**38 N	X210**B**39 N	X210**B**40 N	X210**B**41 N	X210**B**42 N

	Signal Flags	Semaphores	Morse Code	ASL (American Sign Language)	Braille Reader	Braille Touch
O	X210**C**01 Oscar Man Overboard	X210**C**02 O	X210**C**03 O	X210**C**04 O	X210**C**05 O	X210**C**06 O
P	X210**C**07 Papa Blue Peter, About to Sail, All Aboard, Nets Fouled, Your Lights Out or Dim	X210**C**08 P	X210**C**09 P	X210**C**10 P	X210**C**11 P	X210**C**12 P
Q	X210**C**13 Quebec Request Pratique, Healthy Vessel	X210**C**14 Q	X210**C**15 Q	X210**C**16 Q	X210**C**17 Q	X210**C**18 Q
R	X210**C**19 Romeo Way is Off My Ship, Received (Procedural)	X210**C**20 R	X210**C**21 R	X210**C**22 R	X210**C**23 R	X210**C**24 R
S	X210**C**25 Sierra Going Full Speed Astern	X210**C**26 S	X210**C**27 S	X210**C**28 S	X210**C**29 S	X210**C**30 S
T	X210**C**31 Tango Do not pass ahead of me, Keep Clear, Am Pair Trawling	X210**C**32 T	X210**C**33 T	X210**C**34 T	X210**C**35 T	X210**C**36 T
U	X210**C**37 Uniform Standing into Danger	X210**C**38 U	X210**C**39 U	X210**C**40 U	X210**C**41 U	X210**C**42 U

	Signal Flags	Semaphores	Morse Code	ASL (American Sign Language)	Braille Reader	Braille Touch
V	X210**D**01 Victor Require Assistance (not distress)	X210**D**02 V	X210**D**03 V	X210**D**04 V	X210**D**05 V	X210**D**06 V
W	X210**D**07 Whiskey Require Medical Assistance	X210**D**08 W	X210**D**09 W	X210**D**10 W	X210**D**11 W	X210**D**12 W
X	X210**D**13 Xray Stop Your Intention, Watch for Signals	X210**D**14 X	X210**D**15 X	X210**D**16 X	X210**D**17 X	X210**D**18 X
Y	X210**D**19 Yankee Carrying Mail, Am Dragging Anchor	X210**D**20 Y	X210**D**21 Y	X210**D**22 Y	X210**D**23 Y	X210**D**24 Y
Z	X210**D**25 Zulu Require a Tug, Am Handling Nets, (Used to address shore station)	X210**D**26 Z	X210**D**27 Z	X210**D**28 Z	X210**D**29 Z	X210**D**30 Z

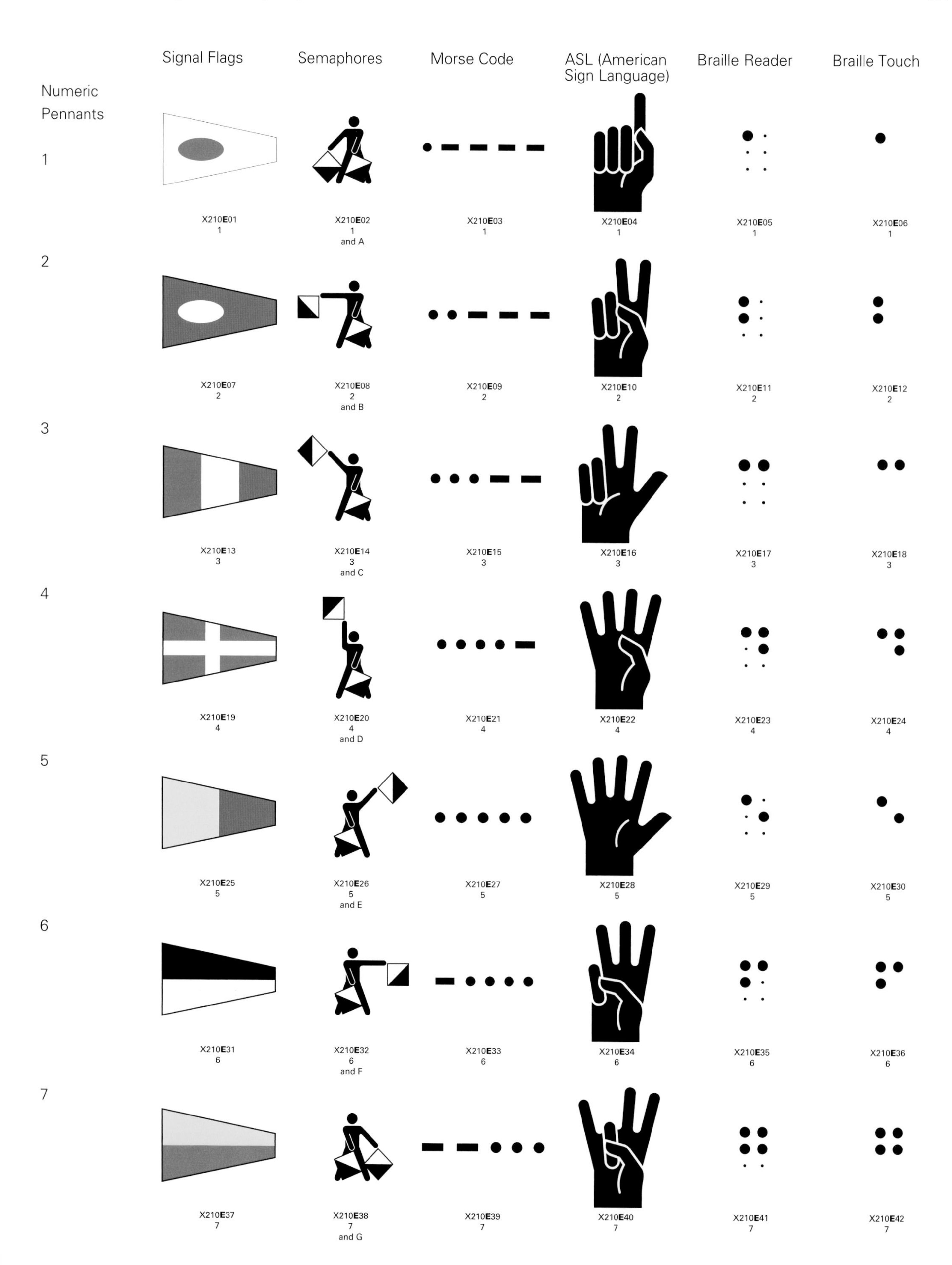
Signal Flags
Semaphores
Morse Code
ASL (American Sign Language)
Braille Reader
Braille Touch
Numeric Pennants
1
X210E01 1
X210E02 1 and A
X210E03 1
X210E04 1
X210E05 1
X210E06 1
2
X210E07 2
X210E08 2 and B
X210E09 2
X210E10 2
X210E11 2
X210E12 2
3
X210E13 3
X210E14 3 and C
X210E15 3
X210E16 3
X210E17 3
X210E18 3
4
X210E19 4
X210E20 4 and D
X210E21 4
X210E22 4
X210E23 4
X210E24 4
5
X210E25 5
X210E26 5 and E
X210E27 5
X210E28 5
X210E29 5
X210E30 5
6
X210E31 6
X210E32 6 and F
X210E33 6
X210E34 6
X210E35 6
X210E36 6
7
X210E37 7
X210E38 7 and G
X210E39 7
X210E40 7
X210E41 7
X210E42 7

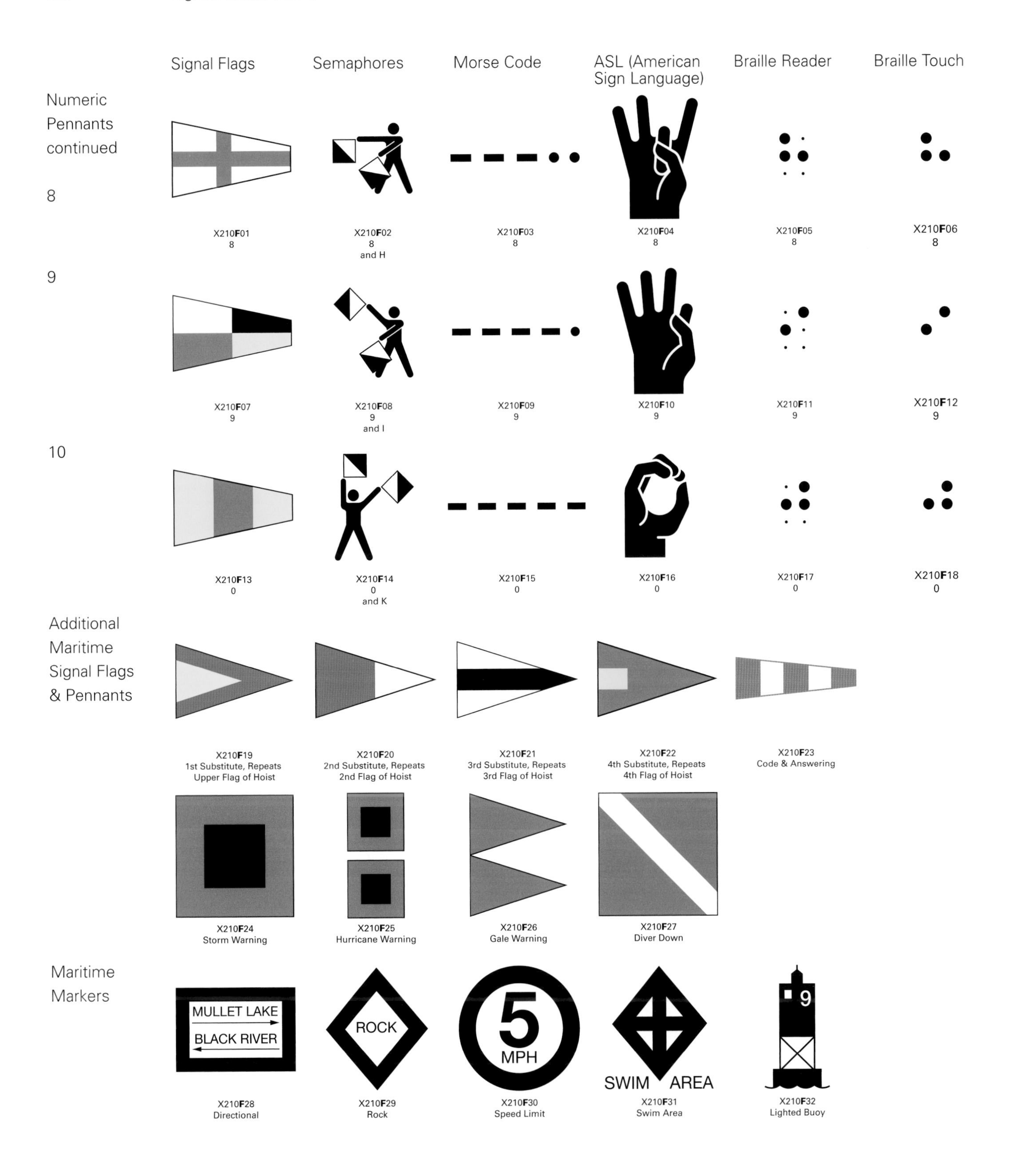

Note: All symbols and signs are available as fully editable vector image files: see page 238 or www.ultimatesymbol.com

Punctuation and Composition Signs

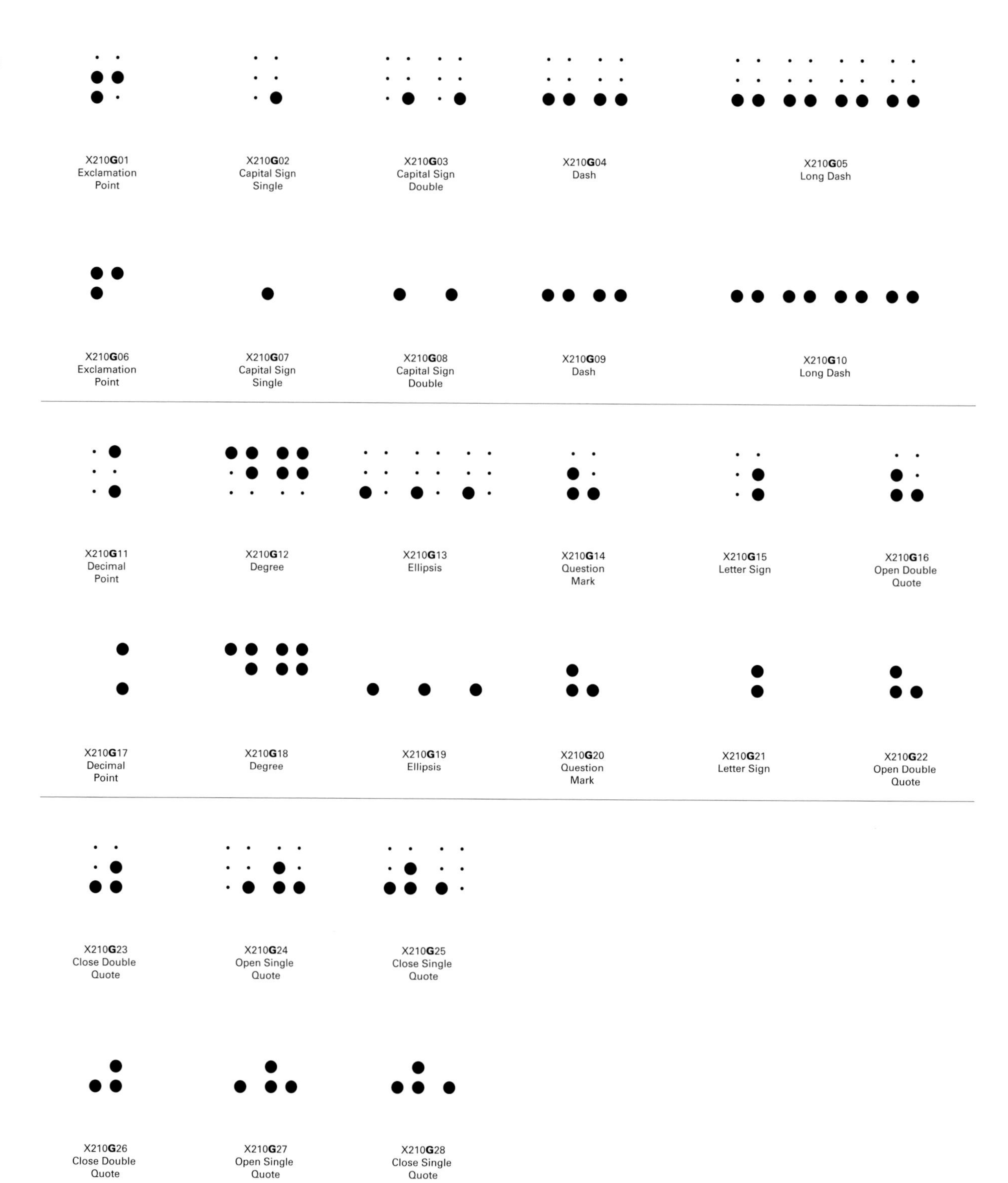

Note: The top row are Braille Reader symbols. Below each one is its corresponding Braille Touch symbol.

Accented Letters

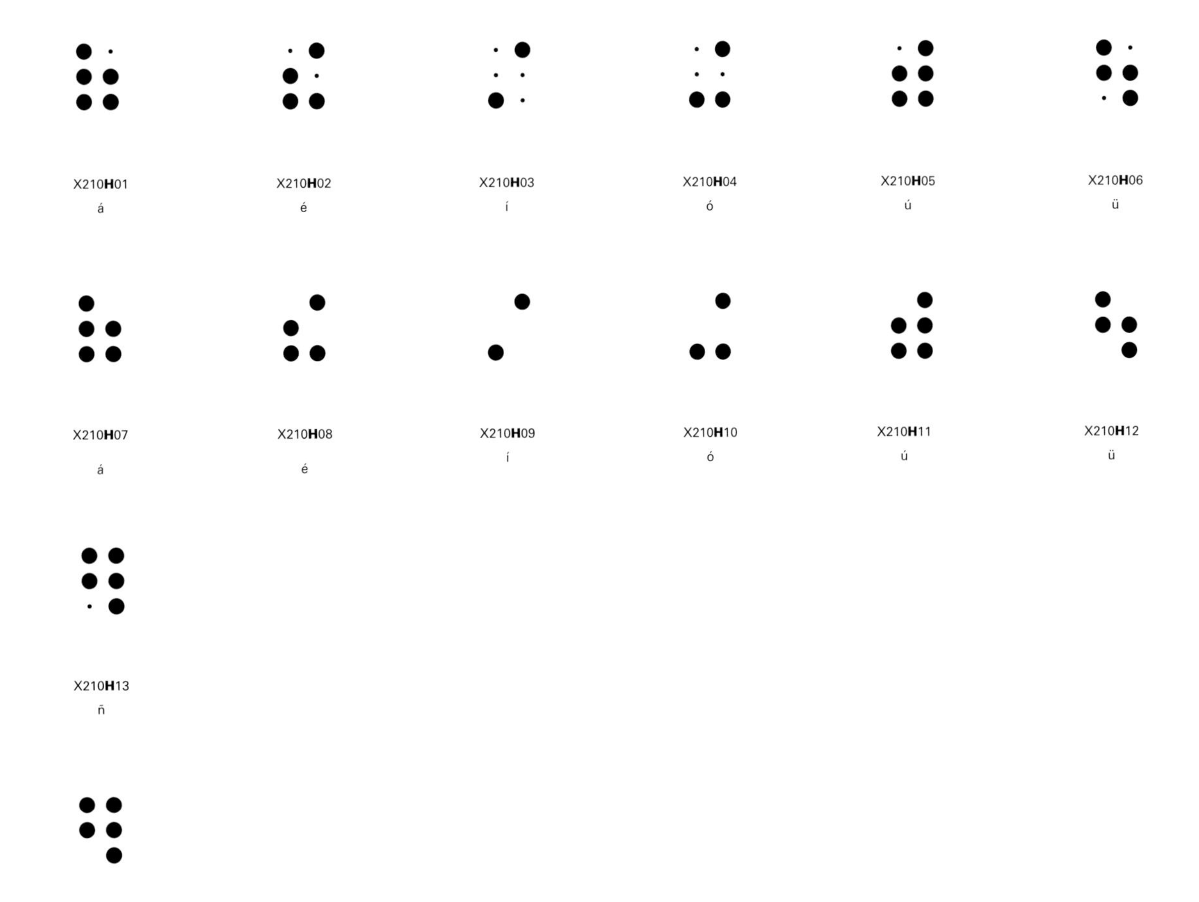

Braille: Contractions Word Signs, and Short-Form Words

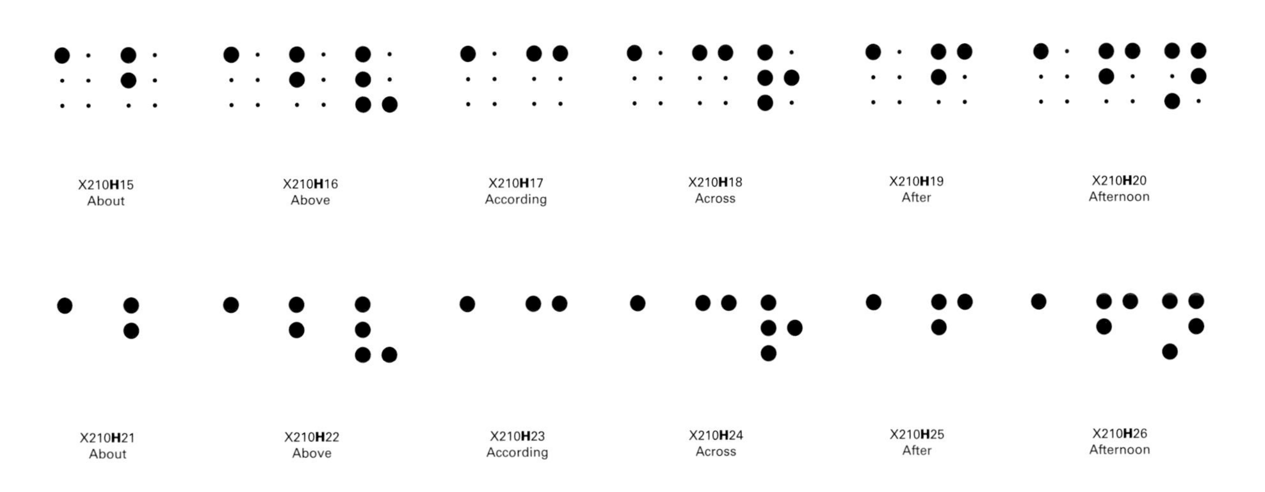

Braille: Contractions, Word Signs, and Short-Form Words continued

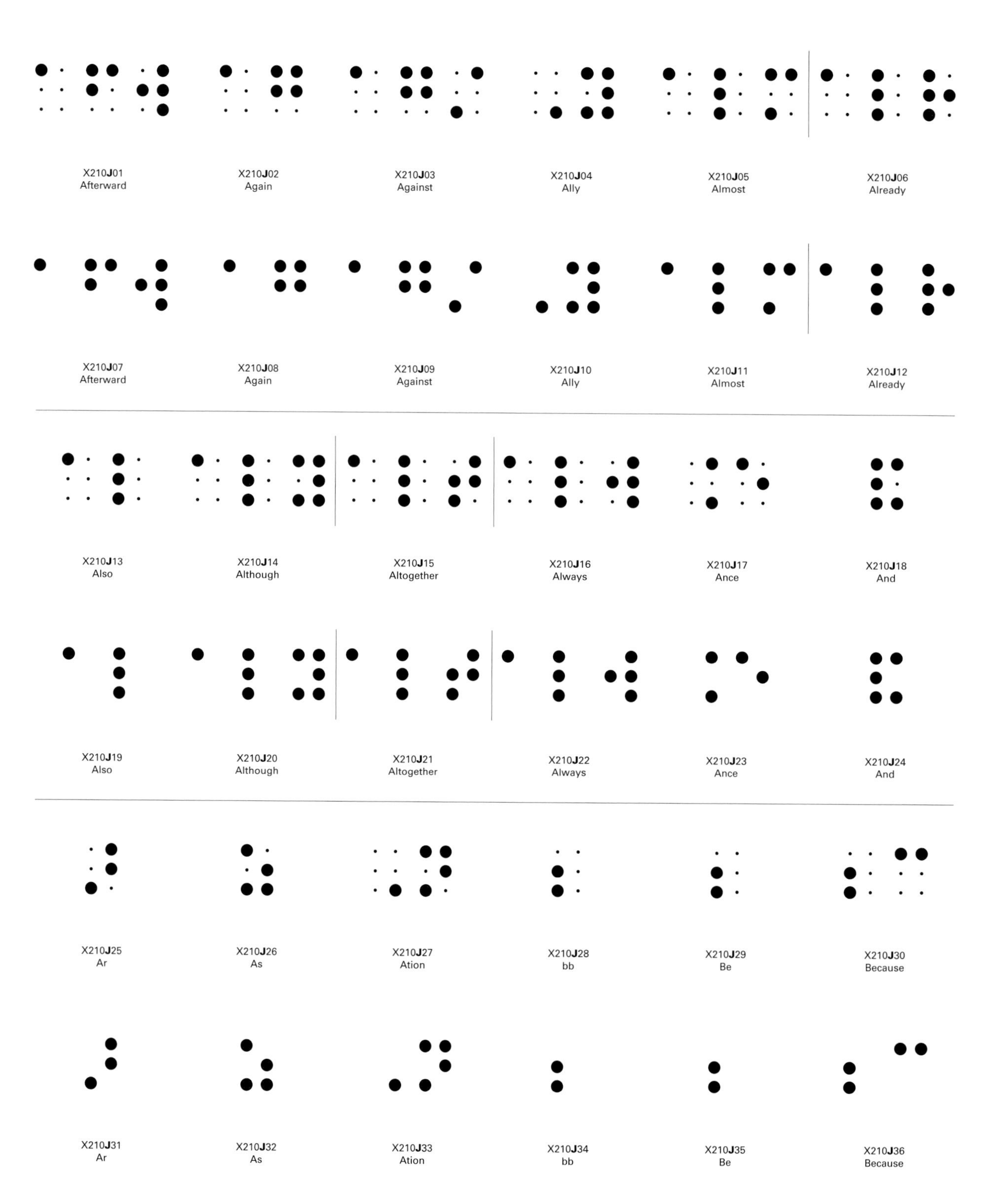

Note: The top row are Braille Reader symbols. Below each one is its corresponding Braille Touch symbol.

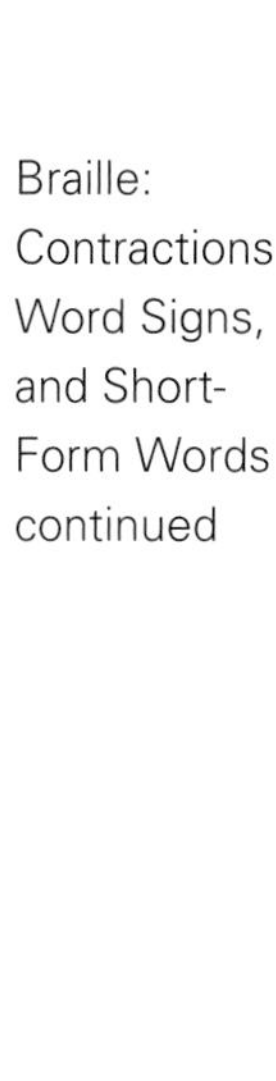

Braille: Contractions Word Signs, and Short-Form Words continued

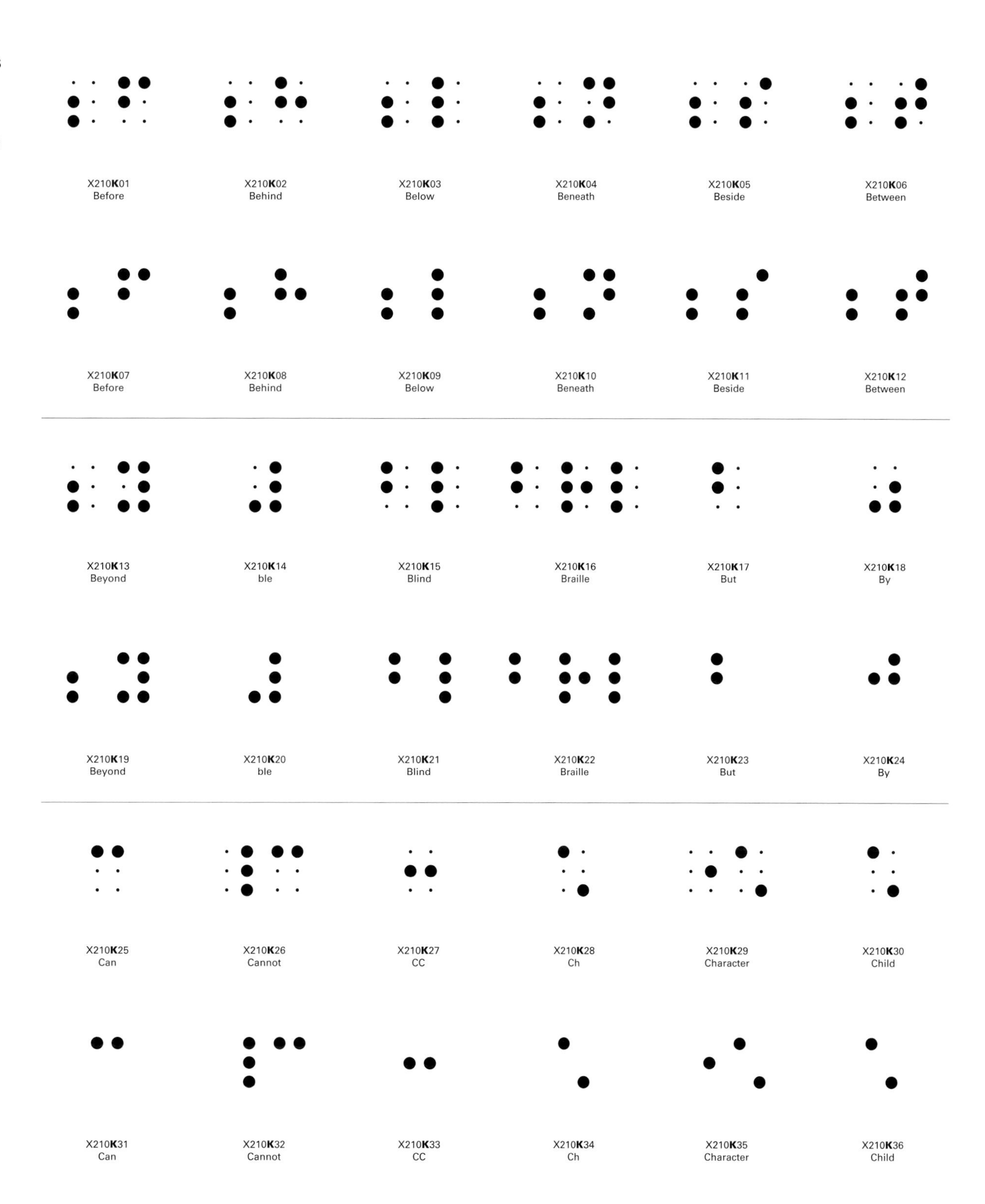

Braille: Contractions, Word Signs, and Short-Form Words continued

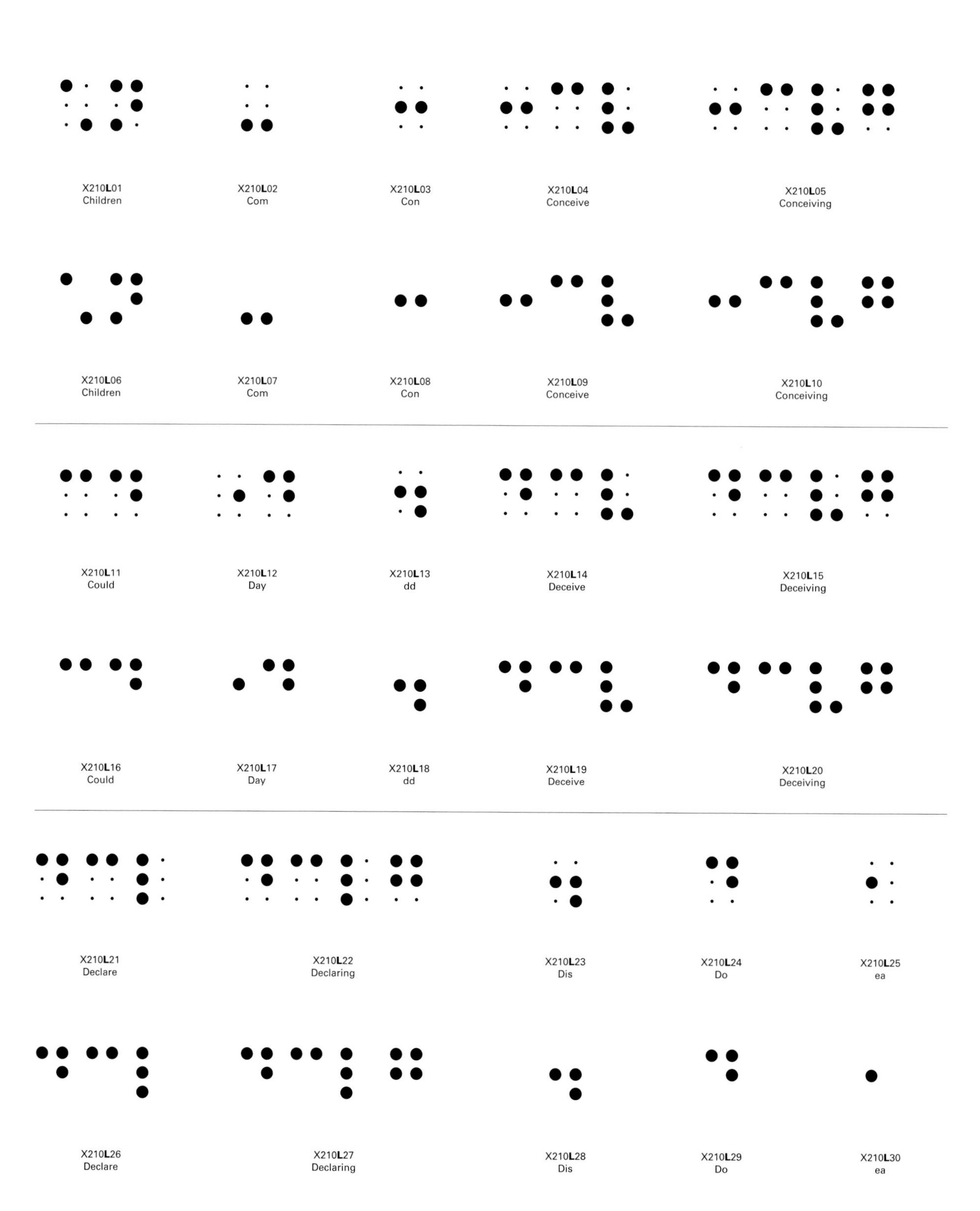

Note: The top row are Braille Reader symbols. Below each one is its corresponding Braille Touch symbol.

Braille: Contractions, Word Signs, and Short-Form Words continued

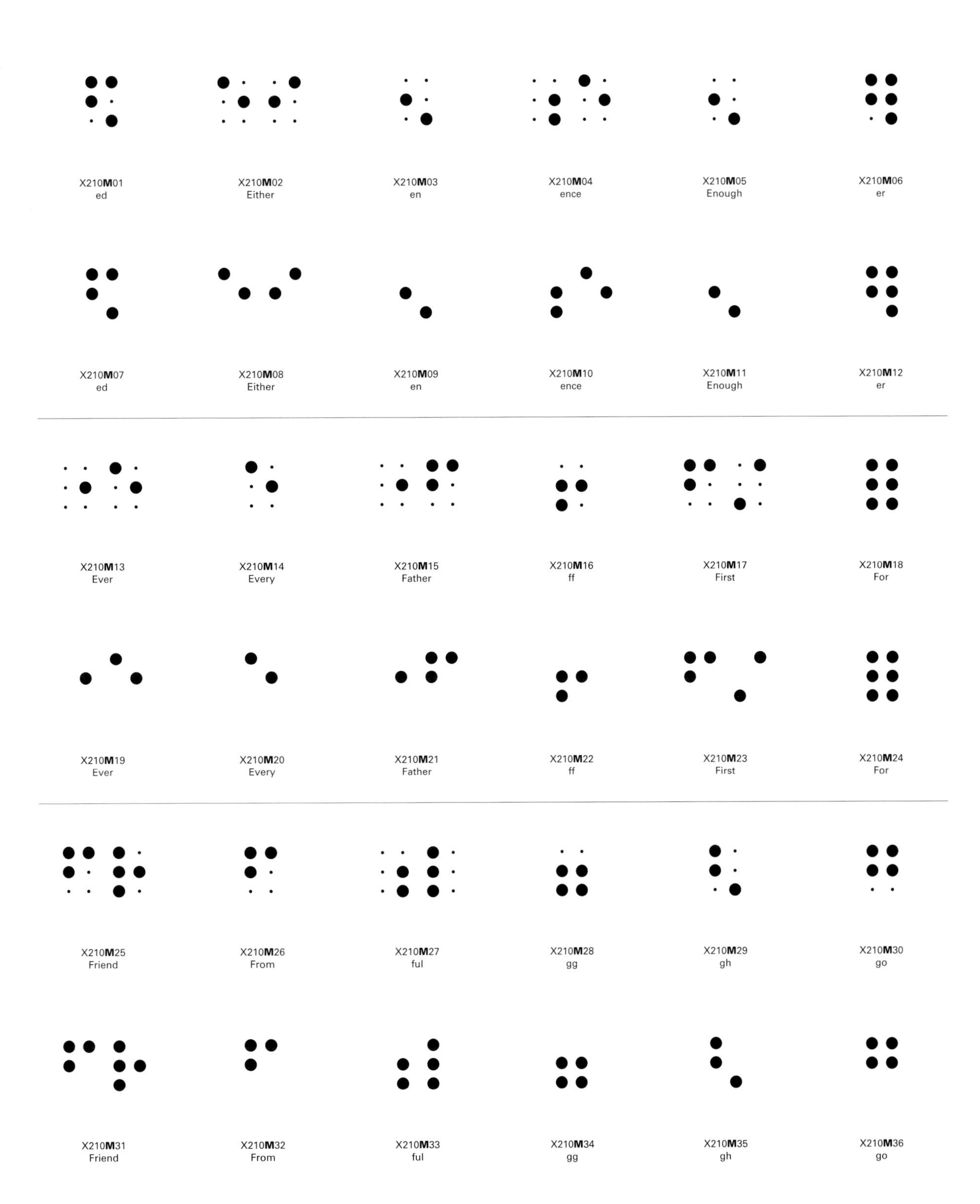

Braille:
Contractions,
Word Signs,
and Short-
Form Words
continued

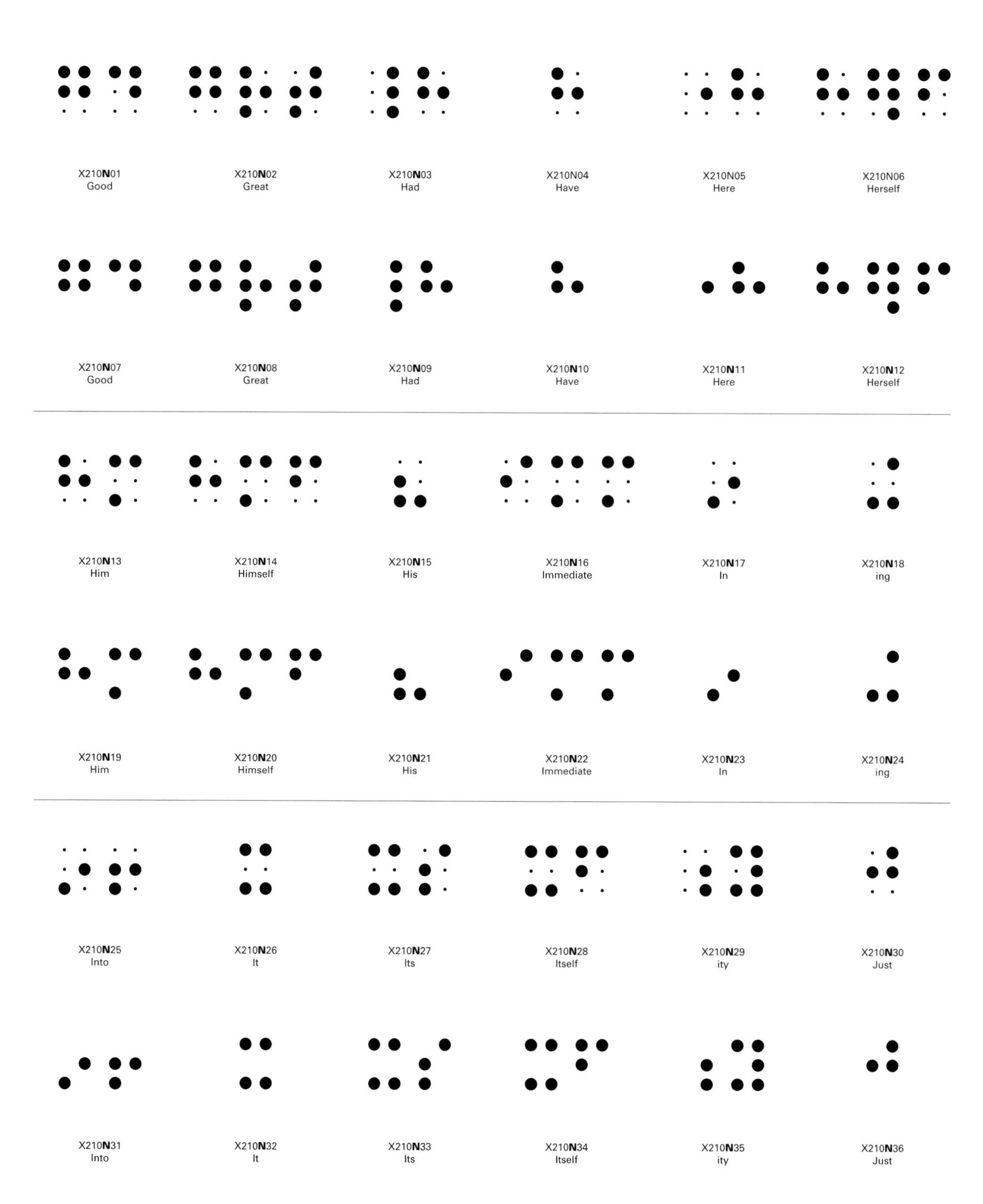

Note: The top row are Braille Reader symbols. Below each one is its corresponding Braille Touch symbol.

Braille: Contractions, Word Signs, and Short-Form Words continued

X210**P**01 Know

X210**P**02 Knowledge

X210**P**03 Less

X210**P**04 Letter

X210**P**05 Like

X210**P**06 Little

X210**P**07 Know

X210**P**08 Knowledge

X210**P**09 Less

X210**P**10 Letter

X210**P**11 Like

X210**P**12 Little

X210**P**13 Lord

X210**P**14 Many

X210**P**15 ment

X210**P**16 More

X210**P**17 Mother

X210**P**18 Much

X210**P**19 Lord

X210**P**20 Many

X210**P**21 ment

X210**P**22 More

X210**P**23 Mother

X210**P**24 Much

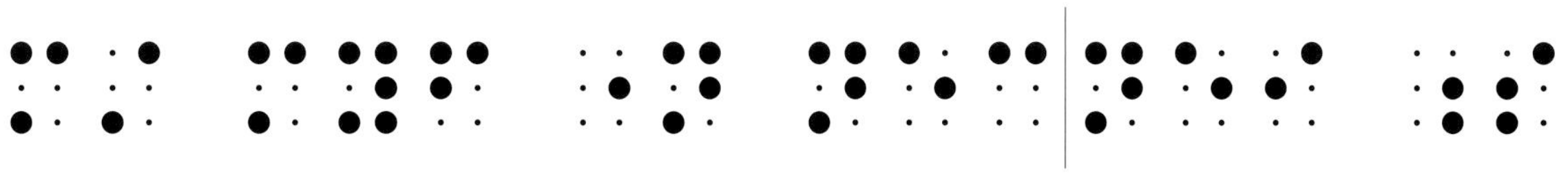

X210**P**25 Must

X210**P**26 Myself

X210**P**27 Name

X210**P**28 Necessary

X210**P**29 Neither

X210**P**30 ness

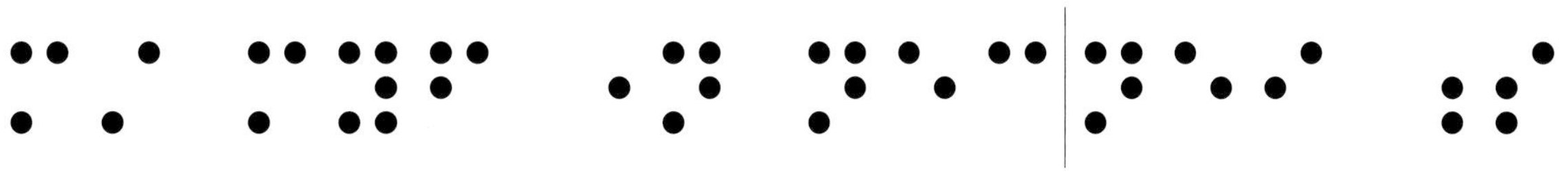

X210**P**31 Must

X210**P**32 Myself

X210**P**33 Name

X210**P**34 Necessary

X210**P**35 Neither

X210**P**36 ness

Braille: Contractions, Word Signs, and Short-Form Words continued

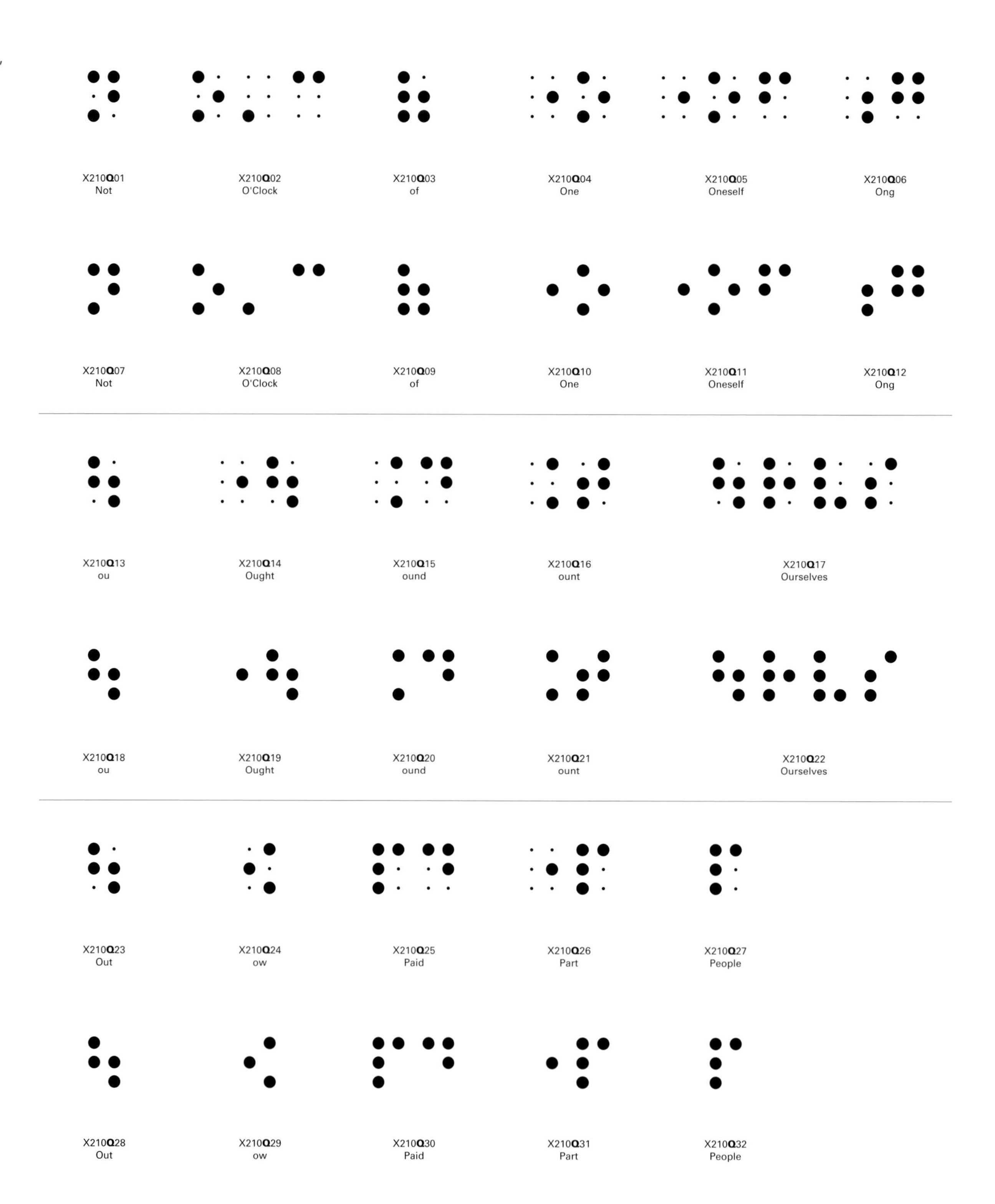

Note: The top row are Braille Reader symbols. Below each one is its corresponding Braille Touch symbol.

Braille: Contractions, Word Signs, and Short-Form Words continued

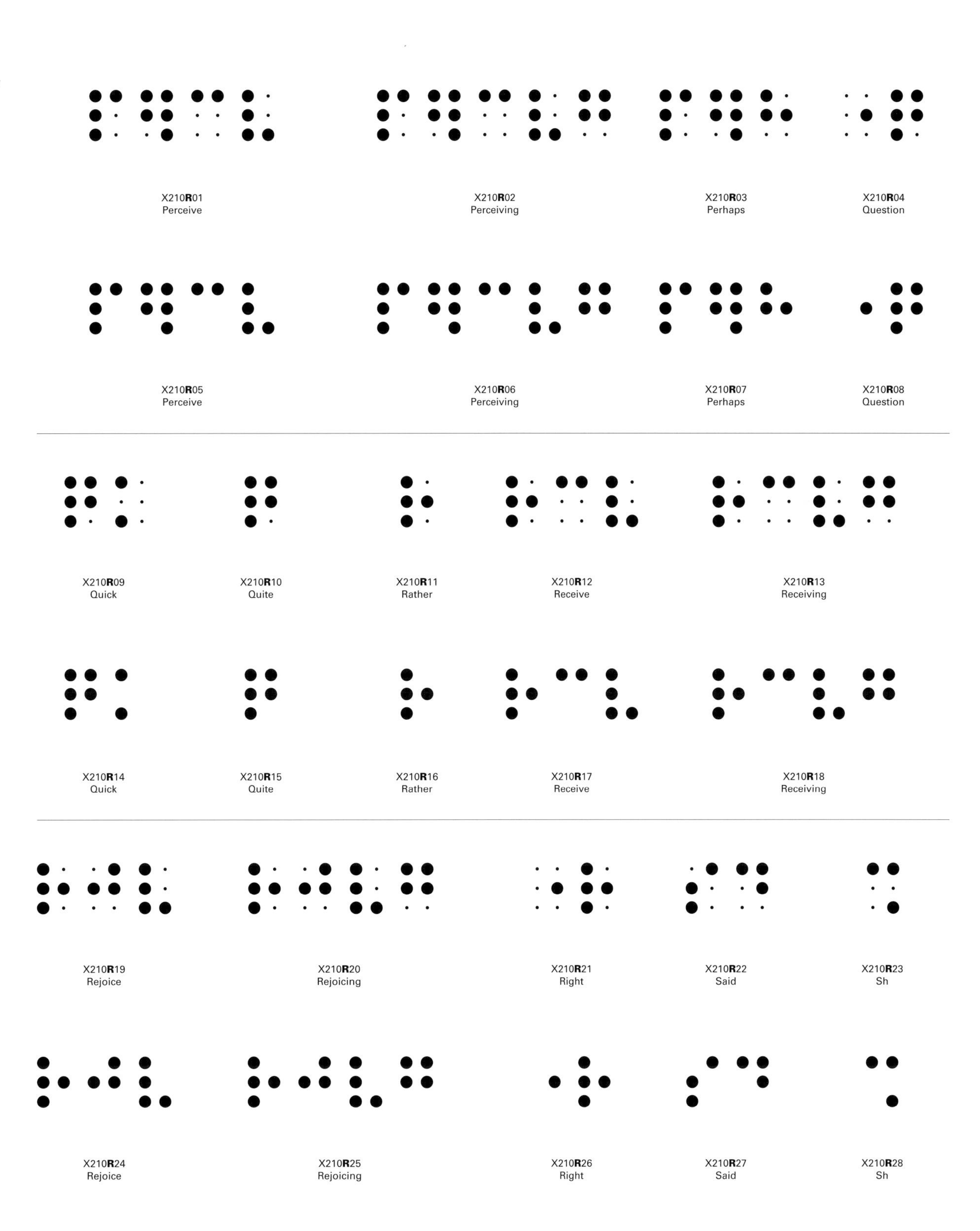

Braille:
Contractions,
Word Signs,
and Short
Form Words
continued

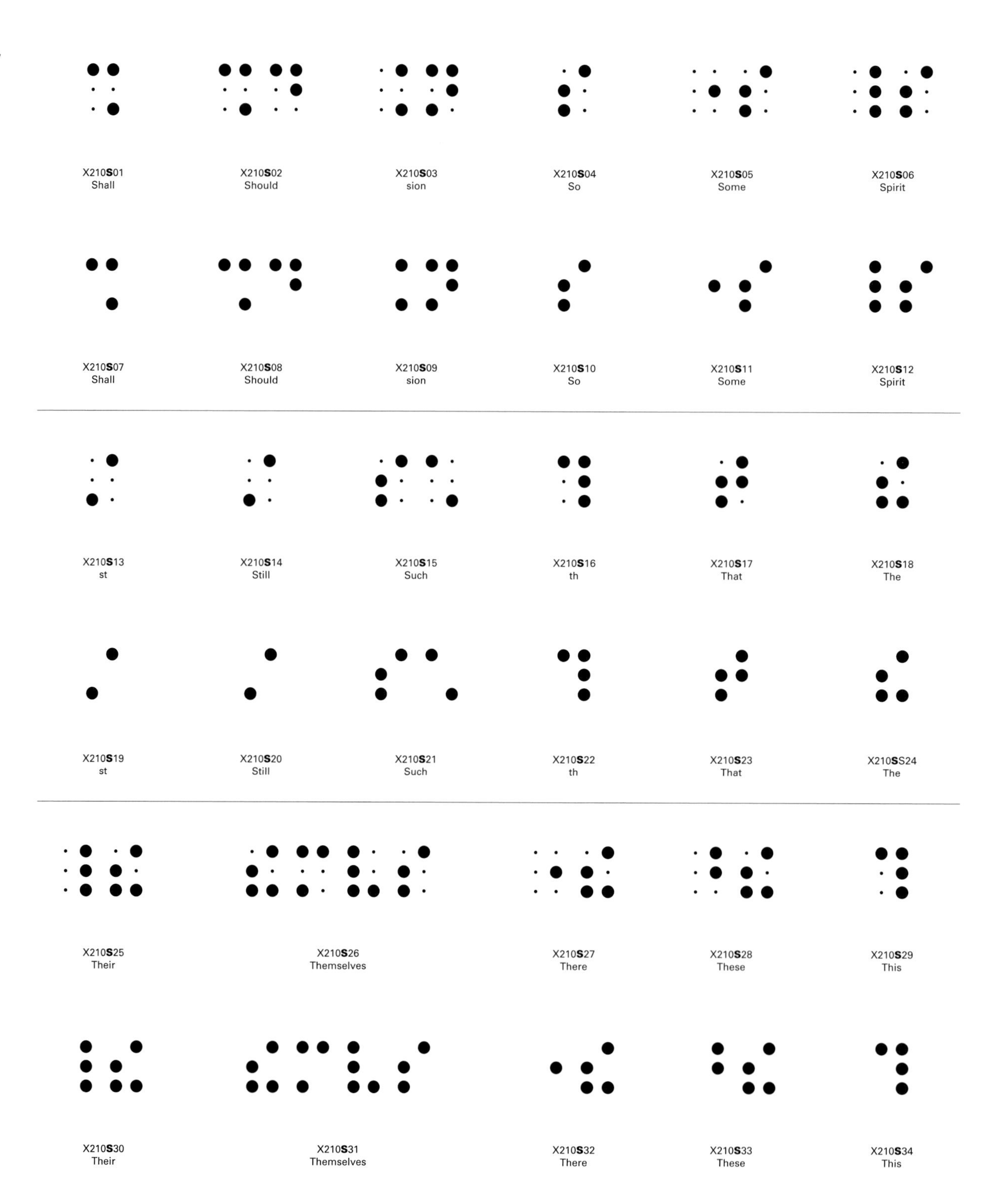

Note: The top row are Braille Reader symbols. Below each one is its corresponding Braille Touch symbol.

Braille:
Contractions,
Word Signs,
and Short-
Form Words
continued

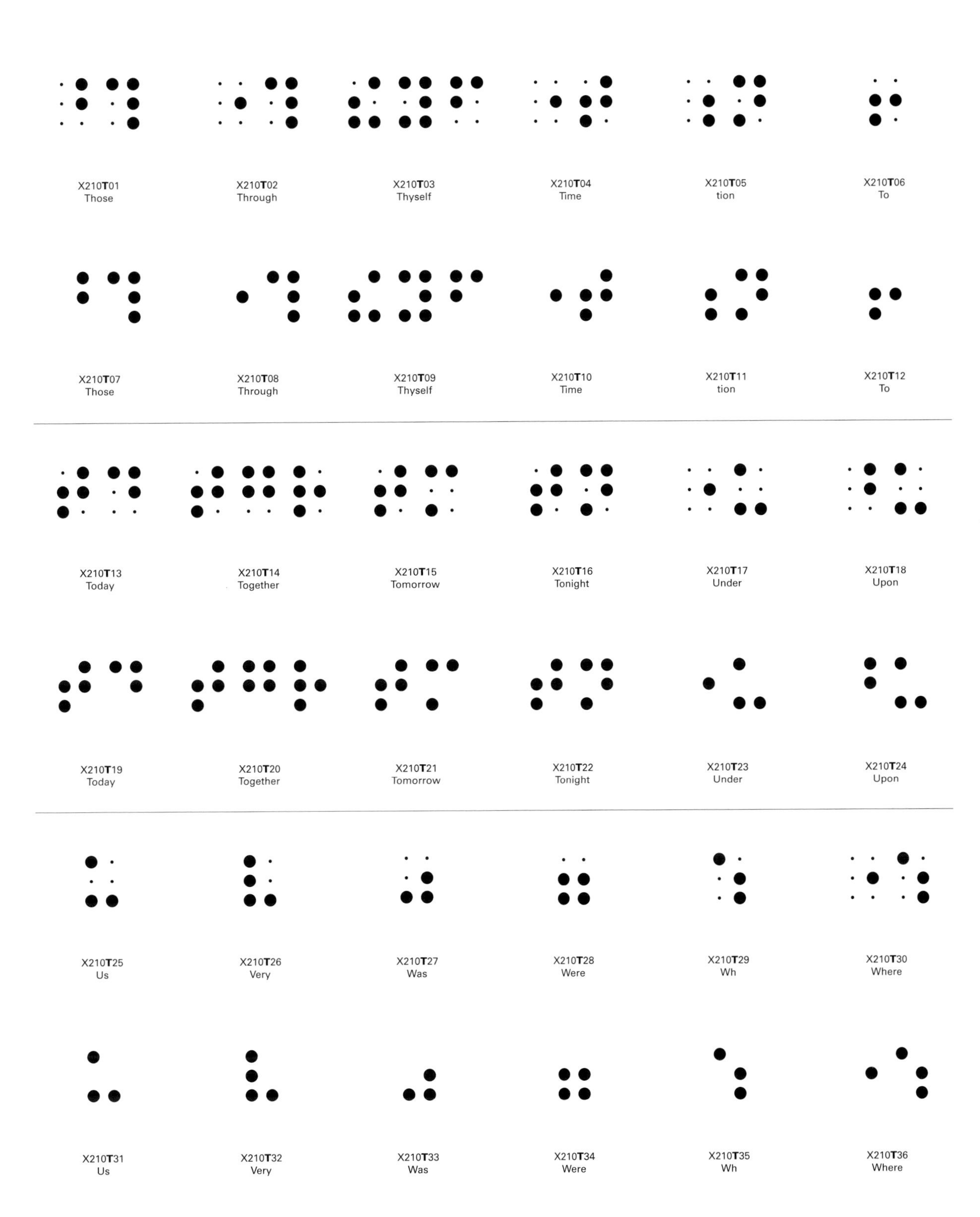

Braille: Contractions, Word Signs, and Short-Form Words continued

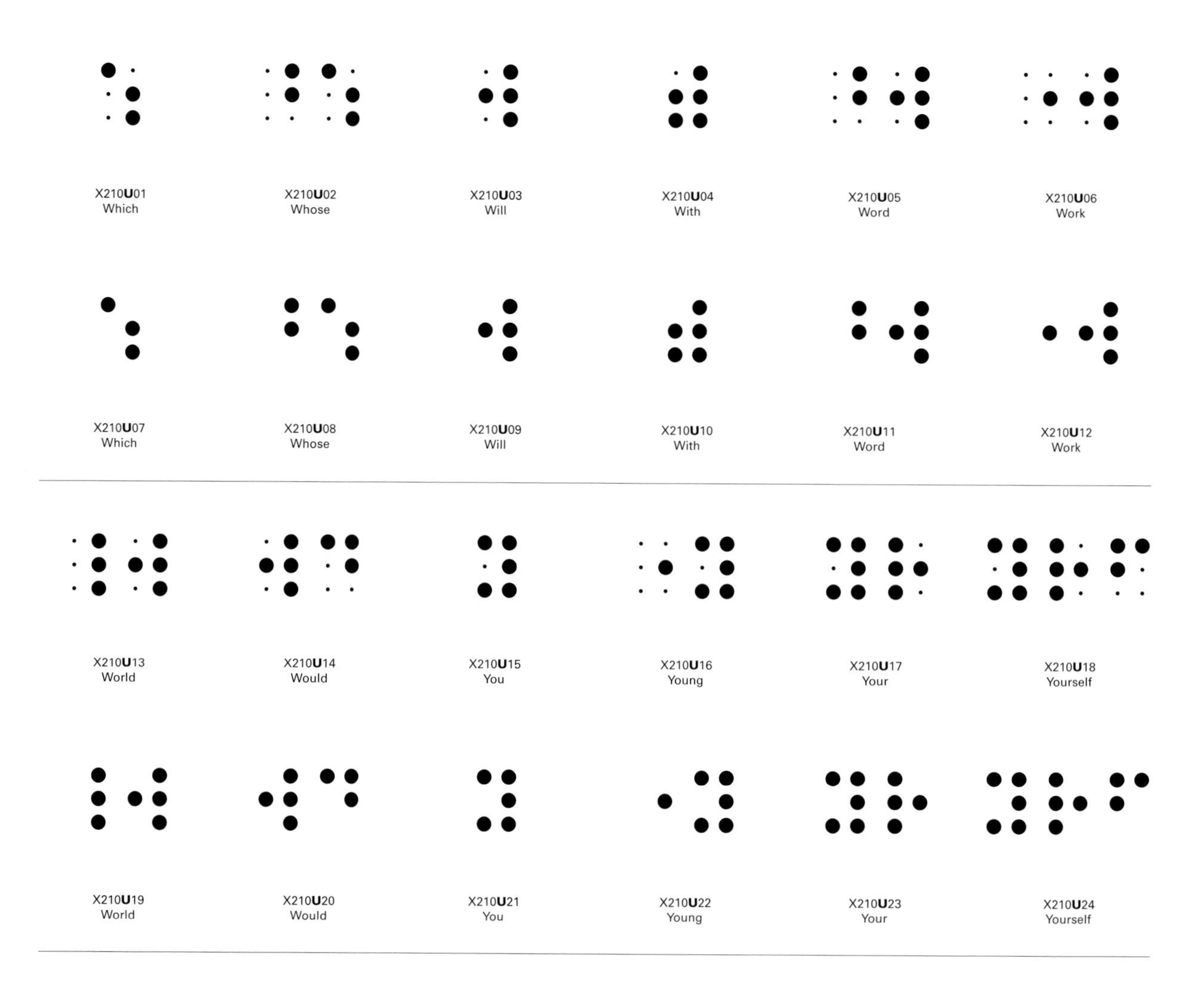

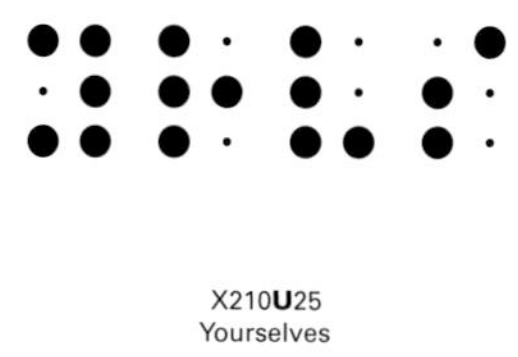

X210U25
Yourselves

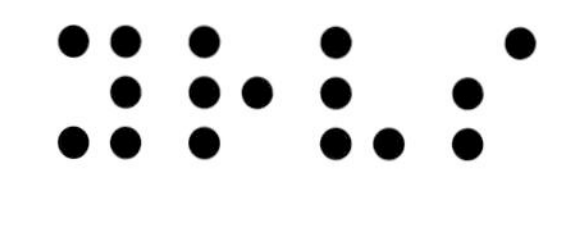

X210U26
Yourselves

Note: The top row are Braille Reader symbols. Below each one is its corresponding Braille Touch symbol.

Meteorological Symbols (WMO)

11

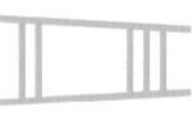

Overview

Meteorological data collection and notation has a long and fascinating historical evolution. The up-to-the-minute weather reports, forecasts, satellite photos, and maps that we take for granted today have as their foundation 2,500 years of observing and recording what is occurring in our constantly changing atmosphere. Finding ways to communicate what is or is about to happen with the weather is closely related to humanity's desire to understand nature's forces, harness them to benefit mankind and lessen the impact of the more powerful and threatening meteorological events that are still beyond our control.

As weather and climate know no national boundaries, international cooperation on a global scale is essential for the development of meteorology and operational hydrology as well as to reap the benefits from their applications. The World Meteorological Organization, based in Geneva, provides the framework for such international cooperation through the work of its members and centers, and via the regular publication of international codes, technical regulations, meteorological analyses, and forecast products.

Graphic Representation of Data on Weather Charts

The elaborate system of symbols collected here are in part derived from the WMO *Manual on the Global Data-processing System, Volume 1.*[1] As is common with most official standards (i.e., electrotechnical, mechanical), the raw message content is presented in the manual as simple line drawings or diagrams. Once again, the Ultimate Symbol design and illustration team has carefully organized and translated this material into a categorized set of symbols with consistent line weight, size, and style. Please note that because the manuals are constantly being annexed and revised, generally they should be obtained and reviewed for complete accuracy.

History

The first known routine weather observations were made during the Golden Age of Greece, approximately 500 B.C. Data gathered using the newly developed rain gauge and wind vane were written down and displayed publicly in the cities and for farmers. Around 350 B.C. Aristotle wrote his book *Meteorologica,* which was the first major weather treatise. The science of meteorology derives its name from the title of that book, which comes from the Greek word root *meteoron* and its plural *meteora*, meaning "things in the air".[2] The thermometer was invented by the Italian Galileo Galilei in 1593 and it was one of his students, Evangilista Torricelli, who developed the barometer 50 years later. In the first half of the 18th century Gabriel Daniel Fahrenheit (Germany) and Andrus Celsius (Sweden) invented their temperature scales, while in the American Colonies notables like George Washington and Thomas Jefferson kept regular weather diaries. Benjamin Franklin made his most important discovery of electricity during that period, and also that there are organized weather systems and that these systems move. The 1800s ushered in a new era of weather classification beginning with the British atmospheric enthusiast Luke Howard, who codified all the types of clouds that exist using a specific system of Latin words. The first weather map was drawn in 1819 by H. W. Brandes at the University of Breslau, identifying areas of high/low pressure and temperature using observations that were taken at the same time and mailed to him.

The development of the telegraph and Morse Code (see page 175 for more) paved the way for weather reports that were more accurate and easier to compile and disseminate across long distances. This lead to the establishment of the U.S. Department of Army's Signal Corps weather observations, and by 1950, the Smithsonian Institution in Washington D.C. began producing the first daily weather reports. The National Weather Service was named in 1970 and became the modern embodiment of the Federal weather bureau that was originally created under Ulysses S. Grant's influence 100 years earlier. Today, a branch of the National Centers for Weather Prediction, part of the NWS, creates computerized numerical forecasts using models first developed during World War I by an Englishman fighting in France, Lewis F. Richardson. Numerical models are used to generate forecast weather maps for the surface, aloft, and for layers of the atmosphere.

Cloud Classification

Clouds develop when moist air cools to its dew point by rising to a higher altitude or by moving over a cooler surface. Water vapor in the air then condenses in liquid or frozen form around minute particles such as pollen or dust. The shapes and altitudes of clouds, as well as sequences in which they develop, help forecast the weather. Prior to the beginning of the 19th century, most weather observers believed that clouds were too transient, too changeable, too short-lived, to be classified or even analyzed. With few exceptions, no cloud types were even named; they were just described by their color and form as each individual saw them: dark, white, grey, black, mare's tails, mackerel skies, woolly fleece, towers and castles, rocks, and oxen eyes. Clouds were used in a few instances as forecast tools in weather proverbs, but mostly by their state of darkness or color: "Red sky in morning, sailor take warning."[3]

Godfather of Clouds[4]

During the winter of 1802-03, Luke Howard (1772-1864), an English manufacturing chemist/pharmacist and amateur meteorologist, presented a paper to the Askesian Society, of which he was a founding member, entitled *On the Modification of Clouds.* In that seminal paper, Howard proposed that one could identify several simple categories within the complexity of cloud forms. The great leap that Howard took was to provide his descriptive categories with Latin names (as Linneaus had done with the plant and animal kingdoms), the language of scholarship, thus transcending national and language borders in its usage. Understandable to all European-derived cultures, the system was both very simple and nearly all-encompassing, enhancing its prospects for success.

Howard believed all clouds belonged to three distinct groups:
Cumulus (Latin for *heap*): "Convex or conical heaps, increasing upward from a horizontal base – wool bag clouds."
Stratus (L. for *layer*): "A widely extended horizontal sheet, increasing from below."
Cirrus (L. for *curl of hair*): "Parallel, flexuous fibres extensible by increase in any or all directions."
To denote "a cloud in the act of condensation into rain, hail or snow," he added a fourth category:
Nimbus (L. for *rain*): "A rain cloud — a cloud or systems of clouds from which rain is falling."

According to Howard: "While any of the clouds, except the nimbus, retain their primitive forms, no rain can take place; and it is by observing the changes and transitions of cloud form that weather may be predicted." Clouds could also alter their forms; thus, he reasoned, when cumulus clouds bunched together so that they crowded the sky, they became:
Cumulo-stratus: "The cirro-stratus blended with the cumulus, and either appearing intermixed with the heaps of the latter, or super-adding a widespread structure to its base." Similarly, he defined other intermediate categories of transformation:
Cirro-cumulus: "Small, well-defined, roundish masses increasing from below." and
Cirro-stratus: "Horizontal or slightly inclined masses, attenuated towards a part or the whole of their circumference, bent downward or undulated, separate, or in groups, or consisting of small clouds having these characters."

Howard's work made a big impression on those interested in the sky, particularly after his papers were reprinted in Thomas Forster's successful *Researches About Atmospheric Phaenomenae* in 1813. The classification system quickly gained wide acceptance both in Britain and other countries. Among its biggest supporters were Constable, Coleridge, and the German poet, philosopher and scientist Johann Wolfgang von Goethe, who wrote: "He was the first to hold fast conceptually the airy and always changing form of clouds, to limit and fasten down the indefinite, the intangible and unattainable and give them appropriate names." Legitimized by the elevation of Howard's new classification and nomenclature, meteorology fast became a respectable science.[5]

Later scientists added terms such as *humilis* (small) and *incus* (anvil) to designate other cloud properties. *The International Cloud-Atlas*, first published in 1896, is based on this classification system. It is published by the American Meteorological Society.

About WMO

The World Meteorological Organization (WMO) is an intergovernmental organization with a membership of 187 Member States and Territories. It originated from the International Meteorological Organization (IMO), which was founded in 1873. Established in 1950, WMO became the specialized agency of the United Nations for meteorology (weather and climate), operational hydrology, and related geophysical sciences.
www.wmo.ch

Cloud Genera

(CL)
Cumulus
Cumulonimbus
Stratocumulus
Stratus

X211**A**01
Cumulus, Cu
genus

X211**A**02
Cumulus, Little
vertical development

X211**A**03
Cumulus, Considerable
development

X211**A**04
Cumulonimbus
Clear-cut tops lacking

X211**A**05
Stratocumulus, Sc
genus

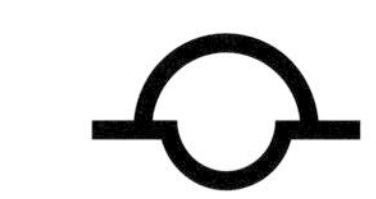
X211**A**06
Stratocumulus
Spreading from cumulus

X211**A**07
Stratocumulus
Not from cumulus

X211**A**08
Stratus, St
genus

X211**A**09
Stratus
Continuous layer or sheet

X211**A**10
Stratus Fractus
Fractocumulus (Scud)

X211**A**11
Cumulonimbus, Cb
genus

X211**A**12
Cumulonimbus
Clear top

X211**A**13
Cumulus
and Stratocumulus

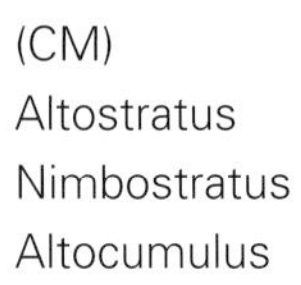
(CM)
Altostratus
Nimbostratus
Altocumulus

X211**A**14
Altostratus
Thin, semi-transparent

X211**A**15
Altostratus, As
genus

X211**A**16
Altostratus
Thick

X211**A**17
Nimbostratus, Ns
genus

X211**A**18
Altocumulus, Ac
genus

X211**A**19
Altocumulus
Thin, semi-transparent

X211**A**20
Altocumulus
Thin, patches

X211**A**21
Altocumulus
In bands and thickening

X211**A**22
Altocumulus
Spreading from cumulus

X211**A**23
Altocumulus
Double- or multi-layered

X211**A**24
Altocumulus
Tufts or turrets

X211**A**25
Altocumulus
of Chaotic Sky

(CH)
Cirrus
Cirrostratus
Cirrocumulus

X211**A**26
Cirrus, Ci
genus

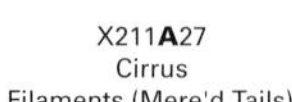
X211**A**27
Cirrus
Filaments (Mere'd Tails)

X211**A**28
Cirrus
Dense, patches, tufts

X211**A**29
Cirrus
Dense, anvil shaped

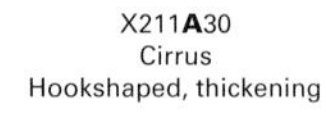
X211**A**30
Cirrus
Hookshaped, thickening

X211**A**31
Cirrus, and Cirrostratus,
< 45° above horiz.

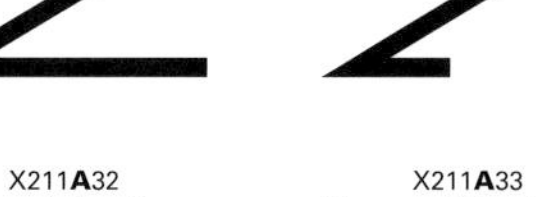
X211**A**32
Cirrostratus, Cs
genus

X211**A**33
Cirrus and Cirrostratus,
> 45° above horiz.

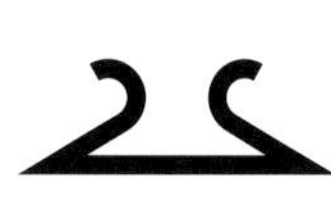
X211**A**34
Cirrostratus
Veil covering sky

X211**A**35
Cirrostratus
Not increasing

X211**A**36
Cirrocumulus, Cc
genus

X211**A**37
Cirrocumulus

WW Series:
Present Weather
Reported from
a Manned
Weather Station

X211**B**01
Visibility Reduced by Smoke

X211**B**02
Haze

X211**B**03
Widespread Dust in Suspension in the Air Not Raised by Wind at Time of Observation

X211**B**04
Dust or Sand Raised by Wind at or Near the Station at Time of Observation

X211**B**05
Well Developed Dust Whirl; Within past hour

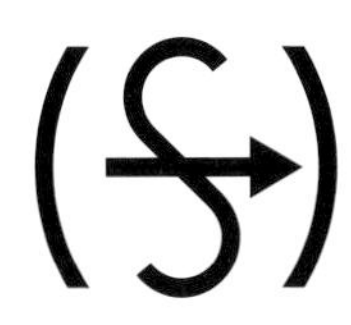
X211**B**06
Dust Storm or Sand Storm; Within sight of or at station during past hour

X211**B**07
Light Fog

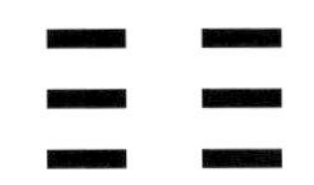
X211**B**08
Patches

X211**B**09
More or Less Continuous

X211**B**10
Lightning Visible; No thunder heard

X211**B**11
Precipitation Within Sight; But not reaching the ground

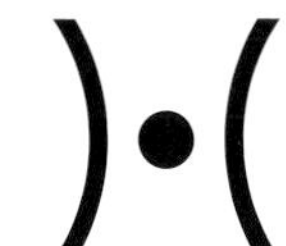
X211**B**12
Precipitation Within Sight; Reaching the ground but distant from station

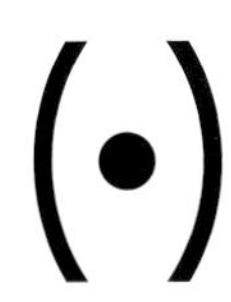
X211**B**13
Precipitation Within Sight; Reaching the ground, near to but not at station

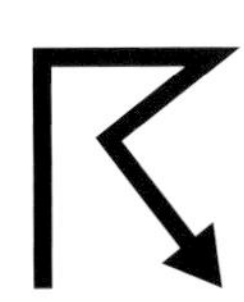
X211**B**14
Thunder Heard; But no precipitation at the station

X211**B**15
Squall; Within sight during past hour or at time of observation

X211**B**16
Funnel Cloud; Within sight of or at time of observaton

X211**B**17
Drizzle or Snow Grains; Not freezing and not falling as showers, during past hour but not at time of observation

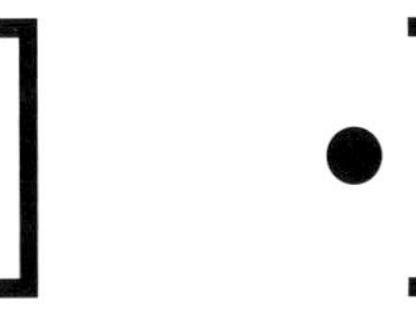
X211**B**18
Rain; Not freezing and not falling as shower during past hour, but not at time of observation

X211**B**19
Snow; Not falling as showers, during past hour, but not at time of observation

X211**B**20
Rain and Snow or Ice Pellets; Not falling as showers, during past hour, but not at time of observation

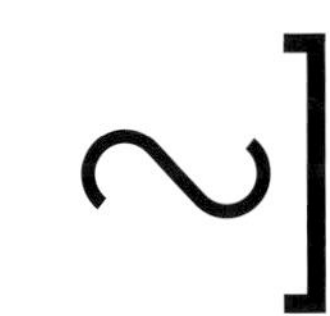
X211**B**21
Freezing Drizzle or Freezing Rain; Not falling as shower, during past hour, but not at time of observation

X211**B**22
Showers of Rain; During past hour, but not at time of observation

X211**B**23
Showers of Snow, or of Rain and Snow; During past hour, but not at time of observation

X211**B**24
Showers of Hail, or of Hail and Rain; During past hour, but not at time of observation

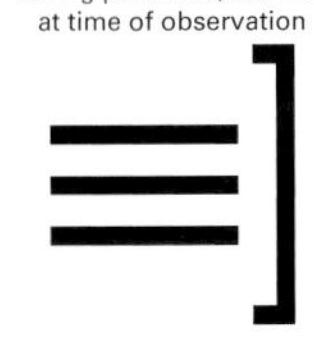
X211**B**25
Fog; During past hour, but not at time of observation

X211**B**26
Thunderstorm; With or without precipitation during past hour, but not at time of observation

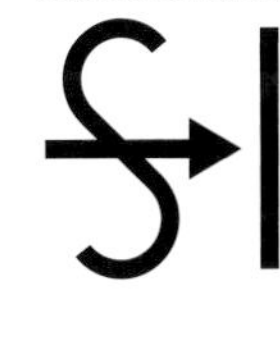
X211**B**27
Slight or Moderate Dust Storm or Sand Storm; Has decreased during past hour

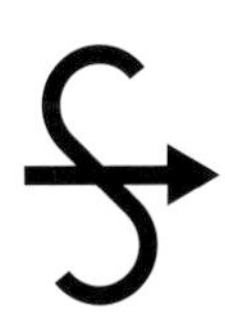
X211**B**28
Slight or Moderate Dust Storm or Sand Storm; No appreciable change during past hour

X211**B**29
Slight or Moderate Dust Storm or Sand Storm; Has begun or increased during past hour

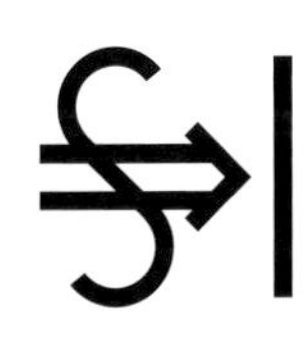
X211**B**30
Severe Dust Storm or Sand Storm; Has decreased during past hour

X211**B**31
Severe Dust Storm or Sand Storm; No appreciable change during past hour

X211**B**32
Severe Dust Storm or Sand Storm; Has begun or increased during past hour

X211**B**33
Slight or Moderate Drifting Snow; Generally low

X211**B**34
Heavy Drifting Snow; Generally low

X211**B**35
Slight or Moderate Blowing Snow; Generally high

X211**B**36
Heavy Blowing Snow Generally high

Note: All symbols and signs are available as fully editable vector image files: see page 238 or www.ultimatesymbol.com

WW Series: Present Weather Reported from a Manned Weather Station continued

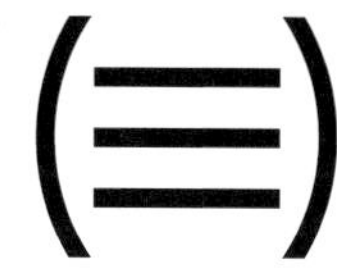
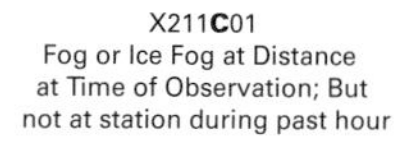
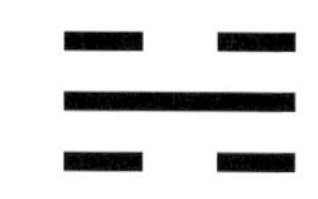

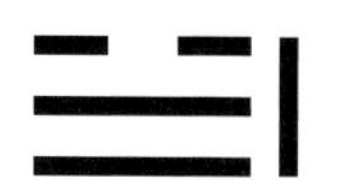

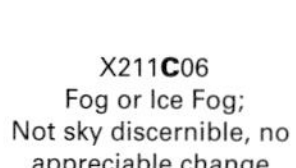

X211C01
Fog or Ice Fog at Distance at Time of Observation; But not at station during past hour

X211C02
Fog or Ice Fog in Patches

X211C03
Fog or Ice Fog; Sky discernible, has become thinner during past hour

X211C04
Fog or Ice Fog Sky; Not discernible, has become thinner during past hour

X211C05
Fog or Ice Fog; Sky discernible, no appreciable change during past hour

X211C06
Fog or Ice Fog; Not sky discernible, no appreciable change past hour

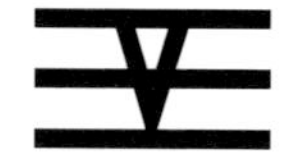

X211C07
Fog or Ice Fog; Sky discernible, has begun or became thicker during past hour

X211C08
Fog or Ice Fog; Sky not discernible, has begun or became thicker during past hour

X211C09
Fog; Depositing rime, sky discernible

X211C10
Fog; Depositing rime, sky not discernible

X211C11
Intermittent Drizzle; Not freezing, slight at time of observation

X211C12
Continuous Drizzle; Not freezing, slight at time of observation

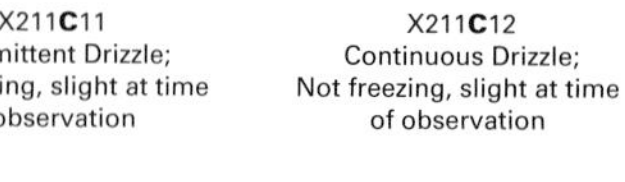

X211C13
Intermittent Rain; Not freezing, moderate at time of observation

X211C14
Continuous Rain; Not freezing, moderate at time of observation

X211C15
Intermittent Rain; Not freezing, heavy at time of observation

X211C16
Continuous Rain; Not freezing, heavy at time of observation

X211C17
Slight Freezing Drizzle

X211C18
Moderate or Heavy Freezing Drizzle

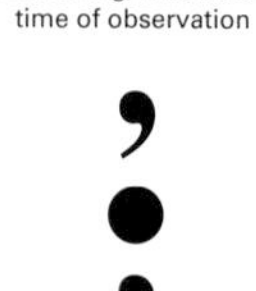

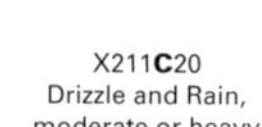

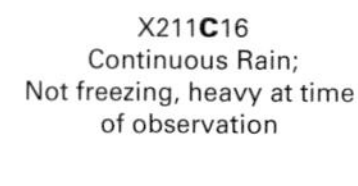
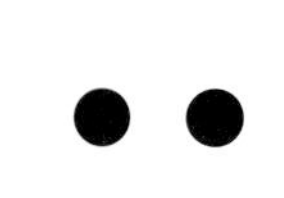
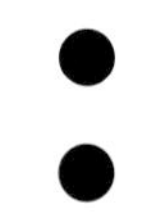

X211C19
Drizzle and Rain, slight

X211C20
Drizzle and Rain, moderate or heavy

X211C21
Intermittent Rain; Not freezing, slight at time of observation

X211C22
Continuous Rain; Not freezing, slight at time of observation

X211C23
Intermittent Rain; Not freezing, moderate at time of observation

X211C24
Continuous Rain; Not freezing, moderate at time of observation

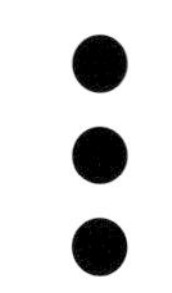

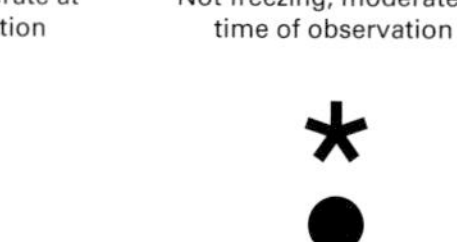

X211C25
Intermittent Rain; Not freezing, heavy at time of observation

X211C26
Continuous Rain; Not freezing, heavy at time of observation

X211C27
Slight Freezing Rain

X211C28
Moderate or Heavy Freezing Rain

X211C29
Rain or Drizzle and Snow, slight

X211C30
Rain or Drizzle and Snow, moderate or heavy

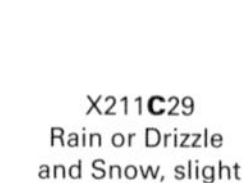
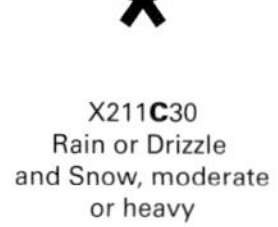

X211C31
Intermittent Fall of Snow Flakes, slight at time of observation

X211C32
Continuous Fall of Snow Flakes, slight at time of observation

X211C33
Intermittent Fall of Snow Flakes, moderate at time of observation

X211C34
Continuous Fall of Snow Flakes, moderate at time of observation

X211C35
Intermittent Fall of Snow Flakes, heavy at time of observation

X211C36
Continuous Fall of Snow Flakes, heavy at time of observation

WW Series: Present Weather Reported from a Manned Weather Station continued

X211**D**01
Ice Prisms;
With or without fog

X211**D**02
Snow Grains;
With or without fog

X211**D**03
Isolated Starlike
Snow Crystals;
With or without fog

X211**D**04
Ice Pellets;
Sleet, U.S. definition

X211**D**05
Slight Rain Shower(s)

X211**D**06
Moderate or Heavy
Rain Shower(s)

X211**D**07
Violent Rain Shower(s)

X211**D**08
Slight Shower(s) of
Rain and Snow Mixed

X211**D**09
Moderate or Heavy Shower(s)
of Rain and Snow Mixed

X211**D**10
Slight Snow Shower(s)

X211**D**11
Moderate or Heavy
Snow Shower(s)

X211**D**12
Slight Shower(s) of Snow Pellets,
or Ice Pellets with or without
Rain or Rain and Snow, Mixed

X211**D**13
Moderate or Heavy Shower(s)
of Snow Pellets, or Ice Pellets,
or Ice Pellets with or without
Rain or Rain and Snow Mixed

X211**D**14
Slight Shower(s) of Hail,
with or without Rain or
Rain and Snow Mixed,
Not Associated with Thunder

X211**D**15
Moderate or Heavy Shower(s)
of Hail, with or without Rain
or Rain and Snow Mixed,
Not Associated with Thunder

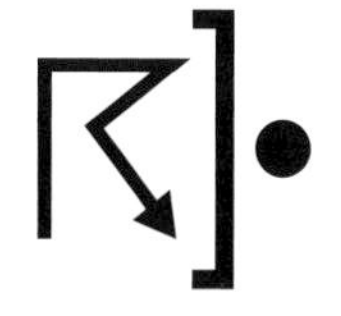

X211**D**16
Slight Rain at Time of
Observation; Thunderstorm
during past hour, but not at
time of observation

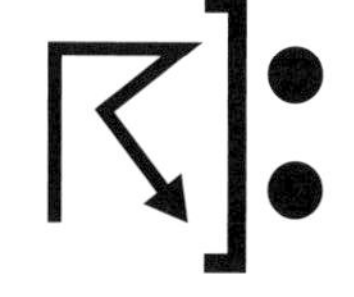

X211**D**17
Moderate or Heavy Rain at Time
of Observation; Thunderstorm
during past hour, but not at
time of observation

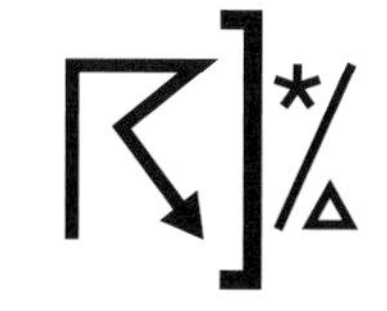

X211**D**18
Slight Snow or Rain and
Snow Mixed or Hail at Time
of Observation; Thunderstorm
during past hour, but not at
time of observation

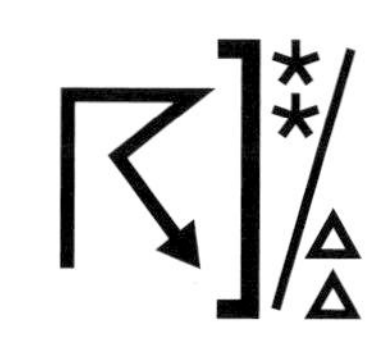

X211**D**19
Moderate or Heavy Snow or Rain
and Snow Mixed or Hail at Time
of Observation; Thunderstorm
during past hour, but not at
time of observation

X211**D**20
Slight or Moderate
Thunderstorm without Hail,
but with Rain and/or
Snow at Time of Observation

X211**D**21
Slight or Moderate
Thunderstorm, with
Hail at Time of Observation

X211**D**22
Heavy Thunderstorm,
Without Hail, but with Rain
and/or Snow at Time of
Observation

X211**D**23
Thunderstorm Combined
with Dust Storm or Sand Storm
at Time of Observation

X211**D**24
Heavy Thunderstorm with Hail
at Time of Observation

WaWa Series: Present Weather Reported from an Automatic Weather Station

X211**D**25
Haze or Smoke, or Dust in
Suspension in the Air; Visibility
equal to, or greater than, 1 km

X211**D**26
Haze or Smoke, or Dust in
Suspension in the Air;
Visibility less than 1 km

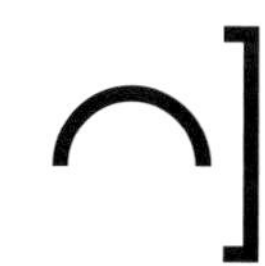

X211**D**27
Precipitation

X211**D**28
Blowing or Drifting Snow
or Sand

X211**D**29
Blowing or Drifting Snow
or Sand; Visibility equal to, or
greater than, 1 km

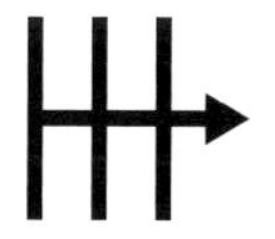

X211**D**30
Blowing or Drifting Snow
or Sand; Visibility less than,
1 km

X211**D**31
Fog

X211**D**32
Fog; Depositing rime

X211**D**33
Precipitation

X211**D**34
Precipitation;
Slight or moderate

X211**D**35
Precipitation;
Heavy

X211**D**36
Liquid Precipitation;
Slight or moderate

WaWa Series:
Present Weather
Reported from
an Automatic
Weather Station
continued

X211**E**01
Liquid Precipitation; Heavy

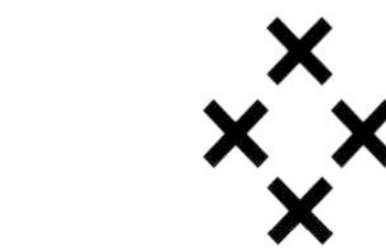
X211**E**02
Solid Precipitation; Slight or moderate

X211**E**03
Solid Precipitation; Heavy

X211**E**04
Drizzle; Freezing, slight

X211**E**05
Drizzle; Freezing, moderate

X211**E**06
Drizzle

X211**E**07
Drizzle; Freezing, heavy

X211**E**08
Rain

X211**E**09
Rain; Freezing, heavy

X211**E**10
Snow

X211**E**11
Ice Pellets; Moderate

X211**E**12
Ice Pellets; Heavy

X211**E**13
Snow Grains

X211**E**14
Ice Crystals

X211**E**15
Shower or Intermittent Precipitation

X211**E**16
Rain Shower or Intermittent Rain; Heavy

X211**E**17
Snow Shower or Intermittent Rain; Heavy

X211**E**18
Hail

X211**E**19
Thunderstorm; Slight or moderate, with no precipitation

X211**E**20
Thunderstorm; Slight or heavy, with no precipitation

X211**E**21
Tornado

W1 Series:
Present Weather
(Addendum)

X211**E**22
Volcanic Ash Suspended in the Air Aloft

X211**E**23
Thick Dust Haze; Visibility less than 1 km

X211**E**24
Drifting Dust

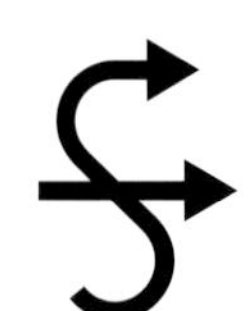
X211**E**25
Wall of Dust or Sand in Distance

X211**E**26
Snow Haze

X211**E**27
Whiteout

X211**E**28
Deposition of Volcanic Ash

X211**E**29
Deposition of Dust or Sand

X211**E**30
Deposition of Dew

X211**E**31
Deposition of Wet Snow

X211**E**32
Deposition of Soft Rime

X211**E**33
Deposition of Hard Rime

W1 Series:
Present Weather
(Addendum)
continued

X211**F**01
Deposition of Hoar Frost

X211**F**02
Deposition of Glaze

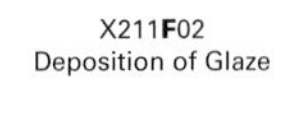

X211**F**03
Deposition of Ice Crust

X211**F**04
Blowing Snow; Impossible to determine whether snow is falling or not

X211**F**05
Fog on Sea

X211**F**06
Fog in Valleys

X211**F**07
Arctic or Antarctic Sea Smoke

X211**F**08
Steam Fog; Sea, lake or river

X211**F**09
Steam Fog; Land

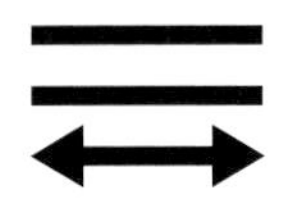

X211**F**10
Fog Over Ice or Snow Cover

/0

X211**F**11
Drizzle, Rate of Fall; Less than 0.10 mm h-1

/1

X211**F**12
Drizzle, Rate of Fall; 0.10-0.19 mm h-1

/2

X211**F**13
Drizzle, Rate of Fall; 0.20-0.39 mm h-1

/3

X211**F**14
Drizzle, Rate of Fall; 0.40-0.79 mm h-1

/4

X211**F**15
Drizzle, Rate of Fall; 0.80-1.59 mm h-1

/5

X211**F**16
Drizzle, Rate of Fall; 1.60-3.19 mm h-1

/6

X211**F**17
Drizzle, Rate of Fall; 3.20-6.39 mm h-1

/7

X211**F**18
Drizzle, Rate of Fall; 6.4 mm h-1 or more

X211**F**19
Drizzle and Snow; ww = 68 or 69

X211**F**20
Not used

X211**F**21
Snow or Ice Crystal Precipitation from a Clear Sky

X211**F**22
Wet Snow; Freezing on contact

X211**F**23
Precipitation of Snow Pellets or Small Hail; with rain

X211**F**24
Precipitation of Snow Pellets or Small Hail; with rain and snow mixed

X211**F**25
Precipitation of Snow Pellets or Small Hail; with snow

X211**F**26
Precipitation of Hail; with rain

X211**F**27
Precipitation of Hail; with rain and snow mixed

X211**F**28
Precipitation of Hail; with snow

X211**F**29
Shower or Thunderstorm Over Sea

X211**F**30
Shower or Thunderstorm Over Mountains

X211**F**31
Over Sea, Lake or River;
Over water

X211**F**32
On or Over Mountains

X211**F**33
In or Over Valleys

Characteristic of Pressure Tendency During the 3 Hours Preceding Time of Observation

X211**G**01
Increasing, then Decreasing; Atmospheric pressure the same as or higher than three hours ago

X211**G**02
Increasing, then Steady; or Increasing, then Increasing More Slowly; Atmospheric pressure now higher than three hours ago

X211**G**03
Increasing, Steadily or Unsteadily; Atmospheric pressure now higher than three hours ago

X211**G**04
Steady;
Atmospheric pressure the same as three hours ago

X211**G**05
Decreasing, then Increasing; Atmospheric pressure the same as or lower than three hours ago

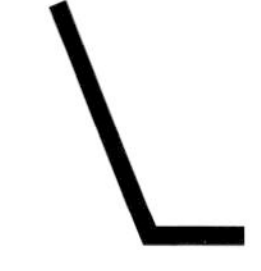

X211**G**06
Decreasing, then Steady; or Decreasing, then Decreasing more Slowly; Atmospheric pressure now lower than three hours ago

X211**G**07
Decreasing Steadily or Unsteadily; Atmospheric pressure now lower than three hours ago

X211**G**08
Steady or Increasing, then Decreasing; or Decreasing, then decreasing more rapidly; Atmospheric pressure now lower than three hours ago

Ground Conditions

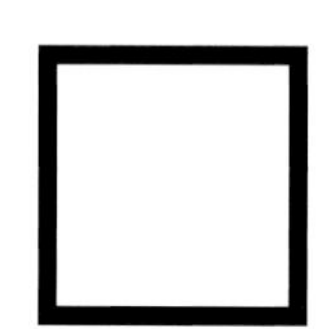

X211**G**09
Surface of Ground Dry; Without cracks and no appreciable amount of dust or loose sand

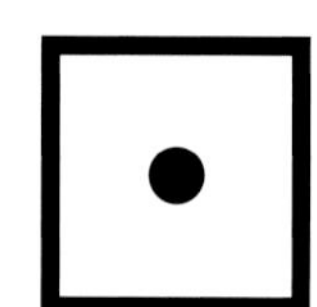

X211**G**10
Surface of Ground Moist

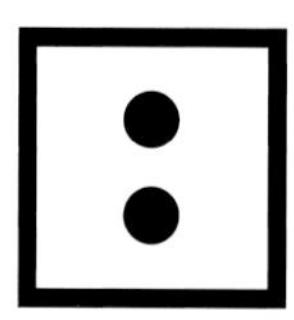

X211**G**11
Surface of Ground Wet; Standing water in small or large pools on surface

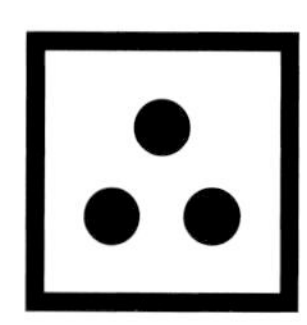

X211**G**12
Flooded

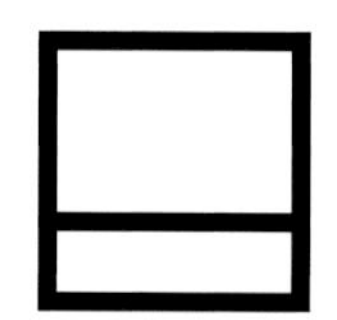

X211**G**13
Surface of Ground Frozen

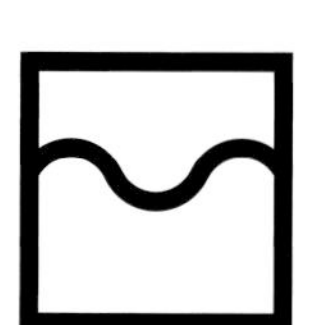

X211**G**14
Glaze on Ground

X211**G**15
Loose Dry Dust or Sand; Not covering ground completely

X211**G**16
Thin Cover of Loose Dry Dust; or Sand covering ground completely

X211**G**17
Moderate or Thick Cover of Loose Dry Dust; or Sand covering ground completely

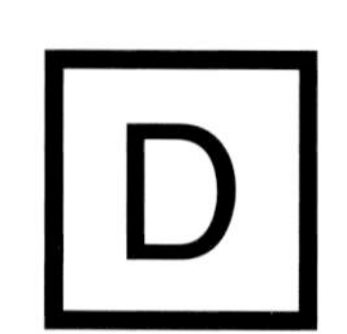

X211**G**18
Extremely Dry with Cracks

X211**G**19
Ground Predominantly Covered by Ice

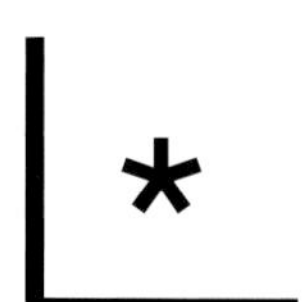

X211**G**20
Compact or Wet Snow; With or without ice covering less than one-half of the ground

X211**G**21
Compact or Wet Snow; With or without ice covering at least one-half of the ground but not completely covered

X211**G**22
Even Layer of Compact or Wet Snow; Covering ground completely

X211**G**23
Uneven Layer of Compact or Wet Snow; Covering ground completely

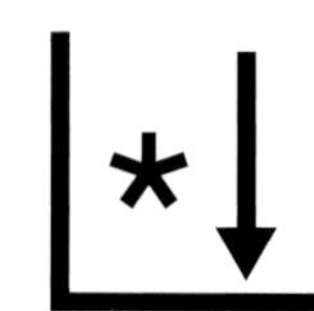

X211**G**24
Loose Dry Snow: Covering less than one-half of the ground

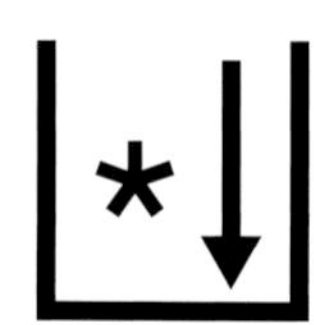

X211**G**25
Loose Dry Snow: Covering at least one-half of the ground but not completely

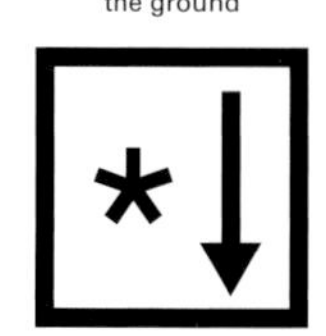

X211**G**26
Even Layer of Loose Dry Snow; Covering ground completely

X211**G**27
Uneven Layer of Loose Dry Snow; Covering ground completely

X211**G**28
Snow Covering Ground Completely; Deep drifts

Analyses & Forecasts on Weather Charts

Description	Symbol	Symbol
Cold front at the surface	X211**H**01	X211**H**02
Cold front above the surface	X211**H**03	X211**H**04
Cold front frontogenesis	X211**H**05	X211**H**06
Cold front frontolysis	X211**H**07	X211**H**08
Occluded front at the surface	X211**H**09	X211**H**10
Quasi-stationary front at the surface	X211**H**11	X211**H**12
Quasi-stationary front above the surface	X211**H**13	X211**H**14
Warm front at the surface	X211**H**15	X211**H**16
Warm front above the surface	X211**H**17	X211**H**18
Warm front frontogenesis	X211**H**19	X211**H**20
Warm front frontolysis	X211**H**21	X211**H**22
Occluded front above the surface	X211**H**23	X211**H**24
Quasi-stationary front frontogenesis	X211**H**25	X211**H**26
Quasi-stationary front frontolysis	X211**H**27	X211**H**28

Analyses & Forecasts on Weather Charts continued

Instability line

X211J01

X211J02

Shear line

X211J03

X211J04

Convergence line

X211J05

X211J06

Intertropical convergence zone

X211J07

X211J08

Intertropical discontinuity

X211J09

X211J10

Axis of trough

X211J11

X211J12

Axis of ridge

X211J13

X211J14

X211J15
Areas of Fog

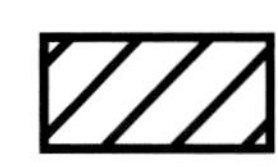

X211J16
Zones of Intermittent Precipitation

X211J17
Zones of Continuous Precipitation

X211J18
Zones of Continuous Precipitation

X211J19
Areas of Dust Storm, Sand Storm, or Dust Haze

X211J20
Snow or Ice Pellets

X211J21
For a Tropical Cyclonic Circulation; With observed or estimated maximum winds of 64 kt(118 km/h) or more

X211J22
For a Tropical Cyclonic Circulation; With observed or estimated maximum winds of 17 to 63 kt (29 to 117 km/h)

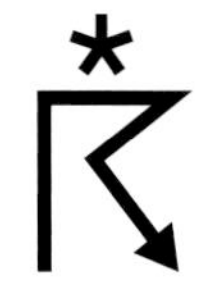

X211J23
Areas of Thunderstorms

X211J24
Visibility Reduced

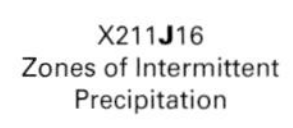

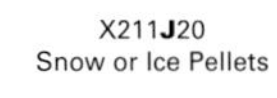

Data on Weather Charts: Total Cloud Cover

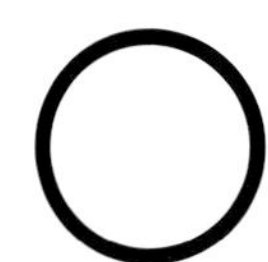
X211**K**01
0 = 0

X211**K**02
1 = 1 Okta or 1/10 or Less; But not zero

X211**K**03
2 = 2 Oktas or 2/10-3/10

X211**K**04
3 = 3 Oktas or 4/10

X211**K**05
4 = 4 Oktas or 5/10

X211**K**06
5 = 5 Oktas or 6/10

X211**K**07
6 = 6 Oktas or 7/10-8/10

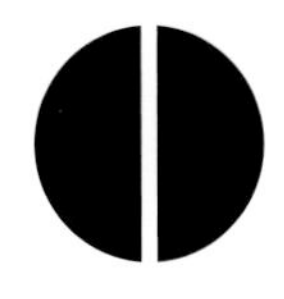
X211**K**08
7 = 7 Oktas or 9/10 or More; But not 8 oktas or 10/10

X211**K**09
8 = 8 Oktas or 10/10

X211**K**10
9 = 9 Sky Obscured; or Cloud amount cannot be estimated

X211**K**11
/ = No Measurements Made

X211**K**12
Calm

Wind Speed & Direction

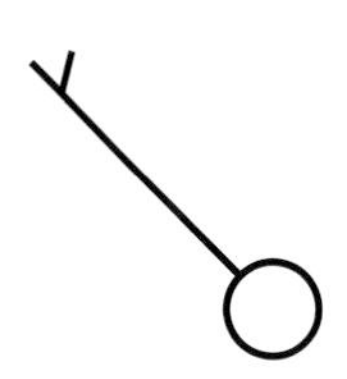
X211**K**13
5 Knots, NW

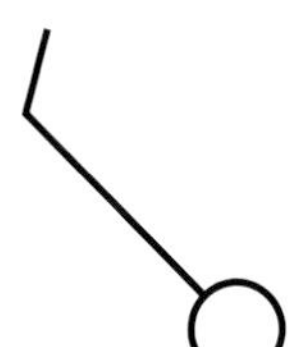
X211**K**14
10 Knots, NW

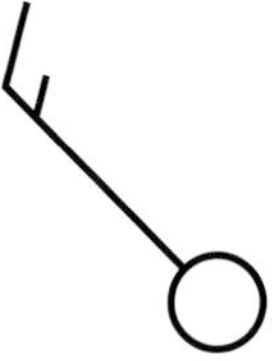
X211**K**15
15 Knots, NW

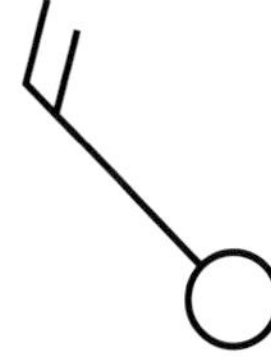
X211**K**16
20 Knots, NW

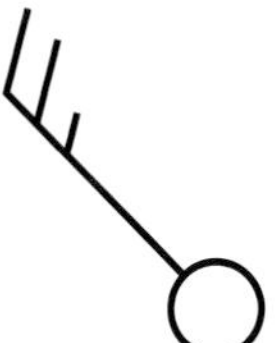
X211**K**17
25 Knots, NW

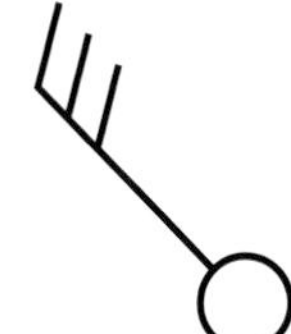
X211**K**18
30 Knots, NW

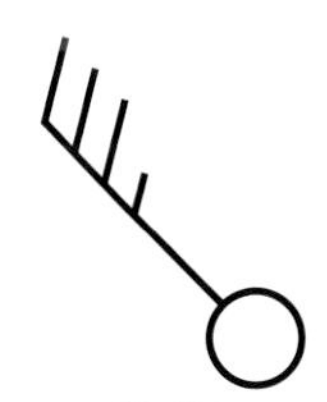
X211**K**19
35 Knots, NW

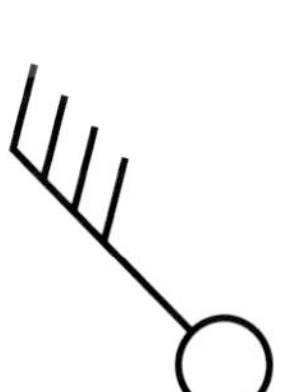
X211**K**20
40 Knots, NW

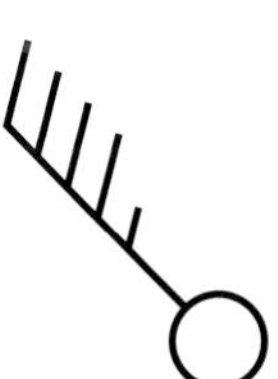
X211**K**21
45 Knots, NW

X211**K**22
50 Knots, NW

X211**K**23
55 Knots, NW

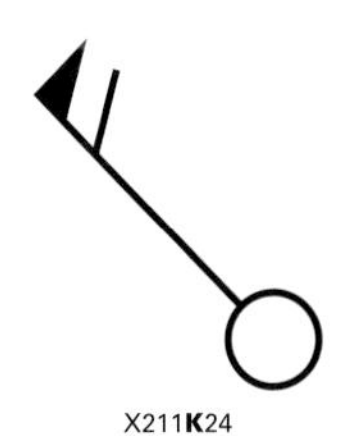
X211**K**24
60 Knots, NW

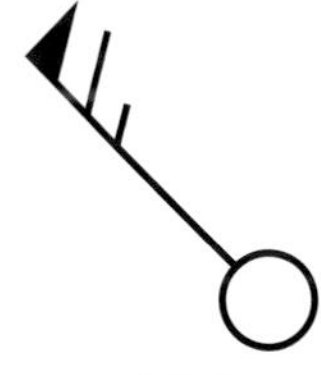
X211**K**25
65 Knots, NW

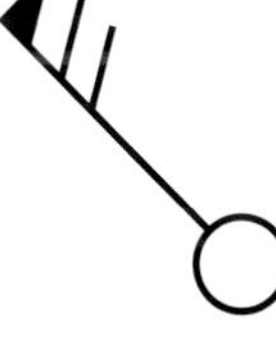
X211**K**26
70 Knots, NW

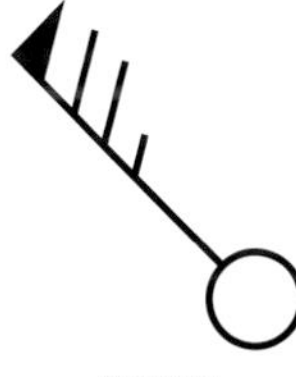
X211**K**27
75 Knots, NW

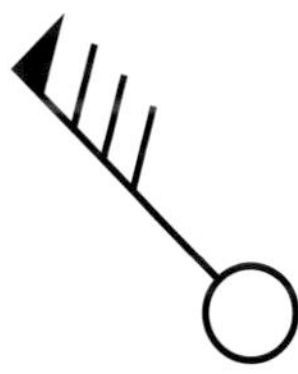
X211**K**28
80 Knots, NW

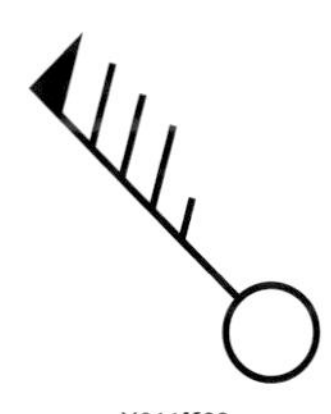
X211**K**29
85 Knots, NW

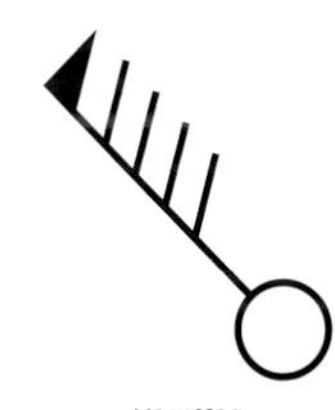
X211**K**30
90 Knots, NW

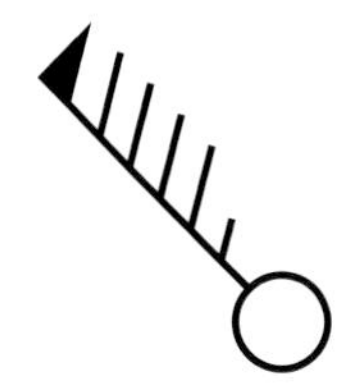
X211**K**31
95 Knots, NW

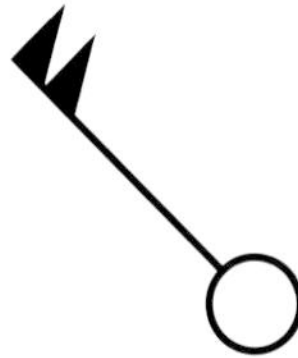
X211**K**32
100 Knots, NW

Appendix

Introduction
1. Dorothy Pollet and Peter C. Haskell, *Sign Systems for Libraries: Solving the Wayfinding Problem*, p. 3 (New York, New York: R.R. Bowker Company, 1979)
2. John Muhlhausen, *Wayfinding Is Not Signage* (Cincinnati, OH: Signs of the Times magazine)

Volume 1 Highway Signs I: U.S. (MUTCD)
1. *The Manual on Uniform Traffic Control Devices (MUTCD)*, (Washington, DC: Federal Highway Administration (FHWA), 2003)

Volume 2 Highway Signs II: International (UNCRT)
1. United Nations, *United Nations Conference on Road Traffic*, Vienna, Oct. 7 - Nov. 8, 1968 (New York, NY: United Nations Publication, 1969)
2. Justin JIH, *Road Traffic Signs* (www.geocities.com/ jusjih, 2005)
3. Merrill J. Allen, *Vision and Highway Safety* (Clifton Park, NY: Chilton Book Company, 1970)

Volume 3 Symbol Signs: Recreational (SEGD)
1. Donald T. Meeker and Peter Reedijk, *Symbol Signs for Recreational Related Facilities: A National System* (New York, New York: SEGD)
2. Joanne Ferria, Office of the General Counsel (Washington D.C.: American Red Cross, 1999)
3. Graphic Artists Guild, *Disability Access Symbols* (New York: www.gag.org/ resources, 2004)

Volume 4 Symbol Signs: Transportation I (AIGA / DOT)
1. *Symbol Signs, Second Edition* (New York, NY: American Institute of Graphic Arts, 1993)
2. *Symbol Signs Repro Art, Symbol Signs Guidelines* (New York, NY: American Institute of Graphic Arts, 1979)
3. *Standards for Symbology and Graphic Signage Aboard Commercial Aircraft, TARC 82-29* [Washington, D.C.: Transport Airworthiness Requirements Committee (TARC) of the Aerospace Industries Association (AIA)]
4. Joanne Ferria, Office of the General Counsel (Washington D.C.: American Red Cross, 1999)

Volume 5 Symbol Signs: Transportation II (TCRP)
1. Joanne Ferria, Office of the General Counsel (Washington D.C.: American Red Cross, 1999)

Volume 7 Safety Symbols Labeling (DOT / ANSI / ISO)
1. Prokepis A. Christou, *How to Select Labels for Your Hazard Package*, 1998
2. Geoffrey Peckham, *Safety Sign Formats* (www.ce-mag.com, 2004)
3. Nora Olgyay, *Safety Symbols Art* (New York, NY: Van Nostrand Reinhold, 1995)
4. *ANSI Z535.4-2002, Product Safety Signs and Labels* (Rosslyn, VA: NEMA, 2002)
5. *Product Safety Labels, ANSI and ISO Formats* (www.safetylabel.com/safety label standards, 1995)
6. *About Workplace Hazardous Materials Information System (WHMIS)* (www.hc-sc.gc.ca/hecs-sesc/whmis, 2005)

Volume 8 International Icons I:
Electronic Labeling (ISO / IEC / JEITA)
1. *Why Standards Matter* (www.iso.org/iso/en/aboutiso/ introduction, 2005)
2. Tim K. Murphy and David Hill, *Graphic Symbols Guideline Proposal* (Chicago, IL: IBM Report, 1991)

Volume 10 Signals Braille
Signal Flags
1. International Marine Signal Flags (www.anbg.gov.au/flags/signal-flags.html, 2004)
2. U.S. Navy Signal Flags (www.chinfo.navy.mil/navpalib/communications/flags/flags.html)

Semaphores
3. *Semaphore Flag Signalling System* (www.anbg.gov.au, 2004)
4. William von Alven, *200-Year Condensed History of Telecommunications* (www.cclab.com/billhist.htm, 2005)
5. *A Brief History of Semaphore* (Grolier Multimedia Encyclopedia, 1997)

Morse Code
6. *History of Morse code* (en.wikipedia.org/wiki, 2005)

American Sign Language
7. Karen Nakamura, *About American Sign Language, Sign Language Linguistics* (www.deaflibrary.org, 2002)

Braille
8. Canadian National Institute for the Blind, *Louis Braille* (www.cnib.ca, 2005)
9. *The Americans with Disabilities Act White Paper, SEGD's Clarification and Interpretation of the ADA Signage Requirements*, Second Edition (New York, NY: SEGD, www.segd.org, 1992)
10. *Merriam-Webster On-line* (www.webster.com, 2004) Enter "brail" to see the derivation.
11. *How Braille Began* (www.brailler.com, 2004)
12. Helen Keller, *Braille, the Magic Wand of the Blind* (New York, NY: American Foundation for the Blind, Helen Keller archive, www.afb.org)

Volume 11 Meteorological Symbols (WMO)
1. *Manual on the Global Data-processing System, Volume I - Global aspects, Annex IV to the WMO Technical Regulations*, 1992 Edition (Geneva, Switzerland: World Meteorological Organization, 1992)
2. Peter R. Chaston, *Weather Maps, Second Edition* (Kearney, MO: Chaston Scientific, Inc., 1999)
3. Keith C. Heidorn, PhD, ACM, *The Weather Doctor*, 1999
4. Dr. John Day, *Luke Howard -The Godfather of Clouds* (www.cloudman.com, 2005)
5. Richard Hamblyn, *The Invention of Clouds* (New York: Farrar, Straus and Giroux, 2001)

Allen, Merrill J., *Vision and Highway Safety* (Clifton Park, NY: Chilton Book Company, 1970)

American Institute of Graphic Arts, *Symbol Signs, Second Edition* (New York, NY: AIGA, 1993)

American Institute of Graphic Arts, *Symbol Signs Repro Art: Reproduction Art and Guidelines for the System of Symbol Signs Developed for the U.S. Department of Transportation* (New York, NY: AIGA, 1979)

American National Standards Institute, *ANSI Series, Z535.1: Safety Color Code; Z535: Criteria for Safety Symbols; Z535.4: Product Safety Signs and Labels* (Rosslyn, VA: NEMA, 2002)

Chaston, Peter R., *Weather Maps, Second Edition* (Kearney, MO: Chaston Scientific, Inc., 1999)

Collins, Belinda L., *The Development and Evaluation of Effective Symbol Signs* (Washington, DC: U.S. Bureau of Standards, Building Science Series, No. BSS 141, 1982)

Danish Design Centre, *Design of the Danish Traffic Signs* (Copenhagen, DK: Dansk Design Center, 1996)

Danish Design Centre, *Finding the Way, by Ear, Hand and Foot* (Copenhagen, DK: Dansk Design Center, 1996)

Dreyfuss, Henry, *Symbol Sourcebook: An Authoritative Guide to International Symbols* (New York, NY: Van Nostrand Reinhold, 1974)

Federal Highway Administration, *The Manual on Uniform Traffic Control Devices (MUTCD),* (Washington, DC: FHWA, 2003)

Follis, John and Dave Hammer, *Architectural Signing and Graphics* (New York, NY: Whitney Library of Design, 1979)

Frutiger, Adrian, *Signs and Symbols: Their Design and Meaning* (London, UK: Studio Editions, 1978)

Hamblyn, Richard, *The Invention of Clouds* (New York: Farrar, Straus and Giroux, 2001)

Hora, Mies, *Official Signs & Icons* (Stony Point, NY: Ultimate Symbol Inc., 1996)

International Organization for Standardization, *Procedures for the Development and Testing of Public Information Symbols* (Geneva, Switzerland: ISO/TC 145, No. 9186, 1989)

Lam, William M.C., *Perception & Lighting as Formgivers in Architecture,* edited by Christopher Hugh Ripman (New York, NY: Van Nostrand Reinhold, 1992)

Laurel, Brenda, *The Art of Human-Computer Interface Design* (Addison Wesley, 1990)

Liungman, Carl, *Dictionary of Symbols* (New York, NY: W.W. Norton & Company, Inc., 1991)

Manual on the Global Data-processing System, Volume I - Global Aspects, Annex IV to the WMO Technical Regulations, 1992 Edition (Geneva, Switzerland: World Meteorological Organization, 1992)

Modley, Rudolf, *Handbook of Pictorial Symbols* (New York, NY: Dover Publications, 1976)

Olgyay, Nora, *Safety Symbols Art* (New York, NY: Van Nostrand Reinhold, 1995)

Ota, Yukio, *Pictogram Design* (Tokyo, Japan: Kashiwa Shobo Publishers, 1987)

Passini, Romedi, *Wayfinding in Architecture* (New York, NY: Van Nostrand Reinhold, 1992)

Paul Aurthur VisuCom Limited, *Picto'grafics* (Toronto, Canada: Visucom Limited, 1967)

Pollet, Dorothy and Peter C. Haskell, *Sign Systems for Libraries: Solving the Wayfinding Problem* (New York, NY: R.R. Bowker Company, 1979)

Schein, Jerome D. and David A. Stewart, *Language in Motion: Exploring the Nature of Sign* (Washington, DC: Gallaudet University Press, 1995)

Society of Environmental Graphic Design, *The Americans with Disabilities Act White Paper, SEGD's Clarification and Interpretation of the ADA Signage Requirements,* Second Edition (New York, NY: SEGD, 1992)

Stiebner, Erhardt D. and Dieter Urban, *Signs + Emblems: A Collection of International Examples* (New York, NY: Van Nostrand Reinhold, 1982)

Studio 7.5, *Navigation for the Internet and Other Digital Media* (Crans-pres-Celigny, Switzerland: Ava Publishing SA, 2002)

Tufte, Edward R., *Envisioning Information* (Chesire, CT: Graphics Press, 1990)

Tufte, Edward R., *Visual Explanations* (Chesire, CT: Graphics Press, 1997)

United Nations, *United Nations Conference on Road Traffic,* Vienna, Oct. 7 - Nov. 8, 1968 (New York, NY: United Nations Publication, 1969)

U.S. Army Corps of Engineers, *Sign Standards Manual* (Washington, DC: U.S. ACE, 1988)

Wildbur and Burke, *Information Graphics: Innovative Solutions in Contemporary Design* (Thames and Hudson, 1998)

Air Transport Association (ATA) of America, Inc.
Headquarters: 1301 Pennsylvania Avenue, NW, Suite 1100
Washington, DC 20004-1707, U.S.A.
www.airlines.org

American Association of State Highway and Transportation Officials (AASHTO)
444 North Capitol Street, NW, Suite 249, Washington, DC 20001
www.transportation.org

American Bus Association (ABA)
700 13th Street NW, Suite 575, Washington DC 20005-5923
www.buses.org

American Foundation for the Blind (AFB)
AFB Headquarters: 11 Penn Plaza, Suite 300, New York, NY 10001
www.afb.org

American Hotel and Lodging Association (AHLA)
1201 New York Ave., NW, #600, Washington, DC 20005-3931
www.ahla.com

American Institute of Architects (AIA)
1735 New York Ave., NW, Washington, DC 20006-5292
www.aia.org

American National Standards Institute (ANSI)
Headquarters: 1819 L Street, NW, 6th Floor, Washington, DC 20036
web.ansi.org

American Public Transit Association (APTA)
1666 K Street, N.W., Suite 1100, Washington, DC 20006
www.apta.com

American Railway Engineering and Maintenance-of-Way Association (AREMA)
8201 Corporate Drive, Suite 1125, Landover, MD 20785-2230
www.arema.org

American Recreation Coalition (ARC)
1225 New York Ave. NW, Suite 450, Washington, DC 20005-6405
www.funoutdoors.com

AMTRAK, Inc.
15 South Poplar, CNOC, 1st Floor, Wilmington, DE 19801
www.amtrak.com

Asia Pacific Economic Cooperation (APEC)
APEC Secretariat: 35 Heng Mui Keng Terrace, Singapore 119616
www.apec.org

Association of American Railroads (AAR)
50 F Street, NW, Washington, DC 20001-1564
www.aar.org

British Standards Institute (BSI)
389 Chiswick High Road, Lomdon W4 4AL United Kingdom
www.bsi-global.com

Canadian National Institute for the Blind (CNIB)
National Office: 1929 Bayview Avenue, Toronto, ON M4G 3E8
www.cnib.ca

Canadian Standards Association (CSA)
865 Ellingham Ave., Pointe-Claire, Quebec, H9R 5E8, Canada
www.csa.ca

Consumer Electronics Association (CEA)
2500 Wilson Blvd., Arlington, VA 22201-3834
www.ce.org

Federal Highway Administration (FHWA)
400 Seventh Street, SW, Washington, DC 20590
www.fhwa.dot.gov

Gallaudet University (for the Deaf)
800 Florida Avenue, NE, Washington, DC 20002 USA
www.gallaudet.edu

Global Engineering Documents
15 Inverness Way East, Englewood, CO 80112
global.ihs.com

Graphic Artists Guild
90 John Street, Suite 403, New York, NY 10038-3202
www.gag.org

Hazard Communication Systems, LLC
190 Old Milford Rd., P.O. Box 1174, Milford, PA 18337
www.safetylabel.com

Illuminating Engineering Society (IES)
120 Wall Street, Floor 17, New York, NY 10005
www.iesna.org

Institute of Makers of Explosives (IME)
1120 19th Street, NW, Suite 310, Washington, DC 20036-3605
www.ime.org

Institute of Transportation Engineers (ITE)
1099 14th Street, NW, Suite 300 West, Washington, DC 20005-3438
www.ite.org

International Council of Graphic Design Associations
Icograda Secretariat: c/o Montréal International, 380 Saint-Antoine Ouest, Suite 8000, Montréal, Québec, Canada H2Y 3X7
www.icograda.org

International Electrotechnical Commission (IEC)
IEC Central Office: 3, rue de Varembé
P.O. Box 131, CH - 1211 Geneva 20, Switzerland
www.iec.ch

International Organization for Standardization (ISO)
ISO Central Secretariat: 1, rue de Varembé, Case postale 56, CH-1211 Geneva 20, Switzerland
www.iso.org

ISEA - The Safety Equipment Association
1901 North Moore Street, Suite 808, Arlington, VA 22209
www.safetyequipment.org

Japan Electronics and Information Technology Industries Association (JEITA), 3rd Fl., Mitsui Sumitomo Kaijo Bldg., Annex 11 Kanda Surugadai 3-chome, Chiyoda-ku, Tokyo 101-0062, Japan
www.jeita.or.jp

Lab Safety Supply, Inc.
PO Box 1368, Janesville WI USA 53547-1368
www.labsafety.com

National Electrical Manufacturers Association (NEMA)
1300 North 17th Street, Suite 1847, Rosslyn, VA 22209
www.nema.org

National Institute of Standards and Technology (NIST)
100 Bureau Drive, Stop 1070, Gaithersburg, MD 20899-1070
www.nist.gov

National Institute on Deafness and Other Communication Disorders
National Institutes of Health
31 Center Drive, MSC 2320, Bethesda, MD USA 20892-2320
www.nidcd.nih.gov

Occupational Safety and Health Administration (OSHA)
U.S. Department of Labor
200 Constitution Avenue, NW, Washington, DC 20210
www.osha.gov

Railway Progress Institute (RPI)
700 North Fairfax Street, #601, Alexandria, VA 22314-2098
www.rpi.org

Society for Environmental Graphic Design (SEGD)
1000 Vermont Avenue, Suite 400, Washington, DC 20005
www.segd.org

TCRP Transit Cooperative Research Program
Transportation Research Board
500 Fifth Street, NW, Washington, DC 20001
www.trb.org/trb/tcrp

Transportation Research Board (TRB)
The National Academies:
2101 Constitution Avenue, NW, Washington, DC 20418
www.nas.edu/trb

Travel Industry Association of America (TIAA)
1100 New York Avenue, NW, Suite 450, Washington, DC 20005-3934
www.tia.org

Underwriters Laboratories Inc.
Corporate Headquarters:
333 Pfingsten Road, Northbrook, IL 60062-2096 USA
www.ul.com

Unz & Company, Safety Compliance Manuals
8 Easy Street, Bound Brook, NJ 08805
www.unzco.com

U.S. Architectural and Transportation Barriers Compliance Board
(The U.S. Access Board)
1331 F Street, NW, Suite 1000, Washington, DC 20004-1111
www.access-board.gov

U.S. Department of Transportation
400 7th Street, S.W., Washington DC 20590
www.dot.gov

Workplace Hazardous Materials Information System (WHMIS)
HECS Publishing, Healthy Environments and Consumer Safety
AL: 3100A, Health Canada
Ottawa, Ontario, Canada K1A 0K9
www.hc-sc.gc.ca/whmis

World Meteorological Organization (WMO)
7 bis, avenue de la Paix
Case postale No. 2300, CH-1211 Geneva 2, Switzerland
www.wmo.ch

0-B

0-9

A

B

B-C

C

C-D

D

D-F

F-H

H-L

L-N

N-P

P-R

Q

R

R-S

S

S-T

T

T-V

U

V

V-Z

W

X

Y

Z

Official Signs & Icons 2
Product Information

P

Overview

Welcome to *Official Signs & Icons 2:* This 11-volume collection of 4,811 high-quality vector files was created by design professionals *for* design professionals. *Official Signs & Icons 2* is part of *The Ultimate Symbol Collection*, a suite of products that provides instant access to a wide variety of inspirational, high-quality, and time-saving designs and icons, in fully editable PostScript™ format. For more about what products are available, please visit www.ultimatesymbol.com

This section contains the following information:

PRODUCT CONTENTS
MAC or PC CD-ROM

1. EPS Files
EPS 3.0 format for Mac or PC.

Vinyl-Ready Signmaking Files The EPS 3.0 files in Mac or PC format on the CD-ROM were designed specifically for sign making applications and vinyl sign cutting. The images have no strokes or overlapping vectors and points. For more information see page 236.

2. End User License Agreement
By using the images on the *Official Signs & Icons 2* CD-ROM, you agree to the terms and conditions of this agreement (also located on pages 233-234 of this book).

4. Adobe Acrobat Reader™
An intuitive screen interface and image browser. Install to view the PDF documents listed below.

5. OS&I2 Catalog.pdf
On-screen display of the *Official Signs & Icons 2 Catalog* may be viewed in Adobe Acrobat Reader.

6. Ultimate Symbol.pdf
An overview of *The Ultimate Symbol Collection*™, a library of more than 20,000 images. Use to view and access the Free Sample Files.

7. FREE Sample Files
FREE sample EPS files from some of the other available products in *The Ultimate Symbol Collection.*

Notice to User:
This is a contract. By breaking the seal on the CD-ROM that accompanies this book, you accept all the terms and conditions of this agreement.

LICENSE AGREEMENT

Software Use: Ultimate Symbol Inc. (Ultimate Symbol) grants you a non-exclusive limited license to use the EPS/WMF Files on one Apple Macintosh or IBM/PC compatible computer. You may not install the EPS/WMF Files on a network server. You may use the EPS/WMF Files as illustrative or decorative material that is included as part of a total graphic design for print or multimedia communication, produced for you, your employer, or a client, that is not for resale or redistribution as a collection of art for reproduction or as any form of stock design. You may not use any of the contents, in whole or in part, for multiple resale in the form of stock proofs, engravings, film, mats, printing, digitized images, etc. without written permission. When using an outside service bureau or high resolution output service, one copy of the EPS/WMF image or images may be made to accompany the document in which the images have been used. This copy is for one time use only and must be removed from the service bureau's possession upon completion of the service.

You may make one (1) copy of the EPS/WMF Files solely for backup purposes. Any permitted copies must include the same proprietary and copyright notices as were affixed to the original. Any unauthorized duplication or use of the EPS/WMF Files, in whole or in part, in print, or in any other storage and retrieval system is strictly prohibited.

Multi User License

If you plan to operate the EPS/WMF Files on a network or use simultaneously on multiple computers, contact Ultimate Symbol at 800-611-4761 regarding volume discounts and Multi User Licenses. If a Multi User License is obtained, only the number of copies needed to run the software simultaneously on the machines covered by Multi User License may be made.

Termination

Ultimate Symbol Inc. reserves the right to terminate this license upon breach. Upon termination, you will be required to cease using the EPS/WMF Files and return all copies of the EPS/WMF Files and accompanying documentation to Ultimate Symbol Inc. In the event you include the EPS/WMF Files or any portion thereof, whether modified or not, in any other Software product for resale as "Clip-Art", this license is terminated and you agree to remove the EPS/WMF Files or any portion of them from the modified program and return it to Ultimate Symbol at the address listed below.

Copyright

The contents of the EPS/WMF Files and accompanying Documentation are the property of Ultimate Symbol Inc. and are copyrighted, with all rights reserved. Under the copyright laws, the EPS/WMF Files may not be copied, in whole or in part, without written consent of Ultimate Symbol Inc., except to make a backup copy. This exception does not allow copies to be made for others, whether or not sold. Under the law, copying includes translating into another language or format. The purchase or use of this Software does not, in any way, transfer ownership or rights to contents, in whole or in part, to you. You are forewarned that Ultimate Symbol Inc. claims protection of the EPS/WMF Files and the symbols contained therein.

Transfer

You may not rent, lease, or sublicense, or lend the EPS/WMF Files or Documentation. You may, however, transfer all your rights to use the EPS/WMF Files to another person or legal entity provided that you transfer this Agreement and transfer (or destroy), the EPS/WMF Files, including all copies, updates and prior versions, and all Documentation to such person or entity and provided that you retain no copies, including copies stored on you computer.

Updates and Upgrades

Updates or upgrades of this software do not convey the right to transfer prior versions to other parties.

LIMITED WARRANTY

Ultimate Symbol Inc. (Ultimate Symbol) warrants to the original purchaser of this Software that:

(1) this Software will perform substantially in accordance with the accompanying written materials, when used with the recommended system configuration, and

(2) the disk or disks upon which this Software is recorded are not defective and have been properly recorded.

90-Day Period

This warranty is for a period of 90 days after the original date of the purchaser's purchase of this package, during which time any disks that become defective under normal use will be replaced at no charge. The product registration form should be registered with Ultimate Symbol in order to provide proof of original purchase.

Returned Goods Policy

Ultimate Symbol Customer Service must be notified before returning the Ultimate Symbol Software Product. Returned Software will not be accepted by Ultimate Symbol unless accompanied by a Returned Merchandise Authorization (RMA) number assigned by Ultimate Symbol Customer Service. Ultimate Symbol's entire liability under this limited warranty and otherwise with respect to the Software is limited to return of the Software and accompanying materials to the dealer or to Ultimate Symbol for replacement or refund, at Ultimate Symbol's option. In no event shall Ultimate Symbol, its suppliers, employees, officers, directors, dealers, or distributors be liable for any damages, including lost profits or lost savings or other incidental or consequential damages, arising out of the use, inability to use, or abuse of this product, even if advised of the possibility of such damages, or for any claim by any other party.

Merchandise

Authorization (RMA) number assigned by Ultimate Symbol Inc. Ultimate Symbol's entire liability under this limited warranty and otherwise with respect to the Software is limited to return of the Software and accompanying materials to the dealer or to Ultimate Symbol for replacement or refund, at Ultimate Symbol's option.

In no event shall Ultimate Symbol, its suppliers, employees, officers, directors, dealers, or distributors be liable for any damages, including lost profits or lost savings or other incidental or consequential damages, arising out of the use, inability to use, or abuse of this product, even if advised of the possibility of such damages, or for any claim by any other party.

Disclaimer

Ultimate Symbol disclaims all other warranties, either expressed or implied, including but not limited to implied warranties of merchantibility and fitness for a particular purpose. Ultimate Symbol does not warrant that the functions contained in this Software will meet your requirements or that the operation of the Software will be uninterrupted or error free.

Some states do not allow limitations of implied warranties, or incidental or consequential damages, so some of the above limitations may not apply to you.

The images in this collection were created, compiled, and collected from a wide variety of sources. Some images were derived from reprinted, secondary or non-original sources. Every attempt has been made to verify that these images are copyright-free. However, in the event that an image has unknowingly infringed a copyright, please alert a representative of Ultimate Symbol Inc. at 800.611.4761.

LOCATING IMAGE FILES

Once you have found the image you want in the Official Signs & Icons 2™ Catalog, take note of the number at the base of the image.

Example:

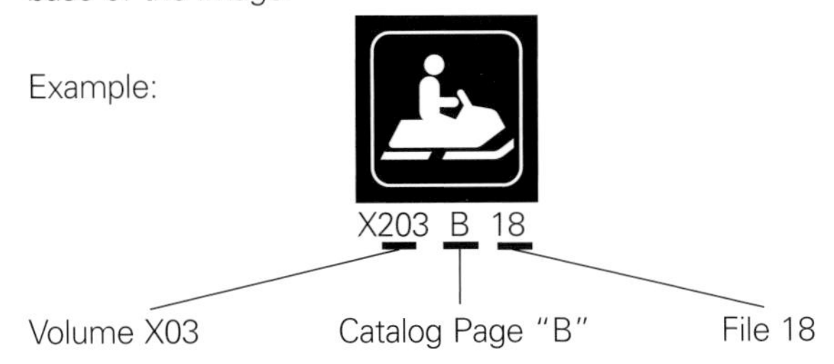

The "2" in "X203B18" denotes that the volume is new to the second edition of *Official Signs & Icons* and/or has new files in it. To find the EPS image, select your CD-ROM drive and locate the EPS or WMF Files folder. Then locate the folder entitled Volume 03, Sub-folder 03B, File Number X203B06.

QUICK TIPS FOR OPENING EPS FILES

The following instructions may vary depending on the version of the application you have. Contact the application manufacturer's tech support or use help menus for up-to-date instructions.

Adobe Illustrator™

From the FILE menu go to OPEN to import the EPS images into your program. If you PLACE the images you will not be able to ungroup or manipulate the files. Select the CD drive and the file you wish to import. Double-click the file to bring it into your program.

Adobe InDesign™

From the FILE menu go to PLACE. Select the image you wish to import into PageMaker. The PS (Post Script) symbol will appear on the screen. Click the mouse to place the image on the screen.

Adobe PageMaker™

From the FILE menu go to PLACE. Select the image you wish to import into PageMaker. The cursor will appear on the screen as the PS (PostScript) or some other symbol. Click the mouse to place the image on the screen.

CorelDRAW!™

From the FILE menu go to IMPORT. From the LIST FILES OF TYPE pop-up select ADOBE ILLUSTRATOR (*.ai, *.eps). DO NOT use the ALL FILES or COREL TRACE option as the files may be incomplete when imported.

Macromedia Freehand™

> Freehand 4.0 and greater: Illustrator 3 files can be opened and edited.

> Freehand 3.x (or earlier versions): Illustrator 3 files are not compatible or require special software to open them. The best option is to upgrade to Freehand 4.0 or greater.

Quark Xpress™

Xpress users must create a graphic box to import the EPS file into. After you have created the graphic box click on the Content Tool, and select Get Picture from the FILE menu.

ABOUT EPS FILES

Official Signs & Icons 2 images are vector outlines, and will print at the very highest resolution on any PostScript™-equipped printer. These images were created in Adobe Illustrator as EPS and saved as grouped, Adobe Illustrator 3.0 (Macintosh), and Adobe Illustrator 3.0 EPS and WMF files (PC/ Windows). The images were not saved in higher versions of Illustrator because of backward compatibility issues.

Display Problems

If you encounter "jaggies" when viewing the images on screen and they appear roughly drawn, check and/or update your computer's Adobe PostScript drivers or make sure that the application you are working in is PostScript-compatible.

Transparency & Compound Paths

Macintosh: Where appropriate, 3.0 images were saved as compound paths, which allows for transparency or the ability to "see through" blank areas of the image.

If a grouped image will not come apart, it may be because the file is a compound path. To release a compound path in Illustrator, select the image, pull down the "Object" menu, select "Compound Paths", then select "Release". Be aware that when releasing a

compound path, some apparently empty or transparent objects/spaces may become solid black or white.
Note: Freehand users, see "Composite Path" in your software manual/help menu.

Images Composed of Separate Shapes
Many of the images in *Official Signs & Icons 2* are composed of separate, grouped shapes which may be pulled apart. To decompose the image, select the image, go to "Object" menu, and select "Ungroup". You are now ready to pull it apart.

ABOUT VINYL-READY SIGNMAKING FILES
Official Signs & Icons 2 images are vinyl-ready and were designed specifically for use by signmakers: they have no strokes (in most cases) or overlapping vectors and points. Exceptions include outlines for some sign surround shapes, which can either be deleted or altered to conform with your sign application(s). The image files were created in Adobe Illustrator as EPS files and saved as grouped, 1-bit, Adobe Illustrator 3.0 files for Macintosh and PC/Windows. You may edit these in any draw or sign making program that accepts EPS files and place or import them into most page layout programs.

Opening EPS Files in Sign Applications
The following instructions may vary depending on the version of the application you have. Contact the application manufacturer's tech support or use help menus for up-to-date instructions.

Arts & Letters Express™
From the FILE menu go to IMPORT. Select EPS from the LIST FILES OF TYPE pop-up. Select the CD drive and the file you wish to import. Double-click the file to bring it into your program.

CASmate™
From the FILE menu go to IMPORT. Select EPS under FILE TYPES. Select the CD drive and the file you wish to import. Double-click the file to bring it in to your program.

EuroCUT™
From the FILE menu go to IMPORT. Select AI ILLUSTRATOR under FILE TYPES. Select the CD drive and the file you wish to import. Double-click the file to bring it in to your program.

FlexiSIGN™
When Flexi is opened, you are presented with a dialog box. Select OPEN and under file type select Adobe Illustrator 3.0. Select your CD drive and double-click the file to open into Flexi. You may get a message "There are objects having the same color as the background." Select "OK". When the drawing is on the screen choose SELECT ALL under the EDIT menu. From the COLOR BAR select the BLACK fill. Then go to the ARRANGE menu and select MAKE COMPOUND. The image is now ready to customize.

GERBER Graphix Advantage™
From COMPOSER go to the FILE menu and select Encapsulated Postcript (EPS) from the Import options. Select your CD drive and locate the EPS image you wish to import. Select the file and CONVERT. Generally the file will open into GA and will be saved in the JOBS directory.

SignLAB™
From the FILE menu go to IMPORT. Select EPS under FILE TYPES to bring images into your program. Select the CD drive and the file you wish to import. (Use MERGE if you want to combine an EPS image with one you are working with currently.)

ABOUT ADOBE ACROBAT READER

With the Acrobat Reader, you can view and navigate any Portable Document Format (PDF) file, including our screen catalog "OS&I2 Catalog.pdf" (Mac); "OS&I2_Cat.pdf" (PC) and "Ultimate Symbol.pdf" (Mac); "Ultimate.pdf" (PC).

IMPORTANT: It is not necessary to load Acrobat Reader or our screen catalog "OS&I2 Catalog.pdf" to begin using the EPS/WMF files. However, the screen catalog will assist you in conveniently viewing and selecting the image files. *Note that the OS&I2.pdf document is locked and not printable for copyright reasons.*

Installing Acrobat Reader

For detailed installation instructions see the "ReadMe" file located in the Acrobat Reader folder on the CD-ROM (Mac) or "readme.txt" located in the Acrobat subdirectory (PC/Windows).

Acrobat Reader Help

Click on the "help" button on the top menu bar for a complete selection of help tools. For the latest information on Acrobat or to download the latest version of the free Acrobat Reader, go online to: www.adobe.com/products/acrobat

Acrobat Reader Features

Once Acrobat Reader is installed, browse PDF files using the following handy Acrobat features:

1. Page by Page
Browse through PDF documents a page at a time using the page forward and back buttons on the tool bar at the bottom of the window.

2. Word or Phrase Search
Search by word or phrase, selecting the "Search" button from the top tool bar.

3. Thumbnail Pages
Click on the "Pages" button on the left hand toolbar to display the pages of the document as thumbnails. You may select a page to jump to by clicking on a thumbnail page, or even select a view or specific area of a thumbnail page.

4. Bookmarks
Click on the "Bookmarks" button on the left hand toolbar to display bookmarks, which serve as an alphabetized index of categories of images. Click on the listing you would like to review.

How to Purchase Electronic Artwork for the Symbols in This Book
All 4,800 symbols displayed in *Official Signs & Icons 2* are available as fully editable EPS vector image files for Mac or PC.

CD Upgrade Discount for Book Owners
If you already own the *Official Signs & Icons 2* Book, you qualify for a special CD upgrade discount.
Call to obtain your discount toll-free: 800.611.4761.

Online Purchases
www.ultimatesymbol.com
Follow instructions to purchase any of the following:

> Single Image Downloads

> Individual Volume Downloads

> *Official Signs & Icons 2,* Book with CD (shipped)

> *Official Signs & Icons 2,* CD only (shipped)

> *Official Signs & Icons 2,* Book only (shipped)

Multi-User Licensing
If you intend to use the *Official Signs & Icons 2* electronic art on more than one computer or on a network, please contact Ultimate Symbol for special multi-user licensing and multiple discount pricing.

Quantity Discounts
Special bulk purchase and educational discount rates are available. Please call 845.942.0003 for information.

Ultimate Symbol Inc.
31 Wilderness Drive
Stony Point, New York 10980-3447
800.611.4761
www.ultimatesymbol.com

Call Toll-Free 800.611.4761
Monday through Friday, 10 am to 6 pm ET (Eastern Time) for information, pricing, and ordering.
Orders received by 1:00 pm ET ship same day.

Outside the U.S. Call: 845.942.0003

Order by Fax: 845.942.0004
24 hours a day, 7 days a week.
Please include name, address, email address, and phone number along with credit card number and expiration date. You will be contacted with any questions. Copies of your invoice will be emailed and included with shipped product.

Order by Mail
Please include name, address, email address, and phone number along with check, money order, or credit card number and expiration date. You will be contacted with any questions. Mail to:
Ultimate Symbol Inc.
Attn: Orders
31 Wilderness Drive
Stony Point, New York 10980-3447

Payment
Visit www.ultimatesymbol.com for current pricing.
Payment options include:
1. Credit Cards:
   MasterCard, Visa, American Express, Discover.
2. Checks:
   Corporate or personal (product ships only upon clearance of check).
3. Purchase Orders:
   Government and educational institutions only.
   Please call 845.942.0003 for more information.

Shipping & Delivery
Orders received by 1:00 pm ET ship same day and are tracked in the U.S. Sorry, no C.O.D. orders.
1. Overnight Priority (delivery by 10:30 am)
   Overnight Standard (delivery by 3:00 pm)
   Two-Day Economy
2. Ground (1-7 days)
3. Foreign: U.S. Postal Service Express Mail